Industrial Air Pollution Control Equipment for Particulates

Louis Theodore
Professor
Chemical Engineering Department
Manhattan College
Bronx, New York

Anthony J. Buonicore
Project Manager
Entoleter, Inc.
New Haven, Connecticut

Published by

CRC PRESS, Inc.
18901 Cranwood Parkway · Cleveland, Ohio 44128

Library of Congress Cataloging in Publication Data

Theodore, Louis.
    Industrial air pollution control equipment for
particulates.

    Includes bibliographical references and index.
    1. Dust – Removal – Equipment and supplies.
I. Buonicore, Anthony J., joint author.
II. Title.
TH7692.T48   628.5'3   76-25095
ISBN 0-87819-068-6

This book represents information obtained from authentic and highly regarded sources. Reprinted material is quoted with permission, and sources are indicated. A wide variety of references are listed. Every reasonable effort has been made to give reliable data and information, but the author and the publisher cannot assume responsibility for the validity of all materials or for the consequences of their use.

International Standard Book Number 0-8493-5132-4
Former International Standard Book Number 0-87819-068-6

Library of Congress Card Number 75-25095
Printed in the United States

PREFACE

In the last two decades, the engineering profession has expanded its responsibilities to society to include the control of air pollution from industrial sources. Increasing numbers of engineers and applied scientists are being confronted with problems in this most important area. The environmental engineer and scientist of today and tomorrow must develop a proficiency and an improved understanding of air pollution control equipment in order to cope with these problems and challenges. It was in this spirit that this book was undertaken.

This book is directed toward the fundamentals and design principles of industrial control equipment for particulate air pollutants. The five basic devices available for controlling the discharge of particulates into the atmosphere — gravity settlers, centrifugal separators, electrostatic precipitators, wet scrubbers, and fabric filters — are discussed in depth. The design of each is considered from both a theoretical and practical viewpoint.

The book begins by considering the overall strategy and general approach employed in the development and application of the subject. Particulate air pollutants are identified and classified, pertinent legislation is discussed, and measurement methods and techniques are treated.

Since particulate air pollutants are dispersed in a gaseous medium, knowledge of their behavior in such an environment is essential, regardless of the type control device being considered. The entire second chapter, therefore, concentrates on the dynamics of fluid-particle systems, with the primary emphasis on the equations describing particle motion.

The remainder of the book is devoted to particle collection in each of the basic control devices. Separate chapters treat gravity settlers, centrifugal separators, electrostatic precipitators, wet scrubbers, and fabric filters. For each system, the design equations for overall collection efficiency and pressure drop are developed from fundamental principles. Empirical correlations, if available, and practical experience are incorporated into the development: Illustrative examples are used to demonstrate the basic concepts and design principles.

The information developed and presented throughout the book is essential to the design of industrial control equipment for particulate air pollutants. It will enable one to follow a design through from fundamental considerations and provide a better understanding of both the system itself and those factors affecting system performance. Such knowledge is essential in view of the stringency of existing and anticipated air pollution control regulations.

Out sincere thanks go to Margit Buonicore and Loretta McGowan for their dedicated efforts in typing and preparing the manuscript. The authors are also indebted to Robert Stanton for preparing the artwork and to Peter Ferenz and Robert DiVincenzo for their contribution to this text.

Louis Theodore
Anthony J. Buonicore

THE AUTHORS

Louis Theodore is presently a professor of Chemical Engineering at Manhattan College. He received a B.Ch.E. degree from The Cooper Union in 1955. The degrees of M.Ch.E. and Eng.Sc.D. were obtained from New York University in 1957 and 1964, respectively.

Dr. Theodore joined the faculty at Manhattan College with the rank of Instructor in the fall of 1960. In 1963 he was appointed Director of the Chemical Engineering Laboratory. In 1964 he was appointed Director of Computer Utilization in the Chemical Engineering Department. He has taught courses in Transport Phenomena, Kinetics, Statistics, Mathematics for Chemical Engineers, and Air Pollution and Its Control, served as a lecturer in Transport Phenomena for industry and education here and abroad, and has presented invited lectures and seminars in the air pollution control area. He has consulted for several industrial companies in the field of computer applications and pollution control, participated as a research consultant on an NAPCA sponsored project, and supervised NSF environmental projects. He is presently Director of Research in Chemical Engineering at Manhattan.

Early in 1967, the Ford Foundation awarded Dr. Theodore a Residency in Engineering Practice for the 1967–68 year. He accepted a position with the Mobil Research & Development Corporation and worked for the Process Simulation Group of the Computer Methods and Control Section, developing and solving mathematical models to simulate and improve the performance of existing refinery process units.

Dr. Theodore received a sabbatical for the 1973–74 academic year. He accepted a position (half-time) with the Air Pollution Training Institute of the Environmental Protection Agency. Part of Dr. Theodore's responsibilities include active participation in the Institute's courses "Control of Gaseous Emissions" and "Control of Particulate Emissions."

Dr. Theodore is a member of Phi Lambda Upsilon, Sigma Xi, American Chemical Society, American Society for Engineering Education, Royal Hellenic Society, Metropolitan Engineers' Council on Air Resources (MECAR), Air Pollution Control Association (APCA), the ACS – Division of Water, Air and Waste Chemistry, and the New York Academy of Sciences.

Anthony J. Buonicore received his B.Ch.E. and M.Ch.E. from Manhattan College in New York, specializing in environmental engineering. His prime area of research has been in the modeling and simulation of air pollution control equipment. Previously he worked as a principal environmental engineer in the Office for Environmental Protection of the Civil Engineering Center at Wright-Patterson Air Force Base, where his primary responsibilities were in the areas of air pollution control and solid waste management. Prior to his work at Wright-Patterson, he had been employed as a Process Design/Environmental Engineer with Stauffer Chemical Company's Eastern Research and Development Center in Dobbs Ferry, New York. He is presently Project Manager for Entoleter, Inc., a major environmental control firm specializing in the engineering, design, and fabrication of control equipment for both gaseous and particulate air pollutants. Mr. Buonicore is a licensed professional engineer in the State of Ohio.

Mr. Buonicore is also a member of the faculty of the Engineering and Science Institute of Dayton, where he offers continuing education courses on air pollution control technology. He has frequently been a guest lecturer on air pollution control at the Air Force Institute of Technology and most recently been invited to lecture on Stack Design for the Dilution of Air Pollutant Concentrations in the National Science Foundation sponsored "Air Pollution Control Equipment Problem Workshop."

Mr. Buonicore is an active member of the American Institute of Chemical Engineers and the Air Pollution Control Association, where he chairs the Technical Committee on Energy/Environmental Interactions. He has also been instrumental in organizing and promoting an AIChE/APCA sponsored annual conference on Energy and the Environment and acted as its first General Chairman. His other affiliations include Tau Beta Pi, Sigma Xi, Society of American Military Engineers, and Citizens' Clean Air Committee.

TO

Patrick George

the last Theodore addition

AND TO

Margit Carleen

the first Buonicore addition

TABLE OF CONTENTS

Chapter 1

INTRODUCTION

1.1. INTRODUCTORY REMARKS

Pollutant discharges to the atmosphere can be classified into two major categories: particulates (often referred to as particles, including both liquid and solid matter) and gases. Although gaseous pollutants comprise approximately 85% of industrial pollutant emissions, it is estimated that about 35 million tons of particulate matter are emitted to the atmosphere each year from man-made sources such as fuel combustion, transportation, solid waste disposal, and various industrial processes. Particulate matter is also produced from natural sources such as the sea, soil, volcanic eruptions, and forest fires. In many cases the contribution from these sources is considerably greater than that associated with human activities. Such sources constitute "background" pollution, that portion of the pollution problem over which control activities can have little, if any, effect.

To reduce or eliminate particulate emissions from man-made polluting operations, five control strategies are available.

1. Elimination of the operation entirely or in part.
2. Modification of the operation.
3. Relocation of the operation.
4. Application of appropriate control devices.
5. Combinations thereof.

The emphasis throughout this book will be on strategy 4 — the selection and design of control equipment for particulates; the companion volume, *Industrial Control Equipment for Gaseous Pollutants*, deals with gaseous pollutants in a similar fashion.[1]

The primary objective of this book is to familiarize the environmental engineering student, the practicing engineer, and responsible environmental control administrators with industrial particulate equipment and design procedures. Although the work is not intended as an extensive theoretical treatment of the subject, the fundamentals of each control unit are reviewed and design equations are discussed. The information presented should provide sufficient material to enable the reader to properly select equipment for a particulate pollution problem, perform a design review, and make a preliminary design prior to discussing the problem with a control equipment manufacturer.

1.2. UNITS, NOTATIONS, AND DEFINITIONS

The basic equations of engineering and applied science are dimensional equations — usually consisting of several terms. For equality to be maintained, each term in the equation must have the same units, i.e., the equation must be dimensionally homogeneous. Throughout the text, with the exception of certain empirical correlations, dimensional consistency is maintained.

Unfortunately, at the time of this writing, two systems of units are employed in this country by the engineering profession. They are referred to as the English (engineering) and metric (cgs) systems. As a rule, the engineer uses the former and the scientist the latter. Since an attempt has been made to retain the accepted nomenclature found in the literature pertaining to each control device, both systems are featured in the equations, examples, and problems in the following chapters. Some of the units and their corresponding notation(s) are presented below.

Quantity	Engineering system	Metric system
Mass	lb	g
Moles	lb_m	g_m
Length	in., ft, etc.	mm, cm, etc.
Time	sec, min, or hr	sec, min, or hr
Temperature	°F or °R	°C or °K
Energy	ft-lb_f or Btu	cal

Other notations used are as follows:

1. The average value of functions is indicated with the notation $\langle \rangle$, e.g., $\langle T \rangle$.
2. ACFM is the actual volumetric gas flow at operating conditions (temperature and pressure) in units of cubic feet per minute.

3. SCFM is the actual volumetric gas flow reduced to standard conditions (usually specified, i.e., atmospheric pressure and 68°F). To convert from SCFM (1 atm, 68°F) to ACFM (at operating pressure, P, in atmospheres and operating temperature, T, in °F), use:

$$ACFM = (SCFM)\left(\frac{T + 460}{528}\right)\left(\frac{1.0}{P}\right)$$

4. ppm is parts per million by weight (e.g., $lb/10^6\,lb$) or volume (e.g., $ft^3/10^6\,ft^3$), depending on how it is specified (for particulates, usually by weight).

5. The concentration of particulates or loading is the weight of solids and/or liquid per cubic foot of gas (e.g., lb/ft^3, $grains/ft^3$, mg/ft^3, or $\mu g/ft^3$).

6. A typical particulate- size analysis is given in the following form:

	+5	μm	40%
−5	+2.5	μm	27%
−2.5	+1.5	μm	20%
−1.5		μm	13%
			100%

This would mean that 40% of the particles by weight are greater than 5 μm in size, 27% are less than 5 μm but greater than 2.5 μm, 20% are less than 2.5 μm but greater than 1.5 μm, and the remainder (13%) are less than 1.5 μm.

Other conversion factors which may prove helpful in solving the design problems are given in Table 1.2.1.

TABLE 1.2.1

Conversion Factors for Common Particulate Air Pollution Measurements

To convert from	To	Multiply by
mg/m^3	g/ft^3	283.2×10^{-6}
	g/m^3	0.001
	$\mu g/m^3$	1000.00
	$\mu g/ft^3$	28.32
	$lb/1,000\ ft^3$	62.43×10^{-6}
g/ft^3	mg/m^3	35.3145×10^3
	g/m^3	35.314
	$\mu g/m^3$	35.314×10^6
	$\mu g/ft^3$	1.0×10^6
	$lb/1,000\ ft^3$	2.2046

TABLE 1.2.1 (continued)

Conversion Factors for Common Particulate Air Pollution Measurements

To convert from	To	Multiply by
g/m^3	mg/m^3	1000.0
	g/ft^3	0.02832
	$\mu g/m^3$	1.0×10^6
	$\mu g/ft^3$	28.317×10^3
	$lb/1,000\ ft^3$	0.06243
$\mu g/m^3$	mg/m^3	0.001
	g/ft^3	28.317×10^{-9}
	g/m^3	1.0×10^{-6}
	$\mu g/ft^3$	0.02832
	$lb/1,000\ ft^3$	62.43×10^{-9}
$\mu g/ft^3$	mg/m^3	35.314×10^{-3}
	g/ft^3	1.0×10^{-6}
	g/m^3	35.314×10^{-6}
	$\mu g/m^3$	35.314
	$lb/1,000\ ft^3$	2.2046×10^{-6}
$lb/10^3\ ft^3$	mg/m^3	16.018×10^3
	g/ft^3	0.35314
	$\mu g/m^3$	16.018×10^6
	g/m^3	16.018
	$\mu g/ft^3$	353.14×10^3
No. of particles/ft^3	No./m^3	35.314
	No./l	35.314×10^{-3}
	No./cm^3	35.314×10^{-6}
ton/mi^2	lb/acre	3.125
	$lb/1,000\ ft^2$	0.07174
	g/m^2	0.3503
	kg/km^2	350.3
	mg/m^2	350.3
	mg/cm^2	0.03503
	g/ft^2	0.03254
lb	gr	7,000.0
μm	in.	3.937×10^{-5}
	mm	1.0×10^{-3}

1.3. NATURE OF PARTICULATES

Particulates may be defined as solid or liquid matter whose effective diameter is larger than a molecule but smaller than approximately 1,000 μm. Particulates dispersed in a gaseous medium are collectively termed an aerosol. The terms smoke, fog, haze, and dust are commonly used to describe particular types of aerosols, depending on the size, shape, and characteristic behavior of the dispersed particles. Aerosols are rather difficult to classify on a scientific basis in terms of their fundamental properties such as settling rate under the influence of external forces, optical activity, ability to absorb electric charge, particle size and structure, surface-to-volume ratio, reaction activity, physiological action, etc. In general, particle size and settling rate have been the most characteristic properties for many purposes. For example, particles larger than 100 μm may be excluded from the category of dispersions because they settle too rapidly. On the other hand, particles on the order of 1 μm or less settle so slowly that, for all practical purposes, they are regarded as permanent suspensions. Despite possible advantages of scientific classification schemes, the use of popular descriptive terms such as smoke, dust, and mist, which are essentially based on the mode of formation, appears to be a satisfactory and convenient method of classification. In addition, this approach is so well established and understood that it undoubtedly would be difficult to change.

Dust is typically formed by the pulverization or mechanical disintegration of solid matter into particles of smaller size by processes such as grinding, crushing, and drilling. Particle sizes of dusts range from a lower limit of about 1 μm up to about 100 or 200 μm and larger. Dust particles are usually irregular in shape, and particle size refers to some average dimension for any given particle. Common examples include fly ash, rock dusts, and ordinary flour. *Smoke* implies a certain degree of optical density and is typically derived from the burning of organic materials such as wood, coal, and tobacco. Smoke particles are very fine, ranging in size from less than 0.01 μm up to 1 μm. They are usually spherical in shape if of liquid or tarry composition and irregular in shape if of solid composition. Due to their very fine particle size, smokes can remain in suspension for long periods of time and exhibit lively Brownian motion. *Fumes* are typically formed by processes such as sublimation, condensation, or combustion — generally at relatively high temperatures. They range in particle size from less than 0.1 μm to 1 μm. Similar to smokes, they settle very slowly and exhibit strong Brownian motion. *Mists* or *fogs* are typically formed either by the condensation of water or other vapors on suitable nuclei, giving a suspension of small liquid droplets, or by the atomization of liquids. Particle sizes of natural fogs and mists usually lie between 2 and 200 μm. Droplets larger than 200 μm are more properly classified as *drizzle* or *rain*. Many of the important

properties of aerosols which depend on particle size are presented in Figure 1.3.1.

When a liquid or solid substance is emitted to the air as particulate matter, its properties and effects may be changed. As a substance is broken up into smaller and smaller particles, more of its surface area is exposed to the air. Under these circumstances, the substance — whatever its chemical composition — tends to physically or chemically combine with other particulates or gases in the atmosphere. The resulting combinations are frequently unpredictable. Very small aerosol particles (from 0.001 to 0.1 μm) can act as condensation nuclei to facilitate the condensation of water vapor, thus promoting the formation of fog and ground mist. Particles less than 2 or 3 μm in size — about half (by weight) of the particles suspended in urban air — can penetrate into the mucous and attract and convey harmful chemicals such as sulfur dioxide. By virtue of the increased surface area of the small aerosol particles, and as a result of the adsorption of gas molecules or other such properties that are able to facilitate chemical reactions, aerosols tend to exhibit greatly enhanced surface activity. Many substances that oxidize slowly in their massive state will oxidize extremely fast or possibly even explode when dispersed as fine particles in air. Dust explosions, for example, are often caused by the unstable burning or oxidation of combustible particles, brought about by their relatively large specific surfaces. Adsorption and catalytic phenomena can also be extremely important in analyzing and understanding particulate pollution problems. The conversion of sulfur dioxide to corrosive sulfuric acid assisted by the catalytic action of iron oxide particles, for example, demonstrates the catalytic nature of certain types of particles in the atmosphere. Finally, aerosols can absorb radiant energy and rapidly conduct heat to the surrounding gases of the atmosphere. These are gases that ordinarily would be incapable of absorbing radiant energy by themselves. As a result, the air in contact with the aerosols can become much warmer.

1.4. LEGISLATION, STANDARDS, REGULATIONS, AND ENFORCEMENT: THE CLEAN AIR ACT

The legislation, standards, and regulations applicable to particulate pollutants are now briefly considered in order to provide an insight into the

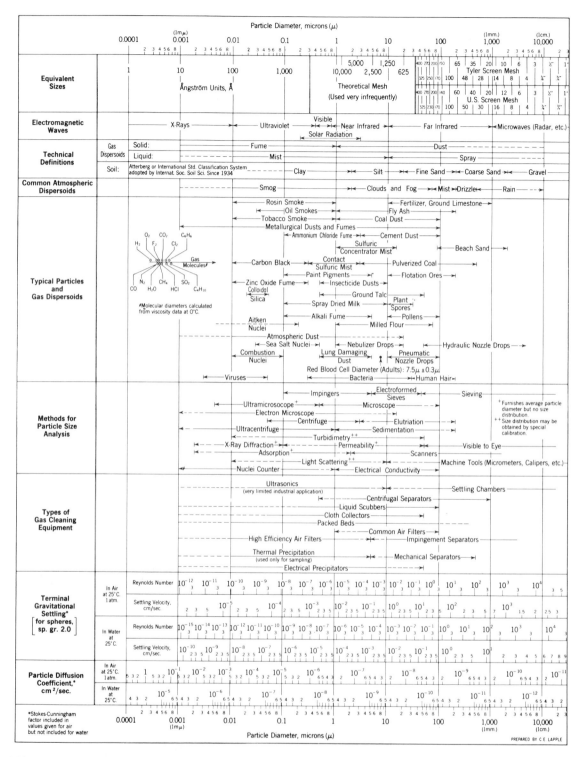

FIGURE 1.3.1. Characteristics of particles and particle dispersoids. (From Lapple, C.E., *Stanford Res. Inst. J.*, 5, 94, 1961. With permission.)

legalistic arena. Although there have been three major pieces of ecological legislation (Public Law 159 in 1955, the Clean Air Act of 1963, and the Air Quality Control Act of 1967), the clean air legislation passed in 1970 under the auspices of the Clean Air Act was the first that had any real bite.

The first federal control act, passed in 1955, was primarily restricted to research into the nature and extent of the nation's air pollution problem. The Clean Air Act of 1963 authorized grants to state and local agencies to assist them in their own control programs. It also provided some limited authority to the federal government to take action to relieve interstate pollution problems. This basic federal control authority was expanded and strengthened by the Air Quality Act of 1967.[2] One of its more significant measures gave citizens a statutory right to participate actively (through public hearings) in the control process. In many communities all over the country, citizens seized this opportunity to become forceful and effective advocates for clean air. The Clean Air Amendments of 1970 provide far stronger legal tools for air pollution control and a larger mandate for citizen participation. Basically, the theory of the federal air pollution control program has been changed only slightly from the statement in the original law of 1955, which stated: "The Congress finds . . . that the prevention and control of air pollution at its source is the primary responsibility of states and local governments." This is still the case. Now, however, if the states fail to meet their control responsibilities, the federal government, acting through the Environmental Protection Agency (EPA), has an increased responsibility and authority to enforce pollution controls.

Most early emission standards limited the concentration of pollutants in the effluent gas from coal-burning power plants. Application of these techniques was later extended to municipal incinerators and industrial processes. These standards only indirectly restricted total emissions; for particulates, they are rapidly being replaced by mass emission rate standards. Concentration standards are not widely used by state or local control agencies because sources can circumvent these regulations by diluting the effluent gas stream with outside air. Application of concentration standards has been limited to specific operations.

Standards based on collection efficiency have been applied to various source categories by a few control agencies. Collection efficiency requirements are similar to concentration standards. They indirectly restrict total emissions and are constant for all sizes of operation (i.e., equal control efficiency required whether small or large operation). These requirements are applicable only to specific sources such as petroleum refineries. The approach is generally weak since the apparent collection efficiency of a collector can often be improved by increasing the throughput (or loading). Although the apparent collection efficiency is increased, the total emissions from the unit also increase.

Most of the more recent standards are variable. Moreover, they are more restrictive on larger sources which usually have greater pollution potential. Some standards also vary the emission limits according to stack height and distance to property line. However, it is important to note that these standards are not affected by changes in gas temperature, pressure, or excess air. They are closely related to the pollution potential and process size.

The standard most used for industrial operations is the "process weight" regulation. It limits mass emission rate which is a function of the total weight of raw materials introduced into the industrial process. This standard requires an increasing degree of control as the process weight increases. There are many variations of the process weight standard, and they differ mainly in the specific emission rate limits. Some agencies have devised more specific regulations for individual processes (e.g., for asphalt plants and foundries) to more nearly reflect attainable emission rates.

The regulations adopted by New York and Pennsylvania are not necessarily restricted to industrial sources or particulates, but they are noteworthy because they limit mass emission rate as a function of "potential emission" rate. Potential emission rate is defined as that quantity of pollutant which theoretically would be emitted if no controls were used. Measurement of the collection efficiency of specific source installations determines the allowable emission rate. The Pennsylvania regulation is a variable standard that applies to different areas of the state. Additional consideration is also given to pollutant toxicity.

Until recent years, the standard most widely accepted for fuel-burning equipment was a concentration standard recommended by the American Society of Mechanical Engineers (ASME). The main reason for its selection was to insure that small combustion units would require no collection equipment. This standard is more lenient but otherwise has the same characteristics attributed to concentration standards for industrial processes.

Concentration standards are rapidly being replaced with a "sliding scale" standard such as that adopted by New York City in 1964. This variable standard has been widely adopted by most major urban and state control agencies, as well as by the federal government for federal facilities. For fuel-burning equipment, this variable standard is a function of equipment capacity rating (million Btu/hr). Indirect restrictions are placed on total emissions. As plant size increases, total allowable particulate emissions also increase, but at a continually decreasing rate.

When compared to a concentration standard, it is apparent that the sliding scale standard has desirable features.

1. It indirectly limits mass emission rate.

2. It varies the control according to the size of the plant.

3. It eliminates the need to standardize flue gas volumes.

4. It varies the control according to modern technology.

Under the Clean Air Act of 1970, the EPA has the increased responsibility and authority to enforce pollution controls. For particulate pollutants, control standards are of two types: national ambient air quality standards and standards of performance.

A national ambient air quality standard is the maximum level which will be permitted for a given pollutant. These standards are classified as either primary or secondary. Primary standards must be sufficiently stringent so as to protect the public health. Secondary standards protect the public welfare. These standards are set by the EPA after it issues a criteria document and a control technology document for a particular pollutant. Each control region must satisfy the standards set forth and is bound by federal enforcement. The primary and secondary standards for suspended particulate pollutants in the ambient atmosphere are presented in Table 1.4.1.

The Clean Air Act of 1970 also requires the EPA to set "standards of performance" for new and "modified" stationary sources of pollution. These standards are distinct from the ambient air quality standards described above. They constitute direct emission limitations for all major pollutants from specified types of sources, such as portland cement plants, municipal incinerators, etc. Any industry planning to construct a potential source of air pollution that is covered by a performance standard will have to design the facility to meet, as a minimum, these federal standards. All standards of performance are applicable nationally to sources in categories specified by the EPA. They apply principally to new pollution sources. They also apply to existing sources whenever "modification" (physical change or change in the method of operation) results in increased emission of old pollutants or in new emission of new pollutants. For all existing unmodified sources in the specified categories, the states are required to set performance standards, under procedures established by the EPA. The EPA also prescribes procedures for state enforcement of federal standards for new and modified sources.

Particulate emission limitations may also be restricted by the density or opacity of the plume discharged to the atmosphere, frequently characterized by the Ringelmann number (see Section 1.5). Opacity regulations have proven to be a most effective enforcement tool in reducing visible particulate emissions. Until 1970 the generally accepted standard for visible emissions in the United States was Ringelmann No. 2 or 40% equivalent opacity. With the requirement of state implementation plans (by Section 110 of the Clean Air Act, as amended in 1970), all states and territories have adopted Ringelmann and equivalent opacity provisions, now commonly referred to as "opacity regulations." The standard predominantly adopted by the states is 20% opacity; however, in new source performance standards a few agencies and the federal government are adopting 10% opacity regulations for many source categories. The limited amount of test data available to support new source performance standards indicates that the 10 to 20% opacity limitation is consistent with the application of "best control technology." It is expected that the pressure for further improvements in air quality will force many control agencies to promulgate the Maryland-type "no visible" or "clear stack" provisions.[5] Tables 1.4.2 and 1.4.3 summarize the federal particulate emission regulations.

Table 1.4.1

Suspended Particulate National Ambient Air Quality Standards[3]

	Primary	Secondary
Maximum annual geometric mean	$75\ \mu g/m^3$	$60\ \mu g/m^3$
Maximum 24-hr concentration not to be exceeded more than 1 day/year	$260\ \mu g/m^3$	$150\ \mu g/m^3$

TABLE 1.4.2

Particulate and Opacity Standards of Performance for New and Modified Stationary Sources (Group I)

Source	Particulate matter (maximum 2-hr average)	Opacity
Fossil fuel-fired steam generators of more than 250 million Btu/hr heat input	0.10 lb/million Btu heat input	20% (except that 40% shall be permissible for not more than 2 min in any 1 hr
Incinerators of more than 50 ton/day charging rate	0.08 grains/SCF corrected to 12% CO_2	
Portland cement plants		
From kiln	0.3 lb/ton feed to kiln	20%
From clinker cooler	0.1 lb/ton feed to kiln	10%
Nitric acid plants		10%
Sulfuric acid plants		10%

From Federal Register, December 23, 1971. Opacity limit from cement kilns revised from 10% to 20% in 1974.

TABLE 1.4.3

Particulate and Opacity Standards of Performance for New and Modified Stationary Sources (Group II)

Source	Particulate matter	Opacity, %
Asphalt concrete plants	0.04 gr/SCF (dry)[a]	20
Petroleum refineries		
From fluid catalytic cracking unit catalyst regenerators	0.027 gr/SCF (dry)	30
Where liquid or solid fuel is used in incinerator waste heat boilers	0.10 lb/million Btu heat input	
Secondary lead smelters (blast or cupola, reverbatory, and pot furnaces of more than 550-lb charging capacity)		
From blast (cupola) or reverbatory furnace	0.022 gr/SCF (dry)	20
From pot furnace		10
Secondary brass and bronze ingot production plants		
From reverbatory furnace (having production capability equal to or greater than 2,205 lb)	0.022 gr/SCF (dry)	20
From an electric furnace (having production capability equal to or greater than 2,205 lb)		10
From a blast (cupola) furnace (having a production capability equal to or greater than 550 lb/hr)		10
Iron and steel plants (basic oxygen furnaces)	0.022 gr/SCF (dry)	
Sewage treatment plants (sludge incinerators)	1.3 lb/ton dry sludge input	<20

[a]gr/SCF (dry) = grains/dry standard cubic foot ($20°C$, 760 mmHg).

From *Fed. Regist.*, 39, 47, 1974.

1.5. MEASUREMENT METHODS

An accurate quantitative analysis of the discharge of pollutants from a process must be determined prior to the design and/or selection of control equipment. If the unit is properly engineered, utilizing the emission data as input to the control device and the code requirements as maximum effluent limitations, most particulate pollutants can be successfully controlled by one or a combination of the methods to be discussed later.

The objective of source testing is to obtain data representative of the process being sampled. The steps followed in obtaining representative data from a large source are:

1. Obtaining a measurement that reflects the time magnitude of the characteristic being measured at the location where the measurement is made.

2. Taking a number of measurements in such a manner that the data obtained from these measurements are representative of the source.

Sampling is the keystone of source analysis. Sampling methods and tools vary in their complexity according to the specific task; therefore, a degree of both technical knowledge and common sense is needed to design a sampling function. Sampling is done to measure quantities or concentrations of pollutants in effluent gas streams, to measure the efficiency of a pollution abatement device, to guide the designer of pollution control equipment and facilities, and/or to appraise contamination from a process or source. A complete measurement requires determination of the concentration and contaminant characteristics, as well as the associated gas flow. Most statutory limitations require mass rates of emission; both concentration and volumetric flow rate data are, therefore, required.

The selection of a sampling site and the number of sampling points required are based on attempts to obtain representative samples. To accomplish this, the sampling site should be at least 8 stack or duct diameters downstream and 2 diameters upstream from any bend, expansion, contraction, valve, fitting, or visible flame. For a rectangular cross section, the equivalent diameter is determined from:

$$\text{Equivalent Diameter} = 2\left[\frac{(\text{length})(\text{width})}{\text{length} + \text{width}}\right]$$

Once the sampling location is chosen, the flue cross section is laid out in a number of equal areas, the center of each being the point where the measurement is to be taken. For rectangular stacks, the cross section is divided into equal areas of the same shape, and the traverse points are located at the center of each equal area, as shown in Figure 1.5.1.A. For circular stacks, the cross section is divided into equal annular areas, and the traverse points are located at the centroids of each area, as shown in Figure 1.5.1.B. When the above sampling site criteria can be met, the minimum number of traverse points should be 12. Some

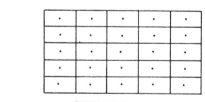

RECTANGULAR STACK
(MEASURE AT CENTER OF AT LEAST 12 EQUAL AREAS).
(A)

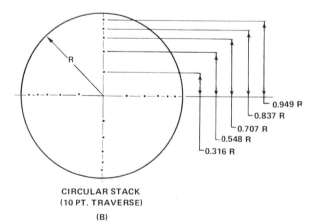

0.949 R
0.837 R
0.707 R
0.548 R
0.316 R

CIRCULAR STACK
(10 PT. TRAVERSE)
(B)

FIGURE 1.5.1. Traverse point locations for velocity measurement or for multipoint sampling in (A) rectangular ducts (25 traverse points) or (B) circular stacks (10-point traverse, with a total of 20 traverse points).

sampling situations, however, render the above sampling site criteria impractical; in this case, choose a convenient sampling location, and use Figure 1.5.2 to determine the minimum number of traverse points. Under no condition should a sampling point that is within 1 in. of the stack wall be selected. To obtain the number of traverse points for stacks or ducts with a diameter less than 2 ft, multiply the number of points obtained from Figure 1.5.2 by 0.67. For circular stack sampling, Table 1.5.1 gives the location of the traverse points as a percentage of stack diameter from the inside wall to the traverse point. The number of traverse points necessary for a particular stack on each of two perpendiculars may also be estimated

from Table 1.5.2. Should a different number of traverse points be required by disturbances upstream and downstream (according to Figure 1.5.2 or Table 1.5.2), choose whichever number is greater. For rectangular stacks, divide the cross section into as many equal rectangular areas as traverse points, so that the ratio of the length to the width of the elemental areas is between one and two.

Example 1.5.1

In order to insure equal annular areas for each point, determine the pitot tube locations (to measure air flow) in a 6-ft I.D. circular duct for an eight-point traverse.

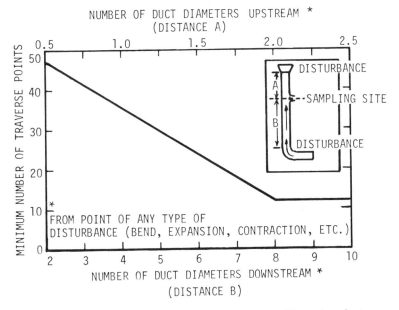

FIGURE 1.5.2. Minimum number of traverse points (total in stack or duct cross section).

TABLE 1.5.1

Traverse Point Locations in Circular Stacks

Traverse point number on a diameter	Number of traverse points on a diameter									
	6	8	10	12	14	16	18	20	22	24
1	4.4	3.3	2.5	2.1	1.8	1.6	1.4	1.3	1.1	1.1
2	14.7	10.5	8.2	6.7	5.7	4.9	4.4	3.9	3.5	3.2
3	29.5	19.4	14.6	11.8	9.9	8.5	7.5	6.7	6.0	5.5
4	70.5	32.3	22.6	17.7	14.6	12.5	10.9	9.7	8.7	7.9
5	85.3	67.7	34.2	25.0	20.1	16.9	14.6	12.9	11.6	10.5
6	95.6	80.6	65.8	35.5	26.9	22.0	18.8	16.5	14.6	13.2
7		89.5	77.4	64.5	36.6	28.3	23.6	20.4	18.0	16.1
8		96.7	85.4	75.0	63.4	37.5	29.6	25.0	21.8	19.4
9			91.8	82.3	73.1	62.5	38.2	30.6	26.1	23.0
10			97.5	88.2	79.9	71.7	61.8	38.8	31.5	27.2
11				93.3	85.4	78.0	70.4	61.2	39.3	32.3
12				97.9	90.1	83.1	76.4	69.4	60.7	39.8
13					94.3	87.5	81.2	75.0	68.5	60.2
14					98.2	91.5	85.4	79.6	73.9	67.7
15						95.1	89.1	83.5	78.2	72.8
16						98.4	92.5	87.1	82.0	77.0
17							95.6	90.3	85.4	80.6
18							98.6	93.3	88.4	83.9
19								96.1	91.3	86.8
20								98.7	94.0	89.5
21									96.5	92.1
22									98.9	94.5
23										96.8
24										98.9

Note: Figures in body of table are precent of stack diameter from inside wall to traverse point.

From Theodore, L. and Buonicore, A. J., *Industrial Control Equipment from Gaseous Pollutants,* CRC Press, Cleveland, 1975.

EXAMPLE 1.5.1 (continued)

Solution (from Table 1.5.1)

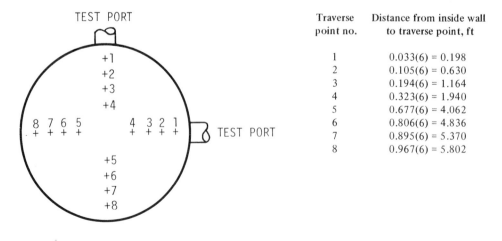

Traverse point no.	Distance from inside wall to traverse point, ft
1	0.033(6) = 0.198
2	0.105(6) = 0.630
3	0.194(6) = 1.164
4	0.323(6) = 1.940
5	0.677(6) = 4.062
6	0.806(6) = 4.836
7	0.895(6) = 5.370
8	0.967(6) = 5.802

Once these traverse points have been determined, gas flow is determined by velocity measurements. The stack-gas velocity is usually determined by means of a pitot tube and differential pressure gauge (see Figure 1.5.3). Figure 1.5.4 shows a typical calculation sheet for the volumetric flow rate using a pitot tube. Where velocities are very low (less than 10 ft/sec) and where great accuracy is not required, an anemometer may be used. For gases moving in small pipes at relatively high velocities or pressures, orifice disk meters or venturi meters may be used. These are valuable as continuous or permanent measuring devices.

Once a flow profile has been established, sampling strategy can be considered. Since sampling collection can be simplified and greatly reduced, depending on flow characteristics, it is best to complete the flow-profile measurement before sampling or measuring pollutant concentrations. Source characteristics may be placed in one of four categories.

1. No time variation, with the emission relatively uniform across the stack cross section. In this case, only one concentration measurement is necessary for accurate results.

2. Steady generation of contaminants, but nonuniform flow across the sampling location. In this case, a traverse is necessary to measure the average concentration. Typically, this is done at the points selected for the velocity traverse. The time of sampling at each point should be the same in order to obtain a representative, composite sample.

3. Cyclical operation in which the actual sampling location is ideal and the variation across the stack is relatively uniform when the operation is running. Because the process involves time variation only, the sampling is conducted at one point for extended periods, usually related to one or more operational cycles.

TABLE 1.5.2

Estimating the Number of Traverse Points

Number of stack diameters downstream and upstream of flow disturbance		Number of traverse points on each diameter
Upstream	Downstream	
8	2	6
7.3	1.8	8
6.7	1.7	10
6.0	1.5	12
5.3	1.3	14
4.7	1.2	16
4.0	1.0	18
3.3	0.8	20
2.6	0.6	22
2.0	0.5	24

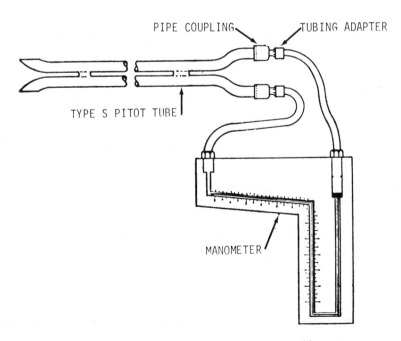

FIGURE 1.5.3.   Pitot tube manometer assembly.

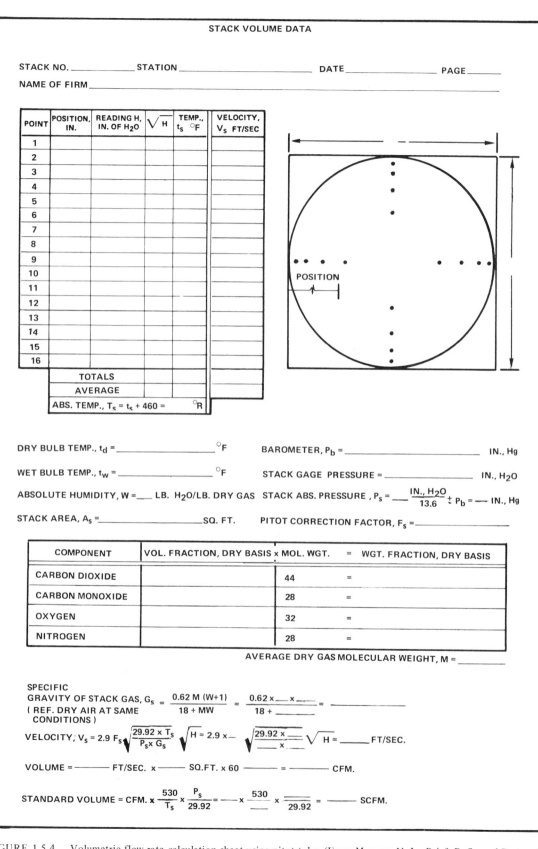

STACK VOLUME DATA

STACK NO. _____ STATION _____ DATE _____ PAGE_____
NAME OF FIRM_____

POINT	POSITION, IN.	READING H, IN. OF H₂O	√H	TEMP., t_s °F	VELOCITY, V_s FT/SEC
1					
2					
3					
4					
5					
6					
7					
8					
9					
10					
11					
12					
13					
14					
15					
16					
	TOTALS				
	AVERAGE				

ABS. TEMP., T_s = t_s + 460 = _____ °R

POSITION

DRY BULB TEMP., t_d = _____ °F   BAROMETER, P_b = _____ IN., Hg

WET BULB TEMP., t_w = _____ °F   STACK GAGE PRESSURE = _____ IN., H₂O

ABSOLUTE HUMIDITY, W =___ LB. H₂O/LB. DRY GAS   STACK ABS. PRESSURE , P_s = ___ $\frac{IN., H_2O}{13.6}$ ± P_b = — IN., Hg

STACK AREA, A_s =_____SQ. FT.   PITOT CORRECTION FACTOR, F_s =_____

COMPONENT	VOL. FRACTION, DRY BASIS	x MOL. WGT.	= WGT. FRACTION, DRY BASIS
CARBON DIOXIDE		44	=
CARBON MONOXIDE		28	=
OXYGEN		32	=
NITROGEN		28	=

AVERAGE DRY GAS MOLECULAR WEIGHT, M = _____

SPECIFIC GRAVITY OF STACK GAS, G_s = $\frac{0.62\ M\ (W+1)}{18 + MW}$ = $\frac{0.62 \times \_\_ \times \_\_}{18 + \_\_\_\_}$ = _____
(REF. DRY AIR AT SAME CONDITIONS)

VELOCITY; V_s = 2.9 $F_s\sqrt{\frac{29.92 \times T_s}{P_s \times G_s}}$ $\sqrt{H}$ = 2.9 x__ $\sqrt{\frac{29.92 \times \_\_}{\_\_ \times \_\_}}$ $\sqrt{H}$ = _____ FT/SEC.

VOLUME = _____ FT/SEC. x ___ SQ.FT. x 60 _____ = _____ CFM.

STANDARD VOLUME = CFM. x $\frac{530}{T_s}$ x $\frac{P_s}{29.92}$ = ___ x $\frac{530}{\_\_}$ x $\frac{\_\_}{29.92}$ = _____ SCFM.

FIGURE 1.5.4.   Volumetric flow-rate calculation sheet using pitot tube. (From Marrow, N. L., Brief, R. S., and Bertrand, R. R., *Chem. Eng.*, 79(2), 84, 1972. With permission.)

4. Nonuniform source and flow conditions. This case requires the most complicated procedure. If there is some measurable cycle related to the process, the sampling can be conducted over this period using simultaneously collected samples. One sample is collected at a reference point and the others at selected traverse points. This is repeated until a complete traverse is made. Results are corrected by using the reference point data as a measure of the time variation.

Depending on the reason for sampling emission sources, the variety and extent of components used in the sampling train will vary. For example, if the chemical and physical characteristics of the aerosols are to be measured, a multicomponent train, or even multiple sampling trains, may be required. On the other hand, if mass loadings alone are being measured, a lesser number of components will be needed.

Representative sampling is obtained only if the velocity of the stack-gas stream entering the probe nozzle is the same as the velocity of the stream passing the nozzle (isokinetic sampling). If the sampling velocity is too high (superioskinetic sampling), there will be a smaller concentration of particles collected since inertia will prevent the larger particles from following the gas stream lines into the nozzle. Alternatively, in subisokinetic sampling, where the sampling velocity is below that of the flowing gas stream, the gas samples would contain a higher-than-actual particulate concentration (heavier particles will enter the nozzle). These conditions are depicted in Figure 1.5.5. The sampling rate should be adjusted to maintain isokinetic sampling conditions and a flow rate of at least 0.5 standard ft^3/min. Inertia effects become more significant when the particle size exceeds about 3 μm. Therefore, if a reasonable proportion of the particles exceeds this size, isokinetic sampling is necessary.

The EPA requires that samples more than 10% from isokinetic, i.e., (nozzle velocity)/(stack velocity) is not between 0.9 and 1.1, be rejected and sampling repeated.[7] Even samples within this range should be corrected by means of a compli-

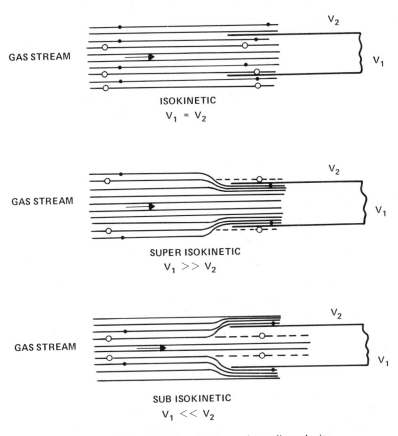

V_2

GAS STREAM

V_1

ISOKINETIC
$V_1 = V_2$

V_2

GAS STREAM

V_1

SUPER ISOKINETIC
$V_1 >> V_2$

V_2

GAS STREAM

V_1

SUB ISOKINETIC
$V_1 << V_2$

FIGURE 1.5.5. Particle collection and sampling velocity.

cated expression. In simplified form, this expression can be stated as follows: (true concentration)/(sampled concentration) = ½[1 + (NV/SV)]. Naturally, correction factors such as this are based on the assumption of a "normal" particle-size distribution (see Section 1.6). If a source contains an unusual distribution, correction factors must be avoided. In many cases, isokinetic sampling (with or without correction factors) is used without particle-size data, since isokinetic conditions are needed to obtain valid samples for particle-size distribution evaluations.

Sampling trains have been mentioned previously and now will be discussed briefly. The typical sequence of components in a sampling train is nozzle, probe, particulate collector, cooling and/or gas collector, flow measurement device, vacuum source. Flow measurements can be made preceding or following the vacuum source. However, vacuum pumps have a tendency to leak, with the result that gas volumes measured downstream may be greater than those actually sampled. Some commonly used components are illustrated in Figure 1.5.6.[8] Ball-and-socket joints and compression fittings allow any desired arrangement of components to be set up rapidly under field conditions.

Although several sampling trains exist today, only the EPA train (shown in Figure 1.5.7) will be considered, as this is the one most commonly used for certification testing. The nozzle and probe direct the sampled particles and gases into the sample box. The pitot tube provides information on the stack velocity. A reverse or S-type pitot tube is normally used because it is less directional than the standard type of pitot tube. The sample box consists of two sections — one heated and one cooled. The heated section, which is connected to the probe, contains a filter holder and a glass fiber filter. It may also contain a cyclone assembly for collecting large particles. The cooled section acts as a moisture condenser and usually consists of modified and regular Greenburg-Smith impingers in an ice bath, followed by an impinger containing silica gel. The sampling box is connected to the meter box by several feet of umbilical cord. The meter box assembly contains a vacuum gauge, an airtight pump, a dry test meter, an orifice meter, an orifice manometer, and a pitot manometer. One of several serious discrepancies that arises in the front half of the EPA train is the failure of the electric heating system to maintain above the

aqueous dew point all the tubing preceding the exterior filter; if condensation occurs, and SO_2 is present, sulfate can form, thereby invalidating the results.[11]

The probe nozzle is selected — after accounting for changes in temperature, pressure, and moisture content (from condensation) in the train — so that the pump can maintain isokinetic velocity. For measurements at a single point, this may not be difficult; however, for multipoint sampling (which is most common), the mathematical and physical manipulations are often troublesome. A simplified procedure uses the null probe, examples of which are shown in Figure 1.5.8. Null probe designs all involve measurement of static pressure perpendicular to flow both inside and outside of the nozzle. The static-pressure taps are connected to opposite sides of an inclined manometer. In operation, the flow through the sampling train is adjusted until there is no pressure differential across the manometer. This is the null condition which in theory presents a situation where isokinetic sampling occurs. Null sampling probes, however, do not guarantee isokinesis. Even though the static pressures are equal, there may be differences in velocity between the inside and outside of the probe. The differences in turbulence for duct and probe flow, the nozzle shape (and its degree of surface roughness), and the location of the static holes may affect the relationship between balanced static pressure and isokinetic flow.

As a check on the stability of gas flow, a pitot tube can be placed at a reference point in the stack or located at the traverse point just prior to sampling. In a design adopted by the EPA, an S-type pitot tube and a hook sampling nozzle are mounted together so as to continuously measure velocity while sampling. Adjustments in sample flow can then be more rapidly applied to meet changes in stack flow conditions and thus more closely approach overall isokinetic sampling. Critics of this system point out that the proximity of the nozzle can influence the pitot tube readings and vice versa, so that the benefits may be outweighed by the effects on sampling results. Regardless of the sampling system used, it is essential that attempts be made to sample isokinetically when particles are greater than about 3 μm.

Adjustments in flow, when using the isokinetic design, require establishment of a prescribed methodology of data collection. A preferred tech-

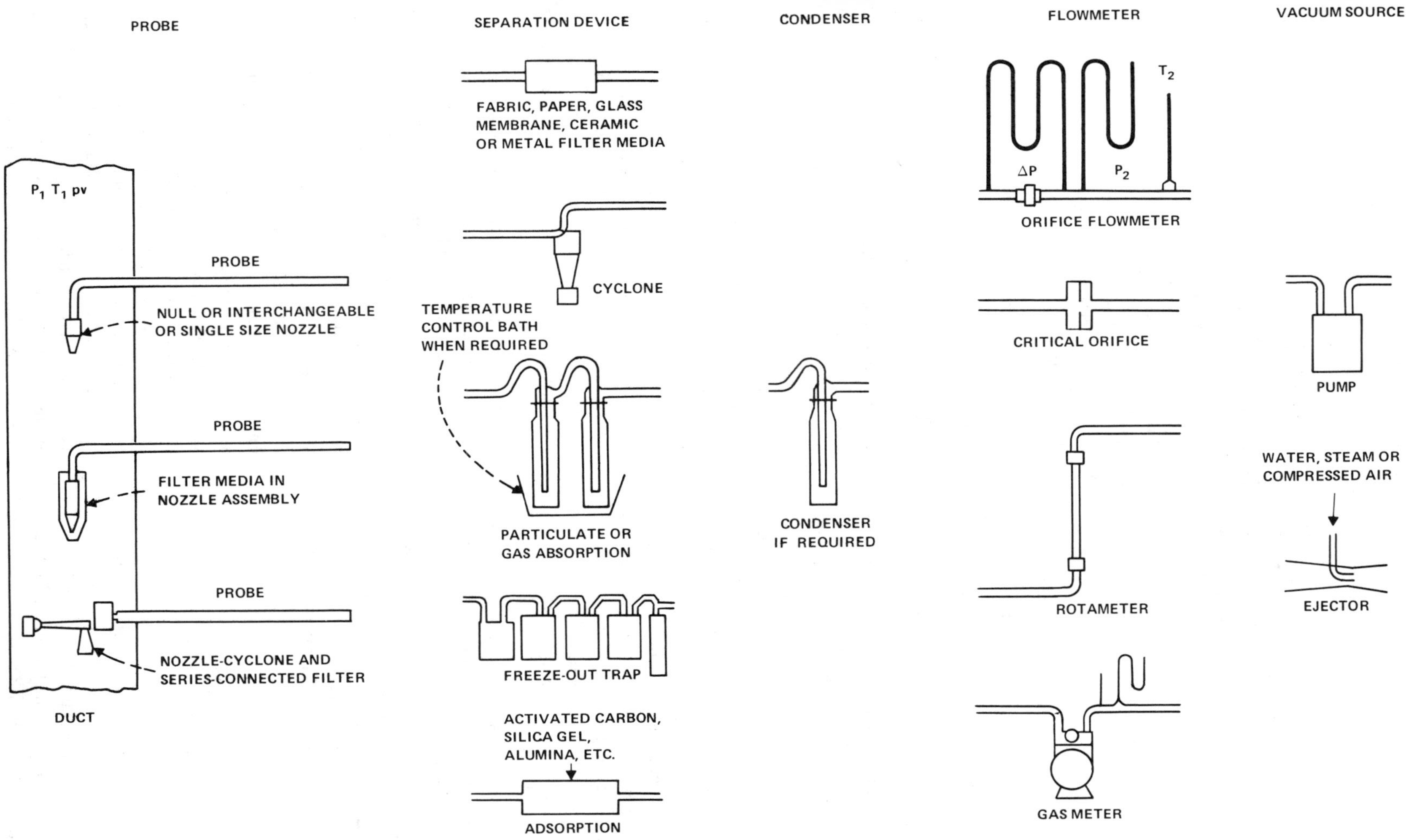

FIGURE 1.5.6. Components of common sampling systems.

15

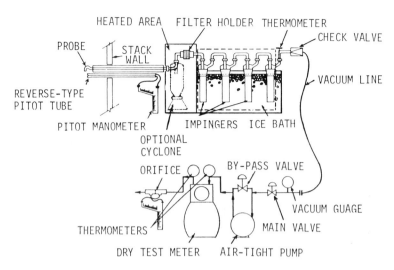

FIGURE 1.5.7. EPA particulate sampling train.

nique involves taking readings at fixed time intervals (e.g., 2 to 5 min) and recording data such as temperature, pressure, and flowmeter readings. Calculation and readjustment of flow rate are then made to meet changing requirements in the sampling system as the result of increased resistance to the air flow when filtration is included. Typically, it is found that the rate of change in resistance is the greatest near the end of the run or where the pump capacity is no longer adequate. This is easily sensed, and the run time can be adjusted accordingly. In this regard, if the run time is too small because the pump size is not adequate, it may be necessary to rerun with either a smaller nozzle size or a larger vacuum source. When possible, the nozzle diameter should not be less than approximately 1/4 in., although many sampling trains operate successfully with 1/8-in. nozzles. The sampling time at each traverse point should be the same for composite samples, regardless of the differing velocities at each point.

The particle-mass rate discharged from the stack (PRS) is extremely sensitive to the particle-mass rate in the nozzle (PRN). The two are related by the expression:

$$PRS = PRN \left(\frac{\text{cross-sectional area of stack}}{\text{cross-sectional area of nozzle}} \right)$$

Hence, if the nozzle diameter is 1/4 in. and the stack diameter is 10 ft, the ratio of the cross-sectional areas is approximately 250,000. It becomes very clear that a small error in PRN can cause erronious results in the PRS.

Temperature corrections are made as needed during the run; there must be a calibration chart for the metering element (viz., pressure drop vs. flow rate) to ensure that isokinetic conditions exist for the full range of sampling conditions.

The moisture correction, which must be applied if condensation occurs prior to metering, can be eliminated if the particulate collection and metering are conducted above the dew point. Rate meters that can be used in this way include orifices and venturi meters. If condensation does occur, it is necessary to determine the condensate's vapor fraction in the total gas-volume samples. This can be done simply by drawing a sample of the hot stack-gas psychrometry, as illustrated in Figure 1.5.9.

At the completion of the run, the sampler must be taken to a clean area, and dust that has been collected in the nozzle, probe, and collecting elements must be washed or brushed into the succeeding collector. The total catch in each stage is measured, and all stages are summed to obtain total particulate-mass loading.

As mentioned earlier, actual particulate flow rate determinations from industrial sources fall into two general categories: opacity measurements and mass measurements. There is no universally acceptable correlation between these two parameters, except in very special cases. Many pollution codes limit emissions of black smoke by setting Ringelmann number limits on the density or opacity of the plume. Smoke density is defined as the degree of blackness (opacity) of a plume expressed in terms of some arbitrary scale. The apparent blackness or stack plume opacity

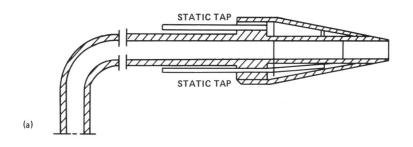

(a)

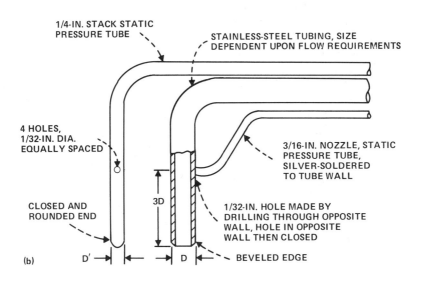

1/4-IN. STACK STATIC
PRESSURE TUBE

STAINLESS-STEEL TUBING, SIZE
DEPENDENT UPON FLOW REQUIREMENTS

4 HOLES,
1/32-IN. DIA.
EQUALLY SPACED

3/16-IN. NOZZLE, STATIC
PRESSURE TUBE,
SILVER-SOLDERED
TO TUBE WALL

CLOSED AND
ROUNDED END

3D

1/32-IN. HOLE MADE BY
DRILLING THROUGH OPPOSITE
WALL, HOLE IN OPPOSITE
WALL THEN CLOSED

(b)   D′   D   BEVELED EDGE

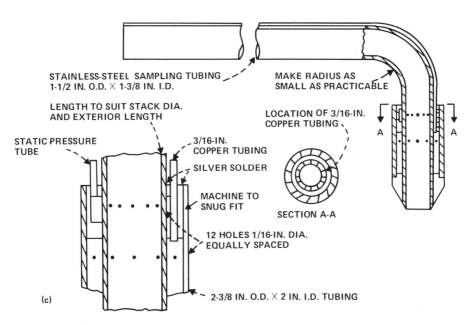

STAINLESS-STEEL SAMPLING TUBING
1-1/2 IN. O.D. × 1-3/8 IN. I.D.

MAKE RADIUS AS
SMALL AS PRACTICABLE

LENGTH TO SUIT STACK DIA.
AND EXTERIOR LENGTH

LOCATION OF 3/16-IN.
COPPER TUBING

A   A

STATIC PRESSURE
TUBE

3/16-IN.
COPPER TUBING

SILVER SOLDER

MACHINE TO
SNUG FIT

SECTION A-A

12 HOLES 1/16-IN. DIA.
EQUALLY SPACED

(c)   2-3/8 IN. O.D. × 2 IN. I.D. TUBING

FIGURE 1.5.8.   Null probes of various configurations.

depends on the concentration of the particulate matter in the effluent, the size of the particulate, the depth of the smoke column being viewed, natural lighting conditions such as the direction of the sun relative to the observer, and the color of the particles. One of the oldest and most common methods of describing the black smoke or opacity from a source is to compare it to the shades of gray on the Ringelmann chart. The Ringelmann system is virtually a scheme whereby graduated shades of gray, varying by five equal steps between white and black, may be accurately reproduced on a white background by means of a rectangular grid of black lines of definite width and spacing.[4] The procedure, given by Professor Maximilian Ringelmann, by which the charts may be reproduced is given in Table 1.5.3. The actual charts are shown in Figure 1.5.10. To use a chart, it is supported on a level with the eye, at a distance

from the observer where the lines on the chart merge into shades of gray and, as nearly as possible, are in line with the stack. The observer glances from the smoke (as it issues from the stack) to the chart and notes the number of the chart most nearly corresponding with the shade of the smoke; then, he records this number with the time of observation. A clear stack is recorded as No. 0; 100% black smoke is recorded as No. 5. In theory, such a number will correspond to the light transmittance of the plume. To determine average smoke emission over a relatively long period of time, such as an hour, observations are usually repeated at ¼- or ½-min intervals. The readings are then reduced to the total equivalent of No. 1 smoke as a standard, with No. 1 smoke considered as 20% density. The percentage "density" of the smoke for the entire period of observation is then obtained by the formula:

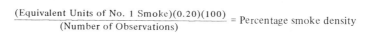

$$\frac{(\text{Equivalent Units of No. 1 Smoke})(0.20)(100)}{(\text{Number of Observations})} = \text{Percentage smoke density}$$

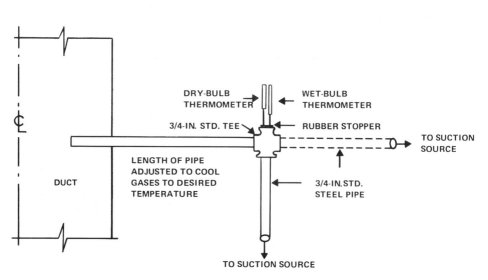

FIGURE 1.5.9.   Hot-gas psychrometry measurement.

TABLE 1.5.3

Spacing of Lines on Ringelmann Chart

Ringelmann chart no.	Width of black lines (mm)	Width of white spaces (mm)	Percent black
0	All white		0
1	1	9	20
2	2.3	7.7	40
3	3.7	6.3	60
4	5.5	4.5	80
5	All black		100

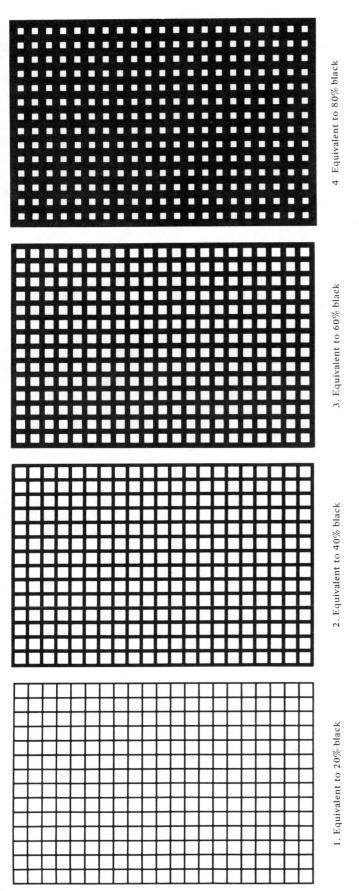

1. Equivalent to 20% black   2. Equivalent to 40% black   3. Equivalent to 60% black   4 Equivalent to 80% black

FIGURE 1.5.10. Ringelmann's scale for grading the density of smoke. (From U.S. Bureau of Mines, Department of the Interior Information Circular No. 6888. With permission.)

19

A convenient form for recording and computing the percentage of smoke density appears in Table 1.5.4. The timing and extent of observations made for the purpose of determining compliance with local smoke abatement ordinances depend on the wording and smoke limitations of these ordinances.

While the chart serves a useful purpose, it should be noted that the data obtained are empirical in nature and have definite limitations. Despite these limitations, the chart still provides the well-trained observer with good practical results. In fact, Ringelmann number criteria are in use almost everywhere in the United States.

Although the Ringelmann chart is only applicable to black smoke, "equivalent opacity" measurements (e.g., Ringelmann No. 1 corresponds to 20% opacity) are also applied to white smoke plumes. Furthermore, all qualified smoke readers must be able to read both white and black smoke.

To help quantify the Ringelmann measurement, a number of opacity measuring devices (photometers) have recently been introduced. While the

TABLE 1.5.4

Ringelmann Chart Reading

Location _____

Hour _____ 9:00–10:00 a.m. _____   Date _____

	0	1/4	1/2	3/4		0	1/4	1/2	3/4	Point of observation
0	–	–	–	–	30	1	1	1	1	
1	–	–	–	–	31	1	1	1	1	
2	–	–	–	–	32	–	–	–	–	
3	1	1	1	1	33	–	–	–	–	Distance to stack_____
4	1	1	1	1	34	–	–	–	–	
5	2	2	2	2	35	1	1	1	1	Direction of stack_____
6	2	3	3	3	36	1	1	1	1	
7	3	3	3	3	37	1	1	1	1	Direction of wind_____
8	2	2	1	1	38	1	1	–	–	
9	1	1	–	–	39	–	–	–	–	Velocity of wind_____
10	–	–	–	–	40	–	–	–	–	Equiv. No. 1 Units
11	–	–	–	–	41	–	–	–	–	_7_ Units No. 5 _____ 35 _____
12	–	–	–	–	42	–	–	–	–	
13	–	–	–	–	43	–	–	–	–	_7_ Units No. 4 _____ 28 _____
14	–	–	–	–	44	1	1	2	2	
15	–	–	–	–	45	2	2	3	3	_27_ Units No. 3 _____ 81 _____
16	–	–	–	–	46	3	3	3	3	
17	–	–	–	–	47	3	3	4	3	_34_ Units No. 2 _____ 68 _____
18	–	–	–	–	48	2	2	2	2	
19	2	2	2	2	49	2	2	2	2	_52_ Units No. 1 _____ 52 _____
20	2	2	2	2	50	2	1	1	1	
21	2	2	2	2	51	1	1	1	1	_113_ Units No. 0 _____ 0 _____
22	3	3	3	3	52	1	1	1	–	
23	3	4	4	4	53	–	–	–	–	_240_ Units _____ 264 _____
24	4	5	5	5	54	–	–	–	–	
25	5	5	5	5	55	–	–	–	–	$\frac{264}{240}$ × 20% =
26	4	4	3	3	56	–	–	–	–	
27	3	3	3	3	57	–	–	–	–	
28	2	2	1	1	58	–	–	–	–	_____ 22% _____ Smoke density
29	1	1	1	1	59	–	–	–	–	

Observer _____

Checked by _____

devices are not yet in widespread use, they are expected to improve the reproducibility of the opacity measurement. They still, however, suffer from the basic problems of this measurement — the requirement of daylight and black smoke.

Many stacks require virtually continuous monitoring to control smoke emissions; consequently, in-stack opacity measurements are attempted. These measurements are not useful when there is a detached plume that is essentially invisible in the stack but becomes visible some distance beyond the stack. Also, when stack gases are opaque due to condensed water vapor, this method does not serve a useful purpose. Steam plumes, although aesthetically unattractive, present no air pollution problem. The in-stack measurement of opacity, however, can still be very valuable in those situations where suspended particulates are the major contributor to opacity. To provide such continuous opacity measurements, a large number of stacks have been equipped with in-stack transmissometers (transmission photometers). A typical installation is shown in Figure 1.5.11. Usually a light or radiant heat beam is projected across the stack. The intensity of radiation reaching the other side is proportional to the number and size of particles obstructing the beam at any time. Once the unit is installed, it can be calibrated in place in terms of stack opacity with visual observations of the stack. The major problems with these systems are their propensity for becoming fouled and the difficulties associated with *in situ* calibration. Attempts to maintain clean and dust-free optics have been directed toward recessing the components away from the stack and continually sweeping clean air over the exposed areas. Often, however, these actions are inadequate and measurement accuracy suffers. After the instrumentation has been in use for some time, the optics can become dirty and scratched, and the detector and light-source characteristics can change. Therefore, regular recalibration is required. The problem is that there is no really acceptable means of accomplishing this recalibration, except for 0% transmission, unless the stack is taken out of use. Where the stack or duct is under negative pressure, it may, however, be possible to hinge the light source and sensor so that they can be easily swung open for lens cleaning. Also, the instruments are frequently equipped with calibration filters which can be dropped into the line of sight, thereby blocking a given portion of the radiation. However, to use the calibration panels, it is usually necessary to shut down the process or maintain the effluent at absolutely zero opacity. Some systems may also use a tubular sleeve to connect the light source and

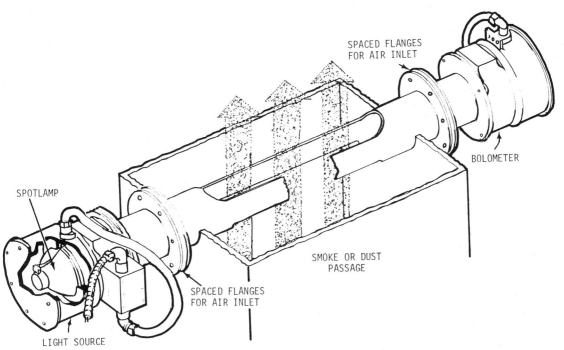

FIGURE 1.5.11.   Stack density transmitter.

detector. A transmission of 100% can be checked by flushing the tube with clean gas.

Misalignment between the light source and the receiver is another difficulty which may arise due to expansion or shifting of the stack. Setting the 100% transmission by removing the detector from the stack and calibrating separately is the normal recalibration procedure. This, though, does not actually represent 100% transmission in the real stack, primarily because of in-stack alignment variations and differing light-source characteristics. Furthermore, no test of intermediate transmission levels is possible, except under laboratory conditions.

There are certain inherent characteristics, common to all opacity instrumentation, which all but preclude their valid application to stack-gas particulate monitoring, the major one arising due to varying optical effects produced by particulates of different size and nature. With present knowledge, it is all but impossible to relate the concentration of particulates in a gas stream with optical opacity or other measurable optical phenomena. This was mentioned previously and warrants emphasis. A given weight concentration of particulate matter in a gas stream will absorb and reflect light to varying degrees, depending on the size and nature of the particles involved. For example, a given concentration of particulate matter of typical magnitude will attenuate a light beam very slightly if the particles are large in size (10 μm or larger). Smaller particles (1 to 10 μm) will have a greater attenuation effect. Attenuation will be very great for those particles having a size which approaches the wavelength of the light source (0.1 to 1.0 μm). Hence, the optical effect measured may vary by several orders of magnitude with no change in particle concentration, only a change in particle-size distribution. A second limitation of this type of instrument is that it "sees" only a limited portion of the total flow area. These instruments should be considered on the basis of what they really are and what they are capable of doing, i.e., indicating major deviations from normal conditions resulting from poor combustion, failure of particulate collection systems, or soot blowing.

Opacity measurements are useful in evaluating particularly bad (and nuisance-type) emissions, such as those found in incinerators and power plants. However, recent air pollution codes are aimed at controlling all particulates, day and night, regardless of color. To achieve this, regulations have been promulgated to control the total mass of emissions.

Many different approaches to particulate-mass measurements are in use. By far, the most common method is collection of the particulates by filtration, followed by drying and weighing. Glass-fiber filters are generally used to collect the particulates because they are relatively inert and because the sample-weight-to-filter-weight ratio is high. Alundum thimbles are also used, but have low sample-weight-to-thimble-weight ratios, making weighing small samples tricky. In addition, since filters are discarded after use but thimbles are cleaned and reused, clogging can be a problem in thimbles. Although it is generally agreed that no completely acceptable filter medium is available, flash-fired glass fiber is usually used in hot service, and paper is commonly used in cool service. The glass-fiber paper itself is usable in temperatures as high as 900°F. Unfortunately, this temperature is misleading because most commercial filter holders have a 400°F limit.

Two of the more common instruments for measuring mass are tape samplers and high-volume samplers. The tape sampler consists of a series of portions of filter paper (usually successive areas of a paper tape) clamped between an intake tube and a vacuum connection. Air is drawn through the filter for a selected time, usually 1 to 4 hr; then, a new portion of tape is moved into position and sampling is resumed. The tape sampler is cheap, simple, and rugged. It should, however, be used with the knowledge that its measurements, in whatever units, are arbitrary, artificial, and without absolute meaning. Their relative values can be useful, though, if the samplers (as well as their locations and installation and the technique used for their measurement) are rigorously standardized. The high-volume sampler, on the other hand, originally consisted of the motor and blower of a tank-type vacuum cleaner, suitably enclosed and fitted with a flat-paper holder in place of a dust bag. Present versions are more refined, but little different in concept. The use of a blower necessitates a filter of large area and low air resistance; it makes the sampling rate very dependent on the mass of material collected.

Considering the cumbersomeness of particulate collection trains and the sampling time needed to obtained a single mass measurement, it is readily apparent why so few good data exist. Obviously, one major improvement would be a continuous measurement. Isokinetic sampling would still be required, as would sampling traverses, but the time at each sampling point and the filter pretreating and weighing times would be considerably reduced. One currently marketed instrument that may achieve this result is the piezoelectric mass monitor. In this device, particles in the sample stream are electrostatically deposited onto a piezoelectric sensor. The added weight of particulate changes the oscillation frequency of the sensor in a known way. This instrument, however, cannot handle the very high particulate loadings found in many stacks without dilution of the sample. This dilution step complicates the sampling problems associated with use of the device by requiring two isokinetic samples: one of the stack and one of the diluted stack sample (see Figure 1.5.12).

Beta attenuation is another continuous monitoring system that is sometimes used on stacks. Commercial instrumentation that permits a particulate measurement every 15 to 30 min is available. In this type of device, the particulate sample is filtered using a continuous filter tape, and the mass of particulate filtered out is determined by measuring its attenuation of beta radiation. Since beta attenuation characteristics are not very different for a wide variety of stack particulate matter compositions, a direct mass measurement is possible.

Another relatively new technique to determine particulate-mass concentration is now under investigation; this procedure uses the narrow, monochromatic light beam of a laser. These characteristics allow the particulate concentration in a stack to be measured without having to put a sensing device within the stack itself. A typical laser light-source opacity monitor is shown in Figure 1.5.13. The laser light source is the heart of the monitor. It emits a well-collimated, linearly polarized light beam at a wavelength of 6,328 Å which is transmitted through the stack or duct to the sample detector cell on the opposite side of the stack. A portion of the laser beam (reflected from the tilted window) is used to illuminate the light-sensitive reference detector cell contained in the laser housing assembly.

Particulate matter in ambient air is measured by high-volume samplers, as described previously. Using this method, results of relatively high precision may be obtainable.

After the particulate matter is collected, its subsequent treatment must be considered. If only the overall weight is required, the use of filtration methods is satisfactory; the collector can be weighed before and after sampling, and the net

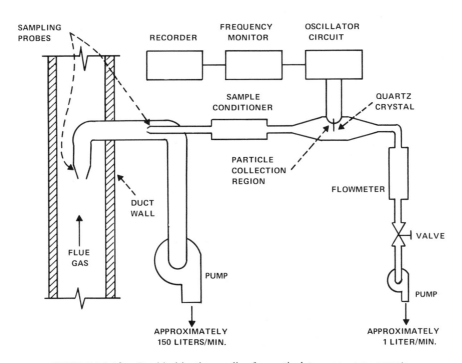

FIGURE 1.5.12.   Dual isokinetic sampling for particulate-mass measurements.

weight is obtained by the difference. If the sample is to be analyzed chemically, it will have to be removed from the filter or collecting medium, usually either by leaching or the use of a soluble filter medium. Perhaps of greatest importance is the sizing of the collected particles; this also presents the greatest technical difficulties. If liquid sedimentation or elutriation is to be used for sizing, leaching the filter with the sedimentation liquid is an acceptable method. However, for both liquid and air elutriation or sedimentation, a major problem lies in redispersing the collected sample into the particles and agglomerates which existed in the gas stream. There is no single unit of measurement of particle size. Rather, there are sizes based on linear dimensions, projected area, surface area, volume, and mass. Some of the instrumentation used to measure such properties

of particles is presented in Table 1.5.5. While the list is not intended to be exhaustive, it does contain the more commonly employed methods.

Physical sizing is one of the most common methods available for classifying (or sizing) particles. This is most often achieved by dry or wet screening with sieves, microscopic analysis, electric-gating techniques, and light-scattering methods. The microscopic technique (in which glass slides are passed through an aerosol and the diameters of the particles collected are measured) is time consuming and tedious. The results are usually biased in favor of the larger particles. In the electric-gating technique, as incorporated in the Coulter counter, particles suspended in an electrically conducting liquid flow through a small aperture between two electrodes. If a relatively nonconducting particle passes between the elec-

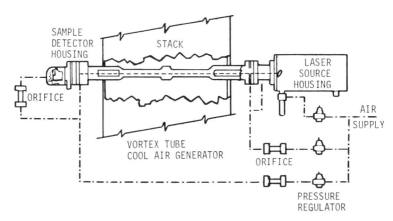

FIGURE 1.5.13.   In-stack laser light source opacity monitor.

TABLE 1.5.5

Some Common Particle Sizing Techniques and Associated Instrumentation

Property measured	Method	Size application (μm)
Length	Optical microscopy	0.5–2,000
	Scanning electron microscopy	0.02–500
	Transmission electron microscopy	0.002–10
Minimum length	Sieving	10–6,000
Projected surface area	Light scattering	0.3–30
	Automatic image analyzing microscopy	0.5–2,000
Surface area	Gas adsorption	0.001 m^2/g and up
Volume	Electrical resistivity	0.5–400
Mass	Sedimentation	0.5–200
	Elutriation	5–100
	Centrifugation	0.01–30
	Impaction	0.2–50
Crystallite volume	X-ray diffraction	0.015–0.050

trodes, a voltage decrease proportional to the size of the particle occurs between the electrodes. Measurement of the light scattered by individual particles has also been found to be a useful technique for particle-size determination. However, the intensity of light scattered by a particle is not only a function of the particle size but also of its index of refraction and shape. As a result, in those instances where a wide and unknown range of indices of refraction and shapes may exist in the sample (such as ambient particulate aerosols), the light-scattering method may give erroneous size values.

Each of the particle sizing methods discussed thus far has its limitations. More realistic determination of particle behavior in any environment must consider the size, shape, and density. The technique best able to accomplish this is aerodynamic sizing. Only by knowing the aerodynamic size of particles is it possible to determine how they will behave in an air stream and the kind(s) of control equipment required to capture them. Consider, for example, a ping-pong ball and a golf ball. Under a microscope they will appear almost equal in size; however, if both were tossed into a moving air stream, they would behave quite differently. Even though the size and shape are similar, the density is quite different, and the behavior of the two objects is far from being similar aerodynamically. This is the primary fallacy in physical sizing. The use of cascade impactors to aerodynamically size particles is probably the most widespread and accepted technique. The cascade impactor is constructed of a succession of jets, each followed by an impaction slide; it is based on the principle that particles in a moving air stream impact on a slide placed in their path if their momentum is sufficient to overcome the drag exerted by the air stream as it moves around the slide. As each jet is smaller than the preceding one, the velocity of the air stream, and therefore that of the dispersed particles, is increased as the aerosol advances through the impactor. Consequently, smaller particles eventually acquire enough momentum to impact on a slide, and a complete particle-size classification of the aerosol is achieved. The principle is demonstrated in Figure 1.5.14; a system developed by the Battelle Memorial Institute is shown in Figure 1.5.15. By timing the exposures and counting the number of particles collected on each slide, a particle-size distribution can be obtained.

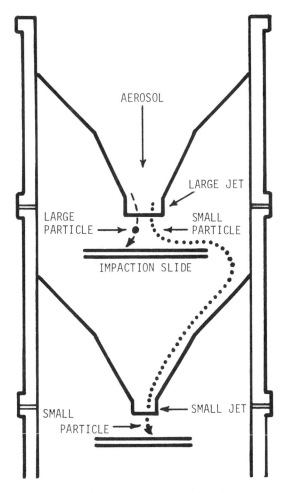

FIGURE 1.5.14. Principle of operation in a cascade impactor.

Some impactors, such as the Andersen sampler, attempt to overcome some of the limitations of single-orifice multistage cascade impactors. The latter collect only a small amount of sample because of the single-orifice stage design. Because of the single opening per stage, very high velocities, which can result in sample reentrainment, are required. The high velocities also usually necessitate a coating on the collection plate (to retain particles), which can adulterate the sample. The Andersen sampler consists of a series of stacked stages and collection surfaces (see Figure 1.5.16). Depending on the calibration requirements, each stage contains from 150 to 400 precisely drilled jet orifices, identical in diameter in each stage but decreasing in diameter on each succeeding stage. A constant flow of air is drawn through the sampler so that as the air passes from stage to stage through the progressively smaller

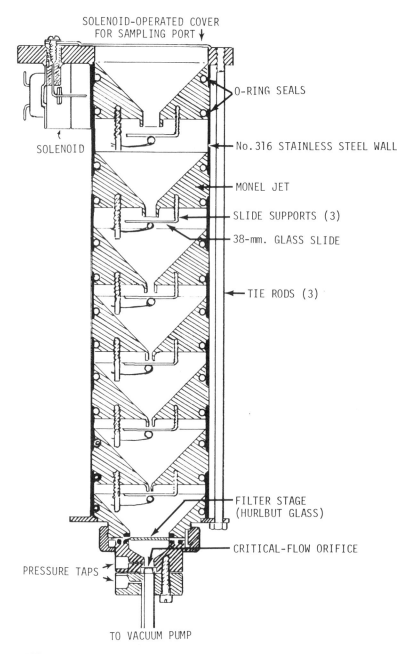

SOLENOID-OPERATED COVER
FOR SAMPLING PORT ↓

O-RING SEALS

SOLENOID

No.316 STAINLESS STEEL WALL

MONEL JET

SLIDE SUPPORTS (3)

38-mm. GLASS SLIDE

TIE RODS (3)

FILTER STAGE
(HURLBUT GLASS)

CRITICAL-FLOW ORIFICE

PRESSURE TAPS

TO VACUUM PUMP

FIGURE 1.5.15.   Cascade impactor developed by Battelle Memorial Institute.

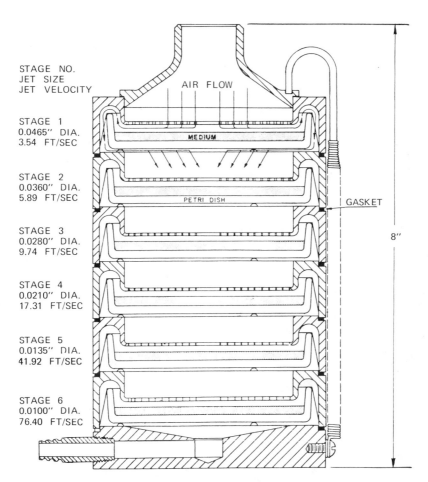

STAGE NO.
JET SIZE
JET VELOCITY

AIR FLOW

STAGE 1
0.0465" DIA.
3.54 FT/SEC

MEDIUM

STAGE 2
0.0360" DIA.
5.89 FT/SEC

PETRI DISH

GASKET

STAGE 3
0.0280" DIA.
9.74 FT/SEC

8"

STAGE 4
0.0210" DIA.
17.31 FT/SEC

STAGE 5
0.0135" DIA.
41.92 FT/SEC

STAGE 6
0.0100" DIA.
76.40 FT/SEC

FIGURE 1.5.16. Cross-sectional drawing of a six-stage Andersen dust sampler. (Courtesy of Andersen 2000, Inc. With permission.)

holes, the velocity increases as the air stream makes a turn at each stage; thus, the particle gains enough inertia to lose the aerodynamic drag. It is hurled from the air stream and impacted on the collection surface. The particle is aerodynamically sized the moment it leaves the turning air stream. Adhesive, electrostatic, and van der Waal's forces hold the particles to each other and to the collection surface. Moreover, the particles are not blown off the collecting plate by the jets of air because these jets follow laminar flow paths so that no turbulent areas exist. This results in complete dead air spaces over and around the samples. Oversampling to the point that the collection will build into the air stream is the only means by which reentrainment can occur. Because of its design, the Andersen concept permits greater volumes of sample to be drawn at much lower jet velocities. Also, due to its design, it is not

necessary to coat the collection plates, which results in an unadulterated sample, insignificant sample loss, and collection of enough sample to analyze accurately. The Andersen "in-stack" sampler (see Figure 1.5.17) permits in-stack iso-kinetic sampling up to $1,500°F$ since the unit features a stainless steel shell. Samples with broad size ranges are collected to produce particle sizes ranging from a minimum of 0.36 μm in the last stage to 20 μm and above in the top stage, depending on flow rate. With a proper backup filter, particles as small as 0.05 μm can be collected with 98% efficiency. Such in-stack samplers are applicable in all stack concentrations up to 1 grain/SCF. A mechanical separator (e.g., cyclone) must be used upstream from the stack head when the stack effluents contain particulates larger than 20 μm.

The previously discussed techniques have been effectively used to analyze particles as small as

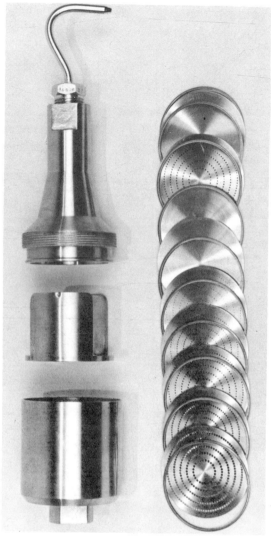

FIGURE 1.5.17. Andersen in-stack dust sampler. (Courtesy of Andersen 2000, Inc. With permission.)

charging of these smallest particles in order to derive numbers and effective sizes.

4. Electron microscopic techniques have been used to obtain particle counts as well as information on the size and morphology of these small particles.

Of these methods, only the electrical mobility separator has been used for chemical characterization of particles below 0.1 μm, but little analytical information is presently available. Electron microscopic methods can provide some insight into the chemical composition of the particles. However, in the most favorable cases, the composition of less than half of the particles observed was able to be determined.

1.6 PARTICULATE EQUIPMENT DESIGN CONSIDERATIONS

Control equipment for particulates falls into five general classes: (1) gravity settlers, (2) centrifugal separators (cyclones), (3) electrostatic precipitators, (4) fabric filters, and (5) wet scrubbers. Such equipment must be matched to the emission to be controlled in terms of variables such as flow rate, temperature, nature and concentration of pollutant, and desired degree of control. It is well recognized that no universal gas cleaning method exists which will satisfy all problems and conditions. The choice of method depends on many technical and economic factors.

Each air pollution problem is unique; therefore, preliminary knowledge of the pollutants is required in order to design compatible equipment. To acquire this knowledge, particulate samples must first be collected. The particulate properties most fundamental to the performance and choice of gas cleaning equipment are particle-size distribution, shape, structure, density, composition, electrical conductivity, abrasiveness, corrosiveness, flammability, hygroscopic properties, flowability, toxicity, and agglomeration tendencies. Also important is knowledge of the gas stream properties including temperature, pressure, humidity, density, viscosity, dew point for condensable components, electrical conductivity, corrosiveness, toxicity, composition, and flammability. The process conditions include the allowable pressure drop, electrical power requirements, collection efficiency requirements, particle concentration, and gas volumetric flow rate. The plant factors

approximately 0.2 μm. To characterize particles less than approximately 0.1 μm, several other techniques have been systematically used.

1. Saturation of the air and subsequent rapid expansion to cause a high supersaturation. The resulting droplet count is assumed to be equal to the total particle concentration.

2. Passage of the air through a long narrow channel. The smallest particles will be removed most rapidly by diffusion, and the extent of the effect can be calculated.

3. Measurement of the mobility of charged particles in an electric field. It is necessary to assume or compute the efficiency of electrical

include maintenance, space limitations, availability of utilities, safety and health protection, disposal facilities, and materials of construction. Finally, knowledge of auxiliary equipment is required, including pumps, fans, compressors, motors, ducting, valves, control instrumentation, storage facilities, and conveying equipment.

Although most of the properties and factors considered in the selection and design of collection equipment are self-explanatory, certain parameters merit further discussion. Particulates discharged from an operation consist of a size distribution ranging anywhere from extremely small particles (less than 1 μm) to very large particles (greater than 100 μm). Data on particle size and particle concentration for some typical industrial dispersoids are given in Table 1.6.1. Particle-size distributions are usually represented by a cumulative weight fraction curve in which the proportion of particles less than a certain size is plotted against the dimension of the particle. Figure 1.6.1 presents typical examples of cumulative weight fraction curves for fly ash and carbon black. The curve rises from 0 to 100% over the range of particle sizes present. To facilitate recognition of the size distribution, it is useful to plot a size-frequency curve (see Figure 1.6.2), which is simply the differential of the cumulative curve. The size-frequency curve shows the number of particles present for any specified diameter. Since most dusts are comprised of an infinite range of particle sizes, it is first necessary to classify particles according to some consistent pattern. The number of particles may then be defined as that quantity within a specified size range having finite boundaries and typified by some average diameter.

The shapes of the curves obtained to describe the particle-size distribution generally follow a well-defined form. If the data include a wide range of sizes, it is often better to plot the frequency (i.e., number of particles of a specified size) against the logarithm of the size. The usual normal-probability equation applies only to distributions which are symmetrical about a vertical axis (Figure 1.6.2, i.e., normal distribution). However, in most cases an asymmetrical or "skewed" distribution (as shown in Figure 1.6.3) exists; normal-probability equations do not apply to this distribution. Fortunately, in most instances the symmetry can be restored if the logarithms of the sizes are substituted for the sizes. The curve is then said to be logarithmic normal in distribution (as shown in Figure 1.6.4).

The equation of the normal-probability curve is given by:

$$y = \frac{\Sigma y}{\sigma \sqrt{2\pi}} \, \exp\left[-\frac{(d_p - \text{arithmetic avg. } d_p)^2}{2\sigma^2}\right] \qquad (1.6.1)$$

where

y = frequency of observations of diameter d_p;

Σy = total number of observations;

σ = = standard deviation =
$$\left[\frac{\Sigma(y(d_p - \text{arithmetic avg. } d_p{}^2))}{\Sigma y}\right]^{\frac{1}{2}}$$

d_p = particle diameter.

The equation of the log-normal distribution is obtained by substituting $\log \sigma$ for σ and $\log d_p$ for d_p. Then:

TABLE 1.6.1

Particle Size and Concentration for Typical Industrial Dispersoids

Industry	Dispersoid	Particle size by wt			Particle loading grains/cu ft (gr/ft³)
		0–1μm	0–5μm	0–10μm	
Electrical power	Fly ash from pulverized coal	1%	25%	50%	3
Cement	Kiln dust	1	20	40	10
Steel	Blast furnace after dry dust catcher	5	30	60	3
Steel	Open-hearth fume	90	98	99	1
Non-ferrous smelters	Copper roaster dust			20	10
Non-ferrous smelters	Converter furnace dust			30	5
Non-ferrous smelters	Reverberatory furnace dust			60	3
Chemical	H$_2$SO$_4$ acid fume	99			0.05
Chemical	H$_3$PO$_4$ acid fume	15	99		20

$$y = \frac{\Sigma y}{\log \sigma \sqrt{2\pi}} \exp \left[-\frac{(\log d_p - \log \text{geometric mean } d_p)^2}{2 \log^2 \sigma_G} \right]$$

$$(1.6.2)$$

where

σ_G = geometric standard deviation;

$$\log \sigma_G = \left[\frac{\Sigma (y(\log d_p - \log \text{geometric mean } d_p)^2)}{\Sigma y} \right]^{1/2}.$$

If the size-frequency data fit Equation 1.6.1 and are plotted on an arithmetic probability grid, the resulting summation curve is a straight line. Similarly, if the curve is asymmetric so that Equation 1.6.2 applies, then the data plot is a straight line on a log-probability grid (see Figure 1.6.5). The two cases are generally referred to as normal and logarithmic-normal distribution.

Equations 1.6.1 and 1.6.2 cover the range $-\infty$ to $+\infty$. Hence, the distribution must be asymptotic at both extremes. For practical reasons, however, the particles measured have a smallest and largest size; therefore, the distribution is not asymptotic, and plots on a probability grid often depart from the straight line at the extremes. This does not warrant much concern since the areas extending from the extremes to infinity are usually negligible compared with the area under the distribution curve within the size range measured.

The use of probability grids is of further value when the arithmetic or geometric mean is required, since these values may be read directly from the 50% point on the arithmetic and logarithmic probability grids, respectively. By definition of Equation 1.6.1, the size corresponding to the 50% point on the probability scale is the arithmetic average diameter. Similarly, since the probability integral shows that 68.26% of the total distribution lies between $(d_p + \sigma)$ and $(d_p - \sigma)$, the standard deviation is easily determined from such a plot as:

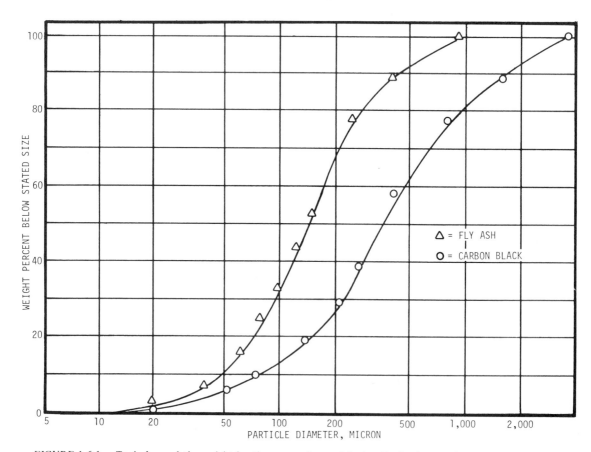

FIGURE 1.6.1.   Typical cumulative weight fraction curves for particle-size distributions of fly ash and carbon black.

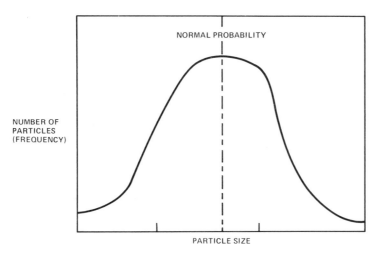

FIGURE 1.6.2.   Size-frequency curve.

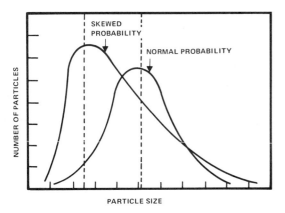

FIGURE 1.6.3. Skewed as compared to normal particle-size distribution.

σ = 84.13% size – 50% size

σ = 50% size – 15.87% size

By the definition of Equation 1.6.2, the skewed probability distribution can be similarly treated as a straight-line plot where the 50% value on the probability scale corresponds to the geometric mean diameter; the geometric standard deviation is given by:

σ_G = 84.13% size/50% size

or

σ_G = 50% size/15.87% size

The representation of particle-size analyses on probability coordinates has the advantage of simple extrapolation or interpolation from a minimum of data. The slope of the line is a

measure of the breadth of the distribution of sizes in the sample. For example, in Figure 1.6.6 curve A represents a batch of uniform-size particles; curve B has the same mean particle size with perhaps a 10-fold variation in diameter between the largest and smallest particles, whereas curve C may have a 20-fold variation. Curve D has the same 10-fold range of sizes as curve B, but in each weight percent category the particles are larger, so that curve D is a coarser grind than curve B but equal in range of sizes.

Efficiency is the other characteristic quantity which warrants further discussion. The efficiency of a particulate control device is usually expressed as the percentage of material collected by the unit compared with that entering the unit. It may be calculated on a particle number basis:

$$\eta_N = \left(\frac{\text{Particles collected}}{\text{Particles entering}}\right) 100$$

or on a total weight basis:

$$\eta = \left(\frac{\text{Inlet Loading} - \text{Outlet Loading}}{\text{Inlet Loading}}\right) 100$$

It is extremely important to distinguish between the two. Larger particles, which possess the greater mass and are more easily removed in a control device, will contribute much more to the efficiency calculated on a weight basis. Thus, if one considers a volume of aerosol which contains 100 1-μm particles and 100 100-μm particles, and if the efficiency of separation is 90% for 1-μm particles and 99% for 100-μm particles, then on a

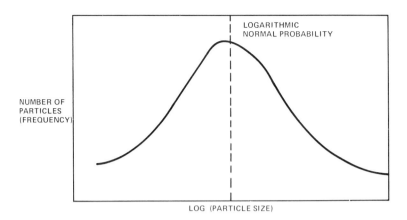

FIGURE 1.6.4.   Logarithmic-normal distribution.

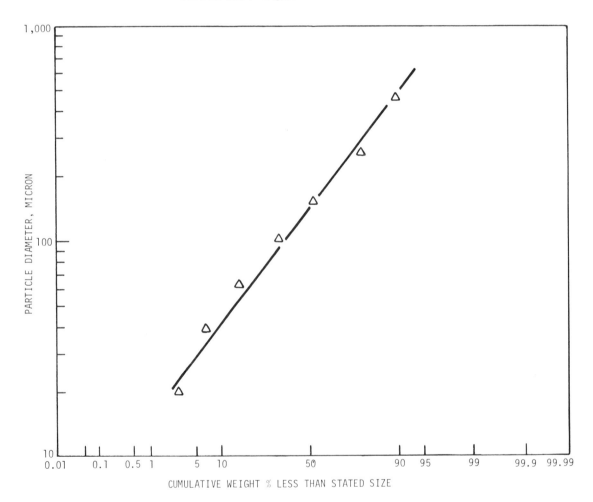

FIGURE 1.6.5.   Log-normal cumulative fly ash particle-size distribution.

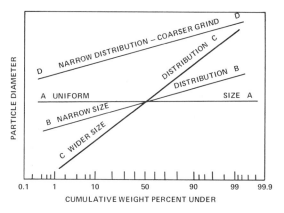

FIGURE 1.6.6. Effect of size distribution on relative probability plots.

particle count basis 90 1-μm and 99 100-μm particles will be removed out of a total of 200. This gives a particle count efficiency of:

$$\eta_N = \left(\frac{189}{200}\right) 100 = 94.5\%$$

On a weight basis, however, if a 1-μm particle has unit mass, a 100-μm particle has 10^6 mass units; the weight efficiency is given by:

$$\eta = \left(\frac{90(1) + 99(10^6)}{100(1) + 100(10^6)}\right) 100 \approx 99\%$$

Any expression of the efficiency of a particulate removal device is therefore of little value without a careful description of the size spectrum of particles involved.

It is interesting to note certain observations. The smaller particles, equivalent in mass to a considerably smaller number of large particles, have a much greater impact on visibility, health, and water droplet nucleation than the larger particles. When large tonnages are involved, the high mass efficiencies often reported for particle collection may lead to overly optimistic conclusions about emissions. The small weight percentages of particles that pass through the collector can still represent large *numbers* of particles escaping to the atmosphere. It would then seem that tonnage-collection figures and weight-removal efficiencies may really not be that adequate to delineate the entire particulate emission problem.

Finally, consider briefly the collection process for particulate control equipment. The overall process may be thought of as occurring in four separate and individual steps.

1. Deposition of particle(s) on a collector or collection surface.
2. Retention of particle.
3. Removal of particle.
4. Ultimate disposal of particle.

Design equations and predictive models are primarily based on step 1. Steps 2 and 3 are important considerations for proper operation and maintenance of the control device. The individual steps, as well as the overall collection process, are considered in detail in later chapters.

1.7. EFFECTS OF PARTICULATE AIR POLLUTANTS

There seems to be little question that during the more serious pollution episodes, air pollution can be a deadly killer. Hundreds of excess deaths have been attributed to incidents in London in 1952, 1956, and 1962; in Donora, Pennsylvania in 1948; and in New York City in 1953, 1963, and 1966. Many of these excess deaths were in failing health, generally by those suffering from lung conditions. Hundreds of thousands of people have suffered from serious discomfort and inconvenience, including eye irritation and chest pains, during these and other such incidents. There is considerable evidence of the chronic threat to human health from air pollution. This evidence ranges from the rapid rise of emphysema as a major health problem to statistical evidence on the reduced life span of individuals exposed to polluted atmospheres over extended periods of time.

Property damage is presently the best documented of the pollution effects. Nylons exposed to polluted atmospheres in Chicago and Los Angeles have disintegrated; historic statues and buildings in Venice and Cologne have been ruined; visibility on roadways and at airports has been affected; fruit, citrus trees, and vegetable crops have been destroyed in California, New Jersey, Georgia, Florida, Washington, and many other states. Even the health of cattle has been affected. Cleopatra's Needle, standing in New York City's Central Park, has deteriorated more in 80 years in that park than in 3,000 years in Egypt.

In 1968 the total national cost of damage resulting from air pollution was 16.1 billion dollars, which includes 5.2 billion dollars for residential property, 4.7 billion dollars for materials, 6.1 billion dollars for health, and 0.1 billion dollars for vegetation.[9] Table 1.7.1 gives the approximate distribution of the cost of the effects of air pollution among specific sources.

The greatest long-term need for a deeper understanding of the air environment lies in the most crucial area: the modes of action and effects of pollutants on man, animals, plants, and inanimate objects. Existing knowledge, buttressed by the clear need for haste, provides the current basis for the establishment of air quality criteria. However, the ability to refine and augment such criteria and standards, to predict the effects of pollutants, and to detect such effects at an early stage requires a more penetrating knowledge of the effects themselves and the mechanisms of contaminant generation.

The environmental effects of particulates are best analyzed in view of the particulate properties, both chemical and physical. Atmospheric particles can scatter and absorb light from the sun, thus reducing the visible radiation available to cities. The emission of fine particles into the atmosphere may also cause changes in the earth's heat balance, resulting in lower surface temperatures. However, the extent to which this occurs is somewhat controversial. Air-borne particles, particularly those with diameters less than 1 μm, can affect local and regional weather by serving as efficient condensation nuclei that influence the formation of clouds, fog, and haze. The clarity of the air or the visual range, or visibility, is reduced by suspended particulate matter. This is primarily the result of light scattering, especially by particles in the range of 1 to 10 μm. When they come into contact with surfaces, air-borne particles contribute to the corrosion of metals, the soiling and damaging of buildings, the discoloration and destruction of painted surfaces, and the deterioration of fabrics and clothing. They can constitute a

health hazard, particularly when associated with sulfur oxides. Numerous epidemiological studies have shown correlations between particulate pollution levels and daily mortality levels (all causes), daily bronchitis mortality, excess infant mortality, cancer mortality, increased incidence of bronchitis and asthma, pneumonia mortality, deaths due to chronic respiratory diseases, mortality from gastric cancer, and increased incidence of respiratory diseases in children. The threshold levels at which these effects first become evident, however, have not been clearly established, nor has it been possible to separate the effects of sulfur dioxide from those of the particulate matter with which it is commonly associated.

Particles with diameters in the approximate range from 0.1 to 10 μm are considered especially dangerous to health. They are small enough to be carried to the lower bronchi and lungs if inhaled, but are large enough that many settle in the lower respiratory tract and are not exhaled. Of particular importance are the chemical composition and solubility of particles in body fluids. These properties largely determine the probability of deposition in the respiratory tract and the ultimate path through, and consequences on, the body. Various studies have suggested that increased incidence of respiratory illness and increased mortality are statistically detectable where annual mean particulate levels are as low as 80 to 100 μg/m^3. The particulate concentration levels corresponding to specific adverse effects are presented in Table 1.7.2.[10]

A study of public reaction to air pollution has concluded that less than 10% of the population would consider air pollution to be a nuisance if the particulate concentrations were held below 75 μg/m^3. However, about 65% of the people would be bothered by a peak concentration of 260 μg/m^3.[10] The EPA has stipulated the danger

TABLE 1.7.1

National Costs of Pollution Damage, by Pollutants (Billion Dollars)

Effects (loss category)	SO$_x$	Part.	Oxidant	NO$_x$	Total
Residential property	2.808	2.392	–	–	5.200
Materials	2.202	0.691	1.127	0.732	4.752
Health	3.272	2.788	–	–	6.060
Vegetation	0.013	0.007	0.060	0.040	0.120
Total	8.295	5.878	1.187	0.772	16.132

TABLE 1.7.2

Particulate Concentration Levels Associated with Specific Adverse Effects

Effect	Particulate concentration level
Adverse health effects	Annual geometric mean level above 80 $\mu g/m^3$
Adverse effect on materials	Annual geometric mean level above 60 $\mu g/m^3$
Visibility reduction to 5 mi	150 $\mu g/m^3$

particulate level — the level at which "significant harm" to the health of individuals might occur during episodes of high air pollution — as 1,000 $\mu g/m^3$, 24-hr average.

The relationship of air contaminants to the ecology, the aggregate of living things as they exist together in nature, is almost a total mystery. It is possible to conceive of ecological cycles in which the specific toxicity of a pollutant for a single species could cause an entire food chain to collapse, but the extent to which this might occur is unknown. Too little is known of the effects of pollutants on too few species to even suggest how such problems might be attacked. That they must be attacked in the long run is certain, but it is equally certain that the attack will require the solution of a variety of difficult problems.

The causes of air pollution are human related, and the most significant effects are those associated with human health, property, and welfare. The solutions, likewise, are all human related and well within the resources of the civilization which created the problems and bears the consequences of their effects.

PROBLEMS

1. Determine the pitot tube locations in an 8-ft I.D. circular stack for a 16-point traverse.
2. For a rectangular duct, 3 ft X 1.5 ft, where would you recommend the pitot tube locations be placed?
3. From previous analysis, particulate matter from a grinding operation is known to have a log-normal distribution. Because of this, only four size fractions were used for a particle-size analysis. For the data given below:

Particle Size Analysis

Particle size (μm)	Total weight in each fraction (%)	Cumulative %
0–10	36.9	36.9
10–20	19.1	56.0
20–40	18.0	74.0
+40	26.0	100.0

a. Determine the geometric mean and geometric standard deviation.
b. Plot a frequency distribution curve.

4. Given the following data for log-normal distribution from various sources, plot the cumulative distribution curve for each source on log-probability graph paper.

Source	Mass mean diameter (μm)	Geometric deviation
Open hearth	0.36	2.14
Fly ash	6.8	4.54
Cement kiln	16.5	2.35
Gray-iron cupola	60.0	17.65
Fly ash, cyclone-type furnace	1.1	7.6

5. Sketch the frequency distribution curve for the following:

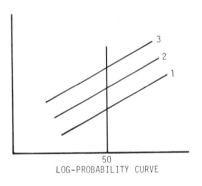

LOG–PROBABILITY CURVE

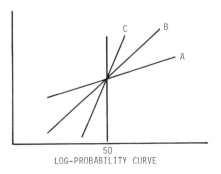

LOG–PROBABILITY CURVE

PROBLEM 5

REFERENCES

1. **Theodore, L. and Buonicore, A. J.,** *Industrial Control Equipment for Gaseous Pollutants,* CRC Press, Cleveland, 1975.
2. The Report of the Secretary of HEW to the U.S. Congress, the Air Quality Act of 1967, U.S. Government Printing Office, March 1970.
3. *Fed. Regist.,* 36, 8186, 1971.
4. U.S. Bureau of Mines Information Circular 6888.
5. **Edmisten, N. G., Stevens, G., and Holzschuk, D. P.,** Effective Enforcement through Opacity Provisions, presented at the 75th Natl. AIChE Meet., Detroit, June 3 to 6, 1973.
6. **Morrow, N. L., Brief, R. S., and Bertrand, R. R.,** *Chem. Eng.,* 79(2), 84, 1972.
7. **Osborne, M.,** personal communication.
8. **Bloomfield, B.,** in *Air Pollution,* Vol. 2, 2nd ed., Stern, A. C., Ed., Academic Press, New York, 1968, chap. 28.
9. **Barrett, L. B. and Waddell, T. E.,** *Cost of Air Pollution Damage: A Status Report,* U.S. Environmental Protection Agency, Publication No. AP-85, February 1973.
10. U.S. Department of Health, Education and Welfare, National Air Pollution Control Administration, Air Quality Criteria for Particulate Matter, Publication AP-49, Washington, D.C., January 1969.
11. **Osborne, M.,** Ten Common Errors and Misconceptions in Source Sampling, presented at the 4th Annu. Env. Eng. Sci. Conf., Louisville, March 4 to 5, 1974.

Chapter 2

FLUID-PARTICLE DYNAMICS

2.1. INTRODUCTION

Most industrial techniques used for the separation of particles from gases involve the relative motion of the two phases under the action of various external forces. The collection methods for particulate pollutants are based on the movement of solid particles (or liquid droplets) through a gas. The final objective is their removal in order to comply with applicable standards and regulations and/or their recovery for economic reasons. In order to accomplish this, the particle is subjected to external forces — forces large enough to separate the particle from the gas stream during its residence time in the control unit.

Prior to any discussion of fluid-particle dynamics, certain pertinent concepts that will be encountered frequently in this and subsequent chapters are now introduced.

The momentum of a system is defined as the product of its mass and velocity:

momentum = mass × velocity

One set of units for momentum is, therefore, lb ft/sec. The units of the time rate of change of momentum are simply the units of momentum divided by time, i.e.,

$$\text{rate of momentum} = \text{mass} \times \text{acceleration}$$
$$= \text{lb ft/sec}^2$$

The above units can be converted to lb_f if multiplied by an appropriate constant. Another defining equation is given by

$$1.0\ lb_f = 32.2\ \frac{lb\ ft}{sec^2}$$

If this equation is divided by lb_f, then

$$1.0 = 32.2\ \frac{lb\ ft}{lb_f\ sec^2}$$

This serves to define the conversion constant, g_c. Note that this conversion constant, like all others, is equal to unity. Any equation or term in an equation may, therefore, be multiplied or divided by g_c since this operation is equivalent to multiplying or dividing by unity. If the rate of momentum is divided by g_c as 32.2 lb ft/lb_f sec^2 — this operation being equivalent to division by unity — the following units result:

$$\text{rate of momentum} = \frac{lb\ ft}{sec^2} \Big/ \frac{lb\ ft}{lb_f\ sec^2}$$
$$= lb_f$$

From the above dimensional analysis it can be concluded that force is equivalent to rate of momentum and is given by the product of mass and acceleration. All theoretical equations must be dimensionally consistent prior to use in any calculation.

The basic principles of particle mechanics that underlie the description, operation, performance, and design of particulate collection devices are now presented.

2.2. THE DRAG FORCE

Whenever a difference in velocity exists between a particle and its surrounding fluid, the fluid will exert a resistive force upon the particle. Either the fluid (gas) may be at rest with the particle moving through it or the particle may be at rest with the gas flowing past it. It is generally immaterial which phase (solid or gas) is assumed to be at rest; it is the *relative* velocity between the two that is important. The resistive force exerted on the particle by the gas is called the *drag*.

In treating fluid flow through pipes, a friction factor term is used in many engineering calculations. An analogous factor, called the drag coefficient, is employed in drag force calculations for flow past particles. Consider a fluid flowing past a stationary solid sphere (see Figure 2.2.1). If F_D is the drag force and ρ is the density of the gas, the drag coefficient, C_D, is defined as

$$C_D = (F_D/A_p)/(\rho v^2/2g_c) \qquad (2.2.1)$$

where A_p is given by $\pi d_p^2/4$. In the following analysis, it is assumed that:

1. The particle is a rigid sphere (with a diameter d_p) surrounded by gas in an infinite medium (no wall or multiparticle effects).

2. The particle or fluid is not accelerating.

(These effects are considered in some detail in Section 2.6.) From dimensional analysis, one can then show that the drag coefficient is solely a function of the particle Reynold's number, Re, i.e.,

$$C_D = C_D(Re) \qquad (2.2.2)$$

where

$$Re = \frac{d_p v \rho}{\mu} \qquad (2.2.3)$$

and

μ = fluid (gas) viscosity;
ρ = fluid (gas) density.

The quantitative use of the equation of particle motion (to be developed in the next section) requires numerical and/or graphical values of the drag coefficient. These are presented in Figure 2.2.2 and Table 2.2.1, respectively.

A brief discussion of fundamentals is appropriate here because of the importance of air flow around particulates. No attempt will be made to develop the expressions for the distribution of momentum flux, pressure, and velocity. However, these expressions will be applied to develop some of the more important relationships.

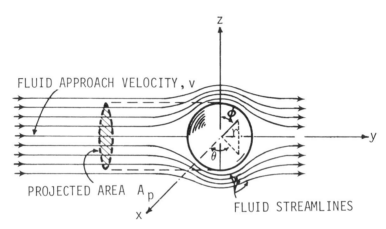

FIGURE 2.2.1. Fluid flow past a solid sphere.

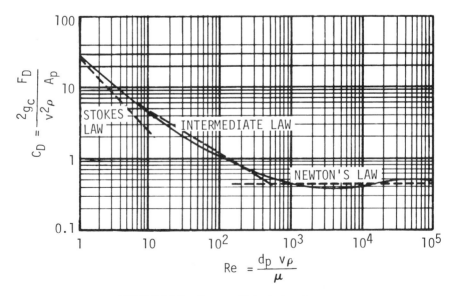

FIGURE 2.2.2. Drag coefficients for spheres.

TABLE 2.2.1

Calculated Versus Experimental Values for the Drag Coefficient as a Function of the Reynolds Number

Range	Re	C_d					
		Equation 2.2.6	Equation 2.2.7	Equation 2.2.8	Equation 2.2.14	Equation 2.2.15	Experimental
Stokes' law	0.01	2,400				2,364	2,100
	0.02	1,200				1,195	1,050
	0.03	820				803	700
	0.05	490				488	420
	0.07	350				352	300
	0.10	290				249	240
	0.20	120				129	120
	0.30	82				88.3	80
	0.50	49				55.0	49.5
	0.70	35				40.5	36.5
	1.00	24			22.4	29.5	26.5
Intermediate	2		12.0			16.2	14.4
	3		9.5		10.5	11.6	10.4
	4		7.8			9.2	8.2
	5		6.9			7.7	6.9
	6		—		6.23	—	5.9
	7		5.4			5.97	5.4
	10		4.5		4.26	4.61	4.1
	20		3.0			2.90	2.55
	30		2.4			2.26	2.0
	40		2.0		1.71	1.93	1.6
	50		1.8			1.71	1.5
	70		1.5			1.45	1.27
	90				1.11		1.14
	100		1.2			1.23	1.07
	200		0.80		0.785	0.93	0.77
	300		0.68			0.82	0.65
	400		0.60			0.76	0.57
	500		0.56		0.568	0.71	0.55
Newton's law	700			0.44	—	0.66	0.50
	900			0.44	0.482	—	0.46
	1,000			0.44	—	0.61	0.45
	2,000			0.44	—	0.54	0.42
	3,000			0.44	0.393	0.51	0.40
	4,000			0.44	—	0.49	0.39
	5,000			0.44	—	0.48	0.385
	7,000			0.44	0.386	0.47	0.39
	9,000			0.44	0.398	—	0.40
	10,000			0.44	—	0.46	0.405
	20,000			0.44	0.451	0.44	0.45
	30,000			0.44	—	0.43	0.47
	40,000			0.44	—	0.42	0.48
	50,000			0.44	—	0.42	0.49
	60,000			0.44	0.520	—	0.49
	70,000			0.44	—	0.42	0.50
	100,000			0.44	0.466	0.42	0.48
	200,000			0.44	—	0.41	0.42
	300,000			—	—	—	0.20
	400,000			—	—	—	0.084
	600,000			—	—	—	0.10
	1,000,000			—	—	—	0.13
	3,000,000			—	—	—	0.20

Consider the very slow flow of a gas about a solid spherical particle (see Figure 2.2.1). The sphere has a diameter, d_p, and a radius, a; the gas has a viscosity and density, μ and ρ, respectively. For the above condition, the inertial terms in the equation of motion are negligible.[1] The momentum flux, pressure distribution, and velocity components in spherical coordinates can then be determined analytically.[2] These equations are given in spherical coordinates (r, θ, ϕ) by

$\tau_{r\theta} = (3\mu v/2a)(a/r)^4 \sin \theta$
$p = p_o - \rho gz - (3\mu v/2a)(a/r)^2 \cos \theta$
$v_r = v [1 - (3a/2r) + 0.5 (a/r)^3] \cos \theta$
$v_\theta = -v [1 - (3a/4r) + 0.25 (a/r)^3] \sin \theta$

where

$\tau_{r\theta}$ = viscous stress;
p = local pressure;
p_o = pressure in the plane z (equal to 0 far away from the sphere);
g = gravitational force.

These equations are valid only for "creeping flow," which occurs for this system when the particle Reynold's number (based on the diameter of the spherical particle) is less than 0.1. This flow region is characterized by the virtual absence of eddying (mixing) downstream from the sphere. The drag force, F_D, exerted on the particle by the gas is computed by integrating the normal (pressure) force (giving rise to "form" drag) and the tangential (viscous) force (giving rise to "skin" drag) over the surface of the sphere. The end result is given by

$$F_D = 6\pi\mu va/g_c = 3\pi\mu vd_p/g_c \qquad (2.2.4)$$

Equation 2.2.4 is known as Stokes' law. However, keep in mind that Stokes' equation is valid only for very low Reynolds numbers — up to Re $\approx$ 0.1; at Re = 1, it predicts a value for the drag force that is nearly 10% too low. In practical applications, Stokes' law is generally assumed applicable up to a Reynolds number of 2.0. By rearranging Stokes' law in the form of Equation 2.2.1, the drag coefficient becomes

$$C_D = (6\pi\mu va/\pi a^2)/(\rho v^2/2) \qquad (2.2.5)$$

Hence, for "creeping flow" around a particle,

$$C_D = 24/Re \qquad (2.2.6)$$

This is the straight-line portion of the log-log plot of C_D vs. Re (Figure 2.2.2). For higher values of the Reynolds number, it is almost impossible to perform purely theoretical calculations. Several investigators have managed to estimate with a considerable amount of effort the drag and/or drag coefficient at higher Reynolds numbers. For example, Oseen[21] linearized the inertial terms and solved the resultant equation of motion to obtain

$$F_D = 6\pi\mu va [1 + (3/8) Re]/g_c$$

Strictly speaking, then, the C_D values for Re greater than 0.1 are experimentally derived.

A qualitative explanation of the drag coefficient (Reynolds number curve, Figure 2.2.2) is now presented. At larger values of the Reynolds number, separation of the flow occurs on the downstream side of the sphere, with the formation of an unsteady eddying wake. At still higher values of Re, the flow in the wake becomes completely turbulent. Under these circumstances it is no longer possible to calculate the drag from the equations of motion, and one must use direct measurement instead. The nature of the flow is illustrated in Figure 2.2.3. As Re is increased beyond the range of Stokes' law, separation occurs at a point just forward of the equatorial plane (as shown in Figure 2.2.3.a), and a wake, covering the entire rear hemisphere, is formed. A wake is characterized by a large friction loss. It also develops a large form drag; in fact, most form drag occurs as a result of wakes. In a wake the angular velocity of the vortices, and therefore their kinetic energy of rotation, is large. The pressure in the wake is less than that in the separated boundary layer; a suction develops in the wake, and the component of the pressure vector acts in the direction of flow. The pressure drag, and hence the total drag, is large. This is shown (see Figure 2.2.2) by the upward trend of the drag coefficient. At larger Re values, a true boundary layer forms, originating at the apex (stagnation point in Figure 2.2.3). The boundary layer grows and separates, flowing freely around the wake after separation. At first the boundary layer is in laminar flow, both before and after separation. As Re is further increased, transition to turbulence takes place, first in the free boundary layer and then in the boundary layer still attached to the front hemi-

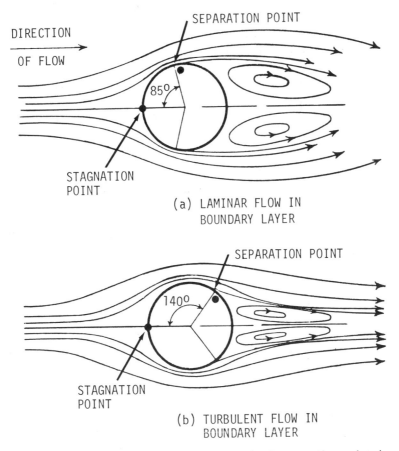

DIRECTION OF FLOW

SEPARATION POINT

85°

STAGNATION POINT

(a) LAMINAR FLOW IN BOUNDARY LAYER

SEPARATION POINT

140°

STAGNATION POINT

(b) TURBULENT FLOW IN BOUNDARY LAYER

FIGURE 2.2.3. Flow past a single sphere, showing separation and wake formation.

sphere of the sphere. When turbulence occurs in the latter, the separation point moves toward the rear of the body, and the wake shrinks (as shown in Figure 2.2.3.b). Both friction and drag decrease, and the remarkable drop in drag coefficient (from 0.45 to 0.10 at a Re of about 250,000) is a result of the shift in the separation point when the boundary layer attached to the sphere becomes turbulent.

In other words, separation of the flow, with the formation of an eddying or turbulent wake as illustrated in Figure 2.2.3, causes failure to achieve the full pressure recovery over the rear half of the sphere; this contributes directly to the form drag. At large values of the Reynolds number, the flow over the front half of a sphere may be divided into a thin boundary-layer region, in which the effects of viscosity are important, and an outer region, in which the flow corresponds to that of an inviscid fluid. The normal pressure distribution over the front half may then be calculated from the theory

of flow of ideal or nonviscous fluids. The tangential shearing stress can be approximately calculated from boundary-layer theory. This method of analysis, however, cannot be extended to flow over the rear half of the sphere.

Over the front half of the sphere the fluid experiences a falling pressure from the front stagnation point to the point of minimum pressure. This favorable pressure gradient has a stabilizing effect on the boundary layer which, therefore, remains laminar. Once the minimum pressure point (halfway around the surface of the sphere) is passed, however, the boundary layer has to face an adverse pressure gradient. This rapidly leads to separation of the boundary layer and the formation of a wake. Laminar separation generally occurs at only a very short distance behind the minimum pressure point. At very large values of the Reynolds number, however, transition to turbulent flow in the boundary layer will take place before laminar separation can occur. In these circumstances the boundary layer with turbulent flow will adhere to the surface for a slightly greater distance before turbulent separation occurs. As indicated earlier, the result of this change in the flow is a net decrease in the total drag due to the smaller form drag. The sudden change in the drag coefficient is shown in Figure 2.2.2, occurring at an Re value between 10^5 and 10^6.[3]

Several simple empirical drag coefficient expressions are available. Three such models are now examined.

In addition to the analytical equation (Equation 2.2.6), one may use

$$C_D = 18.5/Re^{0.6} \; ; \; 2 < Re < 500 \qquad (2.2.7)$$

for the "intermediate" range. This indicates a lesser dependence than Stokes' law on Re; it is less accurate than Stokes' law for Re < 2. At higher Re the drag coefficient is approximately constant. This is the Newton's law range, for which

$$C_D \approx 0.44; \; 500 < Re < 200,000 \qquad (2.2.8)$$

In this region the drag force on the sphere is proportional to the square of the gas velocity. (Note that Newton's law for the drag force is not to be confused with Newton's law of viscosity or Newton's laws of motion.) A simple two-coefficient model of the form

$$C_D = \alpha \, Re^{-\beta} \qquad (2.2.9)$$

can be used over the three Reynolds-number ranges given in Equations 2.2.6 to 2.2.8. The numerical values of α and β are given below.

	α	β
Stokes range	24.0	1.0
Intermediate range	18.5	0.6
Newton range	0.44	0.0

Using the model in Equation 2.2.1, the drag force becomes

$$F_D = (\alpha \pi (d_p v)^{2-\beta} \mu^\beta \rho^{1-\beta})/8g_c \qquad (2.2.10)$$

The above equation reduces to

$$F_D = 3\pi\mu v d_p/g_c \qquad (2.2.11)$$

for the Stokes' law range (Re < 2),

$$F_D = 2.31\pi(d_p v)^{1.4} \, \mu^{0.6} \, \rho^{0.4}/g_c \qquad (2.2.12)$$

for the intermediate range (2 < Re < 500), and

$$F_D = 0.055\pi(d_p v)^2 \, \rho/g_c \qquad (2.2.13)$$

for the Newton's law range (500 < Re < 200,000). This two-coefficient, three-Reynolds-number range model will be used repeatedly for drag force calculations in this and subsequent chapters. Numerical values and experiments for the drag coefficient from the model, Equations 2.2.6 to 2.2.8, are presented in Table 2.2.1. A comparison between the two indicates that these equations are fairly consistent with the experimental values found in the literature.

Another empirical drag coefficient model is given by Equation 2.2.14:[4]

$$\log C_D = 1.35237 - 0.60810 \, (\log Re) - 0.22961 \, (\log Re)^2 + 0.098938 \, (\log Re)^3 + 0.041528 \, (\log Re)^4 - 0.032717 \, (\log Re)^5 + 0.007329 \, (\log Re)^6 - 0.0005568 \, (\log Re)^7 \qquad (2.2.14)$$

This is an empirical equation which has been obtained by the use of a statistical fitting technique. As is evident from Table 2.2.1, this correlation gives excellent results over the entire range of Reynolds numbers. An advantage of using this correlation is that it is not partitioned for application only to a specific Reynolds number range. However, the lengthy calculation warrants its use only as a subroutine in a computer program.

Still another empirical equation[5] is

$$C_D = [0.63 + (4.80/\sqrt{Re})]^2 \qquad (2.2.15)$$

This correlation is also valid over the entire spectrum of Reynolds numbers. Its agreement with literature, as seen from Table 2.2.1, is generally good. However, in the range of 30 < Re < 10,000, there is considerable deviation. For Re < 30 or Re > 10,000, the agreement is excellent. This correlation lends itself easily to manual or computer calculations.

2.3. EQUATION OF PARTICLE MOTION

Consider a solid spherical particle located in a gas stream and moving in one direction with a velocity, v, relative to the gas. The net or resultant force experienced by the particle is given by the summation of all the forces acting on the particle. These forces include drag, buoyancy, and one or more external forces (such as gravity, centrifugal, and electrostatic). In order to simplify the presentation, the direction of particle movement relative to the gas is always assumed to be positive. Newton's law of motion is then

$$F_R = F - F_B - F_D \tag{2.3.1}$$

where

F_R = resultant or net force;
F = external force;
F_B = buoyant force;
F_D = drag force.

The net force results in acceleration of the particle, given by

$$F_R = \frac{m}{g_c} \left(\frac{dv}{dt} \right) \tag{2.3.2}$$

where

m = mass of the particle $(\pi d_p^3 \rho_p / 6)$;
ρ_p = particle density.

The external force per unit mass is denoted as f. The external force, F, on the particle is then

$$F = mf \tag{2.3.3}$$

Unless the particle is in a vacuum, it will experience a buoyant force in conjunction with the external force(s); this is given by

$$F_B = m_f f \tag{2.3.4}$$

where

m_f = mass of gas (fluid) displaced by the particle.

The equation of motion now becomes

$$\left(\frac{dv}{dt} \right) / g_c \quad = f - \left(\frac{m_f}{m} \right) f - \left(\frac{F_D}{m} \right)$$
$$= f \left[1 - (m_f/m) \right] - (F_D/m)$$
$$= f \left[(m - m_f)/m \right] - (F_D/m) \tag{2.3.5}$$

This equation may also be written as

$$(dv/dt)/g_c = (fm_{eq}/m) - (F_D/m) \tag{2.3.6}$$

where

$$m_{eg} = (m - m_f), \text{ or}$$

$$(dv/dt)/g_c = f \left[1 - (\rho/\rho_p) \right] - (F_D/m)$$
$$= f \left[(\rho_p - \rho)/\rho_p \right] - (F_D/m) \tag{2.3.7}$$

For gases, $\rho_p >>> \rho$, so that the bracketed terms in Equations 2.3.5 and 2.3.7 reduce to unity.

The particle may be acted upon by one or more external forces. If the external force is gravity,

$$f_g = g/g_c$$

and

$$F_g = m(g/g_c)$$

The describing equation for particle motion then becomes

$$(dv/dt)/g_c = (g/g_c) - (F_D/m) \tag{2.3.8}$$

If the particle experiences an electrostatic force, F_E, then

$$F_E = m f_E$$

so that

$$(dv/dt)/g_c = f_E - (F_D/m) \tag{2.3.9}$$

where

f_E = the electrostatic force per unit mass of particle.

If the external force is from a centrifugal field,

$$f_C = r \omega^2 / g_c = v_\phi^2 / g_c r$$

with the centrifugal force, F_C, then

$$F_C = m f_C$$

where

r = the radius of the path of the particle;
f_C = the centrifugal force per unit mass of particle;
ω = the angular velocity;
v_ϕ = the tangential velocity at that point.

The describing equation becomes

$$(dv/dt)/g_c = (r\omega^2/g_c) - (F_D/m) \qquad (2.3.10)$$

or

$$(dv/dt)/g_c = (v_\phi^2/g_c r) - (F_D/m) \qquad (2.3.11)$$

The reader is again reminded of the use of g_c. Any term or group of terms in the above equations may be indiscriminately multiplied or divided by this conversion constant.

2.4. TERMINAL SETTLING VELOCITY – STEADY FLOW

If a particle is initially at rest in a stationary gas and is then set in motion by the application of a constant external force or forces, the resulting motion occurs in two stages. The first period (considered in the next section) involves acceleration, during which time the particle velocity increases from zero to some maximum velocity. The second stage occurs when the particle achieves this maximum velocity and remains constant. During the second stage, the particle is not accelerating. The LHS (left-hand sides) of Equations 2.3.5 through 2.3.11 are, therefore, zero. The final, constant, and maximum velocity attained is defined as the terminal settling velocity of the particle. Most particles reach their terminal settling velocity almost instantaneously.

Consider the equations examined in the previous section under terminal settling conditions. Since

$$dv/dt = 0$$

the general equation for particle motion becomes

$$0 = f - (F_D/m)$$

or

$$f = F_D/m \qquad (2.4.1)$$

The units of f in this equation are ft/sec^2. The general equation for the terminal settling velocity is obtained by direct substitution of Equation 2.2.10 into Equation 2.4.1 and solving for v. Thus,

$$f = 3\alpha v^2 \, \mu^\beta \, \rho/4d_p \, (d_p v\rho)^\beta$$

so that

$$v = [4fd_p^{1+\beta} \, \rho_p/3\alpha\mu^\beta \, \rho^{1-\beta}]^{1/(2-\beta)} \qquad (2.4.2)$$

For the Stokes' law range, Equation 2.4.2 becomes

$$v = fd_p^2 \, \rho_p/18 \, \mu \qquad (2.4.3)$$

For the intermediate range,

$$v = 0.153f^{0.71} \, d_p^{1.14} \, \rho_p^{0.71}/\mu^{0.43} \, \rho^{0.29} \qquad (2.4.4)$$

Finally, for Newton's law range,

$$v = 1.74 \, (fd_p \, \rho_p/\rho)^{0.5} \qquad (2.4.5)$$

Keep in mind that f denotes the external force per unit mass of particle. One consistent set of units for the above equations is ft/sec^2 for f, ft for d_p, lb/ft^3 for ρ, lb/ft sec for μ, and ft/sec for v.

Ordinarily, determining the settling velocity of a particle of known diameter would require a trial-and-error calculation since the particle's Reynolds number is unknown. Thus, one cannot select the proper describing drag force equation. This iterative calculation can be circumvented by rearrangement of the drag force equations and solving for the settling velocity directly. Both sides of Equations 2.4.3 and 2.4.5 are multiplied by

$$(d_p \, \rho/\mu)$$

A dimensionless constant, K, is defined as

$$K = d_p(f \, \rho_p \, \rho/\mu^2)^{1/3} \qquad (2.4.6)$$

Equations 2.4.3 and 2.4.5 can now be rewritten, respectively, as

$$Re = K^3/18 \qquad (2.4.7)$$

and

$$Re = 1.74 \, K^{1.5} \qquad (2.4.8)$$

Since K is not a function of the settling velocity, the choice of drag force equations may now be based on calculated K values. These new K range limits are given as follows:

$K < 3.3$	Stokes' law range
$43.6 > K > 3.3$	Intermediate range
$2{,}360 > K > 43.6$	Newton's law range

If K is greater than 2,360, the drag coefficient may change abruptly with small changes in fluid velocity. Under these circumstances, the terminal velocity is calculated from Equation 2.4.1, in view of Equation 2.2.1, using a value of C_D found by trial and error from Figure 2.2.2.

2.5. TIME-VARIABLE MOTION – TRANSIENT FLOW

Although acceleration effects are always present in actual fluid-particle systems, they are usually neglected. The period of acceleration is comparatively short, usually on the order of 100th of a second or less. Nevertheless, this phenomenon should be well understood by the individual striving to achieve a thorough and fundamental understanding of particulate control equipment.

The previous section served to define the terminal settling velocity of a particle. The equation(s) describing particle motion were algebraic, and various solutions were presented for steady flow conditions. However, when the particle is accelerating, the describing equations become differential in time; the acceleration term (dv/dt) is no longer zero and must be retained. These equations are, naturally, more difficult to handle analytically. To simplify the presentation in this section, the drag force equations are still assumed to be applicable (despite the presence of acceleration effects). In addition, the direction of particle movement (relative to the fluid) is assumed to be positive. The equation of motion is now examined under time-variable (transient) flow conditions; solutions will be presented for several specific but appropriate situations.

Consider particle motion without an external force present. The describing equation is

$$(m/g_c)\ (dv/dt) = -F_D$$

Since

$$F_D = C_D A_p\ \rho\ v^2/2\ g_c$$

with

$$A_p = \pi\ d_p^2/4$$

and

$$m = \pi\ d_p^3\ \rho_p/6$$

then

$$(\pi\ d_p^3\ \rho_p/6g_c)\ (dv/dt) = -C_D\ \rho v^2\ \pi\ d_p^2/8g_c$$

Rearranging the above equation gives

$$dv/dt = -3\ \rho\ C_D v^2/4\ d_p\ \rho_p \qquad (2.5.1)$$

Equation 2.5.1 may be rewritten in a different form. Multiplying both sides by $\rho d_p/\mu$ gives

$$d(\rho v d_p/\mu)/dt = -3\ C_D\ \rho^2 v^2/4\ \rho_p \mu$$

or

$$d(Re)/dt = -3\ C_D\ \rho^2 v^2/4\ \rho_p \mu$$

This may be rearranged to

$$d(Re)/C_D\ \rho^2 v^2 = -(3/4\ \rho_p\ \mu)\ dt$$

Multiplying through by $(\mu/d_p)^2$ gives

$$d(Re)/C_D\ (\rho v d_p/\mu)^2 = -(3\ \mu/4\ \rho_p\ d_p^2)\ dt$$

The equation is then written as

$$d(Re)/C_D\ Re^2 = -(3\ \mu/4\ \rho_p\ d_p^2)\ dt \qquad (2.5.2)$$

This is a popular form of the describing equation that appears in the literature for a particle moving through a medium in the absence of any external force.

Equation 2.5.1 may now be solved in the three Reynolds number ranges. Applying Stokes' law to Equation 2.5.1 gives

$$dv/dt = -(18\ \mu/\rho_p\ d_p^2)$$

This equation may be integrated subject to the initial conditions:

$$v = v_o\ at\ t = 0$$

The result is

$$\ln (v/v_o) = -(18\ \mu/d_p^2\ \rho_p)\ t$$

Rewriting this equation in exponential form and multiplying by v_o yields

$$v = v_o\ e^{-(18\ \mu/d_p^2\ \rho_p)\ t} \qquad (2.5.3)$$

For the Newton's law range, the drag coefficient, C_D, is a constant. Rearranging Equation 2.5.1 gives

$$\int_{v_o}^{v} dv/v^2 = -\int_{0}^{t} [3 C_D \rho/4 d_p \rho_p] dt$$

Since the bracketed term on the RHS (right-hand side) of the equation is constant, integration yields

$$(v - v_o)/v v_o = -(3 C_D \rho/4 d_p \rho_p) t \qquad (2.5.4)$$

It is also possible to derive an equation describing particle motion for the creeping motion regime (Stokes' law range) in the presence of a gravitational force field. The particle is assumed to be moving in the upward vertical direction. The describing equation is

$$(m/g_c) (dv/dt) = -F_g - F_D$$

where the direction of the drag force is the same as that for gravity. For "creeping motion" this becomes

$$(m/g_c) (dv/dt) = -m (g/g_c) - (3 \pi \mu v d_p/g_c)$$

Dividing through by (m/g_c) and expressing m in terms of d_p yields

$$dv/dt = -g - (18 \mu v/d_p^2 \rho_p)$$

which is an equation of the form

$$dv/dt = -(A + Bv)$$

This equation can now be integrated as follows:

$$\int_{0}^{t} dt = -\int_{v_o}^{v} dv/(A + Bv)$$

$$t = -(1/B) \ln (A + Bv) \Big|_{v_o}^{v}$$

Substituting the limits yields

$$\ln [(A + Bv_o)/(A + Bv)] = Bt$$

By substituting for A and B, the following equation is obtained:

$$\ln [(g + (18 \mu/d_p^2 \rho_p) v_o)/(g + (18 \mu/d_p^2 \rho_p) v)] =$$

$$(18 \mu/d_p^2 \rho_p) t$$

Since the terminal velocity, v_t, is given by

$$v_t = d_p^2 \rho_p g/18 \mu$$

the above equation may be put in the form

$$(v_t/g) \ln [(v_t + v_o)/(v_t + v)] = t \qquad (2.5.5)$$

Note that this equation only applies while the particle is moving in an upward direction. Similarly, an equation can be derived if the particle is moving in a downward direction. Then

$$(m/g_c) (dv/dt) = +m (g/g_c) - (3 \pi \mu v d_p/g_c)$$

so that

$$dv/dt = g - (18 \mu/d_p^2 \rho_p) v$$

This is now an equation in the form

$$dv/dt = A - Bv$$

Rearranging gives

$$\int_{0}^{t} dt = \int_{v_o}^{v} dv/(A - Bv)$$

Integrating and substituting the limits yields

$$\ln [(A - Bv_o)/(A - Bv)] = Bt$$

Substituting for A and B results in

$$\ln \left[\frac{(gd_p^2 \rho_p/18 \mu) - v_o}{(gd_p^2 \rho_p/18 \mu) - v} \right] = \left[\frac{18 \mu}{d_p^2 \rho_p} \right] t$$

Again, since

$$v_t = d_p^2 \rho_p g/18 \mu$$

then

$$\ln [(v_t - v_o)/(v_t - v)] = [18 \mu/d_p^2 \rho_p] t$$

or

$$t = (v_t/g) \ln [(v_t - v_o)/(v_t - v)] \qquad (2.5.6)$$

If Newton's law is used for the drag in the above development, then

$$(m/g_c)(dv/dt) = m(g/g_c) - (C_D v^2 \rho \pi d_p^2/8 g_c)$$

Multiplying through by (g_c/m) with substitution for m in terms of d_p gives

$$dv/dt = g - (0.75 C_D v^2 \rho/d_p \rho_p)$$

This equation is of the form

$$(dv/dt) = A - Bv^2$$

Rearranging

$$\int_0^t dt = \int_{v_o}^v dv/(A - Bv^2)$$

and integration yields

$$t = (1/2\sqrt{AB}) \ln [(A + v\sqrt{AB})/(A - v\sqrt{AB})] \Big|_{v_o}^v$$

Substituting the limits and simplifying gives

$$\ln \left[\frac{\sqrt{(A/B)} + v}{\sqrt{(A/B)} - v} \right] \left[\frac{\sqrt{(A/B)} - v_o}{\sqrt{(A/B)} + v_o} \right] = 2\sqrt{(AB)}\, t$$

Since

$$v_t = \sqrt{4 g d_p \rho_p/3 \rho C_D} = \sqrt{A/B}$$

then

$$\ln \left[\left(\frac{v_t + v}{v_t - v} \right) \left(\frac{v_t - v_o}{v_t + v_o} \right) \right] = 2\sqrt{AB}\, t$$

Substituting

$$\sqrt{AB} = \sqrt{0.75 C_D \rho g/d_p \rho_p}$$

finally gives

$$\ln \left[\left(\frac{v_t + v}{v_t - v} \right) \left(\frac{v_t - v_o}{v_t + v_o} \right) \right] = 1.732\, t \sqrt{C_D \rho g/d_p \rho_p}$$

$$(2.5.7)$$

The above development (Equations 2.5.1 to 2.5.7) assumes that the particle initially moves with a velocity v_o. If, however, the particle is initially at rest and then acted upon by a constant external force, it will accelerate until it reaches its terminal settling velocity. The equations then reduce to a simpler form since $v_o = 0$.

It should also be noted that an accelerating (or deaccelerating) particle can never reach its terminal settling velocity (since terminal velocity is an asymptotic value). The usual procedure assumes that the particle reaches this ultimate velocity when it achieves a value equal to a percentage of the terminal velocity, e.g., 99%. The 99% value can be used to calculate the distance traveled during the transient period. Since $v = dy/dt$, where y is the position variable in the direction of motion, one can calculate the distance traveled in time t by simply integrating the appropriate equation with respect to time. For example, if it is assumed that a particle is initially at rest in a still fluid (gas), the equation of motion for an accelerating particle (moving in a downward direction) that has covered a distance y in time t is

$$(m/g_c)(dv/dt) = m(g/g_c) - F_D$$

In the Stokes' law range this becomes

$$(m/g_c)(dv/dt) = m(g/g_c) - 3\pi d_p \mu (dy/dt)/g_c$$

Thus, multiplying through by (g_c/m)

$$dv/dt = d(dy/dt)/dt = d^2 y/dt^2 = g - \left(\frac{18\mu}{d_p^2 \rho_p} \right) \left(\frac{dy}{dt} \right)$$

eventually yields the solution (on integration)

$$y = v_t\, t \left\{ 1 - \frac{\rho_p d_p^2}{18\mu t} \left[1 - \exp\left(-\frac{18\mu}{\rho_p d_p^2}\, t \right) \right] \right\} \qquad (2.5.8)$$

where

y = the distance covered at time t;
v_t = the terminal velocity.

To obtain the drag coefficient, C_D', under conditions of acceleration, the following equations are recommended. For particles accelerating from rest and Re $<$ 60, use[19]

$$C_D' = 27/Re^{0.84} \qquad (2.5.9)$$

For Re > 60, use[20]

$$C_D' = 0.217 \, Re^{0.217} \qquad (2.5.10)$$

where

$$Re = \frac{\rho \, |v_r| \, d_p}{\mu};$$
$$|v_r| = \text{the absolute value of the relative velocity between the gas and the particle.}$$

The reader is again reminded that for small particles (less than 10 μm), a velocity approaching the terminal value is attained almost instantaneously; therefore, both the elapsed time and distance traveled during this transient period are negligible. Hence, acceleration effects can generally be neglected.

An important dimensionless number employed in the design of venturi scrubbers is the inertial impaction number, N_I. Interestingly, it can be shown that this dimensionless number is the ratio of a spherical particle's "stopping" distance in air, L, to the collector radius, r_c, i.e.,

$$N_I = \frac{2 \, \rho_p \, a^2 \, V}{9 \, \mu \, r_c} = \frac{L}{r_c} \qquad (2.5.11)$$

The stopping distance is defined as the distance a particle (moving with velocity, V) will come to rest in still air — a condition existing at the surface of the collector. Equating the (de)acceleration term with the drag force gives $F = -F_D$. Assuming that the particle is moving in the Stokes' regime, then

$$m \, dv/dt = -q \, v$$

where

$$m = 4/3 \, (\pi \, a^3 \, \rho_p);$$
$$q = 6 \, \pi \, \mu a.$$

Integrating the above equation subject to the initial conditions

$$v = V \text{ at } t = 0$$

then

$$v = V e^{-(q/m)t}$$

Since

$$v = dy/dt$$

the above equation becomes

$$dy/dt = V e^{-(q/m)t}$$

which may be integrated, subject to the initial conditions y = 0 at t = 0, to give

$$y = (mV/q) \, (1 - e^{-(q/m)t})$$

However, as

$$t \to \infty, \, y \to L$$

so that

$$L = mV/q$$

Substituting for m and q gives

$$L = 2 \, \rho_p \, a^2 \, V/9 \, \mu$$

The inertial impaction number is then

$$N_I = \frac{L}{r_c} = \frac{2 \, \rho_p \, a^2 \, V}{9 \, \mu \, r_c} \qquad (2.5.12)$$

2.6. OTHER FACTORS AFFECTING PARTICLE MOTION

Strictly speaking, the describing equations and calculations presented above are valid only under restricted conditions. The equations are *not* strictly valid if:

1. The particle is "very" small.
2. The particle is not a smooth rigid sphere.
3. The particle is located "near" the surrounding walls containing the gas.
4. The particle is located "near" one or more other particles.
5. The motion of the fluid and particle is multidimensional.

Each of the above topics is treated briefly below. Despite the above limitations, it should be noted that these effects are rarely included in any analysis of a fluid-particle system. It is more common to use an empirical constant or factor that would account for all of these various effects.

Discontinuity of the Fluid

At very low values of the Reynolds number, when particles approach sizes comparable to the mean free path of the fluid molecules, the medium can no longer be regarded as continuous, since particles can fall between the molecules at a faster rate than predicted by the aerodynamic theories which led to the standard drag coefficients. To allow for this "slip," Cunningham[6] introduced a multiplying correction factor to Stokes' law; this alters Equation 2.4.3 to the form

$$v = \frac{f d_p^2 \, \rho_p}{18 \, \mu} \left(1 + \frac{2 A \lambda}{d_p} \right) \qquad (2.6.1)$$

or

$$v = \frac{f d_p^2 \, \rho_p}{18 \, \mu} \ (C)$$

where

λ = mean free path of the fluid molecules;
A = $1.257 + 0.40 \exp(-1.10 \, d_p/2 \, \lambda)$;
C = Cunningham correction factor.

The modified Stokes' law equation, which is usually referred to as the Stokes-Cunningham equation, is then

$$F_D = 3 \, \pi \mu d_p v / C g_c \qquad (2.6.2)$$

As shown in Table 2.6.1, the Stokes-Cunningham correction is less than 1% for particles larger than 16 μm falling freely in air at ambient conditions. The correction factor, however, should definitely be included in the drag force term when dealing with submicron particles.

TABLE 2.6.1

Stokes-Cunningham Correction Factors for Particles in Ambient Air (70°F, 14.7 psia, $\lambda = 6.53 \times 10^{-6}$ cm)

d_p, μm	$(1 + \frac{2A\lambda}{d_p})$
0.01	22.350
0.10	2.870
1.00	1.160
10.00	1.016
16.00	1.010
20.00	1.008

Nonspherical Particles

For particles having shapes other than spherical, it is necessary to specify the size and geometric form of the body and its orientation with respect to the direction of flow of the fluid. One major dimension is chosen as the characteristic length, and other important dimensions are given as ratios to the chosen one. Such ratios are called shape factors. Thus, for short cylinders, the diameter is usually chosen as the defining dimension, and the ratio of length to diameter is a shape factor. The orientation between the particle and the stream is also specified. For a cylinder, sufficient angle is formed by the axis of the cylinder and the direction of flow. The projected area is then determinate and may be calculated. For a cylinder oriented so that its axis is perpendicular to the flow, $A_p = (l)(d_p)$, where l is the length of the cylinder. For a cylinder with its axis parallel to the direction of flow, A_p is $(\pi/4) \, d_p^2$, the same as for a sphere of the same diameter.

Nonspherical bodies generally tend to orient in a preferred direction during fall. For example, at high Reynolds numbers a disk always falls horizontally, with its flat face perpendicular to its motion; a streamlined shape, on the other hand, falls nose down, in its position of least resistance. At low Reynolds numbers a particle such as a disk or ellipsoid, with three perpendicular symmetry planes, will fall in any position;[7] theory predicts that such a particle maintains the orientation which it acquired by chance at the start of its fall. The general tendency is for the shape and surface of irregular particles to influence the rate of fall so that the particle falls at a lower velocity than a sphere of equivalent weight. Figure 2.6.1 gives the curves of drag coefficient for a few regular shapes which have been studied over a range of Reynolds numbers.[8]

As mentioned previously, other factors must be introduced into the fluid resistance equations for spheres if equations of the same form are to be used for nonspherical particles; these include a linear dimension equivalent to the diameter of the sphere and a correction factor based on the surface area of the particle (to adjust the surface area term in Equation 2.2.1). The drag, aerodynamic, or equivalent diameter, incorporates both of these factors on the aerodynamic behavior of the particles. This is defined as the diameter of a sphere having the same resistance to motion as the particle in a fluid of the same viscosity and at the

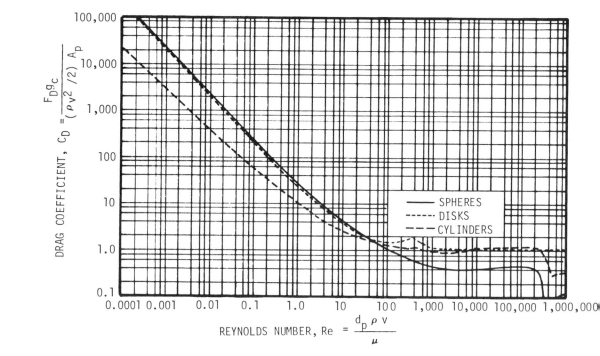

FIGURE 2.6.1. Drag coefficient for spheres, disks, and cylinders.

same velocity. The drag diameter can be substituted for the diameter of the sphere in the fluid resistance equations introduced earlier. However, when the fluid resistance is to be deduced from the geometry of the particles, then the two factors must be considered separately. The equivalent diameter is defined in terms of the particle surface area, volume, or projected area (see Table 2.6.2), while the area correction terms are the dimensionless ratios referred to earlier as shape factors. The most commonly used of the shape factors is the sphericity ($\psi = d_{e,v}^2/d_{e,s}^2$), a surface-volume shape factor defined as the ratio of the surface area of a sphere having the same volume as the particle to the actual surface area of the particle. When the particle is a true sphere, this ratio approaches 1.0 as the upper limit. The other useful shape factor is the circularity (χ), defined as the ratio of the diameter of a circle having the area of the maximum projected area of the particle, to the area of the smallest circle circumscribing this maximum projected area. For most simple irregular particles, the degree of circularity is a very close approximation of the degree of sphericity.

For isometric particles (cubes, spheres, tetrahedrons, and octahedrons), Pettyjohn and Christiansen[9] found a correlation between the drag coefficient and Reynolds number using the

nominal diameter in both terms plus a parameter for the resulting family of curves. The parameter was equal to the ratio of the surface area of a sphere of equal volume to the actual particle surface. Their final correlation is shown in Figure 2.6.2.[8] Squires[8] showed that the correlation of Pettyjohn and Christiansen might be improved by using the equivalent surface diameter, $d_{e,s}$, for the diameter term and by multiplying the drag coefficient by a particle-shape factor, ψ', defined as the ratio of particle volume to the volume of a sphere having the same surface area as the particle. For more irregular particles, Hawksley suggests that the drag coefficient can be calculated from[10]

$$C_D = \frac{4(\rho_p - \rho)g\, d_{e,v}^3}{3\,\rho v^2\, d_{e,s}^2} = \frac{4\,\psi\,(\rho_p - \rho)g\, d_{e,v}}{3\,\rho v^2}$$

with

$$Re = \frac{\rho v d_{e,s}}{\mu} = \frac{1}{\psi^{0.5}}\,\frac{\rho v d_{e,v}}{\mu}$$

Wall Effects

In most particle collection equipment (i.e., settling chambers, cyclones, or electrostatic precipitators) the particles are negligibly small when compared to the dimensions of the unit; therefore,

TABLE 2.6.2

Equivalent Diameters of Particles

Symbol	Name	Definition
$d_{e,s}$	Surface diameter	The diameter of a sphere having the same surface area as the particle
$d_{e,v}$	Volume diameter	The diameter of a sphere having the same volume as the particle
$d_{e,d}$	Drag diameter	The diameter of a sphere having the same resistance to motion as the particle in a fluid of the same viscosity and at the same velocity
$d_{e,a}$	Projected area diameter	The diameter of a sphere having the same projected area as the particle when viewed in a direction perpendicular to a plane of stability
$d_{e,f}$	Free-falling diameter	The diameter of a sphere having the same density and the same free-falling velocity as the particle in a fluid of the same density and viscosity
$d_{e,vs}$	Specific surface diameter	The diameter of a sphere having the same ratio of surface area to volume as the particle

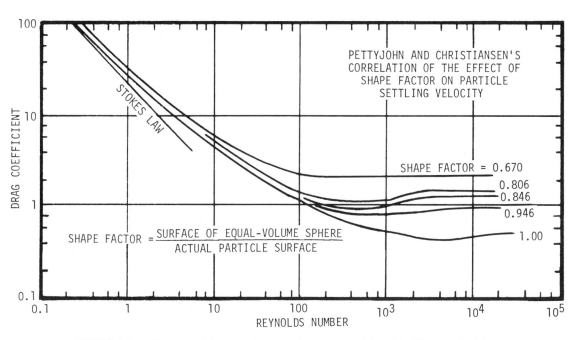

FIGURE 2.6.2. Drag coefficient correlation for isometric particles with different sphericity.

wall effects can usually be neglected. However, in certain other types of collection equipment wall effects can be more pronounced. When the fluid is of finite extent there are two effects: The fluid pulled along by the particle must produce a return flow since it cannot pass through the walls of the containing vessel; since the fluid is stationary at a finite distance from the particle, there is a distortion of the flow pattern which reacts back on the particle.

Theoretical considerations or experimental work has established factors for modifying the Stokes' law equation (2.2.4) to account for wall effects under different sets of circumstances. The fluid resistance near a wall or boundary, F_W, can be calculated by dividing the Stokes' law fluid resistance, F_D, by the boundary correction factor, K',

$$F_W = F_D/K' \qquad (2.6.3)$$

If a spherical particle falls parallel to a single infinite plane wall, K' is given by[11]

$$K' = 1 - 0.5625 \ (d_p/l_W) \qquad (2.6.4)$$

where l_W would represent twice the distance between the particle and the wall. If a spherical particle is falling between two parallel infinite plane walls separated by a distance l, K' is given by[12]

$$K' = 1 - 1.004 \ (d_p/l) + 0.418 \ (d_p/l)^3 - 0.169 \ (d_p/l)^5$$

$$(2.6.5)$$

Equation 2.6.5 is strictly valid when the ratio (d_p/l) is less than 0.05. For larger (d_p/l) ratios, the correction factor results in an underestimation of the fluid resistance. For a spherical particle falling through a narrow (infinitely long) cylinder with a diameter d_c, then K' is given by[13]

$$K' = 1 - 2.104 \ (d_p/d_c) + 2.09 \ (d_p/d_c)^3 - 0.95 \ (d_p/d_c)^5$$

$$(2.6.6)$$

Each extra wall increases the drag by an approximately equal amount; thus, the settling velocity of a spherical particle in a cylinder is much the same over a large part of the central area. The increase in drag is due to displacement towards one side

being offset by the decrease due to displacement from the other side. When particles are not spherical, the correction factor to be used is the same as for spheres with equivalent diameters. It should be emphasized again that the wall-effect correction factors are valid only at very low values of the Reynolds number, probably less than 1.0. Correction factors corresponding to velocities greater than those occurring in the streamline (low Re) region become much more complex, and the reader is referred to the literature.[10,12,15] At very high velocities ($R \approx 10^4$) wall effects are negligible.

Multiparticle Effects

In the removal of particles from gas streams it is almost inevitable that large numbers of particles will be involved. It is also very likely that the particles will influence one another. Therefore, equations for the fluid resistance to the movement of single particles have to be modified to account for such interactions between particles. Particle interactions can become appreciable even at very low concentrations. Even a particle-volume concentration (the ratio of particle volume to total volume) of 0.2% will increase the fluid resistance to particle movement by about 1%.[16] In general, for volume concentrations below 1%, the effect of particle interactions may be neglected.

If two identical particles separated by only a few diameters move through a viscous fluid, the fluid flows around the particles so that the resulting viscous force is greater than that acting on a single particle; thus, the terminal settling velocity is smaller than predicted by Stokes' law. In such hindered settling, the particles are sufficiently close together so as to cause the velocity gradients surrounding each particle to be affected by the presence of the neighboring particles. Also, in settling, the particles displace fluid and generate an appreciable upward velocity. The fluid velocity is, then, greater with respect to the particle than with respect to the apparatus. The effective density of the fluid can be taken as that of the fluid-particle system itself and can be calculated from the composition of the fluid and the densities of the particles and the fluid.

In hindered settling of spherical particles, the drag force given by Equation 2.2.10 is too small. The true drag force corresponds to that which would exist in free settling through a fluid of higher viscosity than that actually used. To find this higher effective viscosity, the actual viscosity, μ, is divided by an empirical correction factor, k', which depends on the fractional volume of the fluid-particle system occupied by the fluid. This is equivalent to the porosity of the aggregation of particles and is denoted by ϵ. Then, mathematically,

$$F_D = \frac{\alpha \pi (d_p \, v_{tr})^{2-\beta} (\mu/k')^\beta \, \rho_m^{\,1-\beta}}{8 \, g_c} \qquad (2.6.7)$$

where

v_{tr} = the terminal velocity of the particle relative to the fluid;
k' = a function of the porosity, ϵ;
ρ_m = the density of the fluid-particle mixture.

The terminal velocity with respect to the apparatus, v_t, is less than that with respect to the fluid, v_{tr}; the relationship between velocities is

$$v_t = \epsilon \, v_{tr} \qquad (2.6.8)$$

The drag is equal to the difference between the external and buoyant forces, so that

$$\frac{\pi \, f d_p^{\,3} \, (\rho_p - \rho_m)}{6 \, g_c} = \frac{\alpha \, \pi (d_p \, v_t)^{2-\beta} \, \mu^\beta \, \rho_m^{\,1-\beta}}{8 \, \epsilon^{2-\beta} \, g_c \, (k')^\beta} \qquad (2.6.9)$$

Solving this equation for v_t gives

$$v_t = \left[\frac{4 \, f d_p^{\,1+\beta} \, \epsilon^{2-\beta} \, (k')^\beta \, (\rho_p - \rho_m)}{3 \, \alpha \, \rho_m^{\,1-\beta} \, \mu^\beta} \right]^{1/(2-\beta)} \qquad (2.6.10)$$

A general relation between ϵ and k' over the entire range of Reynolds numbers has not been determined. A relationship for the settling of spheres in the Stokes' law range has been found and is shown graphically in Figure 2.6.3.[18] This relationship does not apply, without further consideration, to sharp-edged particles. Also, assuming that the Stokes' law range terminates at a Reynolds number of 2.0 (based on velocity, v_{tr}, of the particle relative to the fluid), the criterion for hindered settling in the Stokes' law range is

$$K = d_p \left[\frac{f \rho_m \, (\rho_p - \rho_m) \, (k')^2}{\mu^2} \right]^{1/3} \qquad (2.6.11)$$

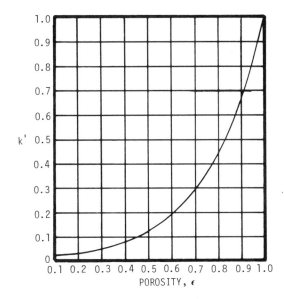

FIGURE 2.6.3. Correction factor k' for the hindered settling of spheres in the Stokes' law range.

If $K < 3.3$, the settling is in the Stokes' law range.

Multidimensional Flow

Previous discussions on particle motion were limited to the unidimensional case, i.e., the parallel movement of a particle relative to the fluid. However, this is not the general case. The actual situation will be defined as multidimensional flow. Equations must then be developed to describe each of the velocity components of the particle. The main complication arises with the drag if more than one relative velocity component exists.

Although the two-dimensional particle flow problem is examined, only one-dimensional drag effects are considered in this text. For example, consider a particle discharged to the atmosphere from a tall stack. The particle, while settling (vertically) under the influence of gravity, may also have a horizontal velocity component due to atmospheric motion (wind). No slip between the particle and air in the horizontal direction is assumed for this situation, i.e., the particle and air are moving with the same velocity in the specified direction. Only drag effects in the vertical direction need to be considered. Using the equations developed earlier, the reader can verify that a 25-μm particle of specific gravity 3.0, discharged from a stack 100 ft high into a 5 mph wind, will reach ground level approximately 3/4 mi downstream from the stack. A 2.5-μm particle in a similar situation will settle about 75 miles downstream.

2.7. BROWNIAN MOTION AND PARTICLE DISPLACEMENT

As a result of bombardment by the molecules of the fluid medium, suspended particles will be subjected to a random motion known as Brownian movement. This effect becomes significant only when the particles are very small and their mass approaches that of the fluid molecules. Einstein[17] showed that the root mean square displacement of a particle, $\bar{l}$, in an interval of time t is given as

$$\bar{l} = (2RT\,C\,t/3\,N_A\,\pi\,\mu d_p)^{0.5} \qquad (2.7.1)$$

where

R = gas constant;
T = absolute temperature;
C = Stokes-Cunningham correction factor;
N_A = number of molecules per unit volume.

Brownian movement, in general, becomes significant only for particles less than about 0.05 μm.

2.8. ILLUSTRATIVE EXAMPLES

The purpose of this section is to apply the material presented in the previous sections. For a few of these examples, solutions can be generated almost immediately by inspection or intuition; however, detailed solutions are presented for the majority of the examples. Unless otherwise specified, the gas density (ρ) is assumed to be negligible as compared to the particle density (ρ_p), and the drag force relationship(s) proposed in Section 2.2 are applicable. Hopefully, the subject matter in this chapter has provided the reader with an understanding of fluid-particle technology and an ability to obtain and solve equations describing particle motion.

Example 2.8.1

Calculate the terminal settling velocity of a 150-μm charcoal sphere in air at ambient conditions. The specific gravity of the charcoal is equal to 0.9. Perform the calculation assuming that the following apply.

1. Stokes' law.

2. The intermediate law.
3. Newton's law.

Comment on the results.

Solution
The particle diameter may be expressed as

$$d_p = 150\ \mu m$$
$$= 4.92 \times 10^{-4}\ ft$$

For Stokes' law

$$v_t = g\,d_p^2\,\rho_p/18\,\mu$$

so that

$$v_t = (32.2)(4.92 \times 10^{-4})^2\,(0.9 \times 62.4)/(18)(1.23 \times 10^{-5})$$
$$= 1.98\ ft/sec$$

For the intermediate range

$$v_t = (0.153)(g\,\rho_p)^{0.71}\,(d_p)^{1.14}/(\rho)^{0.29}\,(\mu)^{0.43}$$

or

$$v_t = (0.153)(32.2 \times 0.9 \times 62.4)^{0.71}$$

$$(4.92 \times 10^{-4})^{1.14}/(0.0775)^{0.29}\,(1.23 \times 10^{-5})^{0.43}$$

$$= 1.44\ ft/sec$$

For Newton's law

$$v_t = 1.74\,(g \times d_p \times \rho_p/\rho)^{0.5}$$

so that

$$v_t = 1.74\,(32.2 \times 4.92 \times 10^{-4} \times 0.9 \times 62.4/0.0775)^{0.5}$$
$$= 5.896\ ft/sec$$

K may be calculated from

$$K = d_p\,[g\,\rho(\rho_p - \rho)/\mu^2]^{1/3}$$

Substituting the data gives

$$K = 4.796$$

Therefore, the intermediate law range applies so that the correct velocity is

$$v = 1.44\ ft/sec$$

Example 2.8.2

A spherical limestone particle is settling in air (at ambient conditions) with a velocity of 0.96 cm/sec. Calculate the diameter of the limestone particle.

Solution

Since the velocity is relatively low, we will assume Stokes' law applies. After determining d_p, this assumption can be checked by calculating K. The velocity is first converted to English units.

$$v = 0.96/2.54 \times 12$$
$$= 0.0315 \text{ ft/sec}$$

For Stokes' law the settling velocity is

$$v_t = g \, d_p^2 \, (\rho_p - \rho)/18 \, \mu$$

After rearranging and assuming $\rho_p \ggg \rho$

$$d_p = (18 \, \mu \, v_t/g \, \rho_p)^{0.5}$$

Substitution of the data gives

$$d_p = (18 \times 1.23 \times 10^{-5} \times 0.0315/32.2 \times 2.67 \times 62.4)^{0.5}$$
$$= 3.61 \times 10^{-5} \text{ ft}$$

Checking K gives

$$K = 3.61 \times 10^{-5} \, [32.2 \times 0.0775 \times 2.67 \times 62.4/(1.23 \times 10^{-5})^2]^{1/3}$$
$$= 0.5$$

The solution is correct.

Example 2.8.3

A spherical particle having a diameter of 0.12 in. and a specific gravity of 2.9 is placed on a horizontal screen. Air is blown through the screen vertically at a temperature of 20°C and a pressure of 1.0 atm.

Calculate the velocity required to just lift the particle, the particle Reynolds number at this condition, the drag force in both engineering and cgs units, and the drag coefficient.

Solution

We first calculate K to determine which drag force equation applies

$$K = d_p \, [g \, \rho(\rho_p - \rho)/\mu^2]^{1/3}$$

Substituting the data and assuming $\rho \lll \rho_p$

$$K = (0.12/12)[32.2 \times 0.0775 \times 2.9 \times 62.4/(0.0182 \times 6.72 \times 10^{-4})^2]^{1/3}$$

Solving for K yields

$$K = 144.5$$

Therefore, Newton's law applies and

$$v_t = 1.74 \, (g \, d_p \, \rho_p/\rho)^{1/2}$$

Substituting into this equation gives

$$v_t = 1.74(32.2 \times 0.01 \times 2.9 \text{`} \times 62.4/0.0775)^{1/2}$$
$$= 47.7 \text{ ft/sec}$$

The Reynolds number is given by

$$Re = d_p \, v_t \, \rho/\mu$$

Substituting the data gives

$$Re = 3,000$$

The drag force is given by

$$F_D = 0.055 \, \pi(d_p \, v_t)^2 \, \rho/g_c$$
$$F_D = 0.055 \times \pi \times (47.7 \times 10^{-2})^2 \times 0.0775/32.2$$
$$= 9.45 \times 10^{-5} \text{ lb}_f$$

This can be converted to cgs units by

$$F_D = 9.45 \times 10^{-5} \times 4.48 \times 10^5$$
$$= 42.4 \text{ dyn}$$

The drag coefficient is

$$C_D = (F_D/A_p)/(\rho \, v_t^2/2 \, g_c)$$

Substituting yields

$$C_D = 0.437$$

Example 2.8.4

A spherical limestone particle 93.7 μm in diameter is allowed to settle in air at ambient conditions. Calculate the particle's terminal settling velocity. How far will the particle fall in 30 sec? The specific gravity of limestone is 2.67.

Solution

The particle diameter is first converted to feet.

$d_p = 93.7/2.54 \times 12$
$\quad = 3.07 \times 10^{-4}$ ft

We now calculate K.

$K = 3.07 \times 10^{-4} [32.2 \times 0.0775 \times 2.67 \times$
$\quad 62.4/(1.23 \times 10^{-5})^2]^{1/3}$
$\quad = 4.3$

This means that the terminal velocity equation for the intermediate range is to be used.

$$v_t = 0.153 (g)^{0.71} (d_p)^{1.14} (\rho_p - \rho)^{0.71}/\rho^{0.29} \times \mu^{0.43}$$

Substituting gives

$v_t = 1.83$ ft/sec

In 30 sec, the distance traveled (neglecting acceleration effects) is

$s = v_t \, t$
$\quad = (1.83)(30)$
$\quad = 54.9$ ft

Example 2.8.5

General Foods, which recently developed a freeze-dried Sanka® product, has hired a consultant to study potential environmental problems that may arise. Information on the effect of diameter on the terminal settling velocity of the Sanka in air is required as an intermediate step in the analysis. Obtain this information. Prepare a table of particle diameter, velocity, Reynolds number, and drag coefficient. The specific gravity of the Sanka is 1.1. Neglect particle slip.

Solution

For air at 60°F and 1 atm, the physical properties are

$\rho = 0.0764$ lb/ft³
$\mu = 0.0175$ cp $= 1.176 \times 10^{-5}$ lb/ft sec

and the particle density is

$\rho_p = 1.1 \times 62.4 = 68.64$ lb/ft³

K is determined to be

$K = d_p [32.2 \times 0.0764 \times 68.64/(1.176 \times 10^{-5})^2]^{1/3}$
$\quad = 1.07 \times 10^4 \, d_p$

Various diameters are selected and K values determined. The appropriate form of the drag force equation is employed to calculate the terminal velocity. The Reynolds number and drag coefficient are obtained from their defining equation. The following table provides the results.

d_p, μm	K	v_t, ft/sec	Re	C_D
1.0	0.0351	1.12×10^{-4}	2.39×10^{-6}	10^7
10.0	0.351	1.12×10^{-2}	2.39×10^{-3}	10^4
25.0	0.8776	0.07	3.73×10^{-2}	643
35.0	1.23	0.1375	0.103	233
55.0	1.931	0.34	0.399	60.15
75.0	2.633	0.632	1.01	23.76
85.0	2.984	0.811	1.47	16.32
100.0	3.51	1.03	2.19	11.6
125.0	4.39	1.33	3.54	8.67
150.0	5.27	1.63	5.21	6.87

Example 2.8.6

What is the settling velocity of a spherical steel particle 1.5 μm in diameter in air at 0°C and 1 atm? The specific gravity of the steel is 7.56. Calculate the velocity if the temperature is changed to 200°C.

Solution

At T = 0°C:

$\rho = 1 \times 29/1.314 \times 273 = 0.081$ lb/ft³
$\mu = 0.0179$ cp $= 1.203 \times 10^{-5}$ lb/ft sec

The conversion for d_p is

$d_p = 15/10^4 \times 2.54 \times 12 = 4.92 \times 10^{-5}$ ft

We again calculate a value for K.

$K = 4.92 \times 10^{-5} [32.2 \times 0.081 \times 7.56 \times$
$\quad 62.4/(1.203 \times 10^{-5})^2]^{1/3}$
$\quad = 1.00$

Stokes' law applies so that

$v_t = g \, d_p^2 \, \rho_p/18 \, \mu$

Substituting the data

$v_t = 0.170$ ft/sec

At T = 200°C

$\mu = 0.025$ cp $= 1.68 \times 10^{-5}$ lb/ft sec

and

$\rho = 1 \times 29/1.314 \times 473 = 0.0467$ lb/ft^3

The value of K is now

K = 0.669

Stokes' law again applies, but on substituting the data, we obtain a substantial difference in the velocity at this temperature.

$v_t = 0.122$ ft/sec

Example 2.8.7

Calculate the ratio of the settling velocities of particles of charcoal and fly ash, 25 μm in diameter. The particles are settling through air at standard conditions and are assumed to be perfect spheres. The specific gravities of charcoal and fly ash are 0.93 and 2.31, respectively.

Solution

At 0°C and 1 atm we again have

$\mu = 1.203 \times 10^{-5}$ lb/ft sec
$\rho = 0.081$ lb/ft^3

and

$d_p = 25\,\mu = 8.2 \times 10^{-5}$ ft

For charcoal, the specific gravity is 0.93 and K is calculated from

$K = d_p (g\,\rho\,\rho_p/\mu^2)^{1/3}$

Substituting the data

K = 0.82

For fly ash, the specific gravity is 2.31, and K may be calculated with the following data:

$K = 8.2 \times 10^{-5}\,[32.2 \times 0.081 \times 2.31 \times$
$\quad 62.4/(1.203 \times 10^{-5})^2\,]^{1/3}$
$\quad = 1.1$

Stokes' law applies for both particles so that

$\dfrac{v_t(\text{char})}{v_t(\text{fly})} = \dfrac{0.93}{2.31}$
$\qquad\qquad = 0.403$

Example 2.8.8

In an attempt to simulate fluidized bed behavior, a 5-μm spherical particle is placed in an air stream. Calculate the particle's terminal settling velocity. How long and how far will the particle travel when it achieves 99% of its steady velocity? Assume the air to be at ambient conditions. The density of the catalyst particle is 97 lb/ft^3. Comment on the results.

Solution

At this condition we are in the Stokes' law regime, and the settling velocity is given by

$v_t = g\,d_p^{\,2}\,\rho_p/18\,\mu$

Substituting the data

$v_t = (1.64 \times 10^{-5})^2\,(97)\,(32.2)/18 \times 1.225 \times 10^{-5}$
$\quad = 0.00381$ ft/sec

To determine how long and how far the particle will have to travel to reach 99% of its terminal velocity, we will use Equation 2.5.6

$\ln\,[(v_t - v_0)/(v_t - v)] = 18\,\mu\,t/d_p^2\,\rho_p$

where

$v_t = g\,d_p^{\,2}\,\rho_p/18\,\mu = 0.00381$ ft/sec

The value of v is 0.99 v_t and therefore

$\ln\,[(v_t - 0)/(v_t - 0.99\,v_t)] = \ln\,(v_t/0.01\,v_t)$
$\qquad = \ln 100$
$\qquad = 4.61$

Substituting the remaining data into the above equation yields

$4.61 = 18\,t(1.225 \times 10^{-5})/97 \times 1.64 \times 10^{-5}$

Solving for t

t = 0.00055 sec

Since

$$\ln\left[(v_t - v_o)/(v_t - v)\right] = 18\,\mu\,t/d_p^2\,\rho_p = t/7.23$$

we may write

$$v_t - v = (v_t - v_o)\,e^{-t/0.00012}$$

or, assuming the particle to be moving in the y direction,

$$\frac{dy}{dt} = -(v_t - v_o)\,e^{-t/0.00012} + v_t$$
$$= v_t - v_t\,e^{-t/0.00012}$$

By integrating over the appropriate limits, we may calculate the distance, y, traveled in reaching 99% of the terminal velocity.

$$\int_0^y dy = \int_0^{0.00055} v_t\,dt - \int_0^{0.00055} v_t\,e^{-t/0.00012}$$

Integrating yields

$$y = v_t\,t|_0^{0.00055} - [-0.00012\,v_t e^{-t/0.00012}\,|_0^{0.00055}$$

Since $v_t = 0.00381$, substituting the limits yields

$$y = 0.00381 \times 0.00055 + 0.00012 \times$$
$$\quad 0.00381 \;\; e^{-0.00055/0.0\,00012} \;\; -0.00012 \times 0.00381$$
$$= 0.00000164 \text{ ft}$$

Example 2.8.9

A new cereal process has been developed by Quaker Oats®. The new cereal (spherical in shape) is prepared by spraying a warm liquid horizontally into the top of a 32-ft column. The average diameter of the liquid leaving the nozzle is 5,000 μm. This diameter remains relatively constant during the solidification process in the column. The specific gravity of the cereal is 0.43.

1. How long will it take for the cereal to achieve 50% of its terminal settling velocity?
2. Calculate the column residence time of the cereal to ascertain if the 1.2 sec required for solidification is achieved.

Solution

The diameter of the particle is

$$d_p = 5,000\ \mu\text{m}$$
$$\quad = 0.0164 \text{ ft}$$

We first calculate K.

$$K = 125$$

For Newton's law (assuming it applies over the entire time interval)

$$\ln\left[(v_t + v)(v_t - v_o)/(v_t - v)(v_t + v_o)\right] = 9.85\,t(C_D\rho/d_p\rho_p)^{1/2}$$

where

$$v_t = (g\,d_p\,\rho_p/0.75\,C_D\,\rho)^{1/2} = (32.2 \times 1.64 \times 10^{-2} \times$$
$$\quad 62.4/0.75 \times 0.44 \times 0.0775)^{1/2}$$
$$\quad = 23.5 \text{ ft/sec}$$

Since v_t is the terminal velocity and $v = 0.5\,v_t$

$$\ln(1.5/0.5) = 9.85\,t(0.44 \times 0.0775/1.64 \times 10^{-2} \times$$
$$\quad 0.43 \times 62.4)^{1/2}$$

or

$$\ln(3) = 2.75\,t$$

Solving for the time

$$t = 0.4 \text{ sec}$$

At these conditions, neglecting the effect of the transient period, the column residence time, θ, is approximately given by

$$\theta = 32/23.5 = 1.3 \text{ sec}$$

Accounting for the transient period, the actual residence time will be slightly higher. Nevertheless, sufficient time for solidification is available.

Example 2.8.10

The discharge into a 3.0 mi/hr wind from a cyclone contains some residual cement dust in the 2.5- to 50.0-μm range. If the cyclone is located 150 ft above ground level, calculate the minimum distance downstream from the source that will be free of cement deposit. Neglect the effect of turbulence. The specific gravity of the cement is 1.96.

Solution

The height of the column is 150 ft, and this

represents the distance, H, which the particles must settle. The smallest particle will travel the greatest horizontal distance. The diameter of this particle is

$$d_p = 2.5 \ \mu m$$
$$= 8.2 \times 10^{-6} \ ft$$

The value of K is

$$K = 0.105$$

For Stokes' law

$$v_t = g \, d_p^2 \, \rho_p / 18 \, \mu = 32.2 \times (8.2 \times 10^{-6})^2 \times$$
$$1.96 \times 62.4/18 \times 1.23 \times 10^{-5}$$
$$= 1.19 \times 10^{-3} \ ft/sec$$

The time for descent is

$$t = H/v_t = 150/1.19 \times 10^{-3} = 126 \times 10^3 \ sec$$

The horizontal distance traveled is

$$d = 126 \times 10^3 \times 3/3{,}600$$
$$= 105 \ mi$$

Note that this calculation has neglected meteorological effects.

Example 2.8.11

As an intermediate step in the design of a gravity settler to treat air containing aluminum oxide dust, the terminal velocity of these spheres in the 1.0- to 500-μm range is required. The air may be assumed to be at 25°C and 1 atm, and the specific gravity of the aluminum oxide dust is 3.98.

Solution

The value of K can be determined by

$$K = d_p (g \, \rho \, \rho_p / \mu^2)^{1/3}$$

Substituting the data

$$K = d_p [32.2 \times 0.074 \times 3.98 \times 62.4/(1.24 \times 10^{-5})^2]^{1/3}$$

Solving in terms of d_p (in microns) gives

$$K = 5.2 \times 10^{-2} \ d_p$$

If $K < 3.3$, Stokes' law applies. The Stokes' law range equation is

$$v_t = g \, d_p^2 \, \rho_p / 18 \, \mu$$

Substituting the data (including the conversion factor for d_p in microns) gives

$$v_t = 32.2 \ (d_p)^2 \ (3.281 \times 10^{-6})^2 \ (3.98) \ (62.4)/18 \times$$
$$1.24 \times 10^{-5}$$

or

$$v_t = 3.88 \times 10^{-4} \ d_p^2 \, ; d_p \ in \ \mu m$$

The intermediate range is given by

$$v_t = 0.153 \ (\rho_p \, g)^{0.71} \ d_p^{1.14} / \rho^{0.29} \ \mu^{0.43}$$

or

$$v_t = 1.39 \times 10^{-2} d_p^{1.14} \, ; d_p \ in \ \mu m$$

The following table gives the final results.

d_p, μm	K	v, ft/sec
1	5.2×10^{-2}	3.88×10^{-4}
10	5.2×10^{-1}	3.88×10^{-2}
50	2.6	0.97
100	5.2	2.64
250	13	7.51
499	20.8	12.83
500	26	16.54

Strictly speaking, the Cunningham correction factor should be included for the 1-μm particle calculation; the factor is given by 1.082.

Example 2.8.12

Consider a settling chamber (treating a liquid/particle stream) located downstream of a venturi scrubber. Sphalerite particles 100 μm in diameter with a density of 250 lb/ft³ are settling under the force of gravity through a slurry consisting of 30% by volume of quartz particles (with a density of 170 lb/ft³) and water. The volumetric ratio of sphalerite to slurry is 0.25. The temperature is 50°F. What is the terminal velocity of the sphalerite?

Solution

The density of the settling medium is that of the slurry. This can be calculated from the composition.

ρ_m = density of slurry = 0.30 × 170 + 0.70 × 62.4
$\qquad\qquad\qquad\quad$ (solids) $\qquad$ (water)

$\qquad$ = 94.68 lb/ft³

$\rho_p - \rho_m$ = 250 – 94.68 = 155.32 lb/ft³

μ_{water} at 50°F = 1.31 cp

ϵ = 1 – 0.30 = 0.70

From Figure 2.6.3, for ϵ = 0.7, k' = 0.29. The criterion K is

$$K = d_p \left[\frac{g \, \rho_m (\rho_p - \rho_m)(k')^2}{\mu^2} \right]^{1/3}$$

$$K = 100 \times 10^{-6} \text{ m} \left(\frac{3.281 \text{ ft}}{\text{m}} \right)$$

$$\left[\frac{32.2 (94.68)(155.32)(0.29)^2}{(6.72 \times 1.31 \times 10^{-4})^2} \right]^{1/3}$$

$$K = 3.281 \times 10^{-4} \left[\frac{39823.3}{7.75 \times 10^{-7}} \right]^{1/3} = 1.22$$

The settling occurs in the Stokes' law range. The terminal settling velocity is then

$$v_t = \left[\frac{4 \, g \, d_p^{1+\beta} \, \epsilon^{2-\beta} \, (k')^\beta \, (\rho_p - \rho_m)}{3 \, \alpha \, \rho_m^{1-\beta} \, \mu^\beta} \right]^{1/(2-\beta)}$$

with β = 1 and α = 24

$$v_t = \left[\frac{4 (32.2)(3.281 \times 10^{-4})^2 (0.7)(0.29)(155.32)}{3(24)(1.31 \times 6.72 \times 10^{-4})} \right]$$

v_t = 0.007 ft/sec

PROBLEMS

1. Classify small particles of charcoal, assumed to be spherical, with a specific gravity of 2.2. The particles are falling in a vertical tower against a rising current of air at 25°C and atmospheric pressure. Calculate the minimum size of charcoal which will settle to the bottom of the tower if the air is rising through the tower at the rate of 15 ft/sec.

2. A spherical particle having a diameter of 0.0093 in. and a specific gravity of 1.85 is placed on a horizontal screen. Air is blown through the screen vertically at a temperature of 20°C and a pressure of 1.0 atm. Calculate the following.

a. The velocity required to just lift the particle.
b. The particle Reynolds number at this condition.
c. The drag force in both engineering and cgs units.
d. The drag coefficient.

3. A spherical mica particle 400 μm in diameter is allowed to settle in air at ambient conditions. Calculate the particle's terminal settling velocity. How far will the particle fall in 5 min? The specific gravity of mica is 3.02.

4. A spherical mica particle is settling in air (at ambient conditions) with a velocity of 110 cm/sec. Calculate the diameter of the mica particle.

5. Air is being dried by bubbling it (in very small bubbles) through concentrated NaOH (specific gravity of 1.34 and viscosity equal to 4.3 cp). The base fills a 4.5-ft tall, 2.5-in. I.D. tube to a depth of 1.0 ft. The air above the base is at ambient conditions. If the air rate is 4.0 ft³/min, what is the maximum diameter of a base spray droplet which might be carried out of the apparatus by entrainment in the air stream?

6. Separate a mixture of quartz (specific gravity of 2.6) and hornblende (specific gravity of 3.5) by free settling in air. The size range of the particles in the mixture is such that the settling will follow Newton's law. If complete separation is to be obtained, the ratio of the diameter of the largest particle in the mixture to the diameter of the smallest particle in the mixture must not exceed a certain value. Calculate the maximum ratio of diameters allowable for complete separation.

7. Calculate the ratio of the settling velocities of particles of sand and galena, 15 μm in diameter. The particles are settling through air at standard conditions and are assumed to be perfect spheres. The specific gravities of sand and galena are 2.24 and 7.51, respectively.

8. Air is being dried by bubbling it (in very small bubbles) through concentrated HCl (specific gravity of 1.640 and viscosity equal to 10 cp). The acid fills a 4-ft tall, 3-in. I.D. tube to a depth of 9 in. The air above the acid is at ambient conditions. If the air rate is 4.5 ft³/min, what is the maximum diameter of an acid spray droplet which might be carried out of the apparatus by entrainment in the air stream?

9. The discharge into a 4.5 mi/hr wind from a cyclone contains some residual fly ash dust in the 2.0- to 100.0-μm range. If the cyclone is located 125 ft above ground level, calculate the minimum distance downstream from the source that will be free of fly ash deposit. Neglect the effect of turbulence. The specific gravity of the fly ash is 2.90.

REFERENCES

1. Theodore, L., *Transport Phenomena for Engineers,* International Textbook Company, New York, 1971.
2. Bird, R. B., Stewart, W. E., and Lightfoot, E. N., *Transport Phenomena,* John Wiley & Sons, New York, 1960.
3. Kay, T. M., *Fluid Mechanics and Heat Transfer,* 2nd ed., Cambridge University Press, Cambridge, 1963.
4. Theodore, L. and Buonicore, A. J., personal notes.
5. Barnea, S. and Mizraki, I., Ph.D. thesis, Haifa University, Haifa, 1972.
6. Cunningham, E., *Proc. R. Soc. London Ser. A,* 83, 357, 1910.
7. Heiss, J. F. and Coult, J., *Chem. Eng. Prog.,* 48, 133, 1952.
8. Zenz, F. A. and Othmer, D. F., *Fluidization and Fluids Particle Systems,* Reinhold, New York, 1960.
9. Pettyjohn, E. S. and Christiansen, E. B., *Chem. Eng. Prog.,* 44, 157, 1948.
10. Hawksley, P. G. W., *B.C.V.R.A. Bull.,* 15, 105, 1951.
11. Lorenz, H., *Abh. Theor. Phys.,* 1, 23, 1906.
12. Faxen, H., *Ann. Phys.* (Leipzig), 68, 89, 1922.
13. Faxen, H., *Ark. Mat. Astron. Fys.,* 17(27), 1, 1922.
14. Lapple, C. E., *Fluid and Particle Mechanics,* University of Delaware, Newark, 1951.
15. Liebster, H., *Ann. Phys.* (Leipzig), 82, 541, 1927.
16. Strauss, W., *Industrial Gas Cleaning,* Pergamon Press, New York, 1967.
17. Einstein, A., *Ann. Physik,* 19, 289, 1906.
18. Steinour, H. H., *Ind. Eng. Chem.,* 36, 618, 1944.
19. Ingebo, R. D., NASA Tech. Note 3762, September 1956.
20. Rabin, S. et al., AFSOR TR 60-15, Rocketdyne, March 1960.
21. Oseen, C. W., *Philos. Mag.,* 6(21), 112, 1911.

Chapter 3

GRAVITY SETTLERS

3.1. INTRODUCTION

Gravity settlers, or gravity settling chambers, have long been utilized industrially for the removal of solid and liquid waste materials from gaseous streams. Advantages accounting for their use are simple construction, low initial cost and maintenance, low pressure losses, and simple disposal of waste materials.

The gravity settler was one of the first devices used by man to control particulate emissions. The device basically consists of an expansion chamber in which the particle velocity is reduced to such an extent that the particle may settle out under the action of gravity. One advantage of this device is that the external force leading to separation is provided free by nature. Its use in industry is generally limited to the removal of the larger sized particles (greater than 40 μm) since the required chamber required to remove dust from the exit of smaller particles. For example, the area of a chamber required to remove dust from the exhaust gases of a cement kiln burning fuel oil at the rate of 350 gal/hr would be at least of the following order of magnitude: for complete elimination of particles greater than 10 μm, 6,000,000 ft^2; for complete elimination of particles greater than 50 μm, 250,000 ft^2.

Although today's demands for cleaner air and stricter emission standards have all but forced this low-efficiency device off the market (replaced mostly by cyclones, fabric filters, wet scrubbers, and electrostatic precipitators), it still finds use in certain areas, primarily testing and research or as a precleaner. Settlers can be designed to allow only a certain range of particles to pass through the unit, and these are used in some air sampling tests. They are also useful in studying the size and flow of aerosol particles, knowledge of which can be applied to the more efficient design of other pollution control devices.

Other control devices that can be considered under the above broad classification depend, to some extent, on another effect, in addition to gravity, to lead to a successful separation process. This other mechanism is an inertial or momentum effect. It arises by changing the direction of the velocity of the gas and imparting a downward motion to the particle. From a calculational point of view, this induced particle motion is superimposed on the motion arising due to gravity. Some of these other control devices are introduced in this chapter. They are reviewed briefly here since the fundamentals and principles of particle collection by this inertial mechanism, along with the design equations that can be applied to these units, are considered in subsequent chapters.

The reader will note that more time is spent on developmental work in this chapter since much of the material and approach is similar to that employed in later chapters, particularly Chapters 4 and 5.

3.2 DESCRIPTION OF EQUIPMENT

Gravity settlers are usually constructed in the form of a long, horizontal parallelepiped with suitable inlet and outlet ports. In its simplest form the settler is an enlargement (large box) in the duct carrying the particle-laden gases; the contaminated gas stream enters at one end, the cleaned gas exits from the other end (see Figure 3.2.1). The particles settle toward the collection surface at the bottom of the unit with a velocity at or near their terminal settling velocity.

There are basically two types of gravity settlers: the simple expansion chamber and the multiple-tray settling chamber. A simple schematic diagram of the first type is given in Figure 3.2.1. Expansion into the large chamber reduces the velocity of the carrier gas so that particles in the gas settle out by gravity. A typical horizontal-flow gravity settling unit is presented in Figure 3.2.2. Several thin horizontal collection plates (see Figure 3.2.3) have been introduced to reduce the excessive volume requirements for the collection of small particles (as small as 15 μm). Although the gas velocity increases slightly, the vertical distance for collection decreases more significantly; therefore, the overall collection efficiency increases. The Howard settling chamber is an example of this type of unit, as shown in Figure 3.2.4. A unit consisting of (n) shelves will essentially consist of (n + 1) gravity settlers, each with a height equal to the distance

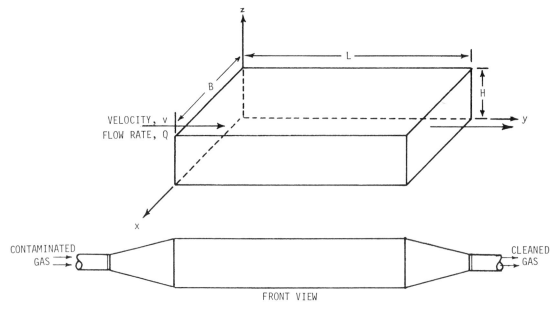

FIGURE 3.2.1 Gravity settling box.

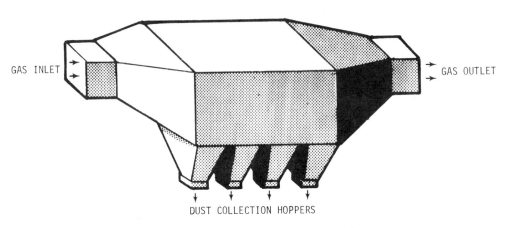

FIGURE 3.2.2. Horizontal flow settling chamber.

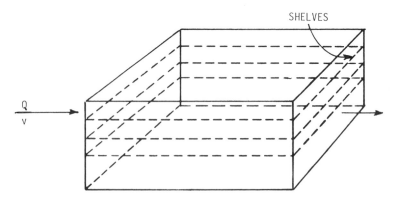

FIGURE 3.2.3. Gravity settling chamber with the addition of multiple horizontal collection plates.

between two adjacent shelves. The vertical distance between shelves may be as little as 1 in. The gas must be uniformly distributed laterally upon entering the chamber; vertical distribution is also critical. Uniform distribution is usually achieved by the use of gradual transitions, guide vanes, distributor screens, or perforated plates. Some of the disadvantages of the multiple-tray settling chambers include the cleaning difficulties arising from closely spaced trays, the tendency of the trays to warp during high-temperature operation, and the tendency of the system to be unable to handle dust concentrations exceeding approximately 1 grain/ft.^{3}

Since the effective settling rate of the dust decreases with increasing gas turbulence, the velocity of the gas stream in the settling chamber is normally kept as low as possible. For practical purposes, the velocity must not be so high that settled particles are reentrained or so low that chamber volume becomes excessive. Gas velocities usually range from 1 to 10 ft/sec. In actual practice, the gravitational settling velocities used in design must be based on experience or tests

conducted under actual conditions, because the terminal settling velocity may be influenced by factors such as agglomeration and electrostatic charge. Pressure drops experienced in settling chambers are quite low, generally less than 0.2 in. of water.

The physical description of a gravity settler includes (1) length, (2) width, (3) height, (4) number of shelves (if applicable), and (5) auxiliary equipment — inlet and outlet ducts, cleaning mechanism, hopper, etc. Three other examples of control equipment that can, in a very broad sense, be considered under the classification of gravity settlers include elutriators, momentum separators, and gravity spray towers. These are briefly discussed below.

Elutriators

An elutriator is a slight modification of the gravity settler. The unit consists of one or more vertical tubes or towers through which the dust-laden gas passes upward at a given velocity. The large particles that settle at a velocity higher than that of the rising air are collected at the bottom of the tube, while the smaller particles are carried out the top. In order to vary the air velocity, several columns of different diameters are used in series to bring about more refined separation (see Figure 3.2.5).

Momentum Separators

These units include another effect, in addition to gravity, to enhance particle separation and collection. This is accomplished by changing the direction of velocity of the gas stream so as to

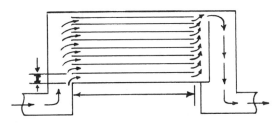

FIGURE 3.2.4. Howard settling chamber (multiple tray).

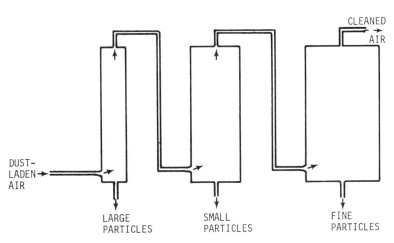

FIGURE 3.2.5. Elutriators in series.

impart an additional downward velocity to the particle. Particles as small as 10 to 20 μm can be collected. The physical arrangement usually involves the insertion of baffles into a gravity settler system. Examples of these devices are shown in Figure 3.2.6, a to c. They are more compact and require less space than the simple gravity settler; however, pressure losses are slightly higher (ranging from 0.1 to 1.0 in. of water).

Gravity Spray Towers

When a moving dust-laden gas stream approaches a body, such as a spherical droplet of water, the gas will be deflected around the droplet. The dust particles, by virtue of their greater inertia, may impact and be collected on the surface of the droplet which is falling under the influence of gravity. The design and operation of the gravity spray tower utilizes this collection phenomenon. The unit consists of a vertical tower or column. The particulate-laden gas is fed to the bottom of the column. A liquid stream (usually water) is introduced at the top of the column, after passing through spray nozzles. The water droplets produced fall vertically downward through the column under the influence of gravity. During their fall the droplets contact and capture the particles in the gas stream. (The collection mechanism is inertial impaction; the basic principles can be presented in terms of a single droplet collection efficiency and the inertial impaction (or target) number. This subject is treated in greater detail in Chapters 6 and 7.) A schematic diagram of this type of unit is shown in Figure 3.2.7. The system is capable of treating larger volumetric gas flow rates and has few mechanical problems. It operates at low pressure drops (usually less than 1 in. of water) with air velocities in the neighbor-

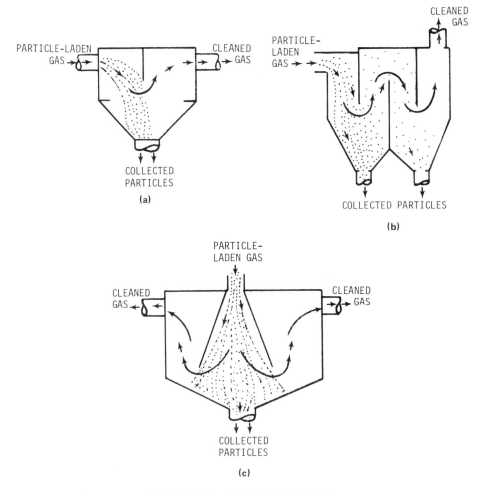

FIGURE 3.2.6. Momentum separators.

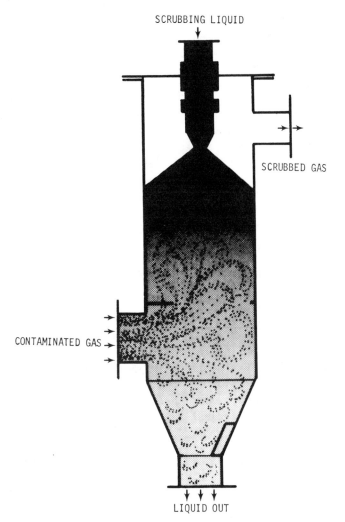

SCRUBBING LIQUID

SCRUBBED GAS

CONTAMINATED GAS

LIQUID OUT

FIGURE 3.2.7. Gravity spray tower.

hood of 2 to 5 ft/sec and residence times of approximately 15 to 30 sec. In addition to the collection of particles (down to the 10- to 20-μm range), the gravity spray tower can also be utilized to absorb noxious pollutant gases (depending on the liquid reagent used and solubility characteristics) and is often employed as a precooler. It is capable of handling relatively high dust loadings (greater than 5 grains/ft^3). The main disadvantage centers on the liquid effluent treatment and/or waste disposal as the air pollution problem is replaced by a water pollution problem. Water usage typically ranges between 5 to 20 gal/1,000 ft^3 gas treated (with a typical value around 18 gal/1,000 ft^3). Another disadvantage is the possibility of liquid entrainment in the gas stream leaving the tower; however, a demister, mist

eliminator, or entrainment separator installed above the spray nozzles (especially when gas velocities are greater than 6 ft/sec) will often eliminate this liquid entrainment problem. Similar to the gravity settlers, gravity spray towers have rather large space requirements.

3.3 LITERATURE REVIEW

A comprehensive review of the literature for this control device is not warranted. Some of the pertinent references on theory and development material are given in the next section.

3.4. FUNDAMENTALS

The fundamentals governing particle collection

in a gravity settler are now presented. Although the settler is initially assumed to contain no trays, the analysis can easily be extended to a multiple-tray unit since the capture height between the trays can be treated as an individual collector. In addition to operating conditions and physical characteristics, this section will discuss the effect of Reynolds number on particle drag, particle-size distribution, particle-mass flow rate gradient, and variable bulk gas velocity profile. Reentrainment effects are also briefly considered.

The analysis begins by examining the behavior of a single spherical particle in a settler in which the bulk flow air velocity profile is plug, i.e., the gas flow over the whole chamber is uniform (see Figure 3.4.1). The particle is assumed to be located at the top of the unit — the most difficult inlet (or initial) position for particle capture. At the inlet condition, it is assumed that the vertical velocity component of the particle is at its terminal settling velocity, i.e., the particle requires a negligible period of time (and consequently travels a negligible distance) to achieve a value approaching this constant terminal velocity. The analysis presented in Section 2.5 can be applied if the particle accelerates over an appreciable period of time. For capture to occur, the particle must reach the collection surface a'b'c'd' during its residence time, t_r, in the unit. For plug flow, t_r is given by

$$t_r = L/v; v = Q/BH$$

or

$$t_r = LBH/Q \qquad (3.4.1)$$

where

v = bulk flow velocity;
Q = volumetric flow rate of gas.

The time required for the particle to settle, t_s, a distance, H, while moving at its terminal velocity, v_t, is

$$t_s = H/v_t \qquad (3.4.2)$$

For capture to occur

$$t_s \leqslant t_r \qquad (3.4.3)$$

In the limit,

$$t_s = t_r \qquad (3.4.4)$$

Substituting Equations 3.4.1 and 3.4.2 into Equation 3.4.4 gives

$$H/v_t = LBH/Q$$

or

$$v_t = Q/LB \qquad (3.4.5)$$

The terminal velocity has previously been determined for the three Reynolds number ranges. For Stokes' law (without the Cunningham correction factor)

$$v_t = g d_p^2 \rho_p/18\mu \qquad (3.4.6)$$

Substituting the above equation into Equation

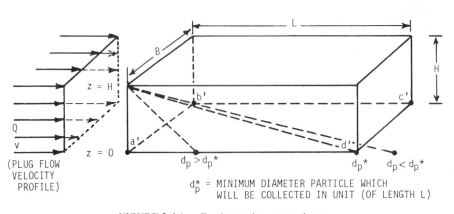

FIGURE 3.4.1. Gravity settler nomenclature.

3.4.5 and solving for the particle diameter, d_p, gives

$$d_p = (18 \mu \, Q/g \, \rho_p \, BL)^{0.5} \qquad (3.4.7)$$

For the intermediate range,

$$v_t = 0.153 \, (g \, \rho_p)^{0.71} \, d_p^{1.14}/\rho^{0.29} \, \mu^{0.43} \qquad (3.4.8)$$

so that

$$d_p = Q^{0.88} \, \rho^{0.254} \mu^{0.377}/0.193 \, (g\rho_p)^{0.623} \, (LB)^{0.88} \qquad (3.4.9)$$

Finally, for the Newton's law range,

$$v_t = 1.74 \, g \, d_p \, \rho_p/\rho \qquad (3.4.10)$$

and

$$d_p = 0.547 \, (\rho/g\rho_p) \, (Q/LB) \qquad (3.4.11)$$

The particle diameters calculated above represent limiting values since particles with diameters equal to or greater than this value will reach the collection surface and particles with diameters less than this value will escape from the unit. This limiting particle diameter may ideally be thought of as the minimum diameter of a particle that will automatically be captured for the above conditions. This diameter is denoted by d_p^* or d_p (min).

The above development assumes the bulk gas velocity profile to be plug. However, the velocity profile can be parabolic, as in laminar flow, or, in the general case, arbitrarily distributed. The calculation for the minimum particle diameter is not affected, provided that the volumetric flow rate of gas processed remains the same and the particle concentration remains uniform. This can be observed directly from Equation 3.4.5. The terminal settling velocity for total collection is the same as a hypothetical volume rate of fluid passing through LB, the collector area $a'b'c'd'$. Based on this analysis, it can be concluded that the performance of a settler depends only on its collection area and is independent of its height. The minimum height, however, is usually established by requiring that the gas velocity through the chamber be low enough to prevent reentrainment of the collected particles.

Collection efficiencies of 100% were used to derive the equations for d_p^*. The collection efficiency, η, for a monodispersed aerosol (particulates of one size) can be shown to be

$$\eta = (v_t BL/Q) \, 100\% \qquad (3.4.12)$$

The validity of this equation is observed by again noting that $v_t BL$ represents the hypothetical volume rate of flow of gas passing the collection area, while Q is the volumetric flow rate of gas entering the unit to be treated. An alternate but equivalent form of Equation 3.4.12 is

$$\eta = (v_t/v) \, (L/H) \, 100\%$$

or

$$\eta = (H^*/H) \, 100\% \qquad (3.4.13)$$

where

H* = the maximum height above the collection area, at inlet conditions, for which particle capture is assured (see Figure 3.4.2).

If the gas stream entering the unit consists of a distribution of particles of various sizes, then frequently a fractional or grade efficiency curve is specified for the settler. This is simply a curve describing the collection efficiency for particles of various sizes (see Figure 3.4.3). If a particle of size d_p will settle a distance h in time t, then (h/H) represents the fraction of particles of this size that will be collected. If h is equal to or greater than H, all the particles of that size or larger will be collected in the settling chamber. A curve of (h/H) vs. d_p over the particle-size distribution range of the incoming particles entrained in the gas stream is the fractional or grade efficiency curve.

The cases considered above are rarely found in industrial applications, so these equations have been of little practical value except to indicate the importance of certain variables. A more realistic approach to the calculation of collection efficiencies for gravity settlers should include several additional and important variables.

A model is now presented to predict the performance of a gravity settler under conditions approaching actual operation. The development treats the effect of the distribution of several system variables. The effects of Reynolds number

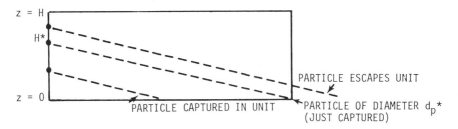

FIGURE 3.4.2. Particle collection in settler.

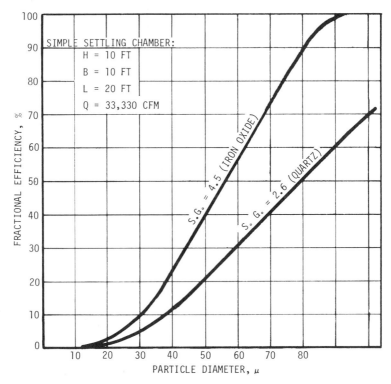

FIGURE 3.4.3. Fractional efficiency curve for dusts from a sinter plant. (Jennings, R. F., *J. Iron Steel Inst.* (London), 164, 305, 1950. With permission.)

on particle drag, particle-size distributions and variations in particle-size distribution, particle-mass flow rate gradients, and variable bulk gas velocity profile are included in the model. A statistical technique using random numbers is employed to account for all the variables in the proposed model. The method of solution is based on the repetitive calculation of the describing trajectory equations for a large number of particles, with the magnitude of the variables determined by the assignment of a random number.

The statistical technique referred to above is the Monte Carlo method. It finds application in describing the behavior of a system which can be subjected to random variations of several system variables. The operation or process is repeated for different sets of conditions — with the magnitude of the variable(s) determined via the random number technique. Since more extensive information can be included in the describing equations, this technique is ideally suited for multidimensional problems. It has found widespread use in the chemical process industry.[2-4]

It was previously shown that the velocity vector of a particle in a gravity settler is the result of two velocity components — one in the direction of bulk gas flow and one perpendicular to the mainstream flow. The equations describing the velocity perpendicular to bulk gas flow were obtained earlier from a force balance on a particle in the settler. The velocity in the direction of bulk gas flow is given by bulk gas velocity profile information. Standard equations are already available for predicting bulk gas velocity profiles in rectangular (or cylindrical) ducts for plug, laminar, and turbulent flow conditions.[5-8] In general, for a gravity settler,

$$dy/dt = v = f(z) \tag{3.4.14}$$

In this analysis, a profile of arbitrary form is assumed. The need for integrating the above equation may be removed by dividing the settler height into j finite sections with the height of each section defined as Δz and the local bulk velocity at each section as v_i (see Figure 3.4.4). Knowing both particle velocity components, it is now possible to calculate a collecting plate length, L^*, needed to capture the particle. This is given by

$$L^* = (\Delta z/v_t)\left(\sum_{i=1}^{1-1} v_i\right) + (q/v_t)\,v_1 \tag{3.4.15}$$

where

1 = the number of sections that the particle is displaced from the collecting plate at the inlet to the settler;

q = the height at which the particle is positioned within section 1.

In order to solve the above equation, the particle's inlet position and size must be known. The details of specifying these variables are presented below.

Since it is necessary to determine the individual paths of a large number of particles entering each section of the settler, a representative set of particles must be used and the inlet position of each particle must be specified. In general, a particle-mass flow rate gradient will exist with a certain percentage of the total mass flow rate passing through the inlet into each section. One such possible mass flow rate gradient is shown in Figure 3.4.5. For the representative set of particles chosen for study, the number of particles initially positioned at each section is proportional to the mass flow rate into each section. The particle is positioned in each section by application of a random number. For example, setting the two-digit numbers 00 and 99 as the limits for each section, the magnitude of a random two-digit number can be used to assign a particle position at an inlet section using a suitable interpolation technique.

The particle size is also specified by the application of the Monte Carlo method. A sample distribution of particle sizes can be represented in a cumulative distribution curve, as shown in Figure 3.4.6. This distribution may be divided into five ranges each representing 20% of the total mass of

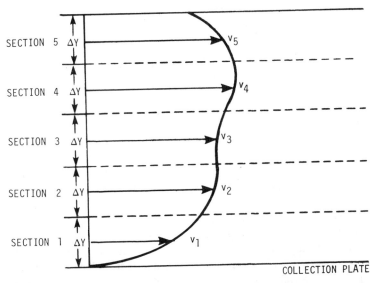

FIGURE 3.4.4.   Arbitrary inlet bulk gas velocity profile.

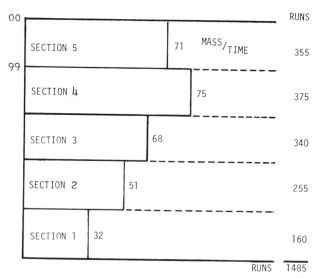

FIGURE 3.4.5. Arbitrary inlet particle-mass flow rate distribution.

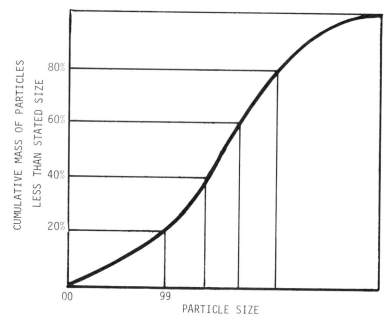

FIGURE 3.4.6. Arbitrary cumulative particle-size distribution for each section.

particles in the entering gas. A different distribution is assumed for each section in order to account for possible variations in the particle-size distribution at the inlet cross section. Thus, for a given inlet particle position (obtained from particle-mass flow rate data), the appropriate particle-size distribution is applied. Since the distribution is arbitrarily divided into five ranges (see Figure 3.4.6), 20% of the trajectory calcula-

tions for each section are made with particle sizes in each of the five ranges. Setting the numbers 00 and 99 as the limits for each range, the magnitude of a random number is used to assign a particle size for each run using a suitable interpolation technique.

In summary, the number of particles to be tested is specified. A specific particle inlet position and size are determined for the first particle to be tested. The trajectory equations are employed to predict whether or not the particle is captured. This procedure is repeated for all particles to be investigated — with the magnitude of the variables evaluated using random numbers.

A running tally is made of the particles tested and collected for each section. The collection efficiency equation for section i is given by

$$\eta_i = (P_i/T_i)\, 100 \qquad (3.4.16)$$

where

P_i = the number of particles collected;
T_i = the total number of particles tested.

The same weighing factor, irrespective of the particle size, is assigned to each particle tested. This sectional efficiency is then extended to include the effects of all the particles on the overall collection efficiency by the equation

$$\eta = \sum_{i=1}^{j} \eta_i\, w_i \qquad (3.4.17)$$

where

w_i = the fractional particle-mass flow rate for section i.

The equations and method of solution to this model can, and have been, incorporated into a program for a digital computer.[9] Although the Monte Carlo method of solution has been presented for gravity settlers, it can also be applied to

determine collection efficiencies for other particulate collection devices.[2,3] It is a useful and versatile tool that can easily provide accurate estimates for a number of various equipment designs and thus be used in optimization studies.

The collection of particles from a gas stream involves three distinct phases: deposition on the collecting surface, retention on the surface, and finally, removal of the collected material. Thus far it has been assumed that once a particle settles to the bottom of the chamber (or onto a tray within the chamber), it is retained there, i.e., reentrainment effects have been neglected. If the bulk flow gas velocity is sufficiently high, a collected particle will not be retained by the surface, but will be picked up and reentrained into the moving air stream. This can substantially reduce the collection efficiency; the consideration of pickup or suspension velocity for horizontal flow is indeed important. Therefore, in a simple gravity settler, the bulk gas velocity should *not* exceed this pickup or suspension velocity. Experimental pickup velocities of various materials are tabulated in Table 3.4.1.[10] Values for this limiting velocity can also be obtained from semitheoretical considerations. By equating the various forces acting on the particle while neglecting interparticle friction, one can derive the equation[11]

$$v_p = (4\, g\, d_p\, (\rho_p - \rho)/3\, \rho)^{0.5} \qquad (3.4.18)$$

where

v_p = pickup velocity.

If the static head arising due to the deposited solids is included, Equation 3.4.18 becomes

TABLE 3.4.1

Pickup Velocities of Various Materials

Material	Density (g/cm³)	Median particle size (μm)	Pickup velocity (ft/sec)
Aluminum chips	2.72	335	14.2
Asbestos	2.20	261	17.0
Nonferrous foundry dust	3.02	117	18.8
Lead oxide	8.26	14.7	25.0
Limestone	2.78	71	21.0
Starch	1.27	64	5.8
Steel shot	6.85	96	15.2
Wood chips	1.18	1,370	13.0
Wood sawdust	—	1,400	22.3

$$v_p = \left\{ \frac{2\,g}{\rho} \left[\frac{2\,d_p\,(\rho_p - \rho)}{3} + \frac{P_s\,\rho\,W}{\rho_p\,G} \right] \right\}^{0.5} \qquad (3.4.19)$$

where

(W/G) = the rate of solids carried as (lb of solids)/(lb of gas);

P_s = the static gas pressure.

3.5. DESIGN PRINCIPLES

It must be stated at the outset that industry's approach to the design of gravity settlers, as well as other particulate control devices, is very pragmatic. Often one will find that the design procedures and equations employed bear little resemblance to those presented in the previous section. It is common practice to modify theoretical equations with coefficients which correlate the results generated from a theoretical analysis with those results obtained from an experimental (or actual) system.

Industrial collection efficiency equations and design procedures almost always include the following assumptions.

1. The bulk gas velocity profile is plug.
2. Particle concentration is uniform.
3. Particles settle at their terminal velocities.
4. The Stokes' settling velocity is valid for the calculation.
5. The Cunningham correction factor effect is assumed negligible.
6. No particle reentrainment.
7. The particle is spherical in shape.
8. The effect of particle-particle interactions is negligible.

Collection efficiencies for gravity settlers are usually calculated by one of the following methods.

1. Estimate or calculate the minimum particle diameter, $d_p{}^*$, that must be captured by the unit. The collection efficiency is then 100% for particle diameters above $d_p{}^*$. (Note, however, that in actual practice some of the particles smaller than $d_p{}^*$ will also be captured).

2. Assume that the particle-size distribution of the dust-laden gas can be represented by the mass median diameter, i.e., the diameter corresponding to 50% on the cumulative size-distribution plot or the diameter at which 50% of the population by mass is greater and 50% is less than. Equation 3.4.12 is then used to calculate the efficiency with the terminal velocity, v_t, based on this diameter.

3. The particle size-distribution curve is divided into several particle-size ranges. An average particle size is assumed for each range i and an efficiency, η_i, similar to (2) is obtained for that range. This is repeated for all the size ranges. For a given unit, operating under a particular set of conditions, an efficiency-particle size curve (referred to as a fractional or grade efficiency curve) can then be generated. The contribution from range i to the overall collection efficiency, η, is

$$\eta_i\,w_i$$

where

w_i = the weight fraction of particles in size range i.

The overall collection efficiency is then

$$\eta = \sum_{i=1}^{l} \eta_i\,w_i \qquad (3.5.1)$$

where

l = the number of size ranges.

The third method discussed above, with its many variations, is the one most frequently used today; as a result, it warrants further elaboration. Most of the presentation to follow, which is directed toward determining the overall collection efficiency, is *also applicable to the other particulate control units to be discussed in subsequent chapters.* Hence, the development will be discussed in full at this time, and referral will be made to it in later chapters. Basically, the techniques enable the overall collection efficiency of the particulate control unit to be determined from particle-size distribution data and fractional or grade efficiency information.

For most particulate control devices it is possible to determine either the theoretical or experimental functional relationship between efficiency and particle size. That is,

Size collection efficiency = $\eta(d_p)$ (3.5.2)

For the gravity settler this was previously shown to be a curve of (h/H) vs. d_p over the particle-size distribution range of the incoming particles entrained in the gas stream. The cumulative size distribution of the particles (i.e., cumulative percent less than stated size by mass vs. particle diameter) in the incoming gas stream can readily be determined from the output of any of several particle-size analyzing instruments such as the Andersen sampler or Coulter counter. The cumulative distribution is the function used to calculate the mass or weight fraction of particles in a given sample having diameters less than a stated diameter, d_p:

Cumulative size distribution = $Y(d_p)$ (3.5.3)

Once known, the cumulative distribution can be used to determine the frequency distribution, which in turn is used to calculate the masses of particulates that fall within various size ranges (size fractions).

The following development adapted from Vatavuk[1][2] shows how the frequency-size distribution, $f(d_p)$, can be found from the cumulative distribution, $Y(d_p)$. Consider a particulate sample of mass, M(lb), with diameters ranging from 0 to ∞. By definition, $Y(d_p)$ equals the mass fraction of particles larger than diameter d_p.

$$Y(d_p) = \int_{d_p}^{\infty} f(x)dx = -\int_{\infty}^{d_p} f(x)dx \quad (3.5.4)$$

This relationship holds because $Y(d_p)$ is the integral of $f(d_p)$. Differentiating $Y(d_p)$ with respect to d_p:

$$d[Y(d_p)]/d(d_p) = \frac{d}{d(d_p)} [-\int_{\infty}^{d_p} f(x)dx] = -f(d_p)$$

(3.5.5)

Now, consider all the particles in the size interval

d_p to $d_p + d(d_p)$. The mass of these particles collected by the device, dM_c, would equal the mass of incoming particles in the interval, $Mf(d_p)d(d_p)$, multiplied by the collection efficiency at size d_p, $\eta(d_p)$:

$$dM_c = Mf(d_p)\,\eta(d_p)\,d(d_p) \quad (3.5.6)$$

To determine the overall collection efficiency, η, one would simply integrate dM_c from 0 to ∞ and divide by the total incoming mass, M:

$$\eta = \frac{1}{M} \int_0^{\infty} dM_c = \int_0^{\infty} f(d_p)\,\eta(d_p)\,d(d_p) \quad (3.5.7)$$

This is the basic equation for the overall collection efficiency. Equation 3.5.7 can be further simplified by the substitution of $f(d_p)$.

For many, if not most, particulate streams, the weight distribution very closely follows a log-normal curve, which is a normal distribution skewed toward very small or very large particle sizes. Substitution of the log-normal distribution function into Equation 3.5.7 would result in an expression that probably could not be integrated to yield a closed-form function. Either numeric or graphic integration would then have to be used to calculate the overall efficiency. A simpler approach can be taken if one recognizes that for values of $Y(d_p)$ ranging from about 0.15 to 0.85, the distribution approximates an exponential of the form

$$Y(d_p) = e^{-\beta d_p} \quad (3.5.8)$$

where

β = slope of the semilog distribution, μm^{-1}.

The parameter β can be obtained by plotting the log of the cumulative distribution of particle-size fractions against the particle diameters. These size-fraction measurements can be obtained from one or more particle separation procedures such as sieving (for coarse particles), elutriation, and sedimentation (for fine particles). Keep in mind that Equation 3.5.8 deviates from the actual weight distribution for relatively small and relatively large particles. Substituting Equation 3.5.8 into Equation 3.5.5 gives

$$f(d_p) = -\frac{d}{d(d_p)}[Y(d_p)] = -\frac{d}{d(d_p)}[e^{-\beta d_p}] = \beta e^{-\beta d_p}$$

$$(3.5.9)$$

Substitution into Equation 3.5.7 yields the total efficiency, η_T,

$$\eta_T = \beta \int_0^\infty e^{-\beta d_p} \eta(d_p)\, d(d_p) \qquad (3.5.10)$$

Equation 3.5.10 can be applied to gravity settling chambers, cyclones, venturi scrubbers, and electrostatic precipitators. Examples of its application will be presented in subsequent chapters. Its application to gravity settlers is demonstrated below.

From Equations 3.4.12 and 3.4.6 for Stokes' law,

$$\eta(d_p) = \left[\frac{g\,\rho_p\,BLN_C}{18\,\mu\,Q}\right] d_p^2 = (k)d_p^2 \qquad (3.5.11)$$

where

g	=	gravitational acceleration, ft/sec^2;
ρ_p	=	particle density, lb/ft^3;
μ	=	gas viscosity, lb/ft-sec;
Q	=	volumetric flow rate, ft^3/sec;
B	=	chamber width, ft;
L	=	chamber length, ft;
N_C	=	number of parallel chambers: 1 for a simple chamber and N trays + 1 for a Howard settling chamber.

In Equation 3.5.11 ρ_p was assumed to be much greater than ρ (the gas density); hence, $(\rho_p - \rho) \approx \rho_p$. Also, the term in brackets in Equation 3.5.11 is often multiplied by a dimensionless empirical factor to correlate theoretical efficiencies with experimental data. If no information is available, it is suggested that 0.5 be used. For a given set of operating conditions, the terms in brackets are considered to be constants. Thus, substitution in Equation 3.5.10 yields the overall collection efficiency:

$$\eta_T = \beta \int_0^\infty (k)d_p^2\, e^{-\beta d_p}\, d(d_p) \qquad (3.5.12)$$

This integral must be evaluated in two parts: first, between the limits of $d_p = 0$ and $d_p = (1/k)^{1/2}$, and second, between the limits of $d_p = (1/k)^{1/2}$ and $d_p = \infty$. This is necessary because the size efficiency remains at a constant value of 100% for all particles having diameters greater than or equal to $(1/k)^{1/2}$. Thus,

$$\eta_T = [\beta \int_0^{(1/k)^{1/2}} (k)\, d_p^2\, e^{-\beta d_p}\, d(d_p)] +$$

$$[\beta \int_{(1/k)^{1/2}}^{\infty} (k)d_p^2\, e^{-\beta d_p}\, d(d_p)]$$

$$= \frac{2\,k}{\beta^2}[1 - e^{-\beta/k^{1/2}}(1 + \beta/k^{1/2})] \qquad (3.5.13)$$

An example of the use of Equation 3.5.13 is presented in Section 3.6 (Example 3.6.13).

Another technique for determining the overall collection efficiency was developed by Sundberg.[13] Essentially, this method permits the overall collection efficiency to be calculated from the four parameters which describe the log-normal properties of the particle-size distribution and the fractional efficiency curve of the collector. Plotting the cumulative size distribution (or percent less than stated size by mass) against the particle diameter on logarithmic probability paper is often adequately represented by a straight line, as was mentioned previously. When this is true, the distribution is log normal, and only two parameters (the median diameter and the geometric standard deviation) are required to completely define the distribution. The mass median diameter (d_{p50}) is the diameter corresponding to 50% on the cumulative size distribution plot or the diameter at which 50% of the population by mass is greater than and 50% less than. The geometric standard deviation (σ_g), as discussed in Chapter 1, is a measure of the spread of the distribution or the slope of the log-normal line. It is the standard deviation of the logarithms of the particle diameters.

$$\sigma_g = \frac{84.13\% \text{ size}}{50\% \text{ size}} = \frac{50\% \text{ size}}{15.87\% \text{ size}}$$

Both of these parameters are easily obtained from the cumulative size distribution plot. The fractional (or grade) efficiency curve, as was also discussed previously, is the plot of collection efficiency as a function of particle size. If this is plotted on logarithmic probability paper, the result is again frequently found to be adequately represented by a straight line or log-normal function. The significant parameters needed to specify the curve are again the 50% point (d'_{ps0}) and the geometric standard deviation (σ'_g). Traditionally, the overall collection efficiency is estimated from graphical integration of the collector fractional efficiency and the particle-size distribution, i.e., the size distribution broken into segments (or histograms) and multiplied by the collection efficiency at the mean of the segment and summed over the range of particle sizes. This procedure is somewhat laborious and frequently inaccurate since it involves a large number of values read from a graph. Sundberg suggests that if the particle-size distribution of the dust and the fractional efficiency of the collector can adequately be approximated by log-normal functions, the collector performance can be completely determined from d_{ps0}, σ_g, d'_{ps0}, and σ'_g, the four parameters required to specify the two log-normal curves. The overall efficiency can be expressed in the integral form as

$$\eta_T = \int_{-\infty}^{+\infty} \Phi_1 (d_p) \, d\left[\Phi_2 (d_p)\right] \qquad (3.5.14)$$

where

$\Phi_1(d_p)$ = log-normal function for the fractional efficiency;

$\Phi_2(d_p)$ = log-normal function for the particle-size distribution;

d_p = particle diameter.

The solution of Equation 3.5.14 is a simple relation between the overall collection efficiency and the error function (erf) or table of areas under the standard normal curve. Then,

$$\eta_T = erf\left[\frac{\ln (d_{ps0}/d'_{ps0})}{(\ln^2 \sigma_g + \ln^2 \sigma'_g)^{0.5}}\right] \qquad (3.5.15)$$

The overall collection efficiency can thus be computed by evaluating Equation 3.5.15 and reading the efficiency from the error function table (a portion of which is presented in Table

3.5.1). An example using Equation 3.5.15 is presented in Section 3.6 (Example 3.6.14).

The process design variables for a gravity settler consist of its length (L), width (B), and height (H). These parameters are usually designed by industry to completely remove all of the particles above a specified particle size, $d_p{}^*$, i.e., method 1 is employed. The volume of the unit should be such that sufficient residence time for the volume rate of gas treated is provided for capture of all the particles. The throughput velocity should not exceed the pickup velocity, i.e.,

TABLE 3.5.1

Error Function

Areas Under the Standard Normal Curve from $-\infty$ to d_p

$$erf(d_p) = \frac{1}{2\pi} \int_{-\infty}^{d_p} e^{-\frac{1}{2} f^2} df$$

d_p	0	2	4	6	8
0.0	0.5000	0.5080	0.5160	0.5239	0.5319
0.1	0.5398	0.5478	0.5557	0.5636	0.5714
0.2	0.5793	0.5871	0.5948	0.6026	0.6103
0.3	0.6179	0.6255	0.6331	0.6406	0.6480
0.4	0.6554	0.6628	0.6700	0.6772	0.6844
0.5	0.6915	0.6985	0.7054	0.7123	0.7190
0.6	0.7258	0.7324	0.7389	0.7454	0.7518
0.7	0.7580	0.7642	0.7704	0.7764	0.7823
0.8	0.7881	0.7939	0.7996	0.8051	0.8106
0.9	0.8159	0.8212	0.8264	0.8315	0.8365
1.0	0.8413	0.8461	0.8508	0.8554	0.8599
1.1	0.8643	0.8686	0.8729	0.8770	0.8810
1.2	0.8849	0.8888	0.8925	0.8962	0.8997
1.3	0.9032	0.9066	0.9099	0.9131	0.9162
1.4	0.9192	0.9222	0.9251	0.9279	0.9306
1.5	0.9332	0.9357	0.9382	0.9406	0.9429
1.6	0.9452	0.9474	0.9495	0.9515	0.9535
1.7	0.9554	0.9573	0.9591	0.9608	0.9625
1.8	0.9641	0.9656	0.9671	0.9686	0.9699
1.9	0.9713	0.9726	0.9738	0.9750	0.9761
2.0	0.9772	0.9783	0.9793	0.9803	0.9812
2.1	0.9821	0.9830	0.9838	0.9846	0.9854
2.2	0.9861	0.9868	0.9875	0.9881	0.9887
2.3	0.9893	0.9898	0.9904	0.9909	0.9913
2.4	0.9918	0.9922	0.9927	0.9931	0.9934
2.5	0.9938	0.9941	0.9945	0.9948	0.9951
2.6	0.9953	0.9956	0.9959	0.9961	0.9963
2.7	0.9965	0.9967	0.9969	0.9971	0.9973
2.8	0.9974	0.9976	0.9977	0.9979	0.9980
2.9	0.9981	0.9982	0.9984	0.9985	0.9986

$$v = (Q/BH) \leqslant v_p \qquad (3.5.16)$$

It is suggested that the experimental data presented in Table 3.4.1, rather than the equations presented in the last section, be used to estimate pickup velocities. If no data are available, the throughput velocity should not exceed 10 ft/sec. In addition, for 100% collection efficiency

$$v_t = Q/LB \qquad (3.5.17)$$

so that

$$LB = Q/v_t \qquad (3.5.18)$$

The volume of the settler is given by

$$\text{Volume} = LBH \qquad (3.5.19)$$

Since LB is fixed from Equation 3.5.18, the volume of the settler is minimized by minimizing H. However, the value of H is limited by cleaning considerations and space requirements (long and narrow vs. short and wide). The minimum height is also limited by the requirement that the gas velocity through the chamber be low enough to prevent reentrainment (or pickup) of collected particles. The above equations must, therefore, be simultaneously considered in the final choice of process design.

In terms of overall design considerations for gravity settlers, advantages include:

    1. Low cost of construction and operation.
    2. Few maintenance problems.
    3. Relatively low operating pressure drops in the range of approximately 0.1 in. of water.
    4. Temperature and pressure limitations imposed only by the materials of construction used.
    5. Dry disposal of solid particulates.

The disadvantages include:

    1. Large space requirements.
    2. Relatively low overall collection efficiencies (typically ranging from 20 to 60%).

In general, most of the gravity settlers found in use today are acting in the capacity of a precleaner — removing the relatively large particles before the gas stream enters a more efficient particulate control device such as a cyclone. Typical installed costs range from \$0.10 to 0.40 per ACFM. Operating costs are typically less than \$0.01 per ACFM per year.

3.6 ILLUSTRATIVE EXAMPLES

The design procedures and equations presented in the previous sections will now be applied to demonstrate their use in gravity settler analysis.

Example 3.6.1
A hydrochloric acid mist in air at $25°C$ is to be collected in a gravity settler. The unit is 30 ft wide, 20 ft high, and 50 ft long. The actual volumetric flow rate of the "acidic" gas is 50 ft^3/sec. Calculate the smallest mist droplet (spherical in shape) that will be entirely collected by the settler. The specific gravity of the acid is equal to 1.6. Assume the acid concentration to be uniform through the inlet cross section of the unit.

Solution
The important data are tabulated below:

$$
\begin{aligned}
T &= 30°C, P = 1 \text{ atm} \\
B &= 30 \text{ ft} \\
H &= 20 \text{ ft} \\
L &= 50 \text{ ft} \\
Q &= 50 \text{ ft}^3/\text{sec} \\
\rho &= 1.6
\end{aligned}
$$

At $25°C$

$$\mu = 0.0185 \text{ cp} = 1.24 \times 10^{-5} \text{ lb/(ft) (sec)}$$

The describing equation (since Stokes' law applies) is

$$d_p(\text{min}) = (18\, \mu\, Q/g\, \rho_p\, BL)^{1/2}$$

Substituting gives

$$d_p(\text{min}) = (18 \times 1.24 \times 10^{-5} \times 50/32.2 \times 1.6 \times 62.4 \times 30 \times 50)^{1/2}$$

or

$$d_p(\text{min}) = 4.82 \times 10^{-5} \text{ ft (or } 14.7\ \mu\text{m)}$$

The reader should verify that the Cunningham correction factor is 1.0 for this diameter.

Example 3.6.2

Calculate the smallest droplet in Example 3.6.1 if the flow rate is tripled.

Solution

If Q is tripled, then the term in parenthesis in the previous example is also tripled. Thus,

$$d_p(min) = (3 \times 23.2 \times 10^{-10})^{1/2}$$
$$= 8.35 \times 10^{-5} \text{ ft (or } 25.4 \text{ } \mu m)$$

Example 3.6.3

Calculate the smallest droplet in Example 3.6.1 if the "acidic" gas is at 200°C.

Solution

At 200°C,

$$\mu = 0.025 \text{ cp} = 1.68 \times 10^{-5} \text{ lb/ft sec}$$

The new volumetric flow rate at this increased temperature is

$$Q = 50(852°R/537°R) = 79.3 \text{ ft}^3/\text{sec}$$

Substituting into the describing equation gives

$$d_p(min) = (18 \mu Q/g \rho_p BL)^{1/2}$$
$$= (18 \times 1.68 \times 10^{-5} \times 79.3/32.2 \times 1.6 \times$$
$$62.4 \times 30 \times 50)^{1/2}$$

Solving yields

$$d_p{}^* = d_p(min) = 7.05 \times 10^{-5} \text{ ft (or } 21.5 \text{ } \mu m)$$

Example 3.6.4

Calculate the smallest droplet in Example 3.6.1 if the length of the unit is doubled.

Solution

If L is doubled, we may simply divide the answer in Example 3.6.1 by $\sqrt{2}$. Thus,

$$d_p(min) = 4.82 \times 10^{-5}/\sqrt{2}$$
$$= 3.41 \times 10^{-5} \text{ ft (or } 10.4 \text{ } \mu m)$$

Example 3.6.5

Estimate the collection efficiency for each of the particle sizes calculated in Examples 3.6.1 to 3.6.4. Justify your answer.

Solution

There must be 100% collection since we are treating a monodispersed aerosol. The development used equated the residence time with the settling time for 100% collection.

Example 3.6.6

A gravity settler 20 cm wide × 50 cm long containing 18 plates with a channel spacing of 0.124 cm is used to trap the particles of a monodispersed latex aerosol of particle diameter 0.81 μm. The gas flow rate is 7.10 l/min. Calculate the operating efficiency of the settler for the data given below:

$$\rho_p = 1.05 \text{ g/cm}^3$$
$$\rho = 1.223 \times 10^{-3} \text{ g/cm}^3$$
$$\mu = 1.82 \times 10^{-4} \frac{g}{cm\text{-}sec}$$

Solution

K is in the Stokes' law range. The Cunningham correction factor is

$$C = 1 + 0.086/0.5 \text{ } d_p$$
$$= 1 + 0.086/0.5 \times 0.81$$
$$= 1.212$$

The settling velocity equation is given by

$$v_t = d_p{}^2 C \rho_p g/18 \mu$$

Substituting the data

$$v_t = (0.81 \times 10^{-4})^2 \times 1.212 \times 1.05 \times 980/18 \times 1.82 \times 10^{-4}$$
$$= 2.498 \times 10^{-3} \text{ cm/sec}$$

The volumetric flow rate is

$$Q = (7.1 \times 1000)/(60 \times 19)$$
$$= 6.228 \text{ cm}^3/(sec)(channel)$$

Therefore

$$\eta = BL \text{ } v_t/Q$$
$$= 20 \times 50 \times 2.498 \times 10^{-3}/6.228$$
$$= 0.401 \text{ or } 40.1\%$$

Example 3.6.7

A gravity settler 20 cm wide × 50 cm long with a channel spacing of 0.124 cm is being used to capture the particles of a polydispersed aerosol whose analysis is given below.

Diameter, μm	Wt %
0.557	20
0.81	20
1.099	60

The settling velocities for each particle have been calculated using the Stokes-Cunningham correction equation and are tabulated below.

Diameter, μm	v_t, cm/sec
0.557	0.0012736
0.810	0.0024977
1.099	0.0043855

Calculate the overall efficiency of the settler when it operates at a gas rate of 6.0 l/min.

Solution

The collection efficiency equation is

$$\eta = v_t \, BL/Q$$

Substituting the data for $d_p = 0.557 \, \mu m$ gives

$$\eta = 1.274 \times 10^{-3} \times 20 \times 50 \times 60 \times 19/6.0 \times 1,000$$
$$= 24.2\%$$

Substituting the data for $d_p = 0.81 \, \mu m$ gives

$$\eta = 2.498 \times 10^{-3} \times 1,000 \times 60 \times 19/6,000$$
$$= 47.46\%$$

For

$$d_p = 1.099 \, \mu m$$

$$\eta = 83.3\%$$

The overall efficiency is then

$$\eta_T = 0.2 \times 24.2 + 0.2 \times 47.46 + 0.6 \times 83.3$$
$$= 64.3\%$$

Example 3.6.8

A gravity settler consists of 19 rectangular channels each 20 cm $\times$ 0.124 cm. Using Stokes' law, with the Cunningham correction factor included, determine the minimum length for 96% collection efficiency with a monodispersed aerosol

0.81 μm in diameter at a flow rate of 2.84 l/min.

$$\mu = 0.0182 \text{ cp}$$
$$\rho_p = 1.05 \text{ g/cc}$$
$$\lambda = 0.1 \times 10^{-4} \text{ cm}$$

Solution

The Cunningham correction factor is again 1.212. The settling velocity equation is given by

$$v_t = d_p^2 \, \rho_p \, gC/18 \, \mu$$

so that

$$v_t = 2.5 \times 10^{-3} \text{ cm/sec}$$

The volumetric flow rate may be calculated by

$$Q = 2.84 \times 1,000/60 \times 19$$
$$Q = 2.49 \text{ cm}^3/(\text{sec}) (\text{channel})$$

Employing the efficiency equation

$$v = Q\eta/BL$$

and solving for L

$$L = Q\eta/Bv$$

gives

$$L = 2.49 \times 0.96/20 \times 2.5 \times 10^{-3}$$
$$= 47.8 \text{ cm}$$

Example 3.6.9

Installation of a gravity settler to help remove fly ash particles (specific gravity = 2.31) from an air stream at ambient conditions has been proposed. The inlet dust loading is 21 grains/ft^3, and the volumetric flow rate is 4,680 ACFM. The inlet size distribution of the fly ash is given below.

Size range, μm	Mass %
0–10	2
10–20	2
20–30	6
30–40	19
50–60	20
60–80	22
80–100	18
100–150	11

The dimensions of the unit are 10 ft wide $\times$ 20 ft

high × 45 ft long. Calculate an average collection efficiency over each size range.

Solution

Converting the volumetric flow rate gives

$Q = 4,680/60$
$\quad = 78 \text{ ft}^3/\text{sec}$

The residence time may be calculated by

$t_r = LBH/Q = (10)(20)(45)/78$
$\qquad = 115 \text{ sec}$

The value of K is calculated from

$K = d_p \, (g \, \rho_p \, \rho/\mu^2)^{1/3}$

Substituting the data

$K = d_p \, [32.2 \times 2.31 \times 62.4 \times$
$\quad 0.075/(1.21 \times 10^{-5})^2]^{1/3} \times 3.281 \times 10^{-6}$

or

$K = 4.38 \times 10^{-2} \, d_p; \, d_p \text{ in } \mu m$

For Stokes' law

$v_t = g \, d_p^{\,2} \, \rho_p/18 \, \mu$

Substituting

$v_t = 32.2 \times (3.281 \times 10^{-6} \, d_p)^2 \times 144/18 \times 1.21 \times 10^{-5}$

so that

$v_t = 2.29 \times 10^{-4} \, d_p^{\,2}, \, d_p \text{ in } \mu m$

For the intermediate range

$v_t = 0.153 \, (g \, \rho_p)^{0.71} \, d_p^{\,1.14}/\rho^{0.29} \, \mu^{0.43}$

Substituting the data gives

$v_t = 9.47 \times 10^{-3} \, d_p^{\,1.14}; \, d_p \text{ in } \mu m$

The decrease in height of each particle is given by

$h = v_t t_r$

and the collecting efficiency by

$\eta = (h/H) \, 100$

The results are tabulated below.

Size range, μm	$\langle d_p \rangle$ μm	K	v_t, ft/sec	h, ft	η, %
0–10	5	0.219	5.73×10^{-3}	0.66	3.3
10–20	15	0.66	5.15×10^{-2}	5.923	29.6
20–30	25	1.09	1.43×10^{-1}	16.44	82.2
30–40	35	1.53	0.28	32.2	100
50–60	55	2.41	0.693	79.7	100
60–80	70	3.06	1.122	129.0	100
80–100	90	3.94	1.6	184	100
100–150	125	5.47	2.33	268	100

Example 3.6.10

Using the data and results of the previous example, estimate the overall collection efficiency of the unit.

Solution

The overall collection efficiency is obtained from the equation:

$$\eta = \sum_{i=1}^{n} w_i \, \eta_i$$

where

w_i = weight fraction in range i;
η_i = collection efficiency in range i.

Results are presented below.

w_i	η_i, %	$w_i \eta_i$, %
0.02	3.3	0.066
0.02	29.6	0.592
0.06	82.2	4.93
0.19	100	19.0
0.20	100	20.0
0.22	100	22.0
0.18	100	18.0
0.11	100	11.0
1.00		95.6%

Note: Overall efficiency = 95.6%.

Example 3.6.11

Using the data and results of the two previous examples, calculate the outlet dust loading, the daily mass of dust collected, and the daily mass of dust discharged from the unit.

Solution

The outlet dust loading may be calculated by

loading out = $(1 - \eta)$(loading in)

Substituting the data

loading out = $(1 - 0.956)21 = 0.924$ grains/ft^3

The daily mass collected is given by

$0.956 \times 21 \times 4,680 \times 60 \times 24/7,000$

or

19.328 lb/day

The daily mass discharged is

$(0.044/0.956)$ 19,328 = 889 lb/day

Example 3.6.12

As a recently hired engineer for an equipment vending company, you have been requested to design a gravity settler to remove all particles greater than 75 μm (specific gravity = 1.91) from a dust-laden gas stream at ambient conditions. The volumetric flow rate is 100 ACFS. Submit your design. The maximum allowable throughput velocity is 10 ft/sec.

Solution

We again calculate K from

$$K = d_p (g \, \rho \, \rho_p / \mu^2)^{1/3}$$

Substituting the data yields

$$K = 2.46 \times 10^{-4} \, [32.2 \times 0.074 \times 119/(1.21 \times 10^{-5})^2 \,]^{1/3}$$

and note that

K < 3.3

Since Stokes' law applies

$$v_t = 32.2 \times (75 \times 3.281 \times 10^{-6})^2 \times 119/18 \times 1.21 \times 10^{-5}$$

or

$$V_t = 1.039 \text{ ft/sec}$$

If V is the volume of the settler

$$t_r = BLH/Q = BLH/100 = V/100$$

The maximum distance to settle, H, is given by

$$H = V \times v_t/100 = V \times 1.039/100$$

The minimum floor area is

$$V/H = BL = 100/1.032$$
$$= 96 \text{ ft}^2$$

Since the throughput velocity is set at 10 ft/sec, the cross-sectional area will be

$$A_c = BH = 100/10$$
$$= 10 \text{ ft}^2$$

Thus,

$$L/H = 96/10$$
$$= 9.6$$

The minimum height required for cleaning purposes is usually 3 ft. If we set H equal to this value, then

$$L = 28.9 \text{ ft}$$

and

$$B = 3.33 \text{ ft}$$

The total volume of the settler becomes

$$V = 3 \times 28.9 \times 3.33$$
$$= 289 \text{ ft}^3$$

(For the most economical design, L should be set equal to B so that L = B = 9.8 ft. Under these conditions the velocity is about 3.4 ft/sec.)

Example 3.6.13

A settling chamber, operating on a heating plant spreader stoker, has the following parameters:

ρ_p = 150 lb/ft³
N_C = 1 (simple chamber)
μ = 1.68 × 10⁻⁵ lb/ft-sec at 400°F, 1 atm
ρ = 0.0462 lb/ft³
Q = 120 ACFS
L = 20 ft
B = 10 ft
g = 32.2 ft/sec²
β = 0.025 μm^{-1} (slope of semilog particle distribution)

Determine the overall collection efficiency using an empirical factor of 0.6 to correlate theoretical with experimental efficiencies.

Solution
From Equation 3.5.11:

$$k = \frac{0.6\, g\, (\rho_p - \rho) L B N_C}{18\, \mu\, Q} = \frac{0.6(32.2)(150)(20)(10)}{18(1.68 \times 10^{-5})(120)}$$

$$= \left(\frac{1.597 \times 10^7}{\text{ft}^2}\right) \left(\frac{\text{ft}^2}{929 \times 10^{-4}\ \text{m}^2}\right) \left(\frac{\text{m}^2}{10^{12}\ \mu m^2}\right)$$

$$= 1.719 \times 10^{-4}\ \mu m^{-2}$$

and

$$\eta_T = \frac{2\,k}{\beta^2} (1 - e^{-\beta/(k)^{1/2}} [1 + \beta/(k)^{1/2}])$$

$$\eta_T = \frac{2(1.719 \times 10^{-4}\ \mu m^{-2})}{6.25 \times 10^{-4}\ \mu m^{-2}} (1 - e^{-0.025/1.31 \times 10^{-2}} [1 + 0.025/1.31 \times 10^{-2}])$$

$$\eta_T = 0.5501\, (1 - e^{-1.908} [1 + 1.908]) = 0.3131$$

$$\eta_T = 31.31\%$$

It is interesting to compare this calculated efficiency with the value obtained from a numerical integration technique. In the graph below, the cumulative distribution function, $Y(d_p)$, is plotted against the particle diameter. The weight fraction of particles falling between 10 and 20 μm, $\Delta Y(d_p)$, is 0.1723. The average size collection efficiency for this size interval corresponds to the average particle size, 15 μm. Thus,

$$\eta\,(15\ \mu\text{m}) = k(d_p)^2_{avg} = (1.719 \times 10^{-4}\ \mu\text{m}^{-2})\,(15\ \mu\text{m})^2$$
$$= 0.0387$$

or 3.87%

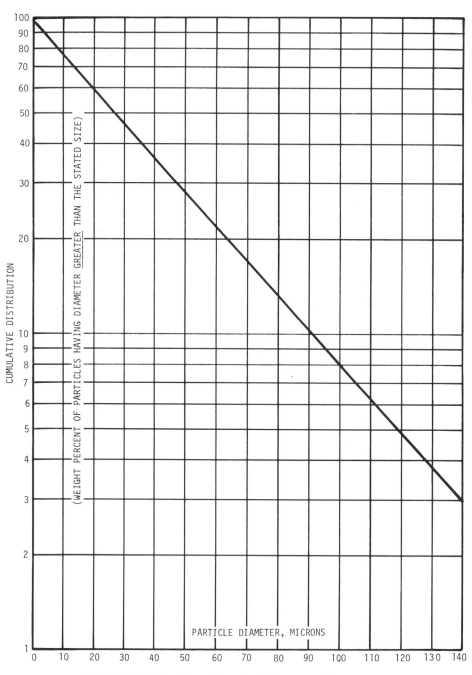

EXAMPLE 3.6.13.   Cumulative distribution vs. particle diameter.

The table below was determined in a similar fashion.

Average Overall Collection Efficiencies

Size range (μm)	$(d_p)_{avg}$ (μm)	$\Delta Y(d_p)$	$\eta(d_p)_{avg}$	$[\Delta Y(d_p)]\,[\eta(d_p)_{avg}]$
0–5	2.5	0.1175	0.00107	0.00013
5–10	7.5	0.1037	0.00967	0.00100
10–20	15.0	0.1723	0.0387	0.00667
20–30	25.0	0.1341	0.1074	0.01440
30–40	35.0	0.1045	0.2106	0.02201
40–50	45.0	0.0814	0.3481	0.02834
50–60	55.0	0.0634	0.5200	0.03297
60–70	65.0	0.0493	0.7263	0.03581
70–76	73.0	0.0242	0.9161	0.02217
>76	–	0.1496	1.0000	0.14960

$$\eta_T = 0.3131$$

Note that this is exactly equal to the value calculated previously.

Example 3.6.14

Consider the particle-size distribution and fractional efficiency curves presented below for a certain gravity settler. Determine the overall collection efficiency.

Solution

Mass median diameter, $d_{p\,50} = 68\ \mu$m

Geometric standard deviation, $\sigma_g = 108/68 = 1.588\ \mu$m

$$d'_{p\,50} = 47\ \mu\text{m}$$

$$\sigma'_g = 78/47 = 1.66\ \mu\text{m}$$

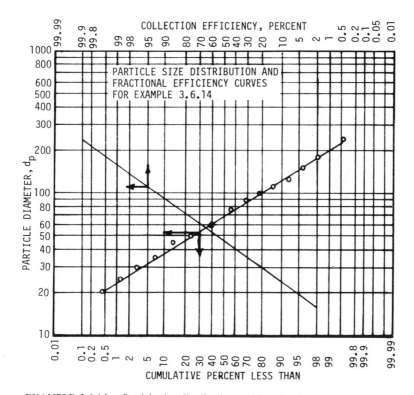

EXAMPLE 3.6.14.   Particle-size distribution and fractional efficiency curves for a certain gravity settler.

Then

$$\eta_T = \text{erf} \left[\frac{\ln{(68/47)}}{(\ln^2 1.588 + \ln^2 1.66)^{1/2}} \right] = \text{erf} \, (0.538)$$

From Table 3.5.1,

$$\eta_T = 70.4\%$$

PROBLEMS

1. In an intermediate step in the design of a gravity settler to treat air containing iron dust, the terminal velocity of iron spheres in the 1.0- to 500-μm range is required. The air may be assumed to be at $25°C$ and 1 atm, and the specific gravity of the iron dust is 7.85.

2. A sodium hydroxide spray in air at $30°C$ is to be collected in a gravity settler. The unit is 30 ft wide, 15 ft high, and 40 ft long. The volumetric flow rate of the gas is 42 ft^3/sec. Calculate the smallest mist droplet (spherical in shape) that will be entirely collected by the settler. The specific gravity of the mist droplets may be assumed to be equal to 1.21.

3. Calculate the smallest droplet in Example 3.6.6 if the flow rate is halved.

4. If the temperature in Example 3.6.6 is $25°C$, calculate the smallest droplet which can be collected if the gas is at $200°C$. Assume that at $200°C$, $\mu = 2.0 \times 10^{-4}$ g/cm-sec.

5. Calculate the smallest droplet in Example 3.6.6 if the length of the unit is halved.

6. A monodispersed aerosol 1.099 μm in diameter is passed through a gravity settler 20 cm wide $\times$ 50 cm long with 18 plates and channel thickness of 0.124 cm. The gas flow rate is 8.6 l/min, and it is observed that it operates at an efficiency of 64.9%. How many plates would be required to have the unit operate at 80% efficiency?

7. An aerosol consisting of particles 0.63 and 0.83 μm in diameter in equal mass amounts passes through a gravity settler at a flow rate of 3.60 l/min. Given the following data, use Stokes' law with the Cunningham correction factor to calculate the efficiency.

length = 50 cm	ρ_p = 1.05 g/cc
width = 20 cm	λ = 0.1 μm
height of channel = 0.124 cm	μ = 0.0182 cP
number of channels = 19	

8. Installation of a gravity settler to help remove limestone particles (specific gravity = 2.67) from an air stream at ambient conditions has been proposed. The inlet dust loading is 17 grains/ft^3, and the volumetric flow rate is 875 ft^3/min. The inlet size distribution of the limestone is given below.

Size range, μm	Mass %
0–5	2
5–20	6
20–50	17
50–100	28
100–500	36
500–	11

The dimensions of the unit are 25 ft wide $\times$ 6 ft high $\times$ 90 ft long. Calculate an average collection efficiency over each size range.

9. Using the data and results of the previous problem, estimate the overall collection efficiency of the unit.

10. Using the results of the two previous problems, calculate (a) the outlet dust loading, (b) the daily mass of dust collected, and (c) the daily mass of dust discharged from the unit.

11. As a recently hired engineer for an equipment vending company, you have been requested to design a gravity settler to remove all the iron particulates from a dust-laden gas stream. The following information is given:

d_p	=	35 μm; uniform, i.e., no distribution
gas	=	air at ambient conditions
Q	=	130 ft^3/sec
ρ_p	=	7.62 g/(cc)

Submit your design.

12. Consider the size efficiency curve below (Figure A) for a certain settling chamber handling a particle-laden gas stream. The particle-size distribution is given in Figure B. (below) Determine the overall collection efficiency.

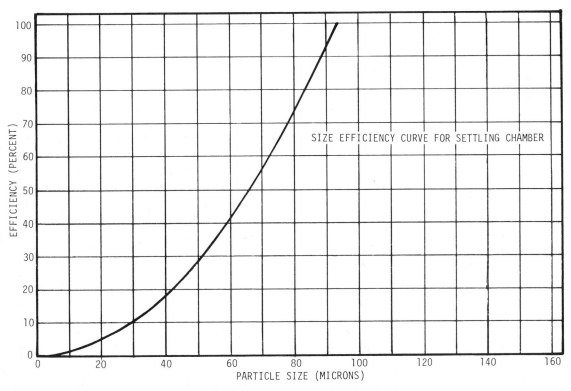

PROBLEM 12.A. Efficiency curve for settling chamber.

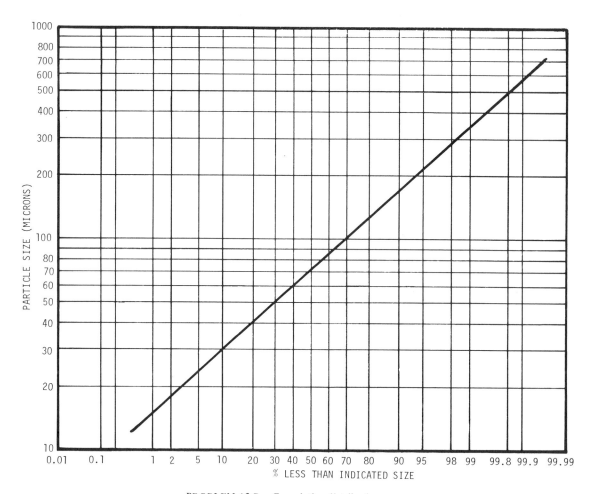

PROBLEM 12.B. Cumulative distribution curve.

REFERENCES

1. Jennings, R. F., *J. Iron Steel Inst.* (London), 164, 305, 1950.
2. Theodore, L. and Buonicore, A. J., A Study of Industrial Air Quality Control Methods for Particulates, Proc. 2nd Annu. Environmental Engineering and Science Conf., University of Louisville, April 20—21, 1972, 573.
3. Buonicore, A. J. and Theodore, L., Monte Carlo Simulation to Predict Collection Efficiencies of Centrifugal Separators, 74th Natl. AIChE Meet., Paper No. 60 d, New Orleans, March 11—15, 1973.
4. Tayyabkhan, M. T. and Richardson, T. C., Chem. Eng. Prog., 61(1), 78, 1965.
5. McCabe, W. L. and Smith, J. C., *Unit Operations of Chemical Engineering,* 2nd ed., McGraw-Hill, New York, 1967.
6. Theodore, L., *Transport Phenomena for Engineers,* International Textbook Company, Scranton, Pennsylvania, 1971.
7. Knudsen, J. and Katz, D., *Fluid Dynamics and Heat Transfer,* McGraw-Hill, New York, 1958.
8. Kay, J. M., *An Introduction to Fluid Mechanics and Heat Transfer,* Cambridge University Press, New York, 1957.
9. Theodore, L., McCarthy, D., and Palmer, A., Simulation of a Gravity Settler, Proc. 3rd Annu. Environmental Engineering and Science Conf., University of Louisville, March 5—6, 1973.
10. Balif, J., Greenburg, L., and Stein, A. C., *Am. Ind. Hyg. Assoc. Q.,* 9, 85, 1948.
11. Zenz, F. A. and Othmer, D. F., *Fluidization and Fluid-Particle Systems,* Reinhold, New York, 1960.
12. Vatavuk, W. M., A Technique for Calculating Overall Efficiencies of Particulate Control Devices, EPA-450/2-73-002, U.S. Environmental Protection Agency, August 1973.
13. Sundberg, R. E., The Prediction of Overall Collection Efficiency of Air Pollution Control Devices from Fractional Efficiency Curves, 66th Annu. Meet. of the Air Pollution Control Association, Paper No. 73-298, Chicago, June 24—28, 1973.

Chapter 4

CENTRIFUGAL SEPARATORS

4.1. INTRODUCTION

Centrifugal separators, commonly referred to as cyclones, are widely used in industry for the removal of solid and liquid (aerosol) matter (hereafter referred to as particles or particulates) from gas streams. Typical applications are found in mining and metallurgical operations, the cement and plastics industries, pulp and paper mill operations, chemical and pharmaceutical processes, petroleum production (cat-cracking cyclones), and combustion operations (fly ash collection).

Particles suspended in a moving gas stream possess inertia and momentum and are acted upon by gravity. Should the gas stream be forced to change direction, these "properties" can be utilized to promote centrifugal forces to act on the particles. In the conventional unit (see Figure 4.1.1) the entire mass of the gas stream with the entrained particles tangentially enters the unit and is forced into a constrained vortex in the cylindrical portion of the cyclone. Upon entering the unit, a particle develops an angular velocity. Due to its greater inertia, it tends to move outward across the gas stream lines in a tangential rather than a rotary direction; thus, it attains a net outward radial velocity. By virtue of its rotation with the carrier gas around the axis of the tube (main vortex) and its higher density with respect to the gas, the entrained particle is forced toward the wall of the unit. Eventually the particle may reach this outer wall where it is carried by gravity, and assisted by the downward movement of the outer vortex and/or secondary eddies, toward the dust outlet at the bottom of the unit. The flow vortex is reversed in the lower (conical) portion of the unit, leaving most of the entrained particles behind. The cleaned gas then passes up through the center of the unit (inner vortex) and out of the collector. The spiral motion of both vortices is in the same direction. The tangential velocity (how fast the gases are swirling) is lowest near the wall and at the center of the cyclone; it reaches a maximum at a point approximately 60 to 70% of the way from the wall to the center. In addition to the tangential velocity variation, there are also vertical eddies and what is called inward drift (see Figure 4.1.2). The inward drift is a radial gas flow which moves toward the center of the cyclone, opposing the movement of particles. While vertical eddies can exist in the cone, the most troublesome are those in the annular region near the gas inlet. The eddies, which are caused by the vortices, can carry particles directly from the gas inlet to the gas outlet with a consequent detrimental effect on collection efficiency. Radial eddies formed at the point where the cylinder joins the cone can also be particularly detrimental to collection efficiency. Eddy currents in the annular region require the gas outlet to extend into the cyclone in order to prevent excessive amounts of dust from passing directly from the inlet to the outlet. Usually, this extension ends just below the bottom of the inlet.

Cyclones may generally be classified into four categories (see Figure 4.1.3), depending on how the gas stream enters the unit and how the collected particles leave the unit.

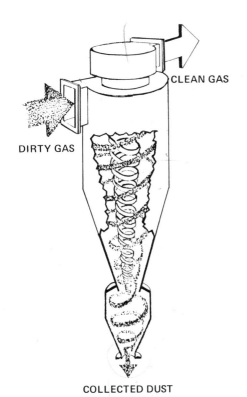

CLEAN GAS

DIRTY GAS

COLLECTED DUST

FIGURE 4.1.1. Conventional centrifugal separator (cyclone).

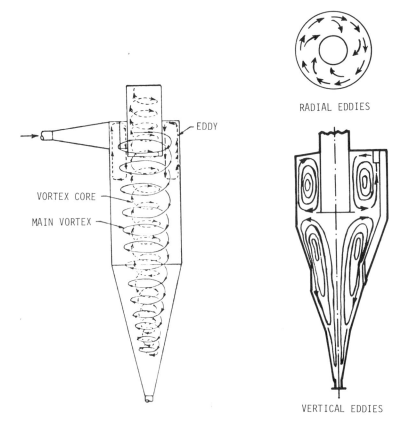

RADIAL EDDIES

VERTICAL EDDIES

FIGURE 4.1.2. Eddy patterns found in typical cyclones.

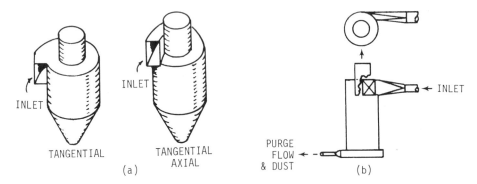

FIGURE 4.1.3. General cyclone categories. (a) Tangential inlet and axial dust discharge. (b) Tangential inlet and peripheral dust discharge. (c) Axial inlet and axial dust discharge. (d) Axial inlet and peripheral dust discharge.

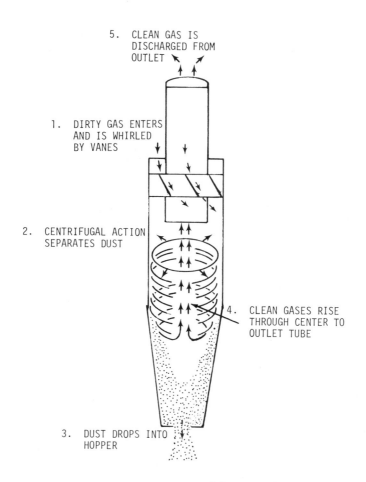

5. CLEAN GAS IS DISCHARGED FROM OUTLET

1. DIRTY GAS ENTERS AND IS WHIRLED BY VANES

2. CENTRIFUGAL ACTION SEPARATES DUST

4. CLEAN GASES RISE THROUGH CENTER TO OUTLET TUBE

3. DUST DROPS INTO HOPPER

FIGURE 4.1.3 (c)

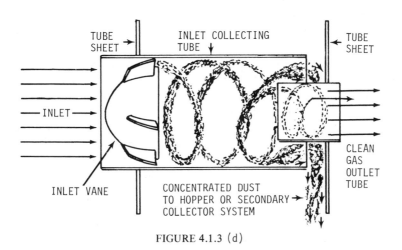

TUBE SHEET

INLET COLLECTING TUBE

TUBE SHEET

INLET

INLET VANE

CONCENTRATED DUST TO HOPPER OR SECONDARY COLLECTOR SYSTEM

CLEAN GAS OUTLET TUBE

FIGURE 4.1.3 (d)

1. Tangential inlet and axial dust discharge.
   a. Conventional (large diameter).
   b. High efficiency (small diameter, less than 10 in.).
2. Tangential inlet and peripheral dust discharge.
3. Axial inlet and axial dust discharge.
4. Axial inlet and peripheral dust discharge.

Types 1 and 3 are the most widely used. Large-diameter cyclones, with body diameters three to five times the diameter of the inlet duct, are useful where large gas handling capacity and moderate particle collection efficiency are required. The ratio of gas volume to capital investment dollar is greater than that for most cleaning devices. As can be deduced from the definition of "high-efficiency" cyclones, decreasing the body diameter will increase the efficiency. This is due to increased separation forces caused by the smaller vortex radius. Individual high-efficiency, small-diameter cyclones have a small capacity, and they must be operated in parallel to handle typical gas volumes. They generally have a common gas inlet, dust hopper, and gas outlet and can be arranged in banks of up to several hundred cyclones each. Typical performance of conventional and high-efficiency cyclones is shown in Table 4.1.1. Cyclone performance often experienced in various applications is shown in Table 4.1.2.

The cone portion of the cyclone is not necessary to convert the downward vortex to an upward one, although its presence does reduce the length of cyclone needed to effect this reversal. The primary purpose of the cone is to deliver the collected particles to a central point for easy handling and disposal. If the cone is too small in diameter at the bottom, the vortex core will contact the walls and reentrain the collected dust. Dust discharge is just as important in reducing this

reentrainment due to the high turbulence and velocities present near the discharge. The static pressure in the vortex core may be slightly negative and tend to draw collected dust up away from the discharge. Mechanical devices (such as rotary valves, double-flop valves, screw conveyers, and dip legs) have been quite successful in minimizing reentrained dust. To be successful, the mechanism must achieve continuous, complete, and immediate removal of the separated particles and prevent the inflow of gas (infiltration) from the hopper.

As the inlet gas stream enters the annular region at the top of the cyclone, it is squeezed by the existing gas to about half of its inlet width. This causes a significant pressure loss, which can be reduced by the addition of vanes to the annular area. The presence of the vanes, however, reduce the efficiency, apparently due to the prevention of vortex formation in the annulus. Helical and involute inlets (see Figure 4.1.4) are attempts to reduce interference between the incoming gas and the vortex already present in the annulus. Axial inlets are free from most of these problems. However, they introduce new problems; the inlet vanes must be designed so that they impart adequate rotation to the gas and yet resist erosion and plugging.

4.2. DESCRIPTION OF EQUIPMENT

There are many different types of dust collection equipment using centrifugal separation collect particles entrained in gas streams. Conventional cyclones (see Figure 4.1.1) can be designed to handle a wider range of chemical and physical conditions of operation than most other types dust collection equipment. Any conditions f which structural materials are available can be m by a cyclone, provided that the degree of collection falls within the operating range of the cyclone and the physical characteristics of the particula are such that no fouling of the cyclone excessive wall build-up will occur. Because of versatility and low cost, and the fact that there no moving parts, the single-cyclone separator probably the most widely used of the dry centrifugal separators. Although many design fact must be considered, the degree of collection efficiency is most dependent on the horsepower expended. Therefore, cyclones with high inlet velocities, small diameters, and long cylinders

TABLE 4.1.1

Cyclone Collection Efficiency

| Particle size (μm) | Efficiency (% by wt) | |
	Conventional cyclone (%)	High-efficiency cyclone (%)
<5	—	50–80
5–20	50–80	80–90
15–50	80–95	90–99
>40	95–99	95–99

TABLE 4.1.2

Cyclone Performance for Various Applications

Efficiency vs. particle size	% of particles below 10 μm in size	Efficiency range
Fly ash (power)		
Spreader stoker-fired boilers	20	90–95
PC-fired boilers	42	75–90
Cyclone-fired boilers	65	55–65
Nonmetallic minerals		
(when collector is part of process		
and collector catch is reusable)		
Cement (kilns and process)	40	70–85
Asphalt plant	10	80–95
Lightweight aggregate (kiln)	30–40	80–90
Refractory clays (kiln)	40–50	70–80
Lime (kiln)	40–50	75–80
Fertilizer plant (process equipment)	40	80–85
Steel (ore beneficiation)		
Pelletizing (vertical shaft and rotary kiln)	10–40	80–95
Foundry (general)	10–40	80–95
Chemical process (drying, calcining)	10–40	80–95
Incinerators (municipal)	20–40	65–75
Coal processing (thermal drying)	10	90–97
Petroleum (catalytic cracking process)	0.6	99+
General industrial application (in plant)	10–60	65–95

generally found to be the most efficient. However, there are limits to all of these parameters (and these will be discussed later in the chapter). Conventional cyclones of medium efficiency (80 to 95%) are capable of handling high throughput at pressure losses typically between 2.0 to 5.0 in. of water. Body diameters are fairly large (4 to 12 ft or larger). High-efficiency (95 to 99%) single-cyclone units are generally long and narrow and seldom have a body diameter larger than 3 ft in diameter. Pressure drop typically ranges from 2 to 6 in. of water.

Multiple-cyclone collectors, another high-efficiency system, consist of a number of small-diameter cyclones operating in parallel (see Figure 4.2.1) with a common gas inlet and outlet. The flow pattern differs from a conventional cyclone in that instead of bringing the gas in at the side to initiate the swirling action, the gas is brought in at the top of the collecting tube and swirling action is then imparted by a stationary vane positioned in the path of the incoming gas. The diameters of the collecting tubes usually range from 6 to 24 in.

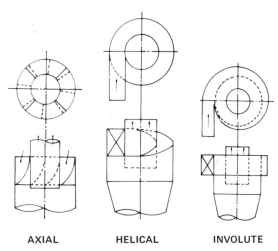

AXIAL   HELICAL   INVOLUTE

FIGURE 4.1.4.   Cyclone inlet configurations.

with pressure drops in the 2–6-in. range. Properly designed units can be constructed and operated with a collection efficiency as high as 90% for particulates in the 5-10-μm range. The most serious problems encountered with these systems involve plugging and flow equalization.

Another type of available collector is that in which centrifugal force is supplied by a rotating vane. The unit, shown in Figure 4.2.2, serves both as an exhaust fan and a dust collector. In operation the rotating fan blade exerts a large centrifugal force on the particles, ejecting them from the tip of the blades to a skimmer bypass leading into a dust hopper. Efficiencies of these systems are somewhat higher than those obtained with conventional cyclones. Mechanical centrifugal collectors are compact; however, they cannot generally be used to collect particles that cake or tend to accumulate on the rotor blades. This can cause clogging and, consequently, unbalancing of the impeller blades with resultant high maintenance costs and shutdowns. Frequently, this is

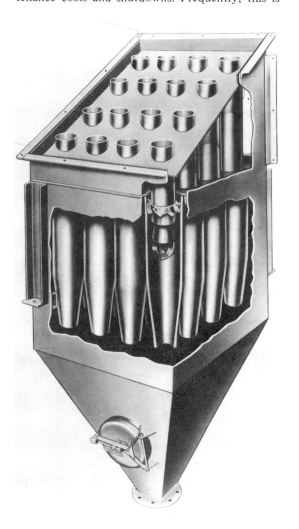

FIGURE 4.2.1. Multiclone centrifugal separation system. (Courtesy of Western Precipitation Division, Joy Manufacturing Company.)

overcome by the simple addition of a water spray at the collector inlet. Impeller blades are also susceptible to erosion.

A modification of the traditional cyclone collector is a cyclonic system which utilizes an air jet-induced particulate/gas separating force incorporated into each cyclone tube. The heart of the system is an air-jet nozzle assembly which imposes a vortex on the primary air flow (see Figure 4.2.3). This air-jet action separates the particulates from the gas stream, prevents solids build-up on tube surfaces, and virtually eliminates system plugging. Each cyclone tube consists of four components: (1) cyclone tube, (2) clean air outlet tube, (3) secondary air flow inlet, and (4) air-jet nozzle hub. Air-conveyed particulate matter enters the cyclone tube axially. Low-pressure secondary air from an independent blower enters the nozzle hub and creates a constant, controlled vortex. Like conventional cyclones, particles are acted upon by an outwardly directed centrifugal force and an inwardly directed drag force. Separated particles are carried downward and discharged. Cleaned air reverses direction in the lower part of the cyclone tube and travels back up through the clean air outlet. The system is capable of providing a significantly greater fine-particle collection efficiency at high, continuous throughputs. The total power requirement is 4 to 7 hp/1,000 SCFM of gas treated. Efficiencies as high as 95% have been reported for particles in the 2-μm size range.

There are many other systems capitalizing on centrifugal forces. Many of these systems utilize water to assist in the collection mechanism, and these are discussed in greater detail in Chapter 6. In cyclonic spray chambers, such as that illustrated in Figure 4.2.4, the dust-laden gas enters tangentially at the bottom and spirals up through a spray of high-velocity fine water droplets. The dust particles are collected on the fine spray droplets which are then hurled against the chamber wall by centrifugal action. Other units utilize water to wet and entrap the particles separated from the gas stream by centrifugal action.

4.3. LITERATURE REVIEW

Throughout the published literature dealing with cyclone design and theory, there has been little significant deviation from that proposed in 1932 by Rosin et al.[1] These investigators simply

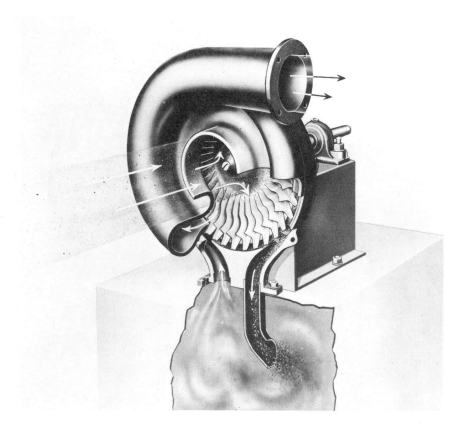

FIGURE 4.2.2.   Mechanical centrifugal collector. (Courtesy of American Air Filter.)

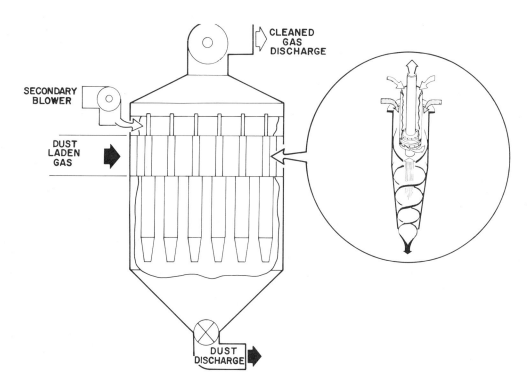

FIGURE 4.2.3.   Air-jet-induced cyclonic system. (Courtesy of the Donaldson Company, Inc.)

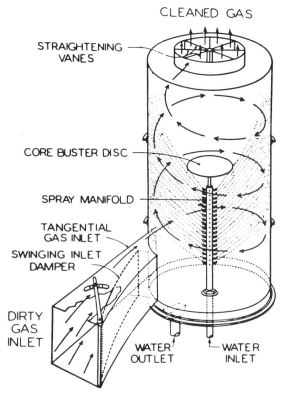

CLEANED GAS

STRAIGHTENING VANES

CORE BUSTER DISC

SPRAY MANIFOLD

TANGENTIAL GAS INLET

SWINGING INLET DAMPER

DIRTY GAS INLET

WATER OUTLET

WATER INLET

FIGURE 4.2.4. Pease-Anthony cyclonic spray scrubber. (Courtesy of Chemical Construction Corporation.)

considered collected particles to be those whose drag in the centrifugal field would permit their crossing the width of gas stream lines (taken as the width of the cyclone inlet port) within the time period of their residence in the cyclone. Though the theory resulted in reasonable agreement with the trends of the variables, it did not adequately account for dramatic changes in performance with variations in dimensions, such as the diameter of the gas outlet tube, or the decrease in collection efficiency with excessive inlet velocity. It might also be criticized for considering terminal velocity as the only pertinent drag force, when the particulate path is principally across a horizontal rather than a vertical plane.

Rosin et al.[1] derived the following equation for the minimum particle diameter, $d_{p,min}$, that should be completely separated from the gas stream in a cyclone.

$$d_{p,min} = [9\,\mu_G B_c / \pi\,N_t v_i\,(\rho_p - \rho_G)]^{1/2} \qquad (4.3.1)$$

where

$d_{p,min}$ = diameter of smallest particle theoretically completely collected, ft;
μ_G = viscosity of the gas, lb/ft sec;
B_c = width of cyclone inlet duct, ft;
N_t = number of turns made by gas stream in cyclone, dimensionless;
v_i = cyclone inlet velocity, ft/sec;
ρ_p = particle density, lb/ft^3;
ρ_G = gas density, lb/ft^3.

Smaller particles are removed to an extent proportional to the initial distance of the particles from the wall. The Rosin et al. derivation is based on Stokes' law, assuming that the gas stream undergoes a fixed number of turns at constant spiral velocity without any mixing action or turbulence.

Lapple extended this analysis to a method for the prediction of overall cyclone collection efficiency.[2] His simplified analysis assumed that the gas path within the cyclone is in the form of a rigid spiral, and the rotational velocity equals the average cyclone inlet velocity. In practice, however, the flow pattern is considerably more complex, leading to deviations from the efficiencies theoretically predicted.[3,4] Other studies have indicated that a "double eddy" at the inlet to the cyclone is superimposed on the double spiral and may, in some instances, affect particulate removal.[3,5,6]

Lapple's method for determining cyclone collection efficiency remained virtually unchallenged until recently when Theodore and Buonicore[7,8] introduced a new technique based on the utilization of a random number approach. They were able to incorporate the effect of particle-size distribution, gas velocity profile, particle-mass flow rate profile, and external force(s) variations on the particle collection efficiency.

At about the same time, Leith and Licht[9] introduced a new approach to predicting cyclone collection efficiency; they incorporated into their development the concept of a continual back-mixing of the uncollected particulates in the gas stream. Their model indicated that three mechanisms tend to cause this back-mixing.

1. As the gas below the exit duct moves radially inward to be drawn off, it will tend to drag particles with it.

2. Turbulence and eddies within the unit will aid in the back-mixing of particles.

3. Particles have been observed[10] to bounce from the wall of a cyclone back into the gas stream.

A somewhat novel approach, introduced by Kalen and Zenz,[11] superimposes an adaptation of saltation velocity phenomenon[12] on the relationship shown in Equation 4.3.1; this is more conventionally applicable to the calculation of fluid particle transport limitations in horizontal ducts. The saltation velocity phenomenon can briefly be defined as the minimum velocity required to maintain a particle in suspension when flowing in a given fluid medium through a given horizontal conduit geometry. If the fluid falls below the saltation velocity, particles will drop out (or salt out) of the flowing medium and settle on the floor of the pipe. Using a pipe coil analogy, Kalen and Zenz found that similarity existed between flow in cyclones and horizontal ducts and presented justification for applying the saltation velocity phenomenon theory to cyclones.

Although there have been several attempts to calculate the friction loss or pressure drop in cyclones from fundamental considerations,[13,14,22] none is very satisfactory. Since the simplifying assumptions have not allowed for entrance compression, wall friction, and exit concentration (all of which have a major effect),[15] the tendency is to rely on empirical relationships.[3,15]

4.4. FUNDAMENTALS

In the conventional unit (see Figure 4.4.1) the entire mass of the gas stream with the entrained particles is forced into a constrained vortex in the cylindrical portion of the cyclone. Upon entering the unit, a particle develops an angular velocity; due to its greater inertia, the particle tends to move outward across the gas stream lines in a tangential rather than a rotary direction, thus attaining a net outward radial velocity (v_r). By virtue of its rotation (v_ϕ) with the carrier gas around the axis of the tube and its higher density with respect to the gas, the entrained particle is forced toward the wall of the tube. Eventually the

particle may reach this outer wall where it is carried by gravity and/or secondary eddies toward the dust outlet at the bottom of the tube. The flow vortex is reversed in the lower (conical) portion of the tube, leaving most of the entrained particles behind. The cleaned gas then passes through the central exit tube (inner vortex) and out of the collector.

Since the particle follows a deterministic path, its trajectory can be predicted by studying the forces acting on it. The equations that follow are developed for a single particle entering the centrifugal separator. The position of a particle at any time, t, and its path inside the separator are best described using the cylindrical coordinate system shown in Figure 4.4.2. The development assumes:

1. No interactive effects arising due to the presence of other particles — the individual particles are sufficiently dispersed (although this assumption will be weak for heavy dust loadings).

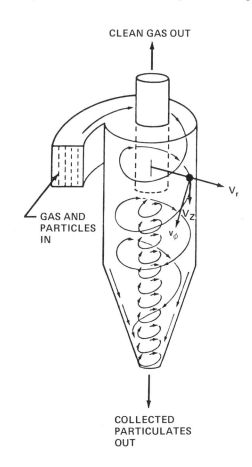

CLEAN GAS OUT

GAS AND PARTICLES IN

V_r

V_z

v_ϕ

COLLECTED PARTICULATES OUT

FIGURE 4.4.1. Conventional centrifugal separator with velocity vectors shown.

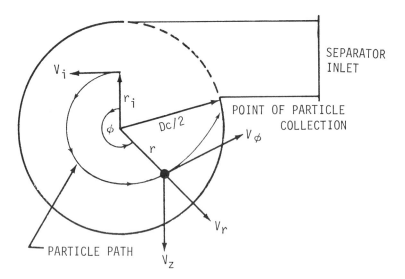

FIGURE 4.4.2. Cross-sectional view of centrifugal separator.

2. The particles do not change the velocity field of the gas.

3. The particles are spherical in shape or can be represented by an "equivalent" diameter.

4. Separation occurs when a particle reaches the outer wall of the separator, i.e., no particle reentrainment (although reentrainment can become a significant problem at high gas through-put velocities).

5. The influence of gas turbulence, Brownian forces, and wall effects on the particles can be neglected (although gas turbulence can seriously affect cyclone efficiency by interfering with particle collection forces).

A force balance on the particle in the three component directions (r, ϕ, z), assuming that Stokes' law is applicable, gives

$$m_p \, dv_r/dt = -6 \, \pi \, \mu_G r_p(v_{r_G} - V_r) \qquad (4.4.1)$$

in the radial direction,

$$m_p \, dv_\phi/dt = 6 \, \pi \, \mu_G r_p \, (v_{\phi_G} - v_\phi) \qquad (4.4.2)$$

in the tangential direction, and

$$m_p \, dv_z/dt = (\rho_G - \rho_p) \, V_p \, g + 6 \, \pi \, \mu_G r_p \, (v_{z_G} - v_z)$$

$$(4.4.3)$$

in the vertical direction, where

$$v_r = dr/dt \qquad (4.4.4)$$

$$v_\phi = r\omega = r \, d\phi/dt \qquad (4.4.5)$$

$$v_z = dz/dt \qquad (4.4.6)$$

and

$$m_p = (4/3)\pi \, \rho_p r_p{}^3 = V_p \rho_p \qquad (4.4.7)$$

The terms ω and v_{rG}, $v_{\phi G}$, and v_{zG} are the particle angular velocity and the velocity components of the gas in the spin region of the separator, respectively. Standard equations are available for predicting these velocity profiles for plug, laminar, or turbulent flow conditions.[3,16-19]

In accordance with Newton's second law, the product of the particle acceleration and mass gives the force on the particle. These forces will be opposed by the resistance of the gas to any relative movement of the particles. The component accelerations of the particle acceleration vector can be derived in cylindrical coordinates and are given by[8]

$$dv_r/dt = (d^2 r/dt^2) - r \, (d\phi/dt)^2 \, ; \, r \text{ component} \qquad (4.4.8)$$

$$dv_\phi/dt = r \, (d^2 \phi/dt^2) + 2 \, (dr/dt) \, (d\phi/dt); \, \phi \text{ component}$$

$$(4.4.9)$$

and for the vertical component

$$dv_z/dt = d^2 z/dt^2 \, ; \, z \text{ component} \qquad (4.4.10)$$

Substitution of the above relationships into Equations 4.4.1, 4.4.2, and 4.4.3 results in the following describing equations:

$$(d^2 r/dt^2) - r (d\phi/dt)^2 + \psi (dr/dt) = 0 \qquad (4.4.11)$$

in the radial direction,

$$r (d^2\phi/dt^2) + 2 (dr/dt)(d\phi/dt) - \psi (v_{\phi_G} - v_\phi) = 0$$

$$(4.4.12)$$

in the tangential direction, and

$$(d^2 z/dt^2) + (\rho_p - \rho_G)(V_p g/m_p) - \psi (v_{z_G} - v_z) = 0$$

$$(4.4.13)$$

in the vertical direction, where

$$\psi = 6\pi \mu_G r_p/m_p \qquad (4.4.14)$$

The simultaneous solution of Equations 4.4.11, 4.4.12, and 4.4.13 with the initial conditions that at t = 0: v_z = dz/dt = 0, z = z_i = 0; v_r = dr/dt = 0, r = r_i; v_ϕ = r_i (dϕ/dt) = v_i, ϕ = 0 will determine the trajectory of a single particle inside the centrifugal separator. The height, Z, necessary to collect this particle is calculated from the vertical distance the particle has traveled until the wall is reached, at which point r = $D_c/2$.

$$Z = \int_0^{t_c} v_z \, dt \qquad (4.4.15)$$

The preceding development assumes the applicability of Stokes' law for the drag force. For the higher Reynold's number ranges, refer to Chapter 2, Section 2.2. for the applicable drag force equation. Incorporating the generalized drag force equation (Equation 2.2.10) into the development will account for those particles outside Stokes' range.

For the smaller particles (less than 10 μm in diameter) it may be necessary to incorporate the Cunningham correction factor into the drag force equation (again, refer to Chapter 2). Whether or not this is performed will have little effect on the outcome since the correction factor only becomes significant for particles less than approximately 1 μm in diameter, and the cyclone is a very poor collector of particles in this size range.

By further assuming that the particle and gas tangential velocities are equal and that the effect of gravity on the vertical component can be ignored, Strauss[20] showed that Equations 4.4.11 through 4.4.13 can be used to determine the time required for a spherical particle to drift from r_i, the particle's initial position in the inlet, to r_o = $D_c/2$, the external radius of the cyclone. Strauss reduced Equations 4.4.11 and 4.4.12 to the following dimensionless form:

$$\frac{d^2\alpha}{d\beta^2} + \delta \frac{d\alpha}{d\beta} - \frac{1}{\alpha^3} = 0 \qquad (4.4.16)$$

where

$$\alpha = r/r_o;$$
$$\beta = tv_{\phi,o}/r_o;$$
$$\delta = 18 \mu_G r_o/d_p^2 \rho_p v_{\phi,o}.$$

Equation 4.4.16 is a nonlinear differential equation which cannot be solved directly. However, if the second-order differential is arbitrarily neglected (which is equivalent to saying that the particle moves radially outward with a constant velocity), Equation 4.4.16 can be solved for the time, t, required for a particle to drift from r_i to r_o.

$$t = 4.5 (\mu_G/\rho_p)(r_o/v_{\phi,o} d_p)^2 (1 - (r_i/r_o)^4) \qquad (4.4.17)$$

The cyclone height necessary to collect this particle is then determined from the product of the vertical velocity, v_z, and the time, t, as calculated in Equation 4.4.17.

The tangential velocity component, v_ϕ, is related to the radial position by the free vortex formula

$$v_\phi r^n = \text{constant} \qquad (4.4.18)$$

For a free vortex in an ideal (perfectly frictionless) fluid, the law of conservation of angular momentum requires that the exponent n be equal to unity. This has been assumed in the development by Strauss. Experimental observations, however, indicate that n may range between 0.5 and 0.9 in a cyclone. Alexander[21] determined that n varied with the size of the cyclone and the temperature. He provided the following empirical equations:

$$n = (12 D_c)^{0.14}/2.5 \qquad (4.4.19)$$

$$(1 - n_1)/(1 - n_2) = (T_1/T_2)^{0.3} \qquad (4.4.20)$$

A more general form of Equation 4.4.17, which takes into consideration values for n other than unity, is given below.

$$t = (9/(n + 1))(\mu_G/\rho_p)(r_o/v_{\phi,o} d_p)^2 \quad (1 - (r_i/r_o)^{2n+2})$$

$$(4.4.21)$$

Equation 4.4.21 reduces to 4.4.17 if n is taken to be unity. In certain cases, it is satisfactory to take $v_{\phi,o}$ as equal to the average velocity of the gas in the inlet duct. Then,

$$v_{\phi,o} = Q/H_c B_c \qquad (4.4.22)$$

Strictly speaking, the tangential velocity of the vortex at the cyclone wall boundary must be zero. However, the boundary layer, a region in which the captured particles slide down the cyclone wall toward the duct outlet, should be very thin. Hence, little error would be introduced by setting $r = r_o$ when $v_\phi = v_{\phi,o}$ as defined above.

Three of the more popular theoretical approaches to the prediction of cyclone collection efficiency are now discussed.

Theodore and Buonicore Model[8]

The model of Theodore and Buonicore incorporates a random number statistical technique into the simultaneous solution of Equations 4.4.11 through 4.4.13. To adequately model the system, information on the particle-size distribution as a function of inlet position, the gas velocity profile, and the particle-mass flow rate gradient must be known. The effect of these parameters is incorporated into the describing particle trajectory equations. This is accomplished by using random numbers (Monte Carlo method) to cope with these important system variables. The method calls for the continuous generation of random numbers to assign magnitudes to these variables. For example, random numbers can be used to assign the particle being studied both a location at the inlet cross section and a size from the corresponding particle-size distribution. These variable magnitudes can then be utilized in the describing particle trajectory equations to determine whether or not the particle is captured in the collector. One possible use of this technique (discussed below) is in evaluating the overall collection efficiency to be expected in a cyclone of specified dimensions.

To obtain the overall collection efficiency, each particle entering the unit should ordinarily be tested. Over a short time interval, this could very well amount to several million particles. In the Theodore and Buonicore model a set of particles is statistically chosen to represent the full spectrum of possible system conditions, and the describing trajectory equations are solved for each particle in this representative set. Obviously, the larger the representative set, the more accurate the solution. Once this representative set is chosen, each particle can be tested. However, prior to any trajectory calculation, the size (or mass) and entrance location of the particle must also be known. These two variables are specified via the application of the Monte Carlo method as follows.

At the separator inlet there exists a particle-size distribution (PSD), a gas velocity profile, and a particle-mass flow rate gradient (PMFRG). Standard velocity profile equations 3,[16-19] are already available for plug, laminar, or turbulent flow conditions. Hence, we are concerned here with the PSD and PMFRG. In order to apply the Monte Carlo technique to this system:

1. The separator inlet cross section is divided into any suitable grid consisting of j sections. Typical examples are shown in Figure 4.4.3.

2. The PSD curve and PMFR in each section are then obtained experimentally (an example is illustrated in Figures 4.4.3.c and 4.4.4).

3. Each PSD curve is then arbitrarily divided into ranges (Figure 4.4.4, for example, shows five ranges) where each range consists of an equal percentage of the total mass of sample collected in the corresponding j-th section.

4. Next, the number of particles to be tested in each inlet section is determined. It is suggested that the number of particles tested in each of the inlet sections be given by the product of an integer constant determined statistically, the mass (flow rate) into the section, and the total number of ranges in the PSD curve corresponding to that section.

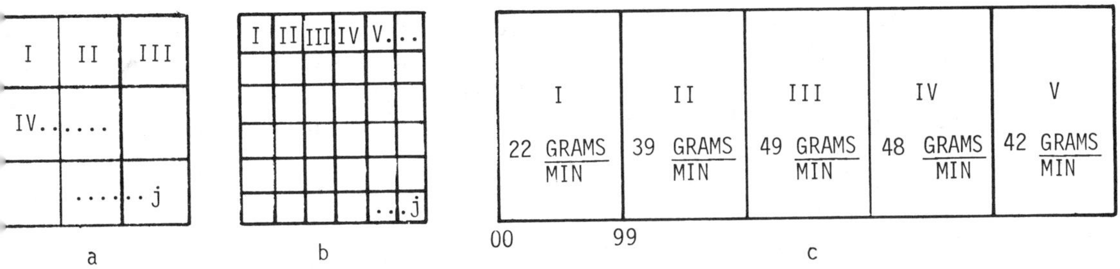

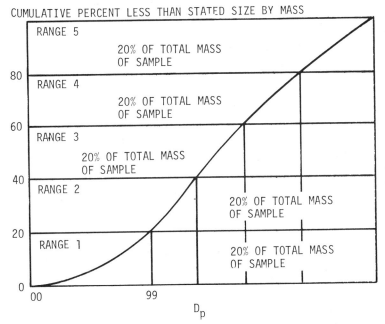

FIGURE 4.4.3. Centrifugal separator inlets divided into typical grids each consisting of j sections. In the last grid (where j = 5), possible particle-mass flow rate data are indicated.

The figure 4.4.3 contains three grids labeled a, b, c. Grid c shows five sections:

I	II	III	IV	V
22 $\frac{GRAMS}{MIN}$	39 $\frac{GRAMS}{MIN}$	49 $\frac{GRAMS}{MIN}$	48 $\frac{GRAMS}{MIN}$	42 $\frac{GRAMS}{MIN}$

CUMULATIVE PERCENT LESS THAN STATED SIZE BY MASS

RANGE 5 — 20% OF TOTAL MASS OF SAMPLE
RANGE 4 — 20% OF TOTAL MASS OF SAMPLE
RANGE 3 — 20% OF TOTAL MASS OF SAMPLE
RANGE 2 — 20% OF TOTAL MASS OF SAMPLE
RANGE 1 — 20% OF TOTAL MASS OF SAMPLE

D_p

FIGURE 4.4.4. Characteristic particle-size distribution curve for any of the separator inlet sections.

5. The number of particles to be tested in the j-th inlet section is then divided by the number of ranges in the corresponding PSD curve. An equal number of particles will then be tested in each size range. In this way a size range has been assigned to each of the particles to be tested in the j-th section.

As an example, suppose that the separator inlet cross section is divided into the type of grid shown in Figure 4.4.3.c with the mass flow rates in each section as shown. Next, the PSD curves corresponding to each inlet section are arbitrarily divided into five ranges (as shown in Figure 4.4.4). Then, assuming an integer constant of one, 110 particles will be tested in Section I, 195 in Section II, 245 in Section III, and so on. Of the 110 particles to be tested in Section I, 22 will be located in each size range of the corresponding PSD curve. Of the 195 particles to be tested in Section II, 39 will be located in each size range of its corresponding PSD curve and so on for the other sections. A random number is then generated to locate the first of the 110 particles to be tested in Section I. The magnitude of the random number is used to specify the particle's inlet position by employing any suitable interpolative technique. For example, if, as in Figure 4.4.3.c, the limits of Section I are set at 00 and 99, and the random number generated is 50, then the inlet location of the particle would be in the center of Section I. After the particle is positioned, it must be assigned a size. Another random number is generated and applied in a manner similar to that used in locating the particle. Its magnitude will determine the particle size in Range 1 of the PSD curve corresponding to inlet Section I. Having positioned the particle and specified its size, the trajectory equations are used to determine its path in the cyclone. Any suitable numerical technique can be used to simultaneously solve the differential equations. When the particle reaches the outer wall ($r_o = D_c/2$), its corresponding height (Z) at that time is compared to the total height of the unit (H). If Z < H, then the particle is considered captured. A running tally of the particles tested and captured is maintained. The collection efficiency for the particles tested in each section j is given by

$$\eta_j = (P_j/N_j)(100) \tag{4.4.23}$$

The sectional efficiency is then extended to include the effects on the overall collection efficiency of all the particles entering the unit in each of the remaining inlet sections. The overall collection efficiency is calculated as the weighted average efficiency of the sections,

$$\eta_T = \sum_{j=1}^{j} \eta_j x_j \tag{4.4.24}$$

A simplified flow chart of the calculation procedure is presented in Figure 4.4.5.

The above approach can easily be modified to enable design of a cyclone which will obtain a specified efficiency on particles with a given size distribution. The technique's inherent flexibility permits one to be as meticulous as necessary in accounting for data variables. The main disadvantage is the computer time required. Experimental verification is currently in progress.[30]

Leith and Licht Model[9]

Leith and Licht postulated that the drag force, turbulent mixing, and particle bouncing or reentrainment are sufficiently prevalent to insure that a uniform concentration of uncollected dust is maintained in the gas flowing through any horizontal cross section of a cyclone, i.e., back-mixing is complete. Consider a horizontal cross section of a cyclone, as shown in Figure 4.4.6. In time dt, all particles a distance dr or less from the

cyclone wall will move to the wall and be collected. Meanwhile, the particles will travel a distance $rd\phi$ tangentially and dz vertically. The number of particles removed, dn', will be

$$-dn' = \frac{d\phi}{2}[r_o^2 - (r_o - dr)^2]\,cdz \tag{4.4.25}$$

where

c = the number concentration of particles.

The total number of particles in the sector from which particles are removed is

$$n' = \frac{d\phi}{2}r_o^2\,cdz \tag{4.4.26}$$

The fraction of particles removed in time dt is, therefore,

$$-\frac{dn'}{n'} = \frac{2r_o\,dr - (dr)^2}{r_o^2} \approx \frac{2\,dr}{r_o} \tag{4.4.27}$$

neglecting the second-order differential.

In order to relate the fraction of particles collected to the average residence time, it is necessary to express Equation 4.4.27 in terms of time. This may be accomplished in view of the following equation which shows the relationship between time and the radial position of a single particle in a vortex.

$$t = \frac{9}{(n+1.0)}\left(\frac{\mu_G}{\rho_p}\right)\left(\frac{r_o}{v_{\phi,o}\,d_p}\right)^2$$
$$\left(\left(\frac{r}{r_o}\right)^{2n+2} - \left(\frac{r_i}{r_o}\right)^{2n+2}\right) \tag{4.4.28}$$

Note that Equation 4.4.28 reduces to Equation 4.4.21 when $r = r_o$. A system of uncollected particles, evenly distributed across the cross section of such a vortex, will have its center of mass at the vortex center. If the system of uncollected particles is instantaneously, continuously, and completely redistributed by back-mixing, as postulated by Leith and Licht, the center of mass of the uncollected particle system will always remain at the vortex center, even though the total number of uncollected particles decreases with increasing gas residence time.

The rate at which the uncollected particle system moves toward the vortex wall as a function

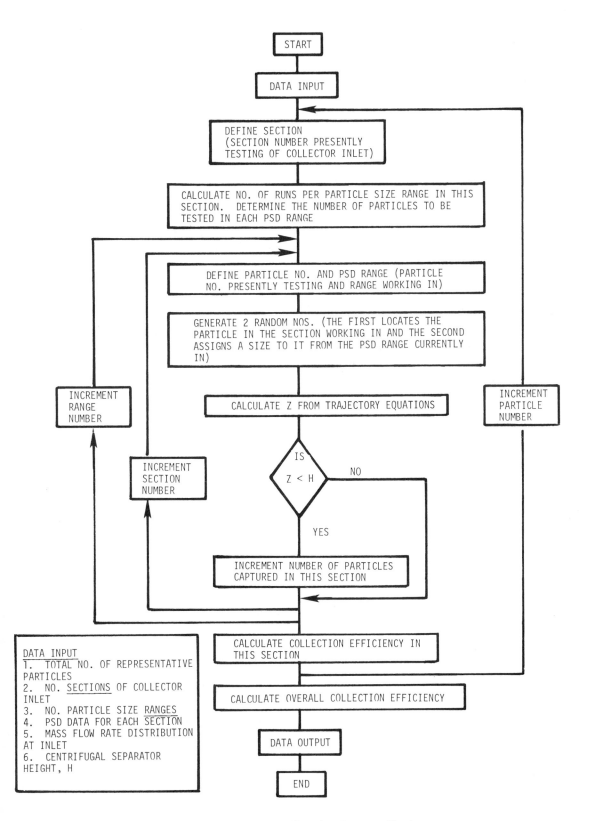

FIGURE 4.4.5. Simplified computer flow chart for a centrifugal separator.

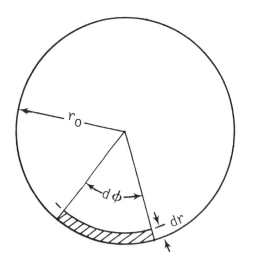

FIGURE 4.4.6. Cross section of cyclone.

of the time the system has spent within the vortex may then be obtained by stating that the radial position of the uncollected particle system is at the vortex center, $r_i = 0$, at zero time. This is obtained by differentiating Equation 4.4.28.

$$\frac{dr}{dt} = \frac{\rho_p}{18\,\mu_G} \left(\frac{d_p\,v_{\phi,o}}{r_o}\right)^2$$

$$r_o \left[\frac{\rho_p(n+1.0)}{9\,\mu_G}\left(\frac{d_p\,v_{\phi,o}}{r_o}\right)^2 t\right]^{-\frac{2n+1.0}{2n+2}} \qquad (4.4.29)$$

Combining Equations 4.4.27 and 4.4.29:

$$\int_{n_0}^{n'} \frac{dn'}{n'} = -\int_0^t \frac{\rho_p}{9\,\mu_G}\left(\frac{d_p\,v_{\phi,o}}{r_o}\right)^2$$

$$\left[\frac{\rho_p(n+1.0)}{9\,\mu_G}\left(\frac{d_p\,v_{\phi,o}}{r_o}\right)^2 t\right]^{-\frac{2n+1.0}{2n+2}} \qquad (4.4.30)$$

Integrating up to the average total residence time of a particle in a cyclone, t_{res}, as given by

$$t_{res} = \frac{1.0}{Q}\,[V_s + (V_{nl}/2)] = K_c D_c^{\,3}/Q \qquad (4.4.31)$$

where

$$V_s = \pi\,[S - (H_c/2)]\,(D_c^{\,2} - D_e^{\,2})/4$$

$$V_{nl} = \frac{\pi\,D_c^{\,2}}{4}\,(L_c - S) +$$

$$\frac{\pi}{4}\,\frac{(l + S - L_c)\,D_c^{\,2}}{3}\left[1.0 + \frac{k}{D_c} + \left(\frac{k}{D_c}\right)^2\right]$$

$$-\frac{\pi}{4}\,(D_e^{\,2}l); \text{ if } 1 < (H - S)$$

or

$$V_{nl} = \frac{\pi\,D_c^{\,2}}{4}\,(L_c - S) +$$

$$\frac{\pi}{4}\,\frac{(H - L_c)\,D_c^{\,2}}{3}\left[1.0 + \frac{J_c}{D_c} + \left(\frac{J_c}{D_c}\right)^2\right]$$

$$-\frac{\pi}{4}\,(H - S)\,D_e^{\,2}; \text{ if } 1 > (H - S)$$

$$k = D_c - (D_c - J_c)\left[\frac{S + 1 - L_c}{H - L_c}\right]$$

$$1 = 2.3\,D_e\,(D_c^{\,2}/H_c B_c)^{1/3}$$

$$K_c = [V_s + (V_{nl}/2)]/D_c^{\,3}$$

yields:

$$\eta = \frac{n'_o - n'}{n'_o} =$$

$$1.0 - \exp\left[-2\,\frac{\rho_p}{9\,\mu_G}\left(\frac{d_p\,v_{\phi,o}}{r_o}\right)^2 (n+1.0)\,\frac{K_c D_c^{\,3}}{Q}\right]^{\frac{1}{2.0n + 2.0}}$$

$$(4.4.32)$$

By defining the following dimensionless parameters

$$\psi = \frac{\rho_p\,d_p^{\,2}\,v_{\phi,o}}{18\,\mu_G\,D_c}\,(n+1.0) \qquad (4.4.33)$$

$$C = 8\,K_c/K_a\,K_b \qquad (4.4.34)$$

where

$$K_a = H_c/D_c$$

$$K_b = B_c/D_c$$

Equation 4.4.32 then becomes

$$\eta = 1.0 - \exp[-2\,C\psi]^{1.0/(2n+2)} \qquad (4.4.35)$$

which is the theoretical equation for collection efficiency based on the back-mixing postulate. Equation 4.4.35, with Equations 4.4.33 and 4.4.34, can then be used to determine a fractional efficiency curve for a cyclone of specified geometry.

Kalen and Zenz Model[11]

Kalen and Zenz were unable to explain satisfactorily the increase in cyclone efficiency with the reduction in outlet (exit) tube area or the decrease in collection efficiency with excessive inlet velocity. They postulated that the enormous acceleration field existing in most industrial cyclones makes it apparent that the orientation of the barrel (cyclone body) may not be overwhelmingly significant, suggesting that the spiraling gas-solids inlet stream can be conceived as a coiled pipe.

Upon entering a cyclone, the largest and/or heaviest particles which reach the barrel wall form a relatively dense and narrow stream which travels down through the barrel and cone in a continuous spiral path. This can easily be demonstrated in a transparent plastic model. The entering gases also initially describe a spiral path within the barrel; however, they eventually follow aerodynamic pressure gradients and travel inward to be exhausted through the upper gas outlet tube, while the stream of collected solids flows out through the hole in the bottom of the cone. This spiraling pattern may be considered analogous to the flow of gas and solids through a coiled pipe with a narrow slit along its inner length to permit gradual dissipation of the gas, as illustrated in Figure 4.4.7.

These authors postulated that, in view of the magnitude of the centrifugal force relative to normal gravitational attraction, the vertical orientation of the model coil (in terms of the particle dynamics) is of almost minor consequence. The effect of the centrifugal force on the particles is equivalent to considering the particles as being heavier, or of a density equal to their normal weight per unit volume multiplied by the number of g's. The pipe coil of Figure 4.4.7 may thus be unrolled and considered as a length of horizontal pipe conveying effectively g-weighted particles, as pictured in Figure 4.4.8.

Cyclone efficiency would presumably be at its maximum when the annular velocity is so low that it cannot carry any particles, i.e., when it is below the minimum saltation velocity. This minimum velocity and hence annular width, or consequent O/I ratio [which represents the relative outlet tube area (of cleaned gas exit) to inlet duct area], can theoretically be calculated for any particle-gas cyclone system from existing correlations of saltation velocity data obtained in conventional horizontal conveying.[12]

The assumptions used in their development are as follows.

1. The solids inlet velocity equals the gas inlet velocity.

2. The width of gas inlet (at the cyclone mouth) is one fourth of the cyclone diameter, i.e., $B_c = D_c/4$.

3. The width of the gas inlet is the effective pipe diameter for calculating saltation velocity.

4. The solids loading is so low that it has a negligible effect on saltation velocity.

5. The acceleration field, expressed as the number of g's (where 1 g = 32.2 ft/sec^2) is based

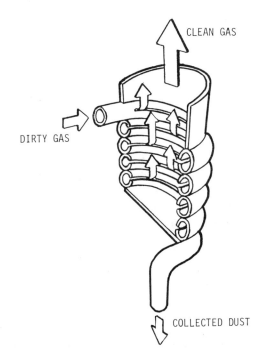

FIGURE 4.4.7. Schematic sketch of pipe coil model.

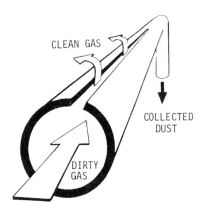

FIGURE 4.4.8. Schematic sketch of unrolled pipe coil model.

on the solids inlet velocity and the cyclone radius from its axis to the midpoint of the inlet width, i.e., radius = $[(D_c/2) - (B_c/2)]$ or $(3 D_c/8)$.

6. The pipe diameter effect on saltation velocity is proportional to the 0.4 power of pipe diameter.

For cyclone diameters of 12 to 36 in., for example, and inlet velocities of 50 to 100 ft/sec, the above assumptions permit calculating the maximum barrel spiraling velocities which can be tolerated while still allowing feed particles to salt out. If these maximum allowable velocities are less than the inlet velocities, then the outlet tube must be decreased in diameter in order to open up the annular area in the barrel and bring the velocities down to the calculated maximum, or if the required reduction in velocity is excessive, then the barrel diameter should be increased. (If the velocity needs to be halved, then the outlet tube diameter would theoretically be squeezed to zero under cyclone dimensional ratios conforming with the second assumption listed above.)

For 161-lb/ft^3 particles in atmospheric air, the denominator of the ordinate of the saltation correlation[12] for 1¼-in. pipe is found to be 2.44 ft/sec at 1-g. The ordinate goes through a minimum at a value of 2.1; therefore, in view of assumption 5, no reentrainment of any size of particles would occur in a 1-g field when $(v_{so}/2.44) = 2.1$. From assumptions 3 and 6, therefore,

$$\frac{v_{so}}{\Phi \ (\text{No. of g's})^{1/3}} = \left(\frac{B_c}{1.25}\right)^{0.4} \quad (2.1) \qquad (4.4.36)$$

where

$B_c =$ the width of the gas inlet duct in inches.

From conditions 1 and 5:

$$\text{No. of g's} = \frac{12 \ v_i^2}{32.2 \ r'} = \frac{12 \ v_i^2 \ (8)}{32.2 \ D_c \ (3)} \approx \frac{v_i^2}{D_c}$$

where

$D_c =$ the cyclone diameter in inches.

Therefore:

$$v_s = \frac{4.7 \ B_c^{0.4} \ v_i^{2/3}}{D_c^{1/3}}$$

or

$$\frac{v_i}{v_s} = \frac{v_i^{1/3} \ D_c^{1/3}}{4.7 \ B_c^{0.4}} = \frac{v_i^{1/3}}{2.7 \ D_c^{0.067}} \qquad (4.4.37)$$

and

$$O/I = \frac{\pi}{4} \left[D_c - \frac{2 \ v_i}{v_s} \left(\frac{D_c}{4}\right) \right]^2 \bigg/ \frac{\pi}{4} \left(\frac{D_c}{2}\right)^2$$

$$= \frac{4}{D_c^2} \left[D_c - \frac{v_i}{v_s} \left(\frac{D_c}{2}\right) \right]^2 \qquad (4.4.38)$$

Equations 4.4.37 and 4.4.38 can be represented graphically, as shown in Figure 4.4.9.

Several rather significant conclusions can be drawn from Figure 4.4.9.[11]

1. The O/I effect becomes more necessary or beneficial with increasing inlet velocity. For the particle-gas conditions chosen in the sample calculations, it appears that outlet tube modification would be beneficial above 32 to 40 ft/sec inlet velocity. In other words, as inlet velocity is increased above these values, collection efficiency becomes less than that normally expected unless the outlet tube diameter is reduced (from the conventional outlet tube diameter).

2. The O/I effect is not strongly dependent on cyclone diameter, particularly as the diameter begins to exceed 3 ft.

3. The benefits of the O/I effect depend on particle diameter. Large particles or high-density particles with a high saltation velocity reflect little gain due to outlet tube modification.

4. At velocities 2 to 2.5 times the saltation rates, particles can be picked up from a deposited layer. For the conditions chosen in Figure 4.4.9, it is expected that, at inlet velocities above 80 to 100 ft/sec, the 36-in. cyclone, for example, begins to show a decline in overall collection efficiency.

Equation 4.3.1 defines the minimum particle size traveling across the full width of the gas stream (the full diameter of the pipe making up the coil in Figure 4.4.8) which can be completely

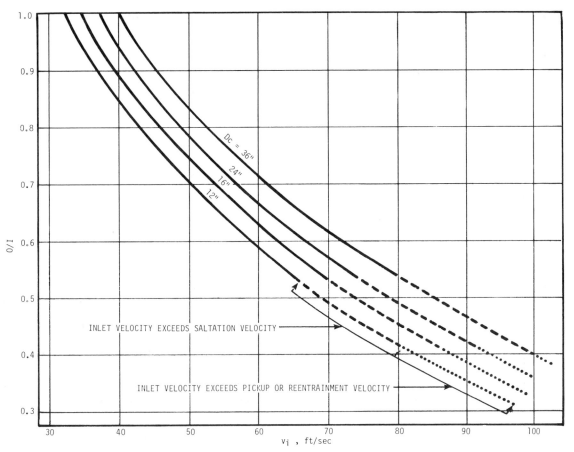

FIGURE 4.4.9. Typical theoretically predicted relationships between inlet velocity and saltation-pickup rates as a function of cyclone diameter and O/I ratio.[11]

collected (i.e., reaches the wall of the cyclone barrel). The smaller $d_{p,min}$, the better the cyclone performance or efficiency. Since some particles will enter the cyclone nearer the wall and must cross a width of gas stream less than B_c, it can be anticipated that a fraction of the feed particles even smaller than the size given by Equation 4.3.1 would also be separated.

According to Equation 4.3.1, the narrower the inlet width (B_c), the better the performance; however, for a fixed barrel height and barrel diameter, it is obvious that if B_c is decreased and H_c is compensatingly increased to maintain the same inlet velocity, then the effective height in which spiraling can take place is reduced; hence, performance in the extreme can be poorer (since N_t is reduced). Only cyclones of a given ratio of H_c:B_c:L_c:Z_c:D_c might be expected to exhibit a fixed characteristic curve of N_t vs. velocity. Also, according to Equation 4.3.1, performance should always improve with increase in inlet velocity. Comparison with operating experience indicates

that this is not entirely true. At sufficiently high inlet velocities there is a general decline in the rate of increase in efficiency; eventually, there is an actual decrease in efficiency with still further increase in velocity.

Kalen and Zenz have proposed that the decline in the rate of increase in efficiency with increasing inlet velocity is attributable to saltation phenomena. If the spiraling gas velocity begins to exceed a particle's saltation velocity, then it becomes more difficult, if not impossible, for the particle to ever reach the barrel wall. This is the basis of Figure 4.4.9.

An experimental investigation was conducted by Kalen and Zenz to verify the proposed model. If, by trial and error, the application of Equations 4.4.37, 4.4.38, and 4.3.1 permitted the satisfying of conditions 1 to 3 with a reasonable matching of calculated against experimental results, this should lend credence to the proposed model. Figure 4.4.10 illustrates the comparison between their experimental data and the results of an empirical

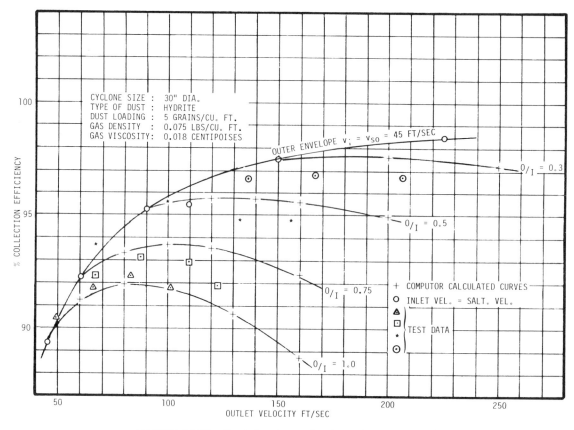

FIGURE 4.4.10.   Typical cyclone collection efficiency results.[11]

correlation program taking into account all conceivable variables. The solid curves represent the calculated results of the computerized correlations carried beyond the theoretical basis to take into account solids loading effects as well as reentraining gas velocities exceeding saltation. The effect of both of these operational variables could be correlated by appropriate adjustment of the effective theoretical or cut point particle diameter defined by Equation 4.3.1. The effect of inlet loading on collection efficiency is related to the cut point diameter by the correction factor λ:

$$d'_{p, min} = [9 \mu_G B_c / \lambda \pi N_t v_i (\rho_p - \rho_G)]^{1/2} \qquad (4.4.39)$$

where

$$\lambda = \left[\frac{89 (1 - \epsilon)^2}{Re (\epsilon)^3} + \frac{0.075 (1 - \epsilon)}{3,300 (\epsilon)^3} \right]^{0.075} \qquad (4.4.40)$$

$$Re = d_{p, min} v_p \rho_G / \mu_G \qquad (4.4.41)$$

and

$$\epsilon = 1 - (e/7,000 \rho_p) \qquad (4.4.42)$$

where

e = the particle entrainment rate in lb/ft^3.

The diameter in Equation 4.4.41 is that calculated from Equation 4.3.1; the particle velocity, v_p, in Equation 4.4.41 is that given by

$$v_p = g [d^2_{p, min} (\rho_p - \rho_G)/18 \mu_G] \qquad (4.4.43)$$

In the theoretical derivation of Equation 4.3.1, the factors N_t and v_i were simply taken as an indeterminate and uncorrelated number of spirals times the inlet velocity. The trail-and-error correlation study, which resulted in the empirically corrected Equation 4.4.39, showed that a single characteristic N_t correlation and an apparently single normalized fractional efficiency curve were obtained if v_i was taken as the highest of either inlet or outlet velocity and if N_t was similarly correlated with either prevailing maximum velocity. This simply reflects the intuitive realization that a high outlet velocity must induce a high inner vortex velocity, with the interfacial gradient dragging on the outer particle-gas spiral at the barrel wall partially increasing this outer spiraling velocity. This results in a greater number of turns penetrating deeper into the cyclone cone.

The effect on overall collection efficiency as inlet velocity exceeds saltation velocity was again empirically related to an effective cut point particle diameter, as represented in Equation 4.4.44 where the d_p and Δ terms are expressed in microns.[11]

$$d''_{p,min} = d'_{p,min} + \frac{0.012 (v_i - v_{so}) \Delta}{\Phi} \quad (4.4.44)$$

The empiricisms of Equations 4.4.39, 4.4.40, and 4.4.44 were derived by a trial-and-error procedure matching experimental data, as in Figure 4.4.10, to a least-squares best-fit fractional efficiency curve (as in Figure 4.4.11) and a cyclone characteristic curve (as shown in Figure 4.4.12).

In summary, then, according to the Kalen-Zenz model, one would first calculate $d_{p,min}$ from Equation 4.3.1 for the cyclone dimensions and Figure 4.4.12. Next v_{so} would be determined from Equation 4.4.36 and $d''_{p,min}$ from Equation 4.4.44. The overall collection efficiency could then be determined from Figure 4.4.11 and the inlet particle-size distribution data.

Pressure Drop

In addition to the ability of predicting particle collection efficiency from fundamental considerations, it is also important to be able to compute the system pressure drop. Lissman[22] developed one of the earliest theoretical expressions proposed for computing pressure drop for a specific cyclone design with fixed dimensional proportions. The theoretical development was based on the assumption that the pressure drop in a cyclone was made up of the energy required to produce the inner spiral plus the total loss of the entrance velocity pressure. On this basis, and assuming a perfectly frictionless fluid moving in a circular path (i.e., the velocity distribution exponent $n = 1$), Lissman obtained the simple result that the friction loss amounted to four inlet velocity heads. The theoretical development does not indicate the effect of variation in the cyclone proportions on friction loss, nor does it account for velocity distribution exponents actually found in practice, i.e., $n = 0.5$ to 0.7. Hence, Lissman's method is not suitable for general application.

In an attempt to explain experimental pressure drop results on a theoretical basis, Shepherd and Lapple[3] proposed a theoretical approach assuming that the loss in a cyclone is equivalent to the energy required to produce the high-velocity inner

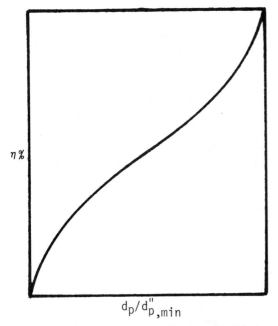

FIGURE 4.4.11. Efficiency as a function of $d_p/d''_{p,min}$ ratio.

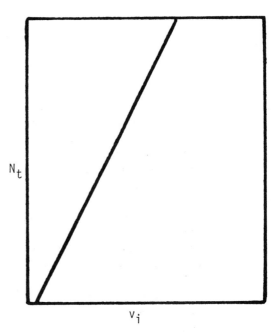

FIGURE 4.4.12. Number of turns as a function of the inlet velocity.

spiral. The derivation is based on a material and energy balance and is presented below.

From Bernoulli's theorem, the head loss, Δh, in a cyclone exceeds the change in velocity head between the exit duct and the cyclone inlet by the loss, F, of mechanical energy due to friction.

$$\Delta h = h_o - h_e = (v_e^2/2g_c) - (v_i^2/2g_c) + F \qquad (4.4.45)$$

where

Δh = pressure drop through cyclone and exit duct, ft;

h_o = pressure head at cyclone entrance, ft;

h_e = pressure head at cyclone exit duct, ft;

v_e = average linear velocity of fluid stream in cyclone exit duct, ft/sec;

v_i = average linear velocity of fluid stream at cyclone entrance, ft/sec;

g_c = gravitational constant;

F = friction loss (cyclone plus exit duct), ft.

Since velocities can be related by cross-sectional areas, Equation 4.4.45 can also be expressed as follows:

$$\Delta h/(v_i^2/2g_c) = \Delta h_v = F_v - 1 + (I/O)^2 \qquad (4.4.46)$$

or

$$\Delta h_v = F_{cv} + F_{ev} - 1 + (I/O)^2 \qquad (4.4.47)$$

where

Δh_v = pressure drop through cyclone and exit duct, expressed as number of cyclone inlet velocity heads;

F_v = friction loss (cyclone plus exit duct), expressed as number of cyclone inlet velocity heads;

F_{cv} = cyclone friction loss, expressed as number of cyclone inlet velocity heads;

F_{ev} = exit duct friction loss, expressed as number of cyclone inlet velocity heads;

I = area of cyclone entrance, ft^2;

O = cross-sectional area of cyclone exit duct, ft^2.

The value of F_{ev} may be computed directly from the usual fluid flow formulas. According to the Fanning equation,

$$F_{ev} = 4f (L/D_e) (I/O)^2 \qquad (4.4.48)$$

where

f = friction factor (read from appropriate curves or as an approximation may be assumed equal to 0.0055 for usual cyclone operating conditions);

L = equivalent length for exit duct (including corrections for bends, etc.), ft;

D_e = cyclone exit duct diameter, ft.

The value, F_{cv}, is not as easily obtained. The following must be taken into consideration to obtain a value for F_{cv}.

1. Loss due to gas expansion upon entering the cyclone chamber.
2. Loss as kinetic energy of rotation in the cyclone chamber.
3. Losses due to wall friction in the cyclone chamber.
4. Any additional frictional losses in the exit duct resulting from the swirling flow above and beyond those incurred by straight flow.
5. Any regain of the rotational kinetic energy as pressure energy.

The latter three factors are usually small for ordinary conventional cyclone designs and, hence, will be neglected.

At the entrance to the cyclone chamber, the gas stream may expand laterally if the inlet width is less than the annular width. In any case, a vertical expansion can occur. The lateral expansion will be inversely proportional to $B_c/(D_c - D_e)/2$, but the magnitude of the vertical is not known and will be represented by some factor k_1. The usual hydrodynamic formula for a sharp expansion loss then applies:

$$F_o = (v_i - v_c)^2/2g_c = v_i^2/2g_c [1 - k_1 (B_c/\Delta')]^2 \qquad (4.4.49)$$

where

F_o = friction loss at cyclone entrance, ft;

v_c = average velocity of fluid stream in cyclone chamber (outer spiral) equivalent to $(v_i k_1 B_c/\Delta')$, ft/sec;

k_1 = expansion factor to correct for vertical expansion of gas stream entering cyclone;

$\Delta' = (D_c - D_e)/2$.

In developing the equation for the rotational kinetic energy of the gas stream in the cyclone, it is assumed that the flow consists essentially of an outer downward spiral and an inner upward spiral. The direction of rotation in both spirals is the same so that little friction is expected at the point of junction. In view of the fact that the reversion from the outer to the inner spiral is rather gradual, it is assumed that the kinetic energy of the outer spiral contributes to the kinetic energy of the inner spiral and induces no loss in itself. The inner spiral is assumed to have a constant height of spiral and a constant angle of inclination to the horizontal, with the same rotational velocity at the same radius on any vertical position. The method of calculation will be to determine the average rotational kinetic energy per unit mass of gas in the inner spiral. Since it is assumed that none of this energy is recovered, this will constitute the friction loss due to the inner spiral. It is further assumed that the rotational velocity distribution in a cyclone can be expressed in the form:

$$\bar{v}_i = k/r_i^n \tag{4.4.50}$$

where

$\bar{v}_i$ = rotational velocity of fluid stream at r_i, ft/sec;

k = constant of velocity distribution;

r_i = distance from cyclone center line;

n = exponent of velocity distribution.

It should be noted that for positive values of n, v_i should approach infinity at zero radius. Since n is positive for a gas, this distribution clearly cannot hold all the way to the center. It is postulated that a core of stagnant fluid exists at the center; hence, the inner radius of the inner spiral is taken as r_d (rather than zero) to allow for any such core or break point in velocity distribution.

The mass flow per unit time in the inner spiral through a plane of unit height, perpendicular to the direction of the stream velocity, is given by the product of the density, the velocity, and the cross-sectional area, or

$$M = \int_{r_d}^{r_e} \rho_G v_a \, dr \tag{4.4.51}$$

where

M = fluid mass flow rate in the inner spiral through a plane of unit height, lb/sec ft;

r_d = inner radius of inner spiral, ft;

r_e = distance from cyclone center line to inner edge of outer spiral (or outer edge of inner spiral) in cyclone, ft;

ρ_G = fluid density, lb/ft^3;

v_a = actual velocity of fluid stream at radius r_i, ft/sec.

The total kinetic energy associated with mass M is the integral of the product of the velocity head, the velocity, and the differential cross-sectional area:

$$KE = \int_{r_d}^{r_e} (v_a^2/2g_c) \rho_G v_a \, dr \tag{4.4.52}$$

where

KE = total kinetic energy associated with mass M, (ft)(lb)/(sec)(ft).

If θ is the angle made with the horizontal by the velocity vector v_a in the inner spiral, the kinetic energy of rotation of mass M is given by

$$KE_r = \int_{r_d}^{r_e} (v_a^2 \cos^2 \theta/2g_c) \rho_G v_a \, dr \tag{4.4.53}$$

where

KE_r = rotational kinetic energy associated with mass M, (ft)(lb)/(sec)(ft);

θ = angle made with horizontal by velocity vector v_a in inner spiral.

The rotational kinetic energy per unit mass inherent in the inner spiral is found by dividing Equation 4.4.53 by Equation 4.4.51:

$$\frac{KE_r}{M} = \frac{(1/2g_c) \int_{r_e}^{r_d} v_a^3 \cos^2 \theta \, dr}{\int_{r_e}^{r_d} v_a \, dr} \qquad (4.4.54)$$

However, since $\bar{v}_i = v_a \cos \theta$ and since θ is assumed independent of r,

$$\frac{KE_r}{M} = \frac{(1/2g_c) \int_{r_d}^{r_e} \bar{v}_i^3 \, dr}{\int_{r_d}^{r_e} \bar{v}_i \, dr} \qquad (4.4.55)$$

By definition, for the inlet velocity

$$v_i = k/r_a^n \qquad (4.4.56)$$

where

r_a = radius at which the spiral velocity $\bar{v}_i$ is equal to the entrance velocity v_i, ft.

It then follows from Equation 4.4.50 that

$$\bar{v}_i = v_i r_a^n / r_i^n \qquad (4.4.57)$$

By substituting Equation 4.4.57 into Equation 4.4.55, the latter may be directly integrated to give (for $n \neq 1$):

$$\frac{KE_r}{M} = \frac{(v_i^2/2g_c)(r_a/r_e)^{2n}(1-n)(r_e^{1-3n} - r_d^{1-3n})}{(1-3n)(r_e^{1-n} - r_d^{1-n})} \qquad (4.4.58)$$

Summing up the significant losses in the cyclone chamber,

$$F_{cv} (v_i^2/2g_c) = F_o + (KE_r/M) \qquad (4.4.59)$$

and from Equations 4.4.49 and 4.4.58,

$$F_{cv} = [1 - k_1 (B_c/\Delta')]^2 + \frac{(r_a/r_e)^{2n}(1-n)[1-(r_a/r_e)^{1-3n}]}{(1-3n)[1-(r_d/r_e)^{1-n}]} \qquad (4.4.60)$$

Equation 4.4.60 represents the generalized form of F_{cv} according to the assumptions made in the derivation. For practical design values, the

value $[1 - k_1 (B_c/\Delta')]^2$ is a relatively small part of the total (typically less than 10%) and may be neglected. This term approaches unity as (B_c/Δ') becomes small; in such a case the entrance loss is the primary one. Such a condition, however, is not even approached in most commercial cyclone designs.

For $n = 0.5$ and neglecting the entrance loss (first term on the right in Equation 4.4.60), Equation 4.4.60 becomes

$$F_{cv} = r_a/(r_e r_d)^{0.5} \qquad (4.4.61)$$

Based upon experimental data, Shepherd and Lapple determined that

$$r_a = 0.47 \, B_c H_c / D_e \qquad (4.4.62)$$

$$r_e/r_d \approx 64 \qquad (4.4.63)$$

and since $r_e = D_e/2$, F_{cv} can then be given by

$$F_{cv} = 7.5 \, B_c H_c / D_e^2 \qquad (4.4.64)$$

In actual practice, the cyclone friction loss, F_{cv}, is approximately given by

$$F_{cv} = K \, B_c H_c / D_e^2 \qquad (4.4.65)$$

where K ranges from approximately 7.5 to 18.4 with a value of 13 found to check with experimental data within 30%.

4.5. DESIGN

The prime considerations in cyclone design are the pressure drop and overall particle collection efficiency. To establish a consistent nomenclature for the dimensions of a cyclone, Figure 4.5.1 gives those proportions commonly used in conventional cyclone design. Cyclones are by no means limited, however, to the proportions specified in Figure 4.5.1; many other configurations exist, such as those shown in Figures 4.5.2 and 4.5.3.

The performance of a cyclone is usually specified in terms of a cut size, d_{pc}, which is the size of the particle collected with 50% efficiency. The cut size depends on the gas and particle properties, the cyclone size and the operating conditions. It may be calculated from

$$d_{pc} = [9 \mu_G B_c / 2 \pi N_t v_i (\rho_p - \rho_G)]^{1/2} \qquad (4.5.1)$$

where

d_{pc} = cut size particle diameter (particle collected at 50% efficiency), ft;

μ_G = gas viscosity, lb/(ft)(sec);

B_c = width of gas inlet, ft;

N_t = effective number of turns the gas stream makes in the cyclone, dimensionless;

v_i = inlet velocity, ft/sec;

ρ_p = particle density, lb/ft³;

ρ_G = gas density, lb/ft³.

Lapple[23] provides a convenient graphical solution to Equation 4.5.1 for typical cyclones (as shown in Figure 4.5.1) having an inlet velocity of 50 ft/sec, a gas viscosity of 0.02 cp, an effective number of turns equal to five, and a cyclone inlet width of $D_c/4$. This is shown in Figure 4.5.4. The cut size may be approximated knowing only the cyclone diameter and the true particle specific gravity. Corrections for viscosity, inlet gas velocity, effective number of turns, and inlet width different from those assumed may be found graphically from Figures 4.5.5 and 4.5.6.

Although the effective number of turns, N_t, in a conventional cyclone with the proportions shown in Figure 4.5.1 has been found to be about 5, this value typically ranges from 3 to 10, but may be as low as 0.5 in some designs. From a theoretical viewpoint,

$$N_t = \frac{t_r v_i}{\pi D_c} = \frac{(V/Q) v_i}{\pi D_c} \qquad (4.5.2)$$

where

t_r = residence time of the gas stream, sec;

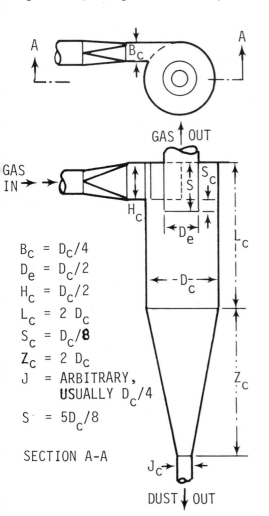

$B_c = D_c/4$
$D_e = D_c/2$
$H_c = D_c/2$
$L_c = 2 D_c$
$S_c = D_c/8$
$Z_c = 2 D_c$
J = ARBITRARY, USUALLY $D_c/4$
S = $5 D_c/8$

SECTION A-A

FIGURE 4.5.1. Typical dimensions of conventional cyclone.

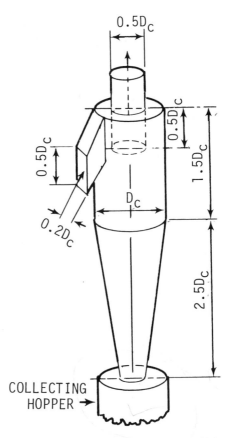

FIGURE 4.5.2. Typical dimensions of a high-efficiency, medium-throughput single cyclone (normal flow rate = 300 D_c^2 ft³/min).

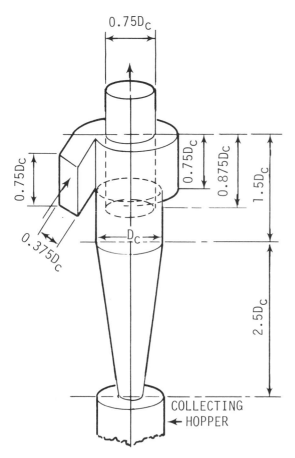

FIGURE 4.5.3. Typical dimensions of a medium-efficiency, high-throughput single cyclone (normal flow rate = 900 D_c^2 ft^3/min).

V = volume of cyclone, ft^3 ;
Q = volumetric flow rate, ft^3/sec.

The effective volume, V, of a cyclone with the dimensions given in Figure 4.5.1 is

$$V = \frac{\pi}{4} \left\{ \left(\frac{Z_c}{D_c - J_c} \right) \left(\frac{D_c^3 - J_c^3}{3} \right) + \right.$$

$$\left. D_c^2 L_c - D_e^2 (H_c + S_c) \right\} \qquad (4.5.3)$$

For a conventional cyclone designed in accordance with the proportions given in Figure 4.5.1, this becomes

$$V = 2.135 \; D_c^3 \qquad (4.5.4)$$

Substituting Equation 4.5.4 into Equation 4.5.2 allows N_t to be solved for directly (assuming that the proportions in Figure 4.5.1 have been used).

$$N_t = \frac{(V/Q) v_i}{\pi \, D_c} = \frac{(2.135 \; D_c^3 / Q) v_i}{\pi \, D_c}$$

Since

$$Q = v_i B_c H_c = v_i (D_c/4)(D_c/2) = 0.125 \; D_c^2 \, v_i$$

then

$$N_t = \frac{(2.135 \; D_c^3 / 0.125 \; D_c^2 \, v_i) v_i}{D_c} = 5.44$$

In actual practice for large-diameter cyclones, the number of turns correlates well with the inlet velocity and may be estimated using Figure 4.5.7.

Particles larger than the cut size d_{pc} will be collected to an extent greater than 50%, while smaller particles will be collected to a lesser extent. This may be represented quantitatively by a curve as shown in Figure 4.5.8,[23] which is essentially a generalized form of the fractional efficiency plot frequently found in commercial literature. The specific values given in Figure 4.5.8 apply for any cyclone of the proportions given in Figure 4.5.1. The calculated particle cut size used in conjunction with the general cyclone efficiency curve as shown in Figure 4.5.8 will determine the particle-size efficiency curve for the cyclone in question. Additional experimental data were used to supplement Lapple's ratios of d_p/d_{pc}.[24] All results compared favorably with Lapple's original curve. Typical manufacturer's efficiency curves for cyclones and multiple cyclones converted to d_p/d_{pc} curves had slightly lower efficiencies than Lapple's correlation for d_p/d_{pc} ratios greater than one. The maximum deviation noted was 5% for the cyclone curve at d_p/d_{pc} of 1.5 and 12% for the multiple cyclone curve at d_p/d_{pc} of 2 to 3. Apparently, Lapple's correlation is accurate enough for an engineering estimation of many cyclone applications. To determine the overall collection efficiency, the particle-size distribution of the feed must be known. An example of the calculational sequence is given in Section 4.6.

A fractional efficiency curve for a geometrically similar cyclone may be constructed from a given fractional efficiency curve using the following procedure.

1. Determine d_{pc} from the fractional efficiency curve for a known cyclone (particle diameter collected at 50% efficiency).

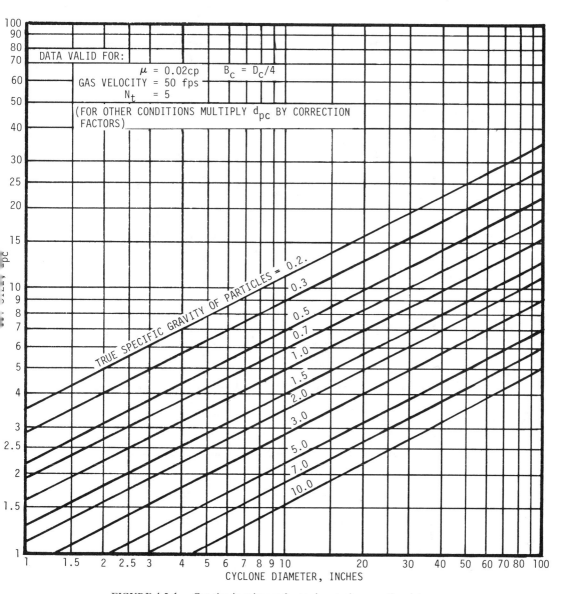

FIGURE 4.5.4.   Cut size in microns for cyclones of conventional type.

2. Replot the fractional efficiency curve as efficiency vs. the ratio d_p/d_{pc}.

3. Calculate d_{pc} for the unknown cyclone from Equation 4.5.1 or Figures 4.5.4 through .5.6.

4. Assume that the efficiency vs. d_p/d_{pc} curve applies to the unknown cyclone. Using the value of d_{pc} for the unknown cyclone and the efficiency vs. d_p/d_{pc} curve, new values of d_p vs. efficiency may be calculated and plotted as the fractional efficiency curve of the unknown cyclone. In most cases, however, a range of d_{pc} for the unknown cyclone is selected instead of a single

value. Then, using the maximum and minimum values for d_{pc}, two size efficiency curves can be plotted. The overall efficiencies obtained from these curves serve as an engineering estimate of the expected cyclone performance.

The overall collection efficiency for the cyclone is determined as follows.

1. Divide the particle-size distribution of the dust to be collected into ranges (if this has not already been done). For example, for the distribution given in Figure 4.5.9,

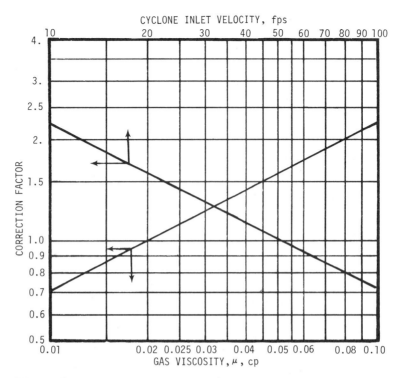

FIGURE 4.5.5. Viscosity and velocity correction factors for cut size particle of conventional cyclones.

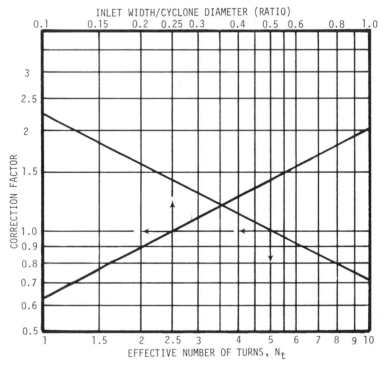

FIGURE 4.5.6. Inlet width/cyclone diameter and effective number of turns correction factors for cut size particle of conventional cyclones.

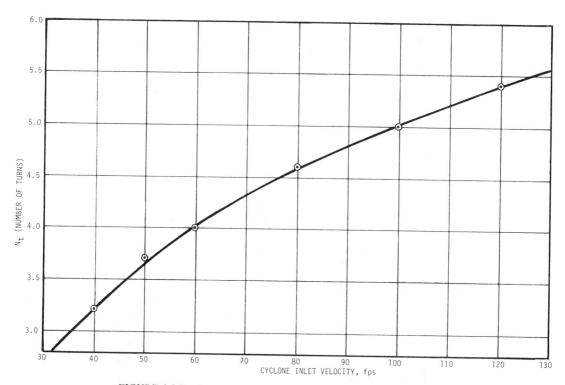

FIGURE 4.5.7. Number of turns as a function of cyclone inlet velocity.

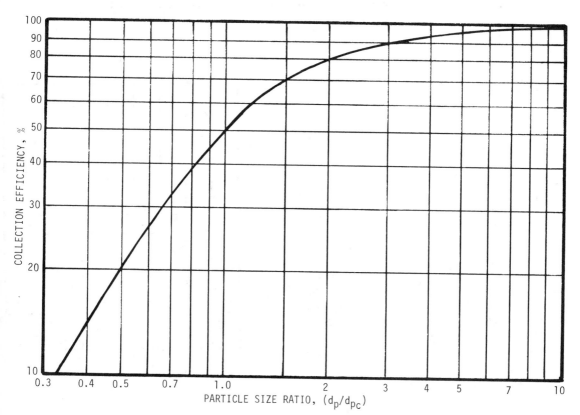

FIGURE 4.5.8. Cyclone efficiency as a function of particle size ratio.

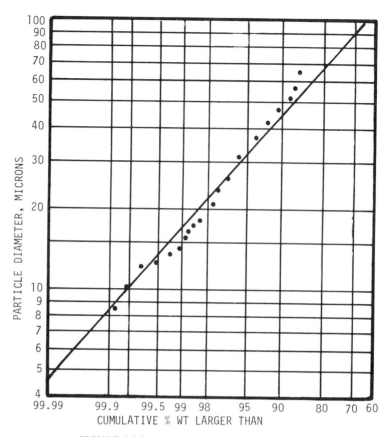

FIGURE 4.5.9.   Typical particle-size distribution.

Particle size, μm		
Range	Avg d_p	Wt %
<6	3	(100.00−99.97) = 0.03
6−8	7	(99.97−99.91) = 0.06
8−10	9	(99.91−99.80) = 0.11
10−12	11	(99.80−99.65) = 0.15
12−15	13.5	etc. 0.35
15−20	17.5	0.90
20−30	25	2.80
30−40	35	3.60
40+	40+	91.90

2. From the fractional efficiency curve, either found experimentally or predicted using Lapple's technique, determine the collection efficiency for the average d_p in each size range of the inlet particle-size distribution.

3. Multiply the weight fraction for each size range by the collection efficiency determined in Step 2. The summation gives the overall collection efficiency.

If the size efficiency curve is plotted on semilog

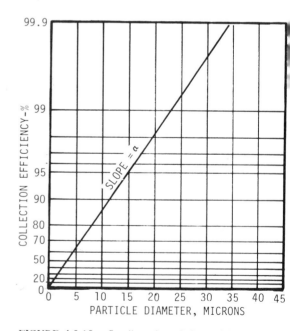

FIGURE 4.5.10.   Semilog plot of size efficiency curve.

paper, as in Figure 4.5.10, a straight line may result.[25] This equation can be represented by

$$\eta(d_p) = 1 - e^{-\alpha d_p} \qquad (4.5.5)$$

where

$\eta(d_p) =$ a collection efficiency for particle size d_p;

$\alpha \quad =$ a constant for the particular cyclone in question.

Direct substitution of Equation 4.5.5 into Equation 3.5.10 results in[26]

$$\eta_T = \beta \int_0^\infty (e^{-\beta d_p})(1 - e^{-\alpha d_p}) \, d(d_p) = \frac{\alpha}{\alpha + \beta} \qquad (4.5.6)$$

Grove[27] developed a method for replacing the constants α and β in this expression with two commonly measured particle diameters, the cut size (d_{pc}) and the mean particle diameter (d_{pm}), defined as the size above which 50% of the particles lie or where the cumulative distribution equals 0.50. Both are expressed in microns. By definition, then,

$$\eta(d_p) = 0.50 = e^{-\alpha d_{pc}} \qquad (4.5.7)$$

$$Y(d_p) = 0.50 = e^{-\beta d_{pm}} \qquad (4.5.8)$$

Combining Equations 4.5.7 and 4.5.8 and solving for α yields

$$\alpha = \beta \, (d_{pm}/d_{pc}) \qquad (4.5.9)$$

Finally, substitution of this expression for α into the overall efficiency equation (Equation 4.5.6) gives

$$\eta_T = \frac{d_{pm}}{d_{pm} + d_{pc}} = \frac{1}{1 + (d_{pc}/d_{pm})} \qquad (4.5.10)$$

The reciprocal efficiency, $1/\eta_T$, is plotted against the ratio $d_{pc}/d_{pm} = \beta/\alpha$ in Figure 4.5.11. This provides a simple means of estimating the overall efficiency.

Another method which can be used to estimate the overall cyclone collection efficiency is that of Sundberg,[28] which utilizes particle-size distribution and fraction efficiency data for the cyclone in question. Again, both the particle-size distribution and fractional efficiency curves must be adequately represented by a straight line when plotted on logarithmic probability paper. This method was discussed in Section 5 of Chapter 3. The overall efficiency is given by

$$\eta_T = \mathrm{erf} \left[\frac{\ln (d_{pm}/d_{pc})}{\sqrt{\ln^2 \sigma_g + \ln^2 \sigma_{gc}}} \right] \qquad (4.5.11)$$

where

$\sigma_g \quad =$ geometric standard deviation of particle-size distribution data;

$\sigma_{gc} =$ geometric standard deviation of fractional efficiency curve.

The above methods for predicting cyclone collection efficiency are, of course, only approximate. However, if utilized correctly, they can be useful for estimation purposes. It is not uncommon in industry to find cases where cyclone performance is considerably less than expected. For example, there are many cases in which large particles, supposedly collected with efficiency approaching 100%, escape the unit. Assuming that the unit has been properly designed, this may be caused by the effect of turbulence and eddies within the unit, particles becoming reentrained in the exiting gas stream, particles bouncing off the wall of the cyclone, and particle-particle interactions.

The pressure drop across a cyclone collector will generally range between 2 and 6 in. of water, and it is usually determined empirically. The method frequently used in industrial practice is to determine the pressure drop of a geometrically similar prototype. As mentioned previously, Lapple[3] suggested the relationship in Equation 4.4.65,

$$F_{cv} = K \, (B_c H_c / D_e^2) \qquad (4.4.65)$$

where K varies from 7.5 to 18.4, with a value of 13 found to check with experimental data within 30%. The friction loss, F_{cv}, is given in units of inlet velocity heads. This inlet velocity head, expressed in inches of water, may be expressed as follows:

$$\text{one inlet velocity head} = 0.003 \, \rho_G v_i^2, \text{ in. } H_2O \qquad (4.5.12)$$

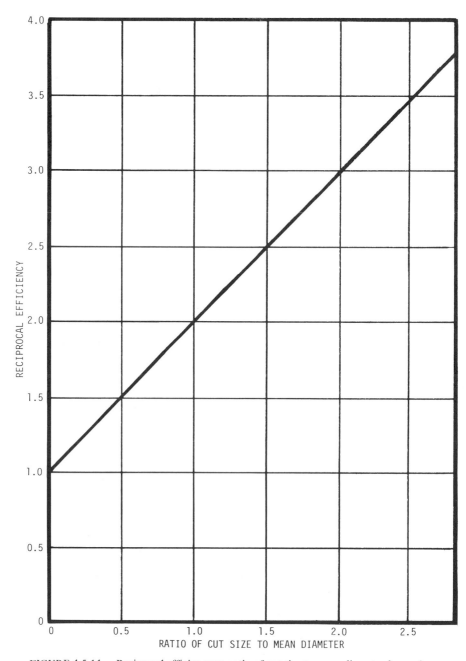

FIGURE 4.5.11. Reciprocal efficiency vs. ratio of cut size to mean diameter for cyclone.

where

ρ_G = the gas density (lb/ft³);
v_i = the inlet velocity (ft/sec).

The friction loss through cyclones encountered in practice may range from 1 to 20 inlet velocity heads, depending on the geometric proportions. For a cyclone of the proportions shown in Figure 4.5.1, the friction loss is approximately 8 inlet velocity heads or, assuming an inlet velocity of 50 ft/sec (typical) and a gas density of 0.075 lb/ft³,

$$\Delta P = 8(0.003)(0.075)(50)^2 = 4.5 \text{ in. } H_2O$$

There is an equation which can be used to relating the pressure drop of a cyclone operating at several different conditions or for geometrically similar cyclones:

$$\Delta P = \frac{0.0027 \, Q^2}{k \, D_e{}^2 B_c H_c (L_c/D_c)^{1/3} \, (Z_c/D_c)^{1/3}} \qquad (4.5.13)$$

where

ΔP = pressure drop, in. H_2O;

Q = volumetric flow rate at the inlet, ft^3/sec;

D_e = diameter of gas outlet, ft;

B_c = inlet width, ft;

H_c = inlet height, ft;

L_c = height of cylinder, ft;

D_c = cyclone diameter, ft;

Z_c = height of cone, ft;

k = dimensionless factor descriptive of cyclone inlet vanes — 0.5 without vanes, 1 for vanes that do not expand the entering gas or touch the gas outlet wall (a in Figure 4.5.12), and 2.0 for vanes that expand and touch the gas outlet wall (b in Figure 4.5.12).

Remember that the cyclone dimensions (B_c, H_c, etc.) are the inner dimensions. For example, B_c is the inside width of the duct, not including any insulation, etc.

Another pressure drop relationship, which attempts to more directly include some of the operating conditions, is given below.[29]

$$\Delta P = KQ^2 P \, \rho_G / T \qquad (4.5.14)$$

where

P = absolute pressure, atm;

T = absolute temperature of the gas, $^\circ R$;

K = proportionality constant (see Figure 4.5.13).

The design factor having the greatest effect on collection efficiency is the cyclone diameter. For a given pressure drop, the smaller the diameter of the unit, the higher the collection efficiency obtained, since centrifugal acceleration increases with decreasing radius of rotation. Centrifugal forces employed in modern designs vary from as low as 5 to as high as 2,500 times gravity, depending on the diameter of the cyclone. The

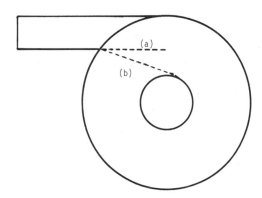

FIGURE 4.5.12.   Inlet vanes.

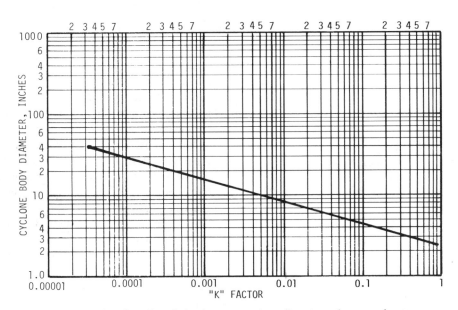

FIGURE 4.5.13.   The relation between cyclone diameter and pressure loss.

ratio of centrifugal force to the force of gravity is frequently referred to as the separation factor S_f given by

$$S_f = v_i^2 / r_o g \qquad (4.5.15)$$

where

v_i = the particle inlet velocity;
r_o = the cyclone radius;
g = the acceleration caused by gravity.

Some typical separation factors for various types of dusts are presented in Table 4.5.1.

For practical applications, cyclone design is usually limited by pressure drops reasonable with commercially available fans. The pressure drop will increase as a function of the inlet velocity squared. This limitation usually dictates that inlet velocities range from 20 to 70 ft/sec; however, equipment is normally designed for an inlet velocity of 50 to 60 ft/sec. Increasing the inlet velocity will increase the efficiency, although the relationship is very complex. There is also an upper limit, about 100 to 120 ft/sec, above which there is increased turbulence which in turn causes reentrainment of the separated particles and reduced efficiencies.

The length of the cyclone body determines the residence time during which particles are subject to the separating forces; increasing this length will

increase efficiency. Also, dust which has been entrained in the vortex core will have more time to become reseparated. Increasing the body diameter-to-outlet diameter ratio will also increase efficiency, although the optimum ratio is between 2 and 3.

The eddy current in the annular region requires that the gas outlet extend into the cyclone to prevent excessive amounts of dust from passing directly from the inlet to the outlet. Usually this extension ends just below the bottom of the inlet. Devices which permit the gases to leave the gas outlet tube tangentially have been successful in reducing the pressure loss without sacrificing the efficiency.

Since the pressure drop in a cyclone is caused by the vortex and not by wall friction, rough walls actually reduce the pressure drop due to suppression of vortex formation. However, they also greatly reduce the collection efficiency due to increased turbulence and reentrainment.

The effects of operating variables on cyclone operation and performance are important in predicting the effect of variations over relatively small ranges. These are summarized in Table 4.5.2. Note also that since the efficiency decreases with increased gas viscosity, and since the gas viscosity increases with an increase in temperature, the cyclone efficiency should decrease with an increase in temperature. It should also be mentioned that particle-size variations have a negligible effect on the pressure drop.

Poor design of the duct system preceding the cyclone can also greatly reduce collector efficiency. For operation at peak performance with minimum maintenance, the physical design must keep dust and gas distribution as uniform as possible. Another reason for poor collection efficiency is air leakage, since most dust collectors operate under negative pressure. Air leaks into cyclone bodies, cones, or disentrainment hoppers should be kept to a minimum, since air drawn into these sections can only escape by the gas outlet and will carry dust which has already been caught, thus reducing the overall efficiency of the cyclone(s). Therefore, it is important to make sure that flange joints are properly constructed and that access doors are correctly fitted and tightened. It is also essential that collected dust is removed from dust hoppers before it reaches the level where it can be reentrained by the cyclone vortex action. Overloading of hoppers will also

TABLE 4.5.1

Typical Separation Factors for Some Dusts

Dust	Dust size analysis, % of total weight	Separation factor
Fly ash	50% less than 50 μm	28
Stone dust	33% less than 20 μm	50
Emery dust	50% less than 50 μm	22
Rock dust	70% less than 35 μm	85
Cement kiln exhaust	73% less than 35 μm	100
Foundry sand	67% less than 45 μm	75
Limestone dust	66% less than 45 μm	93
Soap dust	87% less than 35 μm	85

TABLE 4.5.2

Effect of Operation Variables on Cyclone Operation and Performance

Variable	Effect on efficiency	Effect on pressure drop
Flow rate	$\dfrac{100 - \eta_1}{100 - \eta_2} = \left(\dfrac{Q_2}{Q_1}\right)^{0.5}$	$\dfrac{\Delta P_1}{\Delta P_2} = \dfrac{Q_1{}^2 \rho_{G,1}}{T_1}\left[\dfrac{T_2}{Q_2{}^2 \rho_{G,2}}\right]$
Gas density	$\dfrac{100 - \eta_1}{100 - \eta_2} = \left[\dfrac{\rho_p - \rho_{G,2}}{\rho_p - \rho_{G,1}}\right]^{0.5}$	Same as above
Particle density	Same as above	Negligible
Gas viscosity	$\dfrac{100 - \eta_1}{100 - \eta_2} = \left[\dfrac{\mu_{G,1}}{\mu_{G,2}}\right]^{0.5}$	Negligible
Dust loading	$\dfrac{100 - \eta_1}{100 - \eta_2} = \left[\dfrac{C_{i,2}}{C_{i,1}}\right]^{0.182}$	$\dfrac{\Delta P_d}{\Delta P_c} = \dfrac{1}{0.013 C_i{}^{0.5} + 1}$

Note: 1 = condition 1; 2 = condition 2; Q = gas volumetric flow rate, ft³/sec; η = efficiency; ΔP = pressure drop, in. H_2O (subscript d indicates the gas stream under loading conditions and subscript c, no dust loading or clean conditions); ρ_G = gas density, lb/ft³; T = absolute temperature, °R; μ_G = gas viscosity, lb/(ft)(sec); C_i = inlet dust concentration, grains/ft³.

result in build-up in cyclone cones, and rapid cone wear will result. It is important that an efficient air seal be fitted to hopper dust outlets.

When an installation is handling hot gases, it is necessary to prevent the gas temperature from falling below its dew point; otherwise, condensation will occur causing dust build-up and blockage. Where necessary, the system should be insulated to maintain temperature.

In most plants it is preferable to arrange the fan on the clean air side of the cyclone, since this helps to reduce fan wear.

Typical unerected equipment costs for cyclones may range from $0.20 to 1.50 per ACFM, primarily due to variations in the materials of construction, with the usual around $0.30 per ACFM (for mild steel construction). Installed costs can vary from 50 to over 350% of equipment cost. The operating cost for most cyclone collectors usually runs about $0.015 to 0.030 per ACFM per year. Power costs are typically rated on a pressure drop of about 0.25 hp/in H_2O per 1000 ACFM.

The theoretical annual cost of operation and maintenance for centrifugal collectors can be expressed as follows:

$$\$ = ACFM \left[\frac{0.7457\,(\Delta P)(t)\,P_c}{6356\,\eta_f} + M\right] \qquad (4.5.16)$$

where

ACFM = design capacity of collector, actual ft³/min;

ΔP = pressure drop, in H_2O (typically 2 to 6 in. H_2O);

t = annual operating time (annually 8,760 hr);

P_c = power cost, $/kWh (typically $0.01 to 0.02/kWh);

η_f = fan efficiency (typically 60%);

M = maintenance cost, $/ACFM (typically $0.015 to 0.03/ACFM).

The best cost data, however, are available directly from the manufacturer.

4.6. ILLUSTRATIVE EXAMPLES

The design procedures and equations presented in the previous sections are now applied to demonstrate their use in cyclone design analysis.

Example 4.6.1

Estimate the pressure drop across a 24-in. diameter conventional cyclone (Figure 4.5.1) if the inlet velocity is 60 ft/sec.

Solution

one velocity head = $0.003 \rho_G v_i^2$

Assuming air as the gas stream ($\rho_G = 0.076$ lb/ft^3)

one velocity head = $0.003 (0.076)(60)^2 = 0.82$

Since the conventional cyclone shown in Figure 4.5.1 experiences a friction loss of about 8 velocity heads,

$\Delta P = 0.82 (8) = 6.57$ in. H_2O

Alternately, using Equation 4.4.65

$F_{cv} = K(B_c H_c/D_e^2) = 13(0.5)(1)/1 = 6.5$ inlet velocity heads

$\Delta P = 6.5 (0.82) = 5.33$ in. H_2O

which checks within 20% of the previous result.

Example 4.6.2

Calculate the fan requirement (gas horsepower) in the previous problem if the cyclone units are treating 154,000 ACFM of gas.

Solution

The fan requirement is calculated from

hp = $Q(\Delta P)$

in consistent units. Thus,

$$hp = \frac{(154,000 \text{ ft}^3/\text{min})(6.57 \text{ in. } H_2O)(5.2 \text{ lb/ft}^2/\text{in. } H_2O)}{(60 \text{ sec/min})(550 \text{ ft-lb/sec/hp})}$$

hp = 159 hp

To arrive at the required brake horsepower, the horsepower calculated above would be divided by the fan efficiency.

Example 4.6.3

A cyclone is used to remove the particulates from 18,000 ACFM of dust laden gas at 20°C and 1 atm. The unit is operating at a collection efficiency of 80%. Calculate the collection efficiency of the cyclone if the gas viscosity is decreased by a factor of two.

Solution

The following scale-up equation is employed:

$(100 - \eta_1)/(100 - \eta_2) = (\mu_{G,1}/\mu_{G,2})^{0.5}$

Since $\eta_1 = 80$ and $\mu_2 = 0.5 \mu_1$

$(100 - 80)/(100 - \eta_2) = (2)^{0.5}$

Solving for η_2 gives

$\eta_2 = 86\%$

Example 4.6.4

Calculate a revised collection efficiency for Example 4.6.3 if the pressure is doubled.

Solution

The following scale-up equation is employed:

$(100 - \eta_1)/(100 - \eta_2) = [(\rho_p - \rho_{G,2})/(\rho_p - \rho_{G,1})]^{0.5}$

Since doubling the pressure roughly doubles the gas density, one may calculate η_2 when $\eta_1 = 80$ by

$(100 - 80)/(100 - \eta_2) = [(\rho_p - 2\rho_{G,1})/(\rho_p - \rho_{G,1})]^{0.5}$

Since $\rho_p >>> \rho_{G,1}$, then

$(\rho_p - 2\rho_{G,1})/(\rho_p - \rho_{G,1}) = 1$

or

$\eta_2 = \eta_1$
  $= 80\%$

However, the volume rate of flow would be halved, so that

$(100 - 80)/(100 - \eta_2) = (Q_2/Q_1)^{0.5}$
$= (1/2)^{0.5}$
$\eta_2 = 71.71\%$

This assumes that the two effects are not interdependent.

Example 4.6.5

Calculate a revised collection efficiency for Example 4.6.3 if the inlet dust loading is tripled.

Solution

Using the following scale-up equation

$(100 - \eta_1)/(100 - \eta_2) = (C_{i,2}/C_{i,1})^{0.182}$

one can calculate η_2 when $C_{i,2} = 3C_{i,1}$. Thus,

$$(100 - 80)/(100 - \eta_2) = (3C_{i,1}/C_{i,1})^{0.182}$$

Solving for η_2 gives

$$\eta_2 = 83.6\%$$

Example 4.6.6

Assuming a "base-case" collection efficiency-particle diameter curve, prepare a graph illustrating the effect of volumetric flow rate on collection efficiency.

Solution

Assume the base case to be

$$\eta_1 = 90\%$$

$$Q_1 = 10,000 \text{ ACFM}$$

and using the scale-up equation

$$(100 - \eta_1)/(100 - \eta_2) = (Q_2/Q_1)^{0.5}$$

The effect of volumetric flow rate on collection efficiency may be studied. The following table provides the numerical results.

Q_2, ACFM	η_2, %
1,000	68.5
2,000	77.7
5,000	85.9
7,500	88.5
12,500	91.0
15,000	92.0

The graphical results are shown below.

Example 4.6.7

The size, mass, and cyclone collection efficiency data for a gas containing limestone dust are given below.

Particle diameter, μm	Wt, %	Collection efficiency, %
0–5	2	4
5–10	8	6
10–20	13	20
20–30	26	32
30–50	12	78
50–75	11	89
75–100	9	95
100–200	8	98
200–	11	99+

Calculate the overall collection efficiency of the unit.

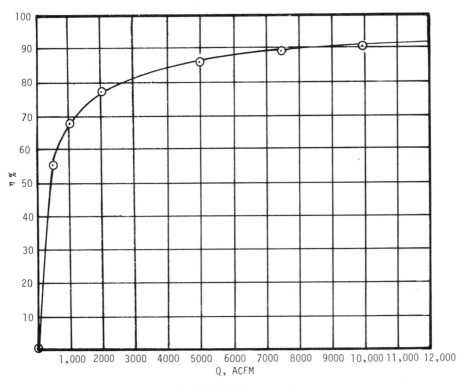

EXAMPLE 4.6.6. η vs. Q.

Solution

The overall efficiency is given by the product of the weight fraction and collection efficiency for each size range. The following table provides the results.

d_p, μm	Wt fraction	η, %	(Wt fraction) $(\eta$, %)
0–5	0.02	4	0.08
5–10	0.08	6	0.48
10–20	0.13	20	2.60
20–30	0.26	32	8.32
30–50	0.12	78	9.36
50–75	0.11	89	9.79
75–100	0.09	95	8.55
100–200	0.08	98	7.84
200–	0.11	99	10.945
			57.97

The overall efficiency is, therefore, approximately 58%.

Example 4.6.8

If the inlet dust loading in the previous problem is 2.2 grains/ft^3 and the quantity of gas processed is 150,000 ACFM, calculate the mass of limestone collected daily.

Solution

Since the inlet loading is 2.2 grains/ft^3, the mass collected per cubic foot of air is given by

2.2 (0.58) = 1.28 gr

The daily mass collected is 150,000 $\times$ 1.28 $\times$ 60 $\times$ 24 or 276,480,000 grains/day.

Example 4.6.9

Calculate the daily mass of limestone discharged to the atmosphere.

Solution

The daily mass discharged is

150,000 (2.20 – 1.28) $\times$ 60 $\times$ 24 =

(198,720,000 grains/day)/(7,000 grains/lb) = 28,390 lb/day

Example 4.6.10

As a recently hired engineer, you have been assigned the job of selecting and specifying a cyclone unit to be used to reduce an inlet fly ash loading with the particle-size distribution given below from 3.1 grains/ft^3 to an outlet value of 0.06. The flow rate from the coal-fired burner is 100,000 ACFM. Fractional efficiency data are presented below for three different types of cyclones (multiclones) already available in the company. Which type and how many are required to meet the above specifications? The optimum operating pressure drop is 3.0 in. H$_2$O; at this condition, the average inlet velocity may be assumed to be 60 ft/sec.

Solution

The required collection efficiency is

$\eta = [(3.1 - 0.06)/3.1]$ 100
$= 98\%$

This requires a trial-and-error calculation. The solution is best presented in tabular form.

Particle diameter range, μm	Average particle diameter, μm	Weight fraction (W_i)	Efficiency for 6-in. tubes, %	$(w_i \eta_i)$ for 6-in. tubes	Efficiency for 12-in. tubes, %	$(w_i \eta_i)$ for 12-in. tubes
5–35	20	0.05	89	4.45	82	4.1
35–50	42.5	0.05	97	4.85	93.5	4.67
50–70	60	0.10	98.5	9.85	96	9.6
70–110	90	0.20	99	19.8	98	19.6
110–150	130	0.20	100	20	100	20
150–200	175	0.20	100	20	100	20
200–400	300	0.10	100	10	100	10
400–700	550	0.10	100	10	100	10
				98.95		97.97

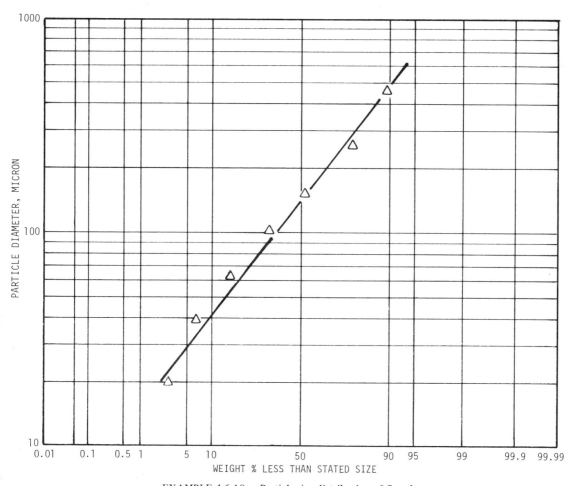

EXAMPLE 4.6.10.   Particle-size distribution of fly ash.

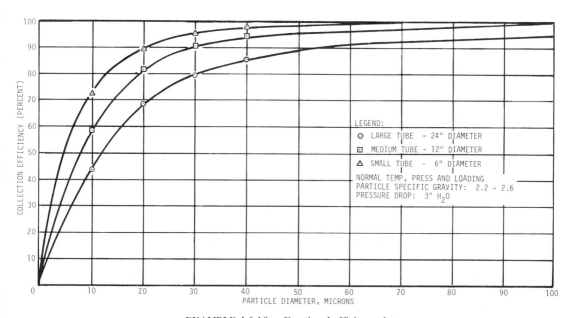

EXAMPLE 4.6.10.   Fractional efficiency data.

Therefore, it will be necessary to use the 6-in. tubes for a conservative design. Assuming a 3-in. outlet tube diameter, the inlet cross-sectional area (for axial flow) for each tube will be

$$A = \pi D^2/4 = 0.785 \, (0.5^2 - 0.25^2)$$

or

$$A = 0.147 \text{ ft}^2$$

Since the velocity in each tube is 60 ft/sec, the number of tubes, n, is given by

$$60 = 100,000/60 \times 0.147 \times n$$

Solving for n

$$n = 190 \text{ tubes}$$

required in this multiple-cyclone unit.

Example 4.6.11

Calculate the daily mass of fly ash collected and discharged to the atmosphere in Example 4.6.10.

Solution

For an efficiency of 98.95%, the fly ash discharged is

$$0.0326 \times 100,000 \times 24 \times 60/7,000 = 670 \text{ lb/day}$$

The fly ash collected is

$$670 \, (3.1 - 0.0326)/0.0326 = 63,042 \text{ lb/day}$$

Example 4.6.12

A dry cyclone is used as a primary cleaner on a heating plant spreader stoker. The following data are available:

$$
\begin{aligned}
B_c &= 1 \text{ ft} \\
\mu_G &= 1.68 \times 10^{-5} \text{ lb/ft sec at } 400^\circ\text{F, 1 atm} \\
N_t &= 10 \\
v_i &= 41.4 \text{ ft/sec} \\
\rho_p &= 150 \text{ lb/ft}^3 \\
\rho_G &= 0.0462 \text{ lb/ft}^3
\end{aligned}
$$

The particle-size distribution is given below. Determine the overall cyclone collection efficiency using Equation 4.5.10 and compare with Lapple's technique.

Solution

$$d_{pc} = \sqrt{\frac{9(1.68 \times 10^{-5})(1)}{2\pi \, 10(150)(41.4)}} \, (30.48 \times 10^4 \, \mu\text{m/ft})$$

$$= 6 \, \mu\text{m}$$

From the particle-size distribution curve,

$$d_{pm} = 28 \, \mu\text{m}$$

Hence, using Equation 4.5.10,

$$\eta_T = 1/[1 + (\beta/\alpha)] = 1/[1 + (d_{pc}/d_{pm})] = 82.35\%$$

According to Lapple's procedure, the overall collection efficiency is determined as follows.

Particle-size range (μm)	(d_p) avg (μm)	Wt fraction	d_p/d_{pc}	η_i,%	Wt fraction × η_i, %
0–5	2.5	0.1175	0.417	15	1.76
5–10	7.5	0.1037	1.250	60	6.22
10–20	15.0	0.1723	2.500	88	15.16
20–30	25.0	0.1341	4.170	95	12.74
30–40	35.0	0.1045	5.830	97	10.13
40–50	45.0	0.0814	7.500	98	7.98
50–60	55.0	0.0634	9.170	99.9	6.33
60–70	65.0	0.0493	10.830	100	4.93
70–76	73.0	0.0242	12.160	100	2.42
76+	76+	0.1496		100	14.96

$$\eta_T = 82.63\%$$

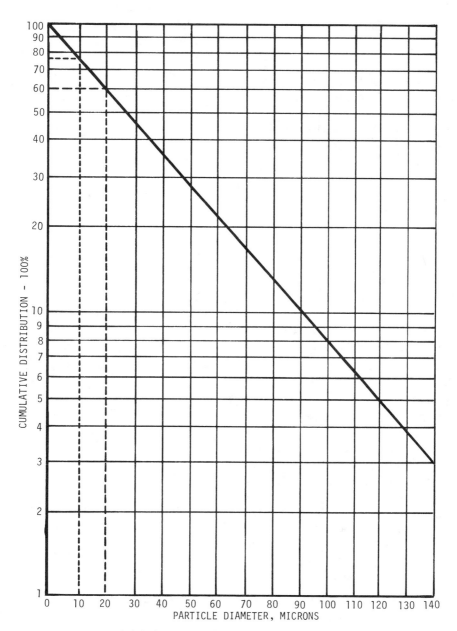

EXAMPLE 4.6.12.   Cumulative distribution vs. particle diameter.

The advantage of using Equation 4.5.10 is evident.

Example 4.6.13

A particular cyclone has a fractional efficiency curve as shown in Figure 4.5.10. Assuming that the same gas is treated as in Example 4.6.12 (i.e., same particle-size distribution), estimate the overall cyclone collection efficiency that can be expected using Sundberg's method.

Solution

d_{pm} = 28 μm
d_{pc} = 3.8 μm
σ_g = 72/28 = 2.57
σ_{gc} = 9.7/3.8 = 2.55

$$\eta_T = \text{erf}\left[\frac{\ln(28/3.8)}{\sqrt{\ln^2 2.57 + \ln^2 2.55}}\right] = \text{erf}(1.13)$$

From Table 3.5.1,

$\eta_T = 87\%$

Example 4.6.14

A large-diameter conventional cyclone (no vanes) handles 5,000 ACFM of a particulate-laden gas exhaust stream (ρ_G = 0.076 lb/ft³) from a certain metallurgical operation. The cyclone diameter is 4 ft. The remaining dimensions may be found from Figure 4.5.1. In an attempt to increase efficiency, a group of new cyclones is to be designed with the same geometrical proportions and pressure drop as the single cyclone. If the diameter of the small cyclone is to be 6 in., what will the dimensions of the new group be? How many will be needed to handle the original flow rate at the same resistance?

Solution

Cyclone Dimensions (ft) – ?

Old		New
4	D_c	0.5
1	B_c	0.125
2	H_c	0.25
2	D_c	0.25
8	L_c	1.0
8	Z_c	1.0

$$\Delta P_{old} = \frac{0.0027\, Q^2}{k\, D_e^{\,2}\, B_c H_c (L_c/D_c)^{1/3} (Z_c/D_c)^{1/3}}$$

$$= \frac{0.0027\,(83.3)^2}{0.5(2)^2\,(1)\,(2)\,(2)^{1/3}\,(2)^{1/3}}$$

$$= 2.95 \text{ in. } H_2O$$

$$\Delta P_{new} = 2.95 = \frac{0.0027\,(Q)^2}{0.5(0.25)^2\,(0.125)\,(0.25)\,(2)^{1/3}\,(2)^{1/3}}$$

Q^2 = 1.7
Q = 1.3 ft³/sec per new 6-in. tube

Thus, the number required will be

$n = 83.3/1.3 = 64$

Note that the inlet velocities for the old and new cyclones will be exactly the same.

$(v_i)_{old}$ = 83.3/(1)(2) = 41.6 ft/sec
$(v_i)_{new}$ = 1.3/(0.125)(0.25) = 41.6 ft/sec

NOMENCLATURE

B_c	Width of cyclone inlet duct, ft (unless specified otherwise)
c	Particle number concentration
C_i	Inlet dust concentration, grains/ft^3
D_c	Cyclone diameter, ft (unless specified otherwise)
D_e	Diameter of outlet gas duct, ft
d_p	Particle diameter, ft (in some cases, μm)
d_{pc}	Particle cut size diameter collected at 50%
d_{pm}	Mean particle diameter, ft or μm
$d_{p,min}$	Diameter of smallest particle theoretically completely collected, ft
$d'_{p,min}$	$d_{p,min}$ Corrected for inlet loading
$d''_{p,min}$	$d_{p,min}$ Corrected for exceeding saltation velocity
e	Particle entrainment rate, lb of solids/ft^3 gas
f	Friction factor
F	Friction loss (cyclone plus exit duct), ft
F_{cv}	Cyclone friction loss expressed as number of cyclone inlet velocity heads
F_{ev}	Exit duct friction loss expressed as number of cyclone inlet velocity heads
F_o	Friction loss at cyclone entrance, ft
F_v	Friction loss (cyclone plus exit duct) expressed as number of cyclone inlet velocity heads
g	Acceleration of gravity, ft/sec^2
g_c	Gravitational constant
H	Overall cyclone height, ft
Δh	Pressure drop through cyclone and exit duct, ft
H_c	Height of cyclone inlet duct, ft
h_e	Pressure head at cyclone exit duct, ft
h_o	Pressure head at cyclone entrance, ft
Δh_v	Pressure drop through cyclone and exit duct expressed as number of cyclone inlet velocity heads
I	Cyclone inlet duct cross-sectional area, ft^2
J_c	Diameter of outlet duct for collected particles, ft
l	Natural length (distance below gas outlet where vortex turns), ft
L	Equivalent length of exit duct, ft
L_c	Height of cylindrical portion of cyclone, ft
m_p	Mass of particle, lb
n	Velocity distribution exponent
n'	Number of particles
N_j	Number of particles tested in inlet section j
N_t	Number of turns made by gas stream in cyclone
O	Cyclone outlet tube cross-sectional area, ft^2
P	Pressure, atm
ΔP	Pressure drop, in. H_2O
P_j	Number of particles collected in section j
Q	Gas volumetric flow rate through cyclone, ft^3/sec or ft^3/min
r	Radial position, ft
r'	Effective cyclone radius, $(D_c - B_c)/2$, ft
Re	Particle Reynolds number, dimensionless
r_i	Inlet radial position of particle, ft
r_o	Radius of the cyclone, ft
r_p	Particle radius, ft
S	Length outlet gas duct extends into cyclone, ft

S_c	Length outlet gas duct extends below inlet duct, ft
S_f	Cyclone separation factor
t	Time, sec (unless specified otherwise)
T	Absolute temperature
t_c	Time it takes for a particle to be captured, sec
t_r	Residence time of gas stream in cyclone, sec
t_{res}	Average residence time of a particle in cyclone, sec
V	Cyclone volume, ft^3
v_c	Average gas velocity in cyclone chamber, ft/sec
v_e	Exit velocity of gas leaving cyclone, ft/sec
v_i	Cyclone inlet velocity, ft/sec
V_{nl}	Volume of cyclone at natural length l, ft^3
v_p	Particle free fall velocity in a 1-g field, ft/sec
V_p	Particle volume, ft^3
v_r	Radial velocity component of the particle (normal to tangential component and normal to the axis), ft/sec
v_s	Suspension saltation velocity, (equals v_{so} at low loadings), ft/sec
V_s	Annular-shaped volume above exit duct to midlevel of extrance duct, ft^3
v_{so}	Single-particle saltation velocity, ft/sec
v_z	Vertical velocity component of the particle, ft/sec
v_{zG}	Vertical velocity component of the gas, ft/sec
v_ϕ	Tangential velocity component of the particle (tangent to gas spiral and normal to axis), ft/sec
$v_{\phi G}$	Tangential velocity component of the gas, ft/sec
$v_{\phi,o}$	Tangential velocity of particle at the cyclone wall, ft/sec
x_j	Inlet mass fraction for section j (equal to the mass entering section j divided by the total mass of particles entering the collector)
z	Vertical position, ft
Z	Vertical distance traveled by a particle entering the collector; determined from the describing trajectory equations, ft
Z_c	Height of cone portion of cyclone, ft
Δ	Constant equal to $[3\mu_G/4\, g\rho_G(\rho_p - \rho_G)]^{1/3}$, dimensionless
ϵ	Fraction voids in flowing gas solids mixture
ρ_G	Gas density, lb/ft^3
ρ_p	Particle density, lb/ft^3
$\eta(d_p)$	Collection efficiency for particle size d_p
η_j	Collection efficiency in inlet section j
η_T	Overall collection efficiency
μ_G	Gas viscosity, lb/(ft)(sec)
ϕ	Angular position, rad
Φ	Constant equal to $(4\, g\mu_G\,(\rho_p - \rho_G)/3\rho_G^2)^{1/3}$, dimensionless
ω	Angular velocity, rad/sec

PROBLEMS

1. The Air Correction Division of Universal Air Products, Inc. provides the fractional efficiency curves for three different cyclone types treating fly ash with the particle-size distribution described below.

Fly Ash Particle-size Distribution

Size range (μm)		% by wt
	+60	8.5
−60	+40	7.0
−40	+30	7.5
−30	+20	12.0
−20	+15	10.0
−15	+10	15.0
−10	+ 7.5	9.5
− 7.5		30.5
		100.0

If the inlet grain loading is 4 grains/ft^3 and the regulation requires 0.5 grains/ft^3, which cylone type will be adequate?

2. What will be the overall collection efficiency of a conventional 6-ft diameter cyclone (Figure 4.5.1) treating fly ash with a particle-size distribution as given in problem 1? The exhaust stream from the boiler is at 400°F and 1 atm. Use an inlet velocity of 50 ft/sec.

3. How many cyclones of the type used in problem 2 will be required to treat 135,000 ACFM?

4. The particle-size distribution of dust from a cement plant is given below.

Particle-size range (μm)	% by wt
0–2.5	15
2.5–5.0	8
5.0–10.0	12
10.0–20.0	13
20.0–30.0	17
30.0–40.0	14
40.0+	11

If a certain cyclone has a cut size of 9 μm, what will be the overall collection efficiency? Plot the fractional efficiency curve of this cyclone.

5. A conventional 5-ft diameter cyclone (Figure 4.5.1) is used to treat an 8,000 ACFM stream. Compare the pressure drop of a cyclone with vanes touching the outlet wall to one with no vanes. If the gas stream is increased by 20%, what effect would this have on the pressure drop?

6. The fractional efficiency curve for a particular cyclone has been found experimentally and is shown below. Determine the overall collection efficiency if the cyclone is treating fly ash with the same particle-size distribution as that in Example 4.5.11.

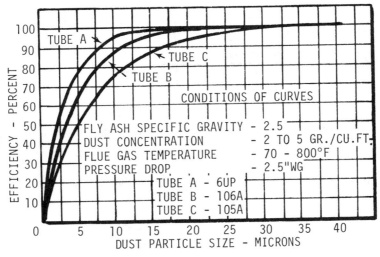

PROBLEM 1. UOP fractional efficiency curves.

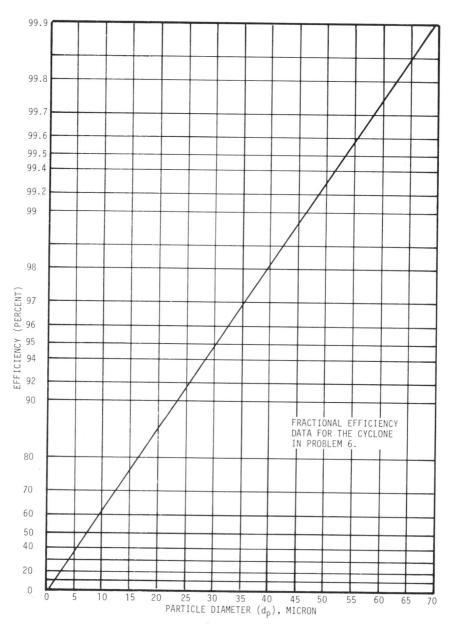

PROBLEM 6. Fractional efficiency data for cyclone.

7. The particle-size distribution of particles emitted from a municipal incinerator is given below.

Particle-size range (μm)	% by wt
0–2	17
2–4	5
4–10	8
10–15	3
15–20	3
20–30	5
30+	59

What is the overall collection efficiency if a conventional cyclone (Figure 4.5.1) with a cut size of 10 μm is used? If the maximum allowable pressure drop is 5 in. H_2O, what should be the dimentions of the cyclone?

8. A cyclone is achieving 90% efficiency on treating a gas stream (μ_G = 0.025 cp) containing 2 grains/ft^3 of dust (specific gravity = 2.8). A dust analysis test produced the following results.

Size range (μm)	Wt % collected	Wt % escaped
0–5	0.5	76.0
5–10	1.4	12.9
10–15	1.9	4.5
15–20	2.1	2.1
20–25	2.1	1.5
25–30	2.0	0.7
30–35	2.0	0.5
35–40	2.0	0.4
40–45	2.0	0.3
>45	84.0	1.1

a. Plot the fractional efficiency curve.
b. Determine the cut size.

9. In a particular operation, a cyclone is used to treat a gas stream containing 5,463 lb/hr of dust. If 1,525 lb/hr of dust escapes, what is the overall collection efficiency? Plot the fractional efficiency curve, given the following data.

Particle-size range (μm)	Size analysis, wt %	
	Inlet	Outlet
0–5	6.2	19.3
5–10	9.4	31.9
10–20	13.8	31.6
20–50	22.9	15.1
>50	47.7	2.1

REFERENCES

1. Rosin, P., Rammler, E., and Intelmann, W., *Z. Ver. Dtsch. Ing.*, 76, 433, 1932.
2. Lapple, C. E., *Chem. Eng.*, 58, 144, 1951.
3. Lapple, C. E. and Shepherd, C. B., *Ind. Eng. Chem.*, 31(8), 972, 1939.
4. Lapple, C. E., Dust and mist collection, in *Chemical Engineers' Handbook*, Perry, J. H., Ed., McGraw-Hill, New York, 1950.
5. Van Tongeran, H., *Mech. Eng.*, 57, 753, 1935.
6. Wallman, X., *Feuerungstechnik*, 26, 137, 1938.
7. Buonicore, A. J. and Theodore, L., A Study of Industrial Air Quality Control Methods for Particulates, Proc. 2nd Am. Environ. Eng. and Sci. Conf., Louisville, 1972, 573.
8. Buonicore, A. J. and Theodore, L., Monte Carlo Simulation To Predict Collection Efficiencies of Centrifugal Separators, 74th Natl. AIChE Meet., Paper No. 60 d, New Orleans, March 1973.
9. Leith, D. and Licht, W., The collection efficiency of cyclone type particle collectors — A new theoretical approach, *AIChE Symp. Ser.*, 68, 196, 1972.
10. Jotaki, T., *Trans. Jap. S.M.E.*, 23, 640, 1957.
11. Kalen, B. and Zenz, F. A., A Theoretical-empirical Approach To Saltation Velocity in Cyclone Design, Bulletin No. C-2071, The Ducon Company, 1973.
12. Zenz, F. A., *Ind. Eng. Chem. Fund.*, 3, 65, 1964.
13. Fiefel, E., *Forsch. Geb. Ingenieurwes.*, 9, 68, 1938; 10, 212, 1939.
14. Fiefel, E., *Arch. Waermewirtsch.*, 20, 15, 1939.
15. Perry, J. H., Ed., *Chemical Engineers' Handbook*, 4th ed., McGraw-Hill, New York, 1963, 68.
16. McCabe, W. L. and Smith, J. C., *Unit Operations of Chemical Engineering*, 2nd ed., McGraw-Hill, New York, 1967, 84, 162.
17. Theodore, L., *Transport Phenomena for Engineers*, International Textbook, Scranton, Pennsylvania, 1971.
18. Knudsen, J. and Katz, D., *Fluid Dynamics and Heat Transfer*, McGraw-Hill, New York, 1958, 69.
19. Kay, J. M., *An Introduction to Fluid Mechanics and Heat Transfer*, Cambridge University Press, New York, 1957, 66.
20. Strauss, W., *Industrial Gas Cleaning*, Pergamon Press, New York, 1966, Chap. 6.
21. Alexander, R., *Proc. Australas. Inst. Min. Eng.*, 152, 202, 1949.
22. Lissman, M. A., *Chem. Met. Eng.*, 37, 630, 1930.
23. Lapple, C. E., *Chem. Eng.*, 58(5), 145, 1951.
24. Air Pollution Engineering Manual, 999-AP-40, 1967, 91.
25. Gallaer, C. A. and Schindeler, J. W., *J. Air Pollut. Control Assoc.*, 13(5), 574, 1963.
26. Vatavuk, W. M., A Technique for Calculating Overall Efficiencies of Particulate Control Devices, EPA-450/2-73-002, U.S. Environmental Protection Agency, 1973.
27. Grove, D. J., Cyclones, in Control of Particulate Emissions, U.S. Environmental Protection Agency, 1971.
28. Sundberg, R. E., *J. Air Pollut. Control Assoc.*, 24(8), 758, 1974.
29. Byers, R. L., Gravitational and dry centrifugal collectors and air pollution control, in *Integrated Engineering Solutions to Overall Pollution Control: Air, Water and Solid Waste Problems*, AIChE, New York, 1971, Chap. 8.
30. Buonicore, A. J. and Theodore, L., Monte Carlo Simulation To Predict Cyclone Performance, 6th Annu. Pittsburgh Conf. on Modeling and Simulation, April 24–25, 1975.

Chapter 5

ELECTROSTATIC PRECIPITATORS

5.1. INTRODUCTION

Electrostatic precipitator technology was developed in the United States by Dr. Frederick Gardner Cottrell at the turn of the century. Cottrell's precipitator was successfully applied in 1907 to the collection of sulfuric acid mist and shortly thereafter proven in a number of ore processing, chemical, and cement plants.

Since Cottrell showed that the electrostatic precipitator could be used for the collection of industrial air contaminants, the use of such systems expanded into many diverse fields. Table 5.1.1 lists some of the early installations and applications,[1] while Table 5.1.2 lists some data that typify a modern electrostatic precipitator installation. Its effectiveness and versatility have contributed immensely to its popularity and widespread use.

With the advent of pulverized coal use in power plant boiler systems around 1924, electrostatic precipitators entered into an intimate association with the power industry. Their usefulness rested on the fact that pulverized coal-fired boilers generated large volumes of flue gas containing a significant proportion of very small dust particles (fly ash) which could not be removed by other more conventional collection devices of the day, such as settling chambers and inertial separators. About 80% of the fly ash particles from a typical pulverized coal-fired boiler are smaller than 30 μm. The problem of cleaning large flue gas volumes containing small particles became even more pronounced in the 1930s with the introduction of the cyclone furnace where typically 80% of the particulate matter released is smaller than 10 μm.

Alone among methods of particle collection, the electrostatic precipitator acts solely on the particles to be collected rather than on the entire gas stream. The gas flow through a precipitator

TABLE 5.1.1

Early Precipitator Installations

Application	Date	Location
Sulfuric acid mist from contact acid plant, 200 ACFM	1907	Pinole, California
Smelter, zinc and lead fumes, 300,000 ACFM	1910	Shasta Co., Balaklala, California
Cement kiln dust, 1 million ACFM	1912	Riverside, California
Copper converter (lead fume), 200,000 ACFM	1912	American Smelting and Refining Co., Garfield, Utah
Gold and silver recovery from furnace treatment of electrolytic copper slimes	1913	Raritan Copper Works, Perth Amboy, New Jersey
Absorption of chlorine gas by powdered lime followed by precipitator collection	1913	Hooker Electro-Chemical, Niagara Falls, New York
Dwight-Lloyd sintering machine lead fume, 20,000 ACFM	1914	International Smelting and Refining Co., Tooele, Utah
Tar removal from illuminating gas, 25,000 ACFM	1915	Portland, Oregon
Cleaning ventilating air in factory not recirculated, 55,000 ACFM	1915	Winchester Arms, New Haven, Connecticut
Paper pulp recovery of alkali salts from waste liquor evaporated gases, 90,000 ACFM	1916	Canada
Central gas cleaning plant, 2 million ACFM	1919	Anaconda Copper Smelting Company, Anaconda, Montana

TABLE 5.1.2

Typical Data on Electrostatic Precipitator Applications

Industry	Application	Gas flow range, ACFM	Temperature range, °F	Dust concentration range, grains/ft^3	Weight % of dust below 10 μm	Usual efficiency, %
Electric power	Fly ash-pulverized coal-fired boilers	50,000−750,000	270−600	0.40−5	25−75	98−99.6
Portland cement	Dust from kilns	50,000−1,000,000	300−750	0.50−15	35−75	85−99+
	Dust from dryers	30,000−100,000	125−350	1−15	10−60	95−99
	Mill ventilation	2,000−10,000	50−125	5−25	35−75	95−99
Steel	Cleaning blast furnace gas for fuel	20,000−100,000	100−150	0.02−0.5	100	95−99
	Collecting tars from coke-oven gases	50,000−200,000	100−150	0.10−1	100	95−99
	Collecting fume from open-hearth and electric furnaces	30,000−75,000	300−700	0.05−3	95	90−99
Nonferrous metals	Fume from kilns, roasters, sintering machines, aluminum pot lines, etc.	5,000−1,000,000	150−1,100	0.05−50	10−100	90−98
	Acid mist	See chemical industry				
Pulp and paper	Soda-fume recovery in kraft pulp mills	50,000−200,000	275−350	0.50−2	99	90−95
	Acid mist	See chemical industry				
Chemical	Acid mist	2,500−20,000	100−200	0.02−1	100	95−99
	Cleaning hydrogen, CO_2, SO_2, etc.	5,000−20,000	70−200	0.01−1	100	90−99
	Separate dust from vapor-ized phosphorus	2,500−7,500	500−600	0.01−1	30−85	99+
Petroleum	Powdered catalyst recovery	50,000−150,000	350−550	0.10−25	50−75	99−99.9
Rock products	Roofing, magnesite, dolomite, etc.	5,000−200,000	100−700	0.50−25	30−45	90−98
Gas	Tar from gas	2,000−50,000	50−150	0.01−0.2	100	90−98
Carbon black	Collecting and agglomer-ating carbon black	20,000−150,000	300−700	0.03−0.5	100	10−35[a]
Gypsum	Dust from kettles, con-veyors, etc.	5,000−20,000	250−350	1.50−5	95	90−98

[a]From Air Pollution Engineering Manual, AP-40, 2nd ed., U.S. Environmental Protection Agency, May 1973, 140.

takes place with little more pressure drop than would be experienced in an equivalent length of straight flue. Through the late 1930's and early 1940's, particle collection efficiency specifications of 94, 95, and 96 percent became common. In 1947 the first guarantee for an efficiency of 97.5% was made.[3] By 1973 individual specifications were as high as 99.8%. Progress from 90% collection efficiency in 1924 to 99% almost a half century later represents much more than an improvement of only 9%. Remember that air pollution discharge is not a result of what is removed from a contaminated flue gas stream; rather, it is a result of what is not removed. A control device of 90% efficiency, therefore, allows 10% of the fly ash to escape, while one of 99% efficiency allows only 1% to escape, a 10-fold reduction in air pollution. More recently, as efficiency requirements have risen to near the theoretical perfection level of 100%, it becomes increasingly difficult to achieve further advances. In a typical modern power plant application, achieving 99% efficiency, as opposed to 98%, requires extracting an extra 100,000th of a pound of ash from a cubic foot of gas that only contains about 1,000th of a pound of fly ash when it leaves the boiler. Nevertheless, the electrostatic precipitator continues to be a principal component in enabling particulate emission sources to comply with the strict air pollution control regulations of today and the even more restrictive regulations anticipated for the future.

5.2. DESCRIPTION OF EQUIPMENT

The electrostatic precipitator (ESP) may be classified as either a high-voltage, single-stage or low-voltage, two-stage system. The high-voltage type is by far the more popular; it has been used successfully to collect both solid and liquid particulate matter from many operations including smelters, steel furnaces, petroleum refineries, cement kilns, acid plants, municipal incinerators, and utility boilers. Low-voltage two-stage precipitators, on the other hand, are limited almost exclusively to the collection of liquid particles discharged from sources such as meat smoke-houses, asphalt paper saturators, pipe-coating machines, and high-speed grinding machines.

High-voltage, Single-stage ESP

The two major types of high-voltage ESP configurations currently used are tubular and plate. Tubular precipitators consist of cylindrical collection electrodes with discharge electrodes located on the axis of the cylinder, as schematically shown in Figure 5.2.1.a. A typical arrangement of a commercial tubular precipitator is shown in Figure 5.2.2. Gas to be cleaned flows around the outside of the cylindrical electrodes and up through the inside of the cylinders where precipitation takes place. The collected dust or liquid is removed from the bottom of the chamber. On occasion, hexagonal tubes (enabling closer packing) may be used to increase the amount of available collecting surface in a given volume. Tubular precipitators are often specified for mist or fog collection or where water flushing is used to remove collected material. Tube diameters typically vary from 0.5 to 1.0 ft, with lengths usually ranging from 6 to 15 ft.

The vast majority of electrostatic precipitators installed are of the plate type. Particles are collected on flat, parallel collecting surfaces spaced 8 to 12 in. apart, with a series of discharge electrodes spaced along the center line of adjacent plates, as shown schematically in 5.2.1.b. A typical arrangement of a commercial plate-type electrostatic precipitator is shown in Figure 5.2.3. The gas to be cleaned passes horizontally between the plates (horizontal-flow type) or vertically up through the plates (vertical-flow type). Collected particles are usually removed by rapping (dry precipitator) or in a liquid film (wet precipitator). They are generally deposited in bins or hoppers at the base of the precipitator (dry-bottom type) or in a liquid (wet-bottom type). Typical design parameters for plate-type precipitators are presented in Table 5.2.1.

The physical components of high-voltage electrostatic precipitators may be generally divided into three groups. The first group includes the discharge and collecting electrodes and their auxiliary parts. Modern precipitators use strong rigid collecting plates which are usually baffled in some manner. The baffling provides shielded air pockets which the dust falls through on its way to the dust hoppers after it is rapped loose from the collecting plates. The shielding also helps to keep the dust from being reentrained into the flue gas stream. Collecting plate auxiliaries include inlet and outlet gas ducts, electrode frames, rappers, supporting framework, dust hoppers, and protective outer shell. An enlargement of collecting plate surface area requires a proportionate expansion in these auxiliaries.

The discharge electrodes, which are almost always energized, provide the corona. Both positive and negative corona are used in industrial gas cleaning operations; however, the negative corona is most prevalent within the temperature range of most industrial applications. Positive and negative corona differ in several important aspects. In appearance, the positive corona is a rather uniform sheath surrounding the discharge electrode. In contrast, the negative corona appears as localized discharges from points on a clean wire and as localized tufts along the dust-coated electrode. The voltage-current characteristics of the negative corona are superior to those of the positive corona at the temperature at which most precipitators operate. Higher operating voltages and currents can be reached prior to disruptive sparking. Negative corona is accompanied by the generation of ozone; therefore, it is usually not used for cleaning air in inhabited space. However, most industrial gas cleaning operations use negative corona because of its inherently superior electrical characteristics which ultimately lead to better efficiencies.

The size and shape of the discharge electrodes are governed by the corona current and mechanical requirements of the system. Where high

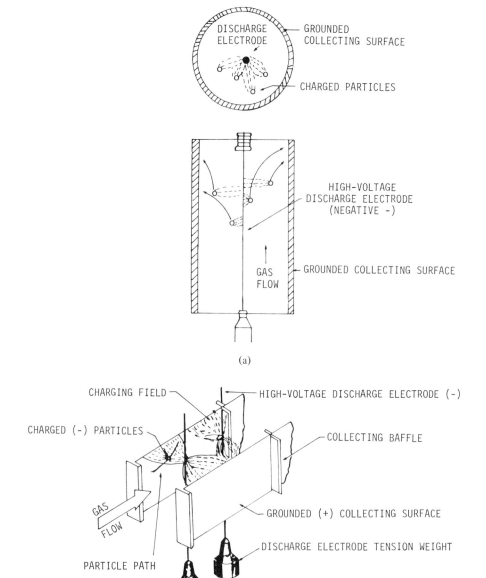

FIGURE 5.2.1. Collecting surface schematic for electrostatic precipitator. (a) Tubular-type precipitator. (b) Plate-type precipitator.

concentrations of fine dusts are encountered, space charge limits the current flow, especially in the inlet sections. In such cases, special electrodes that give higher currents may be used to achieve a high-power density within the inlet sections. Variation in the current flow and electric field is possible, within limits, by controlling the type and size of the discharge electrode. Weighted wire discharge electrodes, as illustrated in Figure

5.2.1.b, consist of vertically hung wires spanning the full height of the collecting electrodes. The wires are typically 0.1 to 0.15 in. in diameter; they are suspended from a support frame at the top and held taut by a weight at the bottom. The principal concern with the wire support is to minimize wire breakage due to mechanical fatigue. The discharge wires move under the influence of both aerodynamic and electrical forces; under severe condi-

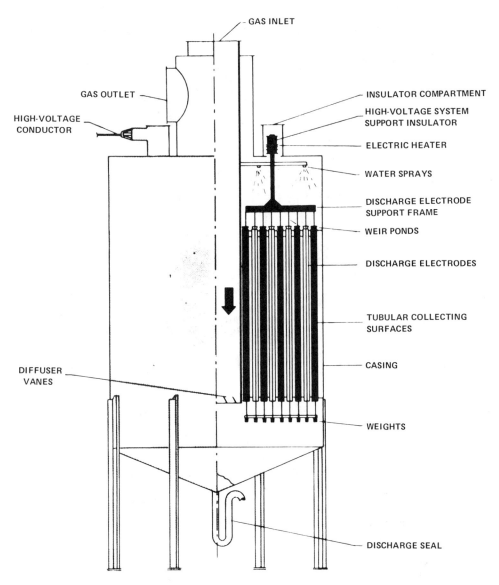

GAS INLET

GAS OUTLET

HIGH-VOLTAGE CONDUCTOR

INSULATOR COMPARTMENT

HIGH-VOLTAGE SYSTEM SUPPORT INSULATOR

ELECTRIC HEATER

WATER SPRAYS

DISCHARGE ELECTRODE SUPPORT FRAME

WEIR PONDS

DISCHARGE ELECTRODES

TUBULAR COLLECTING SURFACES

CASING

DIFFUSER VANES

WEIGHTS

DISCHARGE SEAL

FIGURE 5.2.2. Cross-sectional view of an irrigated tubular blast furnace electrostatic precipitator. (Courtesy of Environmental Elements Corporation, subsidiary of Koppers Company, Inc.)

tions, mechanical fatigue failure can occur. To minimize the fatigue problem, various methods of allowing some movement of the support have been attempted. Some manufacturers, noting the success of European designs, securely mount the discharge electrodes in pipe frames (typically 2 in. in diameter), with pipes welded horizontally at intervals (typically 5 ft) and x-bracing on both sides of each electrical field for added rigidity. Each frame of electrodes is supported from each end by an upper steel framework; this in turn, is supported by steel pipes (typically 2 in. in diameter) running through the centers of four

insulators. The four-point suspension of each electrical field, coupled with the frame construction, virtually eliminates any possibility of pendulum-type movement of the discharge electrode system which can occur with two points of suspension and weighted wires. A comparison of the rigidly supported vs. weighted-wire discharge electrode systems is presented in Figure 5.2.4.

Wires are also subjected to localized sparking regions of high field strength. Shrouds are sometimes used to give a larger diameter and, hence, low field strength in critical regions near the ends of the electrodes. Although twisted or barbed steel

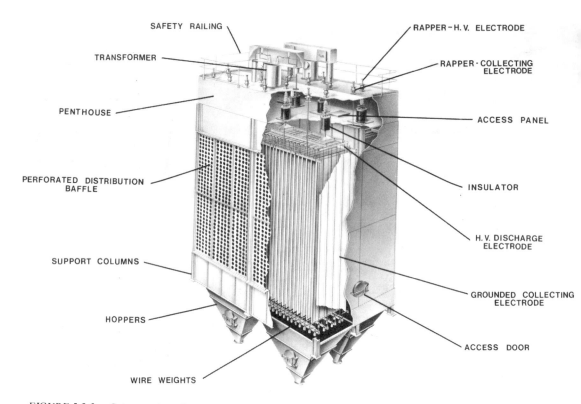

FIGURE 5.2.3. Cutaway view of a plate-type electrostatic precipitator. (Courtesy of UOP, Air Correction Division.)

TABLE 5.2.1

Typical Design Parameters for Electrostatic Precipitators

Parameter	Range of values
Precipitation rate (effective migration velocity)	0.1–0.7 ft/sec
Plate spacing	8–11 in.
Gas velocity	2–8 ft/sec
Plate height	12–45 ft
Plate length	0.5–2.0 times height
Applied voltage	30–75 kV
Corona strength	0.01–1.0 mA/ft of wire
Field strength	7–15 kV/in.
Residence (treatment) time	2–10 sec
Draft loss (pressure drop)	0.1–0.5 in. water
Efficiencies	to 99.9+%
Gas temperature	to 700°F (standard)
	1,000°F (high temperature)
	1,300°F (special)

wires are most common, discharge electrodes can have twisted rod, ribbon, and many other configurations. Some of these are illustrated in Figure 5.2.5. Steel alloys are usually used, although other materials (such as stainless steel, silver, aluminum, copper, lead-covered iron, Nichrome, Hastelloy®, and titanium alloy) have also been specified.

A wide variety of collecting electrode structures have been used in plate-type precipitators. The plates should be (1) designed to minimize reentrainment by scouring from the gas stream, (2) free of points or sharp edges that may cause sparking and reduction in the operating voltage, and (3) mechanically rigid and able to withstand the continuous rapping action. One of the causes

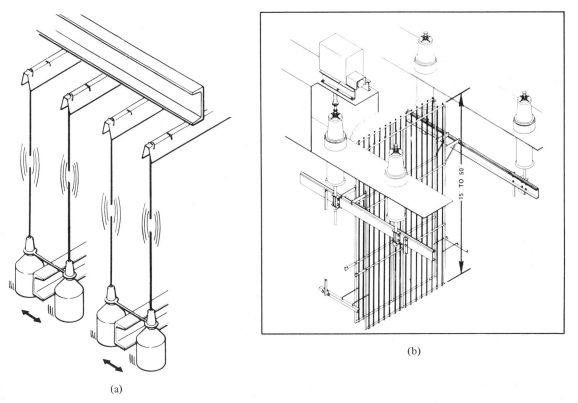

FIGURE 5.2.4. Discharge electrode comparison. (a) Suspension method utilizing free-hanging, weighted wires which, in certain situations, tend to oscillate due to "electric wind" and arc over to collecting surfaces. (b) Rigidly supported discharge electrode system. (Courtesy of Wheelabrator-Frye, Inc.)

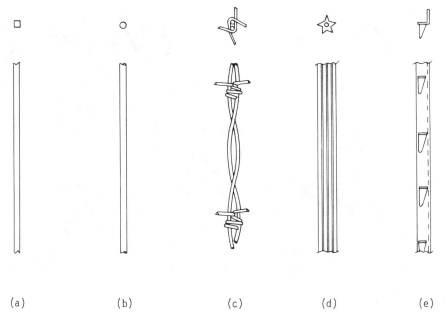

FIGURE 5.2.5. Various types of discharge electrodes: (a) square; (b) round; (c) barbed; (d) star; (e) punched ribbon.

of a drop in collection efficiency is turbulence (induced by the gas flow), which tends to reentrain particles already captured on the collecting surface. Figure 5.2.6 shows the effect that collection electrode configuration can have on the enhancement of turbulence. Recently, the use of smooth plates, with fins to strengthen them and to produce quiescent zones, has become common. Some of the various types of collecting electrodes available are illustrated in Figure 5.2.7. Essentially all tubular collecting surfaces are standard pipe.

The purpose of the protective outer shell is to confine the gas flow for proper exposure to the electrodes, to avoid excessive heat loss, and to provide structural support for the electrodes and rapping equipment. The shell is normally rectangular if plate electrodes are used or cylindrical if tubular electrodes are used. Shell material is usually steel; however, corrosion problems may warrant the use of shells constructed of or lined with tile, brick, concrete, or special corrosion-resistant steels. If the gases contain corrosive materials, insulation is usually required to maintain the shell at a temperature above the dew point. Gas diffuser plates can be provided as part of the shell to improve gas flow. Roof and wall baffles are used to minimize the amount of gas which may bypass the electrodes.

The second group of physical components includes all the electrical components of the precipitator needed for generating and controlling the high-voltage, direct-current corona: transformer rectifiers, various pieces of voltage control equipment, and high-voltage conductors. High-voltage electrostatic precipitators operate on direct current, with voltages ranging from 30 to 100 kV (peak). The precipitators are usually equipped for automatic power control, with electrical power energization and control equipment furnished in the form of several packaged units complete with instrumentation. Transformers, used to provide the high-voltage current, are usually oil cooled and integrally connected to silicon rectifiers. The transformer single-phase output may be rectified to either double half-wave or full-wave direct current.

Recently, for increased performance and reliability, precipitators have been divided into a number of independently energized bus sections. Each bus section has its own transformer rectifier, voltage stabilization controls, and high-voltage conductors which energize the discharge electrodes within that section. The main advantage of sectionalization is to offset the dampening effects on corona power input of heavy flue-gas dust loadings. These heavy flue-gas dust loadings occur

**CONTROLLED TURBULENCE
AND QUIESCENT AREA
RESULTING IN MINIMAL
RE-ENTRAINMENT OF DUST**

**CONSIDERABLE TURBULENCE
WITH DUST
RE-ENTRAINMENT
IN THE GAS STREAM**

FIGURE 5.2.6. Areas of turbulence and quiescence in various types of collection electrodes. (Courtesy of Wheelabrator-Frye, Inc., Air Pollution Control Division.)

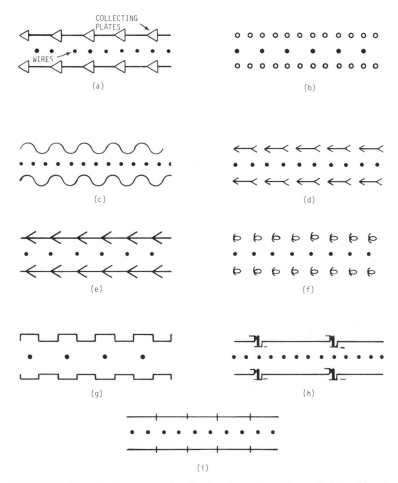

FIGURE 5.2.7. Various types of collection electrodes: (a) opzel plate; (b) rod curtain; (c) zig-zag plate; (d) vee pocket; (e) vee plates; (f) channel; (g) offset plates; (h) shielded plate; (i) expanded metal.

mainly in the inlet sections of a precipitator. By sectionalization, corona power input and particle charging can be increased in the inlet sections, thereby raising overall precipitator collection efficiency.

The third group of components needed for precipitation is external to the precipitator itself; this includes fans for moving the flue gas through the precipitator and equipment used for the removal and disposal of particulate matter discharged from the precipitator hoppers.

Low-voltage, Two-stage ESP

Low-voltage, two-stage electrostatic precipitators were originally designed for air purification in conjunction with air conditioning systems (they are also referred to as electronic air filters). As an industrial collector, the unit is primarily used for the control of finely divided liquid particles, which will readily drain from the collector plates. Difficulty is usually encountered in controlling solid or sticky materials, and the collector often becomes ineffective at dust loadings above 0.4 grains per standard cubic foot (SCF). This has been a deterrent to widespread use of two-stage precipitators in air pollution control applications.

The low-voltage precipitator (schematically shown in Figure 5.2.8) is distinguished from the high-voltage type by the separate ionizing zone located ahead of the collection plates. The ionizing stage (first stage) consists of a series of fine (0.007 in. in diameter) positively charged wires equally spaced 1 to 2 in. from parallel grounded tubes or rods. A corona discharge between each wire and a corresponding tube charges the particles suspended in the air flowing through the ionizer.

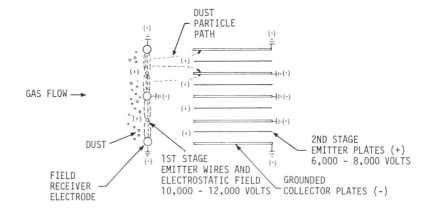

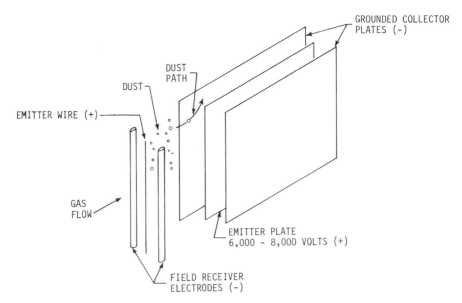

FIGURE 5.2.8. Operating principle of two-stage electrostatic precipitator.

The direct-current potential applied to the wires amounts to 12 or 13 kV. Positive polarity is regularly used to minimize ozone formation. The second stage consists of parallel metal plates usually less than 1 in. apart. In some designs alternate plates are charged positively and negatively, each in a potential of 6 or 6.5 kV of direct current, so that the potential difference between adjacent plates is 12 or 13 kV. In other cases plates are alternately charged to a positive potential of 6 to 13 kV and grounded. This arrangement is shown in Figure 5.2.8. The illustration shows particles entering at the left, receiving a positive charge in the ionizer, and being collected at the negative plates in the second stage. Liquids drain by gravity to a pan located beneath the plates. Rapping or shaking is not usually employed, primarily because of the close spacing.

5.3. THE PRECIPITATION PROCESS

The process of electrostatic precipitation consists of corona formation around a high-tension wire, with particle charging by ionized gas molecules formed in the localized region of electrical breakdown surrounding the high-tension wire. This is followed by migration of the charged particles to the collecting electrodes. Finally, the particles collected from the collecting electrode are removed. Since these aspects have been the subject of extensive treatment in the literature,[4-8,10] a comprehensive discussion in this section is not warranted. Only some of the more pertinent points are discussed below.

Corona is a gas discharge phenomenon associated with the ionization of gas molecules by electron collision in regions of high electric field strength. As the potential difference between the electrodes is raised, the gas near the more sharply curved electrode breaks down at a voltage less than the spark-breakdown value for the gap length in question. This incomplete breakdown, called corona, appears in air as a highly active region of glow (bluish white or possibly reddish in color) extending into the gas a short distance beyond the discharge electrode surface. The process of corona generation requires a nonuniform electric field, which is obtained by the use of a small-diameter wire as one electrode (discharge electrode) and a plate or cylinder as the other electrode (collecting electrode). The application of a high voltage to this electrode configuration results in a high electric field near the wire. The electric field decreases inversely with the square of the radius from the wire surface. The corona process is initiated by the presence of electrons in the high field region near the wire. Electrons for corona initiation are supplied from natural radiation or other sources. Since they are in a region of high electric field, they are accelerated to high velocities; they possess sufficient energy so that on impact with gas molecules in the region, they release orbital electrons from gas molecules. The additional free electrons are also accelerated and join the ionization process. This avalanche process continues until the electric field decreases to the point where the electrons released do not acquire enough energy for ionization.[4]

In the region where ionization is taking place, defined by the corona glow discharge, there are free electrons and positive ions resulting from electron impact ionization. The behavior of these charged particles depends on the polarity of the electrodes. The corona is termed negative corona (if the discharge electrode is negative) or positive corona (if positive). In the case of a negative discharge wire, free electrons in the high-field zone near the wire gain enough energy from the field to produce positive ions and other electrons by collision. These new electrons are, in turn, accelerated and produce further ionization, thus giving rise to the cumulative process termed an electron avalanche. The positive ions formed in this process are accelerated toward the wire. By bombarding the negative wire and giving up relatively high energies in the process, the positive ions cause the ejection of secondary electrons, necessary for maintaining the discharge, from the wire surface. In addition, high-frequency radiation ori-

ginating in the excited gas molecules within the corona envelope may photoionize surrounding gas molecules, likewise contributing to the supply of secondary electrons. Electrons of whatever provenance are attracted toward the anode; as they move into the weaker electric field away from the wire, they tend to form negative ions by attachment to neutral oxygen molecules. These ions form a dense unipolar cloud filling, by far, most of the interelectrode volume; they constitute the only current in the entire space outside the region of corona glow. The effect of this space charge is to retard the further emission of negative charge from the corona, limiting the ionizing field near the wire and stabilizing the discharge. However, as the voltage is progressively raised, complete breakdown of the gas dielectric (i.e., sparkover) eventually occurs.[10] As a rule, in industrial applications the optimum spark rate for maximum efficiency occurs somewhere between 50 to 150 sparks per minute per electrical set.

In positive corona the electrons generated by the avalanche process flow toward the collection electrode. Since the positive ions are the charge carriers, they serve to provide an effective space charge, and the presence of an electronegative gas is not required.

Electrode geometry, gas composition, and gas conditions have important influences on corona generation. In general, the smaller diameter wire requires a higher electric field strength for corona initiation. For a given spacing, however, the onset of corona occurs at a lower voltage for a smaller diameter wire. Also, for a given voltage, higher currents are obtained with smaller diameter discharge electrodes. Temperature and pressure also influence corona generation by changing the gas density. In the avalanche process, the time available for accelerating an electron between collisions is a function of gas density. With increased molecular spacing, higher velocities can be achieved between collisions. Thus, ionizing energy can be achieved with low electric fields for low gas densities.

When gases laden with suspended particulate matter are passed through an electrostatic precipitator, the great bulk of the particles acquire an electric charge of the same polarity as that of the discharge electrodes. This preferential charging occurs because the region of corona, (i.e., the region of intensive ion-pair generation) is limited to the immediate vicinity of a discharge wire, thus occupying only a small fraction of the total cross section of the precipitator.

Two distinct particle-charging mechanisms are generally considered to be active in electrostatic precipitation: (1) bombardment of the particles by ions moving under the influence of the applied electric field (field-dependent charging) and (2) attachment of ionic charges to the particles by ion diffusion in accordance with the laws of kinetic theory (diffusion charging).

Particles in an electric field cause localized distortion of the field so that electric field lines intersect the particles. Ions present in the field tend to travel in the direction of maximum voltage gradient, which is along the electric field lines. Thus, ions will be intercepted by the dust particles, resulting in a net charge flow to the particle. The ion will be held to the dust particle by an induced image charge force between the ion and dust particle. As additional ions collide with and are held to the particle, it becomes sufficiently charged to divert the electric field lines so that they do not intercept it. Under this condition, no ions contact the dust particle, and it receives no further charge. The electrostatic theory of the process shows that the saturation value of the charge on the particle is related to the magnitude of the electric field in the region where charging takes place, particle size and particle dielectric constant. The saturation charge is proportional to the square of the particle diameter. Thus, larger particles are more easily collected than small ones. This mechanism of charging is called field-dependent charging.

For small particles (diameter less than 0.2 μm), the field-dependent charging mechanism is less important, and collision between the particles and gas ions is governed primarily by thermal motion of the ion. As the charge on a particle increases, the probability of impact decreases, so that there is a decreasing charging rate associated with an increasing particle charge. This second charging process is called diffusion charging. Since the range of thermal velocities has no upper boundary, there is no saturation value associated with diffusion charging.

Field charging is the dominant mechanism for large particles with a diameter greater than about 0.5 μm, while diffusion charging predominates for small particles with diameters less than approximately 0.2 μm. In the intermediate range, both mechanisms contribute significant charge and,

therefore, must be considered simultaneously. For the range of particle sizes encountered in most industrial applications, charging by ion bombardment (field-dependent charging) predominates. An expression developed for particle charging, considering both field-dependent and diffusion charging, is given below in differential form.[9]

$$\frac{dq}{dt} = \frac{N_o e\, b q_s}{4\,\epsilon_o} \left[1 - \frac{q}{q_s} \right]^2 + \pi r^2 e\, \bar{v}\, N_o \exp \left[-\frac{qe}{4\pi\epsilon_o rkT} \right]$$

(5.3.1)

where

q = charge, C;
N_o = free ion density, no./m^3;
e = electronic charge, C;
ϵ_o = permittivity of free space, C^2/N-m^2;
b = ion mobility, m^2/V-sec;
$\bar{v}$ = mean thermal speed of ions, m/sec;
r = particle radius, m;
k = Boltzmann's constant, J/$^\circ$K;
T = temperature, $^\circ$K;
t = time, sec;
q_s = saturation charge.

In Equation 5.3.1, the first term on the left-hand side represents the contribution from field charging, and the second term represents that from diffusion charging.

The maximum charge, q_s, a spherical particle can obtain is shown to be given by

$$q_s = 4\pi\epsilon_o p\, r^2 E_c$$

(5.3.2)

with

$$p = 2[(K - 1)/(K + 2)] + 1$$

(5.3.3)

where

ϵ_o = permittivity of free space; 8.86×10^{-12} F/m;
r = particle radius, m;
E_c = charging electric field, V/m;
K = relative dielectric constant of the particle

The local or instantaneous particle charge, q, is a function of time, t, but can be related to the maximum charge.

$q = q_s [t/(t + \tau)]$

where

τ = the particle-charging time constant.

Since τ is extremely small in practice,

$q \approx q_s$

In addition, the dielectric constant may be almost an order of magnitude greater than unity; for most materials, however, it ranges from 2.0 to 8.0. Thus, the value of p may vary from 1.5 to 2.40, with an average value of approximately 2.0. In the limit when $K \to \infty$, p = 3, as in Equation 5.3.3. The electrostatic force, F_E, experienced by a charged particle in an electric field is given by

$$F_E = qE_p \qquad (5.3.4)$$

where

E_p = the collection field intensity.

As mentioned previously, small particles are more difficult to collect than large ones. This is true for several reasons. First, smaller particles absorb smaller corona charges (charging is proportional to the radius). This means that charged particles of a small size must come closer to the collecting plates than larger particles if they are going to be attracted to the collecting plates. Second, smaller sized particles tend to build up on the wire discharge electrodes. When this happens, corona current is suppressed by an effective increase in the discharge electrode diameter and by the voltage drop due to current flowing through a resistive dust layer.

The fundamentals of particle collection in an electrostatic precipitator are considered in the following section.

5.4. FUNDAMENTALS OF PARTICLE COLLECTION

Fundamental electrostatic theory establishes that a force will act on a charged particle under the influence of an electric field. The magnitude of this force is dependent on the charge on the particle and the electric field strength. The direction of the force depends on the polarity of the

particle charge and the direction of the electric field. Both electrostatic and aerodynamic forces act on the particles. For particles smaller than approximately 10 μm in diameter, the motion of the gas stream (aerodynamic forces) may completely determine the particle trajectory through the precipitator. Near the collection plate gas turbulence is reduced, and electrostatic forces predominate.[4] Most of the existing theories of particle collection have been built upon the probability of an individual particle entering this region where the electrostatic forces result in its deposition on the collection surface.

On entering the precipitator, the particles become highly charged within a fraction of a second and begin migrating toward the grounded collecting surface. This electrical attraction is opposed by inertial and friction forces, but may be reinforced by electric wind effects. A number of other forces also act upon the charged particles. Random forces are set up by collisions between neutral gas molecules and the negative and/or positive ions driven by the electrical field. This creates general turbulence in the gas stream itself and leads to some mixing of the charged particles. Unfortunately, it has been theorized that a dust particle in the turbulent flow gas stream, even though it is negatively charged, will be pushed about randomly by the turbulence in most of the space between the discharge electrode and collecting plate; it will only be captured when it wanders into a narrow band which is in very close proximity to the collecting plates. It is further concluded that in this narrow band electrical attraction between the charged particle and the grounded collecting plate dominates any counter forces of gas turbulence; as a result, the particle is captured by the collecting plate. This is discussed further below, along with the details of the capture process.

Collection Efficiency Models

Industrial calculations of collection efficiency for electrostatic precipitators almost always involve the use of the Deutsch-Anderson model. The Deutsch equation, as it is more commonly known, can be derived in the following manner. Consider a tubular precipitator of cross section A_c, perimeter S, and length L, as illustrated in Figure 5.4.1. Subdivide the precipitator pipe into n equal wafer slope sections, where

$n = L/z$

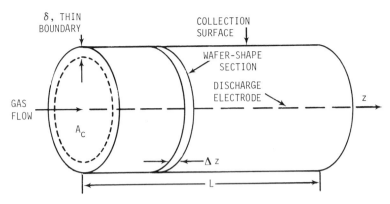

FIGURE 5.4.1. Tubular precipitator for a derivation of the Deutsch equation.

A particle entering the precipitator may be captured in any one of these sections or may travel the complete length of the precipitator without being captured.

The following assumptions can be made.

1. Particle charging time is negligible.

2. Particle migration velocity is constant for all particles and is large compared with the average bulk flow gas velocity near the collecting surface.

3. There is uniform particle concentration at any cross section of the precipitator.

4. There is uniform bulk flow velocity of the gas through the precipitator, except for boundary regions near the collecting surface.

5. There are no disturbing effects such as particle reentrainment, particle-particle interactions, and back corona.

These assumptions guarantee that a particle has an equal probability of capture in any of the n sections.

In the thin boundary region of thickness δ, the gas flow will be laminar because of the friction between the gas stream and the wall. Consequently, the resultant velocity for a dust particle will be the vector sum of the gas velocity, v, and the particle migration velocity to the collection surface, w. Therefore, in an increment of time, Δt, all the dust particles in zone δ will be driven to the collection surface if $\delta = w(\Delta t)$. During the same time interval, the gas stream will have moved through the precipitator a distance of $\Delta z = v(\Delta t)$ where v is the average gas velocity. The effective thickness of the boundary capture ring is, therefore, $\delta = w(\Delta t) = w(\Delta z)/v$. The probability of particle capture, P, is then just the probability of

being in a boundary capture ring of this thickness, i.e.,

$$P = \frac{S\delta}{A_c} = \frac{Sw\Delta z}{A_c v} = \frac{SwL}{A_c v n} \tag{5.4.1}$$

It follows that the probability of escape within each wafer section is

$$P_n = 1 - \frac{SwL}{A_c v n} \tag{5.4.2}$$

and that the probability of escape through the entire precipitator is

$$P = (P_n)^n = \left[1 - \frac{SwL}{A_c v n}\right]^n \tag{5.4.3}$$

Taking the limit, Equation 5.4.3 can be rewritten as

$$\lim_{n\to\infty} (P_n)^n = \lim_{n\to\infty} \left(1 - \frac{SwL}{A_c v n}\right)^n = e^{-\frac{SL}{A_c v}w} \tag{5.4.4}$$

SL is the total collecting area of the pipe, A, and $A_c v$ is the gas flow rate, Q. By substitution, the collection efficiency, η, is, therefore,

$$\eta = [1 - e^{-\frac{A}{Q}w}] \, 100 \tag{5.4.5}$$

Although derived for a tubular precipitator, the above equation can be directly applied to a plate precipitator, with the term A representing the collection area of the plates.

Further light can be shed on the precipitation

process, based on the above model, by considering the equation for particle migration velocity. The electrostatic force acting on a particle results in the lateral motion of the particle to the grounded electrode. The equation describing this motion is obtained by a force balance on this single particle.

$$F = F_E - F_D \qquad (5.4.6)$$

F is the net or resultant force that is given by Newton's law.

$$F = m\alpha = m(dw/dt) \qquad (5.4.7)$$

where

α = particle acceleration;
m = mass of particle.

F_E is the electrostatic force, defined by

$$F_E = qE_p \qquad (5.4.8)$$

F_D is the drag force on the particle. If Stokes' law is assumed to apply,

$$F_D = 6\,\pi\mu r w \qquad (5.4.9)$$

Substituting Equations 5.4.7 to 5.4.9 into Equation 5.4.6 gives

$$m(dw/dt) = q\,E_p - 6\,\pi\mu r w \qquad (5.4.10)$$

Rearranging this equation and integrating subject to the initial conditions (IC)

w = 0, t = 0

yields the following:

$$w = [q\,E_p/6\,\pi\mu r]\,[1 - e^{-(6\,\pi\mu r/m)t}] \qquad (5.4.11)$$

The term $(m/6\pi r\mu)$ denotes the time constant τ of the motion. The velocity, w, essentially reaches its terminal value within five time constants. Thus, the relative residence times necessary for various particle sizes to acquire a terminal velocity can be determined.

$$\tau = \frac{m}{6\,\pi r\mu} = \left[\frac{2\,\rho_p}{9\,\mu}\right] r^2, \text{ sec} \qquad (5.4.12)$$

Actual residence times for particles in a precipitator typically range from 2 to 10 sec.

Since

$$w = dy/dt$$

Equation 5.4.11 can be integrated so that

$$y = At + (A/B)e^{-Bt} - (A/B) + y_0 \qquad (5.4.13)$$

where

A = $qE_p/6\pi\mu r$;
B = $6\pi\mu r/m$;
y_0 = initial lateral position of the particle;
y = lateral position of the particle at time t.

White[6] and Theodore[11] have shown that the acceleration incurred by a particle immediately after it is charged can be neglected under normal operating conditions. It can also be seen from Equation 5.4.12 that for particles up to about 0.5 μm in diameter, the acceleration time is short compared to the residence time in the collector. The larger particles (greater than 50 μm) are generally collected entirely, and the residence time for smaller particles is long compared to the acceleration time; therefore, the exponential part of Equation 5.4.11 can normally be neglected. This is equivalent to ignoring the Newtonian acceleration force. Equation 5.4.11 then becomes

$$w \approx q\,E_p/6\,\pi r\mu \qquad (5.4.14)$$

Equation 5.4.5 may, therefore, be written in the following form:

$$\eta = [1 - e^{-(A/Q)(q\,E_p/6\,\pi\mu r)}]\,100 \qquad (5.4.15)$$

Equation 5.4.15 indicates that any change which suppresses corona current, such as build-up of small dust particles on the discharge electrodes or excessive sparking and back corona due to highly resistive dust, will reduce q and hence w. Consequently, the probability of particle capture, loosely speaking, will decrease. This reduces overall precipitator collection efficiency. On the other hand, any event which increases corona charging, such as increased useful corona power, will increase q and w and raise precipitator collection efficiency.

A rather substantial difference between this theory and actual practice has been observed.[6,12-14] There are many drawbacks to the theory and the final form of the describing equation. Some of the effects not included in the analysis are as follows.

1. The particle-concentration distribution through the cross section of the precipitator. The Deutsch equation assumes that since industrial units operate in the turbulent flow regime, perfect mixing occurs, resulting in a uniform particle concentration.

2. Particle-size distribution. One characteristic size is assumed to represent the distribution of this parameter.

3. Particle-size distribution variation through the cross section of the precipitator.

4. Electrostatic force distribution and its variation in the precipitator.

5. Drag force dependency on particle Reynolds number.

6. The Cunningham correction factor for "small" particles.

7. Bulk flow velocity variation through the cross section of the precipitator.

Perhaps the main drawback can be attributed to item 1 above, since it is unreasonable to apply one-phase turbulent flow theory to a two-phase medium, i.e., the inertia of the particle should not be neglected. Many outstanding researchers have unfortunately concluded that due to the statistical nature of the derivation of the Deutsch-Anderson model, the equation is not subject to assumption 1. A careful review of Deutsch's original work and White's statistical derivation indicates that both derivations are subject to this assumption. Earlier investigations[15,16] have shown that the inertia of the particle should not be neglected, and the fluctuation velocities of the particle, perpendicular to the direction of bulk flow, should not be absent. The particle trajectory is, therefore, deterministic; an exponential efficiency equation, similar to the Deutsch-Anderson model, will not accurately describe the nature of the precipitation process — except perhaps for very fine particles. Since the mass represented by these fine particles is a small fraction of the total mass, it is unlikely that an overall efficiency equation would be given by an exponential relationship.

On those occasions when the engineer finds it necessary to perform statistical analyses of experimental data, he usually has little or no knowledge of the form of the describing equation. Therefore, he is often more interested in obtaining information on (1) how good a proposed model is, rather than (2) how good the data fit the proposed model or obtaining the best fit of the data to the model. A least-squares analysis, or the equivalent, provides *no* information for answering the first statement; an analysis of variance (if possible) must be performed to answer this. Researchers and design engineers in the precipitator field have always assumed that the Deutsch equation applies. It has yet to be subjected to a rigorous statistical analysis; only least-squares studies have been performed. For example, consider the final form of the Deutsch equation.

$$\eta = 1 - e^{-Aw/Q} \tag{5.4.16}$$

$$1 - \eta = e^{-Aw/Q} \tag{5.4.17}$$

Taking the log of both sides of the above equation yields:

$$\ln(1 - \eta) = -w(A/Q) \tag{5.4.18}$$

which is an equation of the form

$$Y = (B)(X) \tag{5.4.19}$$

where

$$Y = \ln(1 - \eta);$$
$$B = -w;$$
$$X = A/Q.$$

Assume (η, A, Q) data are available. If a least squares calculation is performed on the data to the above model, one obtains a value of w resulting in a "best" fit of the data to the model. There will be deviation between the experimental data and the predicted values from the model since *a* measurements are subject to experimental error. Suppose that the *true* relationship between Y and X *is* a straight line. Then the failure of the experimental values to lie directly along this line must be solely a function of the experimental errors: metering errors, reading errors, and multiplicity of other errors almost impossible to enumerate. A measure of this experimental error provided by the differences between the exper mental values and the values predicted by the equation with the calculated value of w. Suppose, however, that the true relationship is *not* a straight line, which undoubtedly is the case with the Deutsch equation. The differences between the calculated values from the model and the experimental values are now the result of two factors: the experimental error and the *selection of an incorrect model* (describing equation). The question now arises: "How can one determine if the failure of the calculated values to equal the experimental values is a function of experimental errors *and* an inadequate model"? Very simply, the answer is to obtain an estimate of the experimental error that is independent of the proposed model. Independent estimates of experimental error are obtained by *repeating* experiments and/or from values of the dependent variable, η, at fixed values of the independent variable, A/Q. This estimate will then provide an answer to the above question. The reader is referred to any one of several recent statistics texts for the details of this "analysis of variance" calculation. Although it is a rather standard mathematical tool employed by researchers and process engineers, the Deutsch equation has somehow managed to survive this test — perhaps due to the lack of (or unwillingness on the part of industry to part with) meaningful operating data and information.

More recently, Theodore et al.[17-20] presented a mathematical model and its solution which more realistically describes the behavior of particles in an electrostatic precipitator and predicts collection efficiency. A statistical technique using random numbers (similar to that presented in Chapters 3 and 4) is employed to deal with some of the more significant system variables not previously treated in the literature. These include the particle-size distribution as a function of inlet position, particle-mass flow rate gradient, gas velocity profile, and the particle electrostatic force distribution as a function of particle size and inlet position. The calculated results for collection efficiencies are in reasonable agreement with the limited experimental data available in the literature. Variation of precipitator geometry and electrostatic force produced results that are in qualitative agreement with what one would expect; it was found that for a given efficiency, the drift velocity in the model differs considerably from that calculated by the Deutsch-Anderson

method. A substantial difference was found between collection efficiencies that are calculated using particles of a single characteristic size and those calculated assuming a distribution of sizes. The model has also been employed to generate performance curves[21] for 12 industries using electrostatic precipitators. These include the electric power, cement, pulp and paper, steel, chemical, and petroleum industries.

The methods of Vatavuk[27] and Sundberg,[28] as discussed previously, may also be applied to estimate overall collection efficiency in electrostatic precipitators under the appropriate circumstances. The procedure is analogous to that described for gravity settlers and cyclones.

Energy and Power Requirements

Before concluding this section on fundamentals, another important consideration — the calculation of energy and power requirements — will be briefly discussed.

The energy in the form of work, W, required to move a particle experiencing an electrostatic force, F_E, through a distance, s, is given by

$$W = F_E s$$

It can be assumed that the particle is moving at its terminal settling velocity, so that

$$F_E = F_D$$

If Stokes' law applies

$$F_D = 6 \pi \mu r w$$

then

$$W = 6 \pi \mu r w s \qquad (5.4.20)$$

This represents the work requirement per particle, subject to the assumptions above. If n such particles are contained in a cubic foot of gas to be processed, the work expended per cubic foot of gas becomes

$$W/ft^3 = 6 \pi r w s n \mu \qquad (5.4.21)$$

By definition, the power, P, is given by the product of the applied voltage, V, and the current, I.

$$P = VI \qquad (5.4.22)$$

Typical (V, i) data[6] include:

for $V = 30$ kV, $i \approx 0.01$ mA/ft

for $V = 75$ kV, $i \approx 1.0$ mA/ft

where

i = the current per foot of wire.

This apparently suggests a logarithmic relationship between V and I, since as V is approximately doubled, the current increases by a factor of $(10)^2$. If H is the height of the wire and n is the number of wires in the precipitator, the current is then given by

$$I = niH \qquad (5.4.23)$$

If V is in volts and I is in amperes, the unit of power is watts.

Unfortunately, the energy and power requirement for electrostatic precipitators is substantially higher than that predicted by the equations above. Soo[26] has recently investigated power requirements for typical control devices, including the electrostatic precipitator, and has shown that there are possibilities for substantial power savings.

5.5. DESIGN PRINCIPLES

Electrostatic precipitator design and specification involve many parameters that must be taken into consideration. The more important ones are summarized in Table 5.5.1. Design methodology in this section will focus on those parameters which must be specified to achieve the desired collection efficiency.

The goal in precipitator design and operation should be an economic balance between collecting plate area and power input, with consideration given to other performance determinants such as resistivity and other particle characteristics. The interrelationship among collecting plate area, power input, and these performance determinants is discussed below.

The approach taken by industry to size electrostatic precipitators for various applications makes use of a modified form of the Deutsch-Anderson equation.

TABLE 5.5.1

Design Factors Requiring Consideration for Electrostatic Precipitator Specification

1. Collection electrodes: type, size (area), mounting, and mechanical and aerodynamic properties
2. Discharge electrodes: type, size, spacing, and method of support
3. Shell: dimensions, insulation requirements, and access
4. Rectifier sets: ratings, automatic control system, number, instrumentation, and monitoring provisions
5. Rappers for corona and collecting electrodes: type, size, range of frequency and intensity settings, number, and arrangement
6. Hoppers: geometry, size, insulation requirements, number, and location
7. Hopper dust removal system: type, capacity, protection against air inleakage, and dust blowback
8. Inlet and outlet gas duct arrangements, gas handling, and distribution system
9. Degree of sectionalization
10. Support insulators for high-tension frames: type, number, and reliability

$$\eta = 1 - \exp\,(-wA/Q) \qquad (5.5.1)$$

In Equation 5.5.1 the term w, formerly the particle migration velocity, now represents the effective migration velocity or precipitation rate parameter which is selected on the basis of experience with a particular dust. Precipitator manufacturers usually have a specific experience from which precipitation rate parameters can be selected for various applications and conditions. Average values of precipitation rate parameters for various applications, and the range of values that might be expected, are presented in Table 5.5.2. Since the desired collection efficiency (η) and gas flow rate (Q) are usually specified, the required collecting area (A) can be determined once an appropriate precipitation rate parameter (w) has been chosen.

The power required for a particular application is usually determined on an empirical basis, with past experience playing the key role. Performance curves for a given application typically relate power requirements to the efficiency and gas volume handled. The degree of sectionalization required is also determined on an empirical basis. Performance curves for a given application have been developed to show the variation in collection efficiency with the number of independently powered bus sections.

The type and number of rappers for the collecting and discharge electrodes depend on the properties of the dust and gas, the current densities, and the configuration of the electrodes and electrode support structures. High-resistivity dust is usually more difficult to remove because of the increased force holding it to the plate. Dust thickness build-up of 0.5 to 1.0 in. prior to dislodging is common. Typical rapper accelerations range from 10 to 100 g. With fly ash, for example, accelerations of 10 to 30 g's may be satisfactory, while highly resistive dust (difficult to remove) may require accelerations as high as 200 g's. Table 5.5.3 shows the number of rappers per unit area of collecting electrode and the number per unit length of discharge wire for various applications.[4]

Empirically derived performance curves relating the precipitation rate parameter and the power density for various applications have also been used in design specification.

Typical performance curves for electrostatic precipitator design specification in various applications are now being presented. Design procedures will be illustrated in the example problems in the next section.

Utilities

Electrostatic precipitators in the utility or electric power generation industry are used principally for emission (fly ash) control from coal-fired steam generating plants. Precipitation parameter, w, typically ranges from 3 cm/sec (0.1 ft/sec) to 17 cm/sec (0.56 ft/sec), with most designs in the 8 to 16 cm/sec range. Many parameters can affect the precipitation parameter. The general effects of fly ash resistivity and sulfur content of the fuel are shown in Figures 5.5.1 and 5.5.2, respectively. In view of the large number of variables involved, it has become common practice to use regression analysis schemes to correlate data.[4,23] Factors such as sulfur content, ash content, moisture, temperature, etc. are assumed to be important and are entered into a standard regression analysis computer program. The data from many installations are then entered, and the statistical importance of each term in the equation is tested. Terms that appear to be random are rejected, and the coefficients for the remaining terms are computed.

The aspect ratio is defined as the height to length of gas passage. Lower aspect ratios generally result in better performance. Aspect ratios in fly ash precipitators typically range between 1 and 1.5.

The rappers used for dust removal are typically specified as follows.

1. Number required — 1,200 to 6,000 ft²/ collection electrode rapper; 1,000 to 7,000 ft/ discharge electrode rapper.

TABLE 5.5.2

Typical Precipitation Rate Parameters for Various Applications

Application	Precipitation rate (ft/sec)
Utility fly ash	0.13–0.67
Pulverized coal fly ash	0.33–0.44
Pulp and paper mills	0.21–0.31
Sulfuric acid mist	0.19–0.25
Cement (wet process)	0.33–0.37
Cement (dry process)	0.19–0.23
Gypsum	0.52–0.64
Smelter	0.06
Open-hearth furnace	0.16–0.19
Blast furnace	0.20–0.46
Hot phosphorous	0.09
Flash roaster	0.25
Multiple hearth roaster	0.26
Catalyst dust	0.25
Cupola	0.10–0.12

TABLE 5.5.3

Typical Rapping Practices for Various Applications

Application	Collection electrodes, rappers/1,000 ft²	Discharge electrode, rappers/1,000 ft
Utilities	0.25–0.90	0.09–0.66
Pulp and paper	0.25–0.99	0.21–0.32
Metals	0.11–0.82	0.28–0.50
Cement	0.33–0.52	0.19–0.33

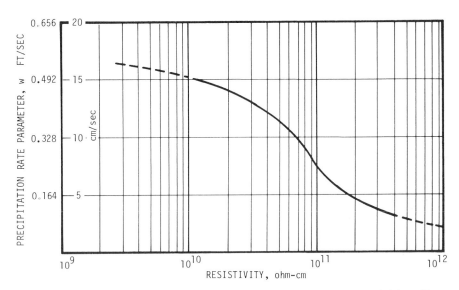

FIGURE 5.5.1. Relationship between precipitation rate parameter and resistivity. (From White, H. J., *Industrial Electrostatic Precipitation,* Addison-Wesley, Reading, Mass., 1963. With permission.)

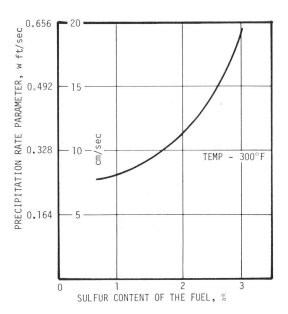

FIGURE 5.5.2. Relationship between precipitation rate parameter and sulfur content for electric utility installations at a temperature of 300°F. (From Ramsdell, R. G., *Proc. Am. Power Conf.,* 30, 129, 1968. With permission.)

2. Size — 25 to 50 ft-lb$_f$ per cycle.
3. Times — 30 to 600 sec between raps.
4. Acceleration — 30 to 50 g's typical.

Input power typically ranges from 50 to 150 W/1,000 ACFM. The relationship between the precipitation rate parameter and the power density is shown in Figure 5.5.3 and that between collection efficiency and input power is shown in Figure 5.5.4. The relationship between collection efficiency and collecting surface area to gas flow ratio for various coal sulfur contents is given in Figure 5.5.5. The relationship between collection efficiency and the degree of sectionalization for a 1.8% sulfur coal is shown in Figure 5.5.6. Typical design parameters for fly ash precipitators are summarized in Table 5.5.4.

Pulp and Paper Industry

Electrostatic precipitators are used in the pulp and paper industry primarily to remove particulates carried by the effluent gases from black liquor recovery boilers.

The gas velocity may range from 3 to 6 ft/sec, usually 4 to 5 ft/sec. The input power ranges from 100 to 200 W/1,000 ACFM (see Figure 5.5.7). As a rule of thumb, minimum input power levels are 0.2 kW/1,000 ACFM for 90% efficiency and about 0.8 kW/1,000 ACFM for 99.9% efficiency. Design electrical field strength (average electric field strength per plate separation) is usually 8 to 13 kV/in. The precipitation parameter often ranges from 6 to 10 cm/sec (see Figure 5.5.8) and the collecting area from 150 to 300 ft²/1000 ACFM (see Figure 5.5.9).

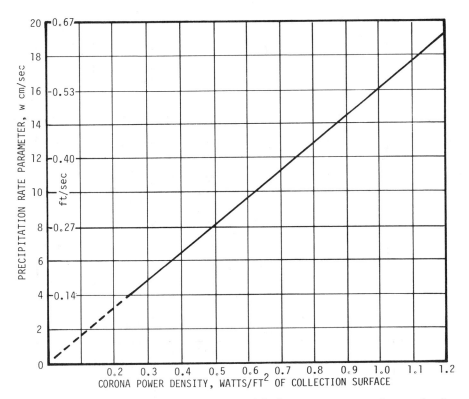

FIGURE 5.5.3. Linear relationship between precipitation rate parameter and power density for fly ash collectors.[4]

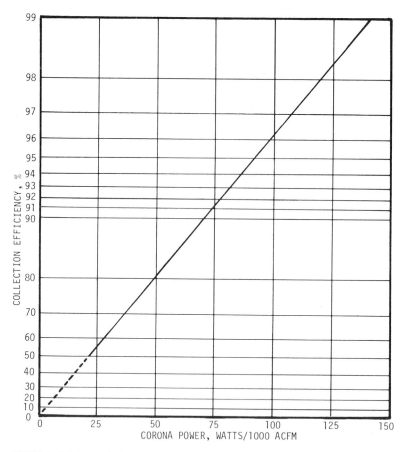

FIGURE 5.5.4.   Relationship between collection efficiency and corona power for fly ash precipitators.[4]

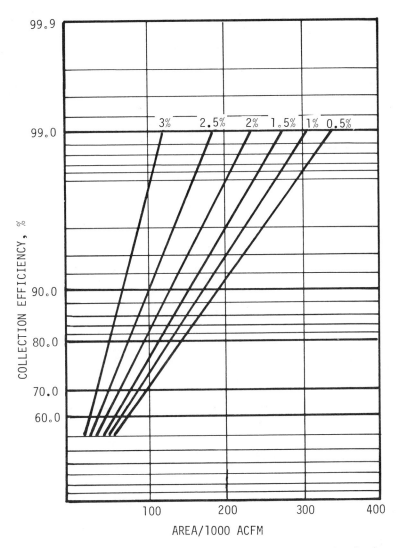

FIGURE 5.5.5. Relationship between collection efficiency and collecting surface area to gas flow ratio for various coal sulfur contents.[4]

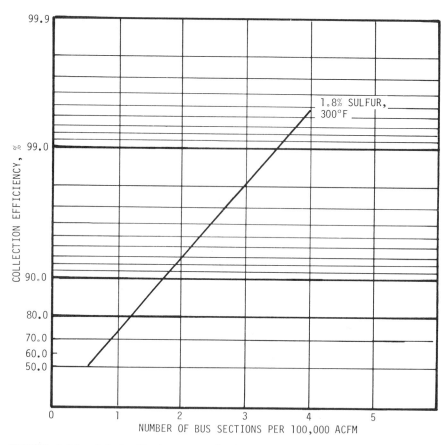

FIGURE 5.5.6. Relationship between collection efficiency and sectionalization. (From Ramsdell, R. G., *Proc. Am. Power Conf.*, 30, 129, 1968. With permission.)

TABLE 5.5.4

Typical Design Parameters for Fly Ash Electrostatic Precipitators

Parameter	Range of values
Precipitation rate (effective migration velocity)	0.05−0.6 ft/sec
Plate spacing	8−12 in.
Collection surface/volumetric gas flow rate, (A/Q)	100−800 ft²/1,000 ACFM
Gas velocity	4−8 ft/sec
Aspect ratio (Plate length-to-height ratio)	0.5−1.5
Corona power/volumetric gas flow rate	50−500 W/1,000 ACFM
Corona current/plate area	5−70 mA/ft²
Plate area per electrical set	5,000−80,000 ft²/electrical set
Number of high-tension sections in gas flow direction	2−8
Degree of high-tension sectionalization	0.4−4 bus sections/100,000 ACFM

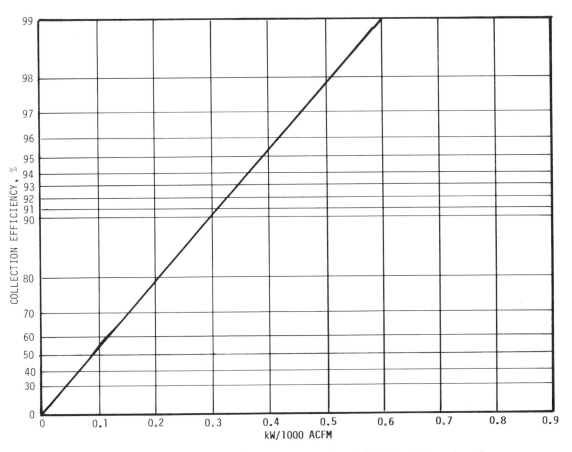

FIGURE 5.5.7. Collection efficiency vs. input power per 1,000 ACFM in pulp and paper installations.[4]

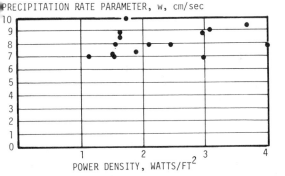

FIGURE 5.5.8. Relationship between precipitation rate parameter and power density in pulp and paper installations.[4]

Iron and Steel Industry

Electrostatic precipitators are used in the iron and steel industry principally for the cleaning of gaseous effluents from steel-making furnaces, foundry cupolas, sinter machines, and byproduct coke ovens.

Coke Ovens — Electrostatic precipitators are utilized to remove suspended oil, tars, and particulate matter from the gases prior to hydrocarbon recovery. Tubular-type precipitators are usually specified with collection electrodes typically 6 to 8 in. in diameter and 6 to 9 ft long. Discharge electrodes are suspended axially through the pipes. Precipitators are maintained at a temperature high enough so that collected tar drains from the plates and no rapping is required. Typical design parameters are given in Table 5.5.5.

Sinter Plants — Electrostatic precipitators are frequently specified to remove particulate matter emitted from the sintering process as a result of the mechanical handling of the raw material and combustion of the coal or coke. Single-stage, horizontal-flow plate-type precipitators are usually preceded by mechanical collectors. The average gas velocity is usually 4 to 5 ft/sec. The average electric field is about 8.1 kV/in. The average power-to-gas volume ratio is often in the range of 70 to 80 W/1,000 ACFM. The precipitation

163

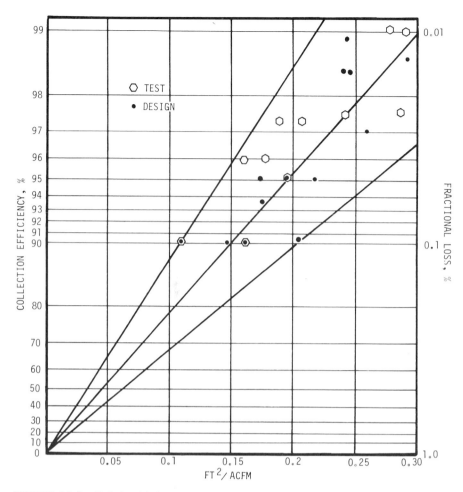

FIGURE 5.5.9. Relationship between design and test collection efficiencies vs. A/Q ratio for 11 electrostatic precipitators for pulp and paper installations.[4]

TABLE 5.5.5

Typical Design Parameters for Electrostatic Precipitators Used in Detarring Byproduct Coke Gas

Parameter	Range of values
Gas volumes treated	5,000–20,000 ACFM
Design efficiencies	95–99%
Precipitation rate parameter	0.20–0.55 ft/sec
Discharge electrode	¼-in. square twisted wire
Collection electrode	8-in. diameter steel cylinder
Voltage	50–70 kV peak
Average electric field	11.5 kV/in.
Average gas velocity	8 ft/sec
Power-to-gas volume ratio	100–200 W/1,000 ACFM

rate parameter is usually in the range of 0.33 to 0.39 ft/sec.

Blast Furnaces — Electrostatic precipitators are typically used for particulate removal of effluent gases from the blast furnace, which is frequently precleaned by a mechanical collector and/or wet scrubber. Vertical-flow tubular precipitors are conventionally specified, although horizontal-flow, plate-type precipitators have also been used. Typical design parameters are provided in Table 5.5.6. Rapping is not usually required since collecting electrodes are flushed with liquid. The relationship between collection efficiency and specific collection area for a number of installations is shown in Figure 5.5.10.

Open-hearth Furnaces — Single-stage, horizontal-flow, plate-type precipitators are frequently used to control particulate emissions in the exhaust gases from open-hearth steel-making furnaces. In addition to the use of electrostatic precipitators for particulate control, cyclone collectors and/or wet scrubbers may also be used. Figure 5.5.11 shows the relationship between collection efficiency and the collecting area-to-gas volume ratio for a group of eight installations. The

TABLE 5.5.6

Typical Design Parameters for Blast Furnace Tubular Electrostatic Precipitators

Parameter	Value
Gas velocity	9−12 ft/sec
Average precipitator field strength	11−14 kV/in.
Input power	50−150 W/1,000 ACFM
Precipitation rate parameter	0.25−0.45 ft/sec
Collection electrode tubes	8−12 in. diameter, 15 ft long
Discharge electrodes	3/16−¼ in. diameter, twisted square bars

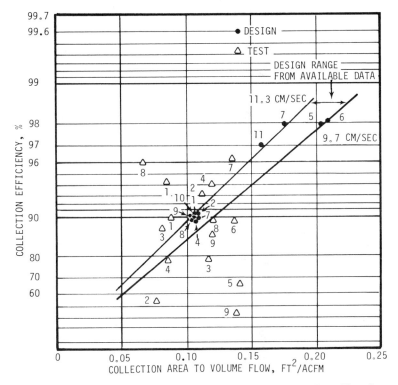

FIGURE 5.5.10. Relationship between collection efficiency and specific collection area for electrostatic precipitators operating on blast furnace installations.[4]

curves show a range of design precipitation rate parameters from 0.23 to 0.30 ft/sec.[4] Power supplied for a group of open-hearth furnace precipitators is shown in Figure 5.5.12 in terms of installed power per 1,000 ACFM.

Basic Oxygen Converters − Fumes from the basic oxygen furnace (BOF) containing particulate matter primarily composed of the oxides of iron are generally cleaned using either high-energy venturi scrubbers or electrostatic precipitators (plate type, horizontal flow). The relationship between collection efficiency and collection area to volume flow rate for a group of three BOF precipitators is shown in Figure 5.5.13. Other design parameters are presented in Table 5.5.7.

Electric Arc Furnaces − Plate-type electrostatic precipitators have been used to control particulate emissions from several electric furnace installations. Typical design parameters are as follows. The gas velocity is usually 2 to 4 ft/sec. The specific collecting area is often 350 to 400 ft²/1,000 ACFM. The precipitation rate parameter is in the range of 0.12 to 0.16 ft/sec.

Scarfing Machines − During the scarfing operation, iron oxide particulate matter is generated. Horizontal-flow, plate-type precipi-

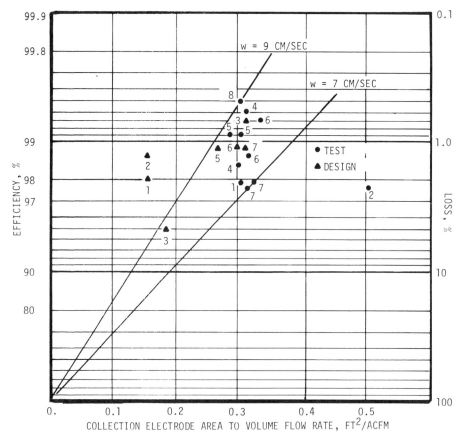

FIGURE 5.5.11. Relationship between collection efficiency and collection electrode to volume flow ratio for open-hearth furnaces.[4]

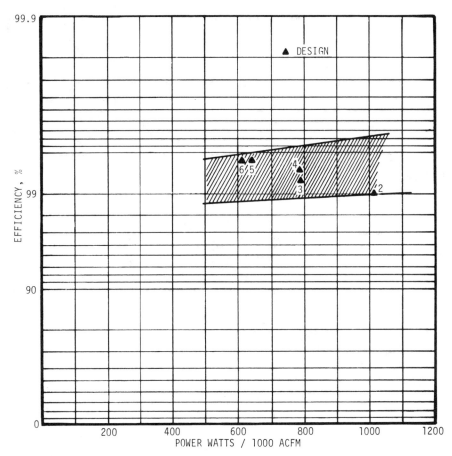

FIGURE 5.5.12. Relationship between installed power per 1,000 ACFM and collection efficiency for five open-hearth installations. (Adapted from Reference 4.)

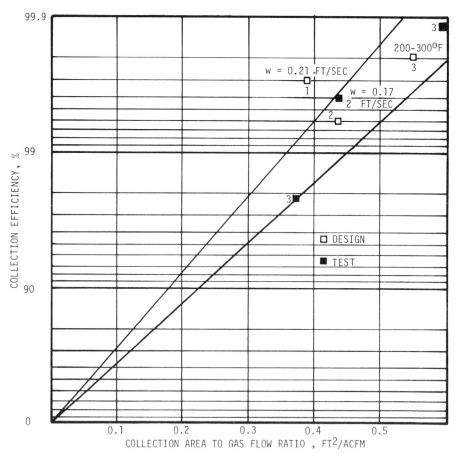

FIGURE 5.5.13. Relationship between collection efficiency and collection area to volume flow rate for BOF installation.[4]

TABLE 5.5.7

Typical Design Parameters for BOF Precipitators

Parameter	Values
Precipitation rate parameter	0.17–0.65 ft/sec
Specific collecting area (SCA)	450–600 ft^2/1,000 ACFM
Collecting electrode length	30–45 ft
Collecting electrode rappers (number)	32–36
Discharge electrode rappers (number)	8–24
Power input	200–300 W/1,000 ACFM
Number of high-tension sections in gas flow direction	4–7

tators have been used for control of these emissions. The average gas velocity is usually 4 to 5 ft/sec. The average field strength is often 11 kV/in, and the average power input may be in the range of 250 to 300 W/1,000 ACFM.

Iron Cupolas — The characteristics of particulate emissions from cupola furnaces (such as the high resistivity, small particle size, and particle-size distribution variability) limit the use of electrostatic precipitators in this area. Based on limited experience, high specific collection areas (900 to 1,100 ft²/1,000 ACFM) are required in view of the low precipitation rate parameters (0.03 to 0.06 ft/sec). Stainless steel construction is usually required.

Rock Products Industry

Electrostatic precipitators are used in the rock products industry to collect dusts from cement kilns, gypsum calciners, and mills and dryers used in preparation of the raw material feed to the kilns and calciners.

Portland Cement — Particulate matter carried by the calcining kiln gases originates from the abrasion of the charge as it tumbles through the kiln. Discharges due to the gas release are associated with calcination, the ash from the kiln if the kiln is coal-fired, and the fume resulting from the vaporization and condensation of alkali. Electrostatic precipitators used on cement kilns are of the horizontal flow, plate type with insulated steel shells. Figure 5.5.14 shows the relationship between collection efficiency and specific collection area for various installations. Due to the moisture content of the contaminated stream and the dust fineness, more frequent and severe rapping is required. The design gas velocities are usually 3 to 5 ft/sec. The precipitation rate parameter is often in the 0.25- to 0.45-ft/sec range. The average field strength is typically 6 to 7 kV/in. The installed power is usually 250 to 1,000 W/1,000 ACFM (see Figure 5.5.15).

Gypsum — Particulate matter from the gypsum processing plant is presently handled using single-stage, horizontal-flow precipitators with shielded flat-plate collecting electrodes. Mechanical collectors are often used upstream of the precipitator. The relationship between collection efficiency and specific collecting surface is shown in Figure 5.5.16 based on data from a limited number of

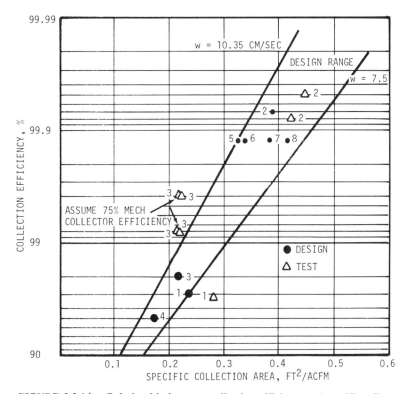

FIGURE 5.5.14. Relationship between collection efficiency and specific collection area for cement industries.[4]

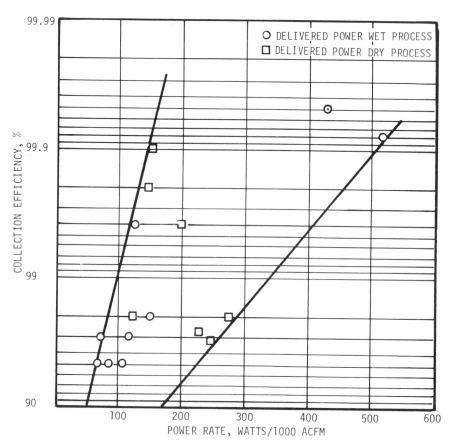

FIGURE 5.5.15.   Efficiency vs. power rate for cement plants.[4]

Chemical Industry

Electrostatic precipitators in the chemical industry find primary application in the manufacture of sulfuric acid, phosphorous, and phosphoric acid, and in carbon black production.

Sulfuric Acid Production – Single-stage, vertical-upflow, tubular-type electrostatic precipitators are used for sulfuric acid mist collection. Cylindrical shells constructed of sheet lead supported by steel banding are frequently specified, although all-steel construction has been used in recent years without apparent difficulty. Discharge electrodes are of lead or steel construction with a four-pointed star cross section, typically ½ in. across the points. Collecting electrodes are tubular, approximately 10 in. in diameter, and constructed of lead or steel. The precipitation rate parameter is usually in the range of 0.20 to 0.30 ft/sec. The specific collection surface area commonly used is 200 to 400

ft^2/1,000 ACFM. The average gas velocity is often 3 to 5 ft/sec. The corona power may range from 300 to 400 W/1,000 ACFM. The corona power density may range from 0.5 to 2.0 W/ft^2. The rectifier voltage is about 75 to 100 kV peak, and the average field strength is about 10 to 13 kV/in.

Elemental Phosphorous (Electric Arc Furnace Process) – Electrostatic precipitators are used for particulate removal from the furnace exhaust gases. Vertical-flow, single-stage tubular precipitators are usually used. The collecting electrode tubes are typically 11 in. in diameter and 16 ft long. Discharge electrodes are generally 3/16- or ¼-in. square bars held taut by weights. Gas design velocity is typically 4 to 5 ft/sec.

Phosphoric Acid Production – Although single-stage, vertical-flow, tubular-type precipitators have been used for phosphoric acid mist collection, the present trend is toward the use of high-energy variable orifice scrubbers.

Carbon Black Industry – Single-stage, horizontal-flow, plate-type precipitators have been used to agglomerate the fine carbon black particles

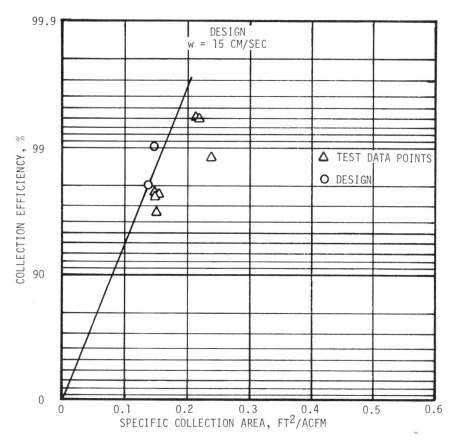

FIGURE 5.5.16. Collection efficiency vs. specific collecting surface for gypsum rock dryer plant preceded by mechanical collector. Efficiency of mechanical collector assumed to be 75%.[4]

from the furnace. The shell is heat insulated and provided with a preheat system, purge vents, and explosion hatches. A variety of collection control devices are generally used in series with the precipitator, i.e., cyclones and filter baghouses. In view of the high conductivity of the carbon black particles, which inhibits good collection in a precipitator, the trend is toward the use of filter baghouses.

Municipal Incinerators

In view of the stringency of current air pollution regulations, the use of electrostatic precipitators for particulate emission control from municipal incinerators is becoming popular. Precipitators used for fly ash collection from waste incinerators are generally of the single stage, plate type with horizontal gas flow. Insulation is generally required on the shell to minimize corrosion due to condensation of the incinerator gases. Size and power requirements are determined from

past experience. The relationship between collection efficiency and specific collection area and power rate for various installations is shown in Figures 5.5.17 and 5.5.18, respectively. Precipitation rate parameters generally vary from 0.13 to 0.33 ft/sec. A range for the precipitation rate parameter and the power density is shown in Figure 5.5.19. The variation between precipitation rate and gas temperature is evident in Figure 5.5.20.

Petroleum Industry

The principal uses of electrostatic precipitators in the petroleum industry are for the collection of particulate emissions from fluidized bed catalytic cracking units and for tar removal from various gas streams such as fuel gases, acetylene, and shale oil distillation gases.

Cat-cracking — The precipitator for the collection of catalyst in the petroleum cracking process is generally a single-stage, horizontal-flow, plate-

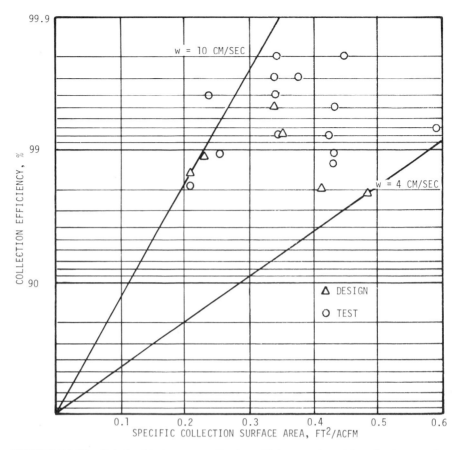

FIGURE 5.5.17. Relationship between collection efficiency and specific collection area for municipal incinerators.[4]

type unit which typically acts as a secondary collection system (cyclones being the primary). The precipitation rate parameter varies from 0.1 to 0.4 ft/sec, with the required specific collection area usually ranging between 350 and 400 ft²/1,000 ACFM.

Detarring — The precipitator most commonly utilized for detarring is a single-stage, tubular type with a cyclindrical shell. Since oil and tar mist are being collected, rapping is not required. Typical precipitation rate parameters range between 0.32 and 0.55 ft/sec.

Nonferrous Metals Industry

The use of electrostatic precipitators has been standard practice by copper, lead, and zinc smelters in cleaning off-gases from the extraction processes. Precipitators are also used in the electrolytic reduction of bauxite to produce aluminum. Design data are dependent on the particular application, and the reader is referred to Reference 4 for additional information. The data compiled by the

Southern Research Institute for the Environmental Protection Agency[4] provide an excellent source of information on the design and use of electrostatic precipitators in various industrial applications.

Recommended Design Precedure

1. Select a precipitation rate parameter from past experience, pilot data, or published data for a similar application.

2. Determine the required collection efficiency to comply with air pollution standards.

3. From Equation 5.5.1 and the volume gas flow handling, calculate the required collection area. The collection area can also be determined if a relationship between the precipitation rate parameter and the power density (such as that in Figure 5.5.3) has been established for this particular application. Both approaches must obviously give compatible results.

4. Total power requirements can be computed if an experimentally derived relationship

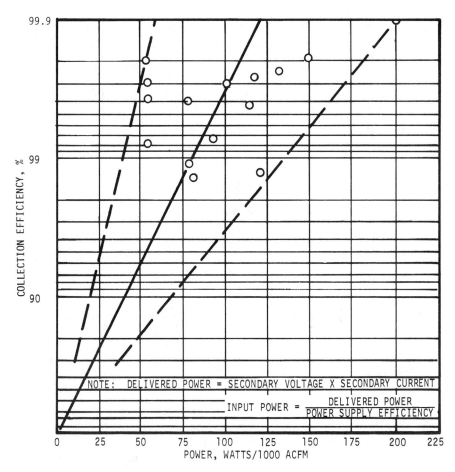

FIGURE 5.5.18. Relationship between collection efficiency and delivered corona power for municipal incinerators.[4]

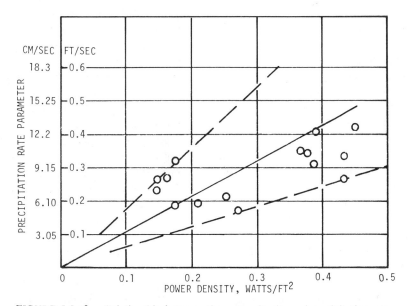

FIGURE 5.5.19. Relationship between the power density and precipitation rate parameter for electrostatic precipitators operating on effluents from municipal incinerators.[4]

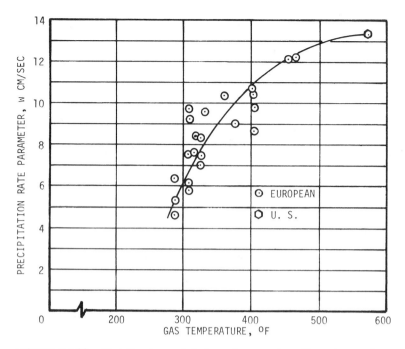

FIGURE 5.5.20. Variation in precipitation rate parameter with gas temperature for municipal incinerator precipitators.[4]

between collection efficiency and power rate (watts per 1,000 ACFM) has been established for this particular application (for example, as shown in Figure 5.5.4). The collection efficiency desired and the gas flow rate will define the power requirements.

5. The number of bus sections is also determined from past experience using curves such as those depicted in Figure 5.5.6.

The remaining design parameters (such as the number of rappers, the rapping frequency, the rapping force, etc.) are usually specified on the basis of past experience with the particular application. For these, it is best to directly contact the manufacturer.

Electrical Sectionalization

The maximum voltage at which a given field can be maintained depends on the properties of the gas and the dust being collected. These parameters may vary from one point to another within the precipitator, as well as with time. In order to keep each section of the precipitator working at high efficiency, a high degree of sectionalization is recommended. This means that many separate power supplies and controls will produce better performance on a precipitator of a

given size than if there are only one or two independently controlled sections. This is particularly true if high efficiencies are required.

Modern precipitators have voltage control devices which automatically limit precipitator power input. A well-designed automatic control system tends to keep the voltage level at approximately the value needed for optimum particle charging by the corona current.

The controls operate on the following principles. The higher the voltage, the greater the spark rate between the discharge electrodes and the collecting plate. As the spark rate increases, however, a greater percentage of input power is wasted in the spark current; consequently, less useful power is applied to dust collection. There is, however, an optimal sparking rate where the gains in particle charging from increased voltage are just offset by corona current losses from sparkover. Measurements on commercial precipitators have determined that this optimal sparking rate is between 50 to 150 sparks per minute per electrical section. The objective in corona power control is to maintain corona power input at this optimal sparking rate. This is usually accomplished by momentarily reducing precipitator power input whenever excessive sparking occurs.

The need for series sectionalization in a precipitator arises mainly because power input needs differ at various locations in a precipitator. In the inlet sections of a precipitator, concentrations of particulate matter will be relatively heavy. This requires a great deal of power input in order to generate the corona discharge required for optimal particle charging: heavy concentrations of dust particles tend to suppress corona current. On the other hand, in the downstream sections of a precipitator dust concentrations will be lighter. As a consequence, corona current will flow more freely and particle charging will tend to be limited by excessive sparking, moreso here than in inlet sections of the precipitator. Hence, excessive sparking is more likely to occur first in downstream sections; if the precipitator has only a single power set, then this sparking, under spark rate-limited control, will limit power input to the entire precipitator, including the inlet sections. This will result in insufficient power being supplied to the discharge electrodes in the inlet sections, with a consequential fall in precipitator collection efficiency in the inlet sections of the precipitator.

A remedy for this situation is to divide the precipitator into a series of independently energized electric bus sections (see Figure 5.5.21.a). Each bus section has its own transformer rectifier, voltage stabilization controls, and high-voltage conductors which energize the discharge electrodes within that section. This would allow greater power input and increased particle charging of dust and particulate precipitation than in the previously described underpowered inlet sections.

Parallel sectionalization (see Figure 5.5.21.b) provides the means for coping with different power input needs due to uneven dust and gas distributions which usually occur across the inlet face of a precipitator. Nevertheless, the gains in collection efficiency from parallel sectionalization are likely to be very small.

Typical limits of sectionalization for utility plants are given below.

Efficiency	Number fields deep	Degree of sectionalization
95	1	Low
95–99	2	Moderate
99–99.5	3	High
99.5+	4	High

Rapping

To maintain a continuous process of precipitation, it is necessary to continuously or periodically remove the precipitated material from the collecting electrodes. In the case of dry dusts, this is usually done by vibrating or rapping the collecting electrodes in order to dislodge the material so that it will fall into the hopper. Since the material must fall through the gas stream in order to reach the hopper, some reentrainment may occur; every effort must be made to minimize this. The following guidelines are recommended.

1. Design the electrodes for low reentrainment.

2. Do only the minimal amount of rapping necessary to clean the electrodes.

3. Rap only a small section of the precipitator at any one time.

4. Provide more than one precipitating field in the direction of flow when high values of collection efficiency are required.

Resistivity

Resistivity is a term that is used to describe the resistance of a medium to the flow of an electrical current. By definition, the resistivity is the electrical resistance of a dust sample 1 cm^2 in cross-sectional area and 1 cm thick. For ease of precipitation capture, dust resistivity values can be classified roughly into three groups.

1. Below 5.0×10^3 Ω-cm.

2. Between 5.0×10^3 and 2.0×10^{10} Ω-cm.

3. Above 2.0×10^{10} Ω-cm (this value is frequently referred to as the "critical resistivity").

Particulates in group 1 are difficult to collect.

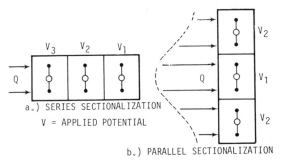

a.) SERIES SECTIONALIZATION

V = APPLIED POTENTIAL

b.) PARALLEL SECTIONALIZATION

FIGURE 5.5.21. Typical arrangements for separately energized bus sections.

They are easily charged and precipitated; upon contacting the collection electrode, however, they lose their discharge electrode polarity and acquire the polarity of the collection electrode. The particulates are then repelled into the gas stream to either escape from the precipitator or become recharged by the corona field. Examples are unburned carbon in fly ash and carbon black. If the conductive particles are coarse, they are usually removed upstream from the precipitator with another collection device, e.g., a cyclone. Baffles are often designed on the collection walls to limit this precipitation-repulsion phenomenon. Particulates with resistivities in group 3 cause back-ionization or back-corona, which is a localized discharge at the collection electrode due to the surface being coated by a layer of nonconductive material. A weak back-corona will merely lower the sparkover voltage, but a strong back-corona produces a positive ion discharge at the electrode. Back-corona phenomenon becomes severe with a bulk particle layer resistivity greater than 10^{11} Ω-cm. Particulates with resistivities in group 2 have been shown by experiment and experience to be the most acceptable for electrostatic precipitation. The particulates do not rapidly lose their charge on contact with the collection electrode or cause back-corona. Back-corona phenomena can be decreased by treatment of the gas stream, such as altering the temperature, moisture content, or chemical composition.

Particle resistivity decreases with both high and low temperatures (see Figure 5.5.22). The moisture content of the gas also affects particle collection by altering the resistivity. The moisture is absorbed on the solid particulates at lower temperature; in many circumstances, a moisture content of 20% or less will insure that the particle resistivity will be lower than the critical 2.0 $\times$ 10^{10} Ω-cm. (For example, inlet gas humidification systems have been developed to reduce the normally high resistivity values associated with the dry-process cement rotary kiln.) The presence of SO_3 in the carrier gas has also been shown to favor the electrostatic precipitation process. For a number of dusts, the resistivity is reduced below the critical limit with as little as 5 to 10 ppm of SO_3. Strauss[5] presents a number of resistivity-temperature graphs from the work of Sproull.[24] Additional data are available in the Southern Research Institute Study.[4]

The effect of chemical conditioning agents

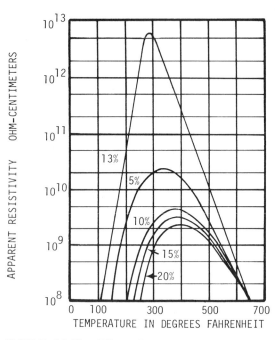

FIGURE 5.5.22. Effect of temperature and moisture content on apparent resistivity of precipitated cement dust.

seems to be to bind moisture to the particles. For example, in fly ash a thin film of sulfate usually is present on the particles. This in turn greatly increases the moisture absorbed by the particles. In this instance the sulfate is present naturally in the flue gas as a result of the burning of the sulfur in the coal, so that fly ash in many cases has adequate conductivity for good electrical precipitation. Other chemical conditioning agents which may be mentioned are (1) ammonia gas used for conditioning the powdered-catalyst dust from the petroleum cracking process and (2) chlorides for the conditioning of certain oxide dusts and fumes.

In practice, it is usually best to determine particle resistivity directly in plant flues because it is not feasible to duplicate the gaseous environment in the laboratory.

Current sulfur dioxide restrictions have encouraged the use of low-sulfur coal. In certain types of low-sulfur coal, the fly ash resistivity encountered is extremely high for the usual operating temperature range (250 to 300°F), as shown in Figure 5.5.23. If the precipitator is not properly designed for this situation, the efficiency may be much less than expected. In such cases (assuming "less resistive" coal is not available), design engineers must choose between various alternatives.

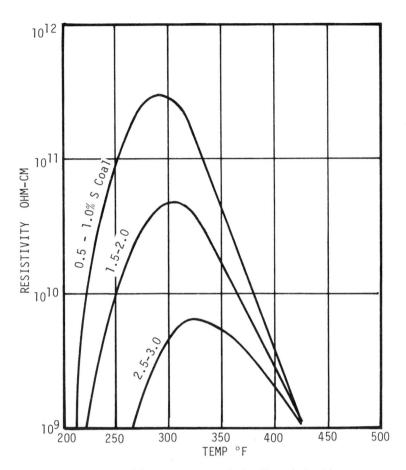

FIGURE 5.5.23. Resistivity, temperature, fuel sulfur relationships – eastern bituminous coals.

1. Run the precipitator hot, i.e., before the economizer, so that the gas temperature is in the 600 to 700°F range. As is evident from Figure 5.5.23, the resistivity curves drop sharply as the temperature increases. Note that this will increase the gas volume to be treated significantly and, consequently, increase precipitator size and cost.

2. Use conditioning agents such as those mentioned previously. This will also increase capital and operating costs, i.e., generating the agent on site and the raw materials involved.

3. Overdesign the precipitator, i.e., increase the collection surface area. This also will increase costs.

4. Run the precipitator cold (in the lower temperature range, if possible, where the resistivity drops sharply). This, however, increases the likelihood of condensation (and sulfuric acid can be terribly corrosive). Operation above the acid dew point is a necessity.

Although none of these alternatives is especially

attractive, there is a current trend toward hot precipitators when the fly ash is highly resistive. In fact, it is primarily due to this resistivity problem that fabric filters are beginning to be specified for fly ash collection at power plants. Based on economic analysis, it seems that fabric filters may be more economical than hot electrostatic precipitators when highly resistive, low-sulfur coal is burned.

It is highly recommended that precipitator applications be considered on an individual basis. Quite often, generalizations can be misleading (for example, that all low-sulfur coals are highly resistive). A comprehensive evaluation of the physical and chemical properties of the particulate matter must be made in order to obtain a correct perspective.

Gas Distribution

Depending on gas and dust conditions, and the required collecting efficiency, the gas velocities in an industrial electrostatic precipitator are between

2.5 and 8.0 ft/sec. A uniform gas distribution is of prime importance for the precipitator operation, and it should be achieved with a minimum expenditure of pressure drop. This is not always easy, since gas velocities in the duct ahead of the precipitator may be 30 to 100 ft/sec in order to prevent dust build-ups.

The economic and technical advantage of conducting three-dimensional flow model studies for this purpose is apparent because providing good gas distribution is an art; model studies are the best means available for obtaining the necessary confidence in the design for these high-cost installations. Suitable distribution models must be tested; the results must be related to the full-size unit considering the laws of dynamic similarities. The results of these tests can be plotted on coordinates in the open duct or precipitator area. These so-called velocity profiles can now be compared and the most suitable one chosen for the final installation. The results of these tests may be so close together that it is quite difficult to decide which arrangement to use. For this purpose, a calculation program can be used, which sets a scale by establishing comparable local collecting efficiencies for different parts of the cross-sectional area of the precipitator. Although model studies are standard procedure for large-scale precipitator installations, smaller installations may not be able to justify a model study. However, certain basic rules have become apparent and are available in the literature.[25]

Advantages and Disadvantages

The electrostatic precipitator has several advantages and disadvantages relative to other particulate collectors. The advantages include:

1. High collection efficiency on removal of submicron particulates (as low as 0.01 μm).
2. Low operation costs.
3. Low pressure drop (usually below 0.5 in. H_2O).
4. Relatively large gas flows can be effectively handled (to 2,000,000 + ACFM).
5. Operation under high pressure (to 150 psi pressure) or vacuum conditions.
6. Use under corrosive particulate conditions.
7. Removal of precipitator units from operation for cleaning is unnecessary.

8. High-temperature gases can be handled (to 1,200°+F).

The disadvantages of the electrostatic precipitator include:

1. High initial cost.
2. Large space required for installation.
3. Explosion hazard when collecting combustible gases or particulates.
4. Ozone (O_3) produced by a negatively charged discharge electrode during gas ionization.
5. Complicated operation procedure which involves precipitator adjustments for gas flow distribution, particulate resistivity values, and corona sparkover rate.

Economics

Initial cost for electrostatic precipitators in the 100,000 ACFM range is about $0.80 to 1.50/ACFM. In the 1,000,000 ACFM range the initial cost is approximately $0.50/ACFM. Installed costs typically run from three quarters to one and one half times the initial cost. Total installed costs from $1.00 to 3.00/ACFM are not unusual. The only operating cost considered in the operation of electrostatic precipitators is the power cost for ionizing the gas and operating the fan. As the pressure drop across the equipment is usually less than ½-in. of water, the cost of operating the fan is, for all practical purposes, negligible. Operating cost is usually quite low, amounting to about $.03 to 0.05/year/ACFM capacity. Maintenance cost ranges from $0.02 to 0.03/year/ACFM capacity.

The theoretical annual cost for operation and maintenance of electrostatic precipitators is given below.

$$\$ = ACFM [j t p + M] \qquad (5.5.2)$$

where

ACFM	= design capacity of precipitator, actual ft^3/min;
j	= power requirements, kW/ACFM;
t	= annual operating time, hr;
p	= power costs, $/kW-hour;
M	= maintenance cost, $/ACFM.

The best cost information is available directly from the manufacturer.

5.6. ILLUSTRATIVE EXAMPLES

One major stumbling block in applying electrostatic precipitator theory to practice is the choice of conversion units. This requires some development — particularly for the beginner. Before proceeding to the illustrative examples, it is appropriate to present this material. The units are consistent with those adopted by the engineering profession in this country. Some of these units, conversion factors, and corresponding notation(s) are presented below.

Quantity	Notation	Relationship
Length	1	$1.0\ \mu m = 10^{-6}$ m
		1.0 in. $= 0.0254$ m
		1.0 ft $= 0.3048$ m
Velocity	v	1.0 ft/time $= 0.3048$ m/time
Volume	V	$1.0\ cm^3 = 10^{-6}\ m^3$
Density	ρ	$1.0\ lb/ft^3 = 16.02\ kg/m^3$
Acceleration (gravity)	g	$32.2\ ft/sec^2 = 9.81\ m/sec^2$
Viscosity	μ	$1.0\ \mu p = 10^{-6}$ p
		$= 10^{-7}$ kg/(m) (sec)
		1.0 p $= 1.0$ g/(cm) (sec)
Charge	q	1.0 electrons/part $= 1.6 \times 10^{-19}$ Coulomb
		260 electrons/part $= 4.2 \times 10^{-7}$ C/part
		1.0 stat V $= 3.33 \times 10^{-10}$ C
		$= 299.8$ V
Capacitance	C	1.0 F $= 1.0$ (C) (V)
Emissivity	ϵ	1.0 F/m $= 1.0$ (C/V)/(m)
Electric field	E	1.0 V/m $= 10^{-5}$ kV/cm
Force	F	1.0 N $= 1.0$ (C) (V/m)
		$= 10^5$ dyne
		$= 1.0$ (kg) (m)/(sec)
		$= 0.22481\ lb_f$
		$1.0\ lb_f = 22481$ (C) (kV/cm)
		1.0 dyne $= 1.0$ (C) (kV/cm)
Power	P	1.0 W $= 1.0$ (V) (A)
		$= 1.0$ (V) (C/sec)

Some of the properties of air at ambient conditions include:

$T = 25°C$
$p = 1.0$ atm $= 1.013 \times 10^6$ dyne/cm² $= 1.013 \times 10^5$ N/m²
Mol Wt $= 29.0$ g/g$_m$ $= 29.0$ kg/kg$_m$
$\rho = 0.0740\ lb/ft^3 = 1.185 \times 10^{-3}$ g/cm³ $= 1.185$ kg/m³
$\mu = 1.84 \times 10^{-4}$ p $= 1.84 \times 10^{-5}$ kg/(m) (sec)

The describing equations for electrostatic precipitators are dimensional equations and a few involve several terms. For the equality to hold, each term in the equation must have the same dimensions, i.e., the equation must be dimensionally homogeneous. This condition can easily be proven. Throughout the previous sections (and in particular in the illustrative examples to follow) care is exercised to maintain the dimensional formulas of all terms and the dimensional homogenity of each equation. The following example problems apply the principles discussed previously to electrostatic precipitator design.

Example 5.6.1

A 10-μm fly ash particle receives a 1.63×10^{-6} esu charge in an electric field. The resulting electrostatic force on the particle gives rise to a velocity of 9.4 cm/sec. Calculate the field strength in kilovolts per inch.

Solution

We assume that Stokes' law applies. The drag force is given by

$$F_D = 6\ \pi \mu w r$$

Substituting the data gives

$$F_D = 6\ \pi\ (183 \times 10^{-7}\ \text{N-sec/m}^2)(0.094\ \text{m/sec})(5 \times 10^{-6}\ \text{m})$$
$$= 1620 \times 10^{-13}\ \text{N}$$

This may also be expressed as

$$F_D = 1.620 \times 10^{-10}\ \text{C-V/m}$$

The charge, in coulombs, on the particle is

$q = 1.63 \times 10^{-6} \text{ esu} \times 3.334 \times 10^{-10} \text{ C/esu}$

$\quad = 5.43 \times 10^{-16} \text{ C}$

Since

$F_E = F_D$

and

$F_E = qE$

then

$E = 1.62 \times 10^{-10}/5.43 \times 10^{-16}$

$\quad = 0.3 \times 10^6 \text{ V/m}$

or

$E = 0.3 \times 10^6 \times 2.54/100 \times 1{,}000$

$E = 7.62 \dfrac{kV}{in.}$

We finally check our initial assumption regarding Stokes' law by calculating the Reynolds number (or K).

$Re = v\, d_p \rho/\mu$

$Re = (9.4/30.48) \times 10 \times 3.28 \times 10^{-6} \times 0.074/1.23 \times 10^{-5}$

$Re < 1$

Example 5.6.2

A horizontal parallel-plate electrostatic precipitator consists of a single duct 24 ft high and 20 ft deep with an 11 in. plate-to-plate spacing. A collection efficiency of 88.2% is obtained with a flow rate of 4,200 ACFM. The inlet loading is 2.82 grains/ft^3. Calculate the following.

1. The bulk velocity of the gas (assume a uniform distribution).
2. The outlet loading.
3. The drift velocity for this system.
4. A revised collection efficiency if the flow rate is increased to 5,400 ACFM.
5. A revised collection efficiency if the plate spacing is decreased to 9 in.

Solution

The bulk flow velocity is given by

$v = Q/A$

$\quad = 4{,}200/24(11/12)$

$\quad = 191 \text{ ft/min}$

The outlet loading is

$2.82\,(1 - 0.882) = 0.333 \text{ grains/ft}^3$

We first back calculate ϕ from the equation

$\eta = 1 - e^{-\phi} = 0.882$

Solving yields

$\phi = 2.14$

Since

$\phi = wA/Q$

We may substitute the data and calculate w.

$2.14 = w \times 24 \times 20 \times 2/(4{,}200/60)$

Solving gives

$w = 0.156 \text{ ft/sec}$

If Q = 5,400 ACFM, then a new ϕ can be calculated assuming the same drift velocity.

$\phi = 0.156 \times 960/(5{,}400/60) = 1.67$

The efficiency then is

$\eta = 1 - e^{-1.67}$

$\quad = 0.812 = 81.2\%$

Since Q, w, and A are all constant, the Deutsch equation predicts that the efficiency does not change if the plate spacing is 9 in.

For the sake of convenience, a graph of efficiency vs. the exponent ϕ is provided below.

Example 5.6.3

A horizontal parallel-plate electrostatic precipitator consisting of four gas passages 24 ft high and 20 ft deep with an 11-in. plate spacing is to treat 41,800 ACFM of air containing 4.3 grains/ft^3 of fly ash. Using an average drift velocity for the system, calculate the collection efficiency of the unit.

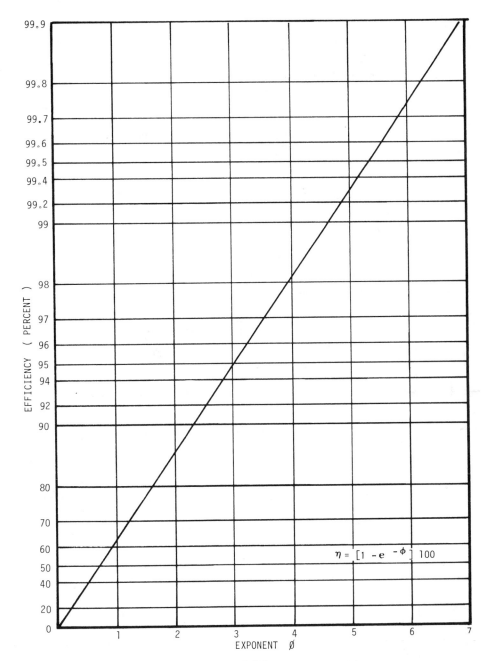

EXAMPLE 5.6.2. Efficiency vs. exponent ϕ.

$$\eta = \left[1 - e^{-\phi} \right] 100$$

Solution

The average drift velocity is obtained from the particle-size distribution and drift velocity curves provided below. These yield the following data:

$\langle d_p \rangle = 154$
$\langle w \rangle = 0.605$ ft/sec = 36.3 ft/min

The area for each collecting surface is

$20 \times 24 = 480$ ft²

Since there are eight collecting surfaces

$A = 8 \times 480$
$= 3,840$ ft²

The value of ϕ is (dropping the average value notation)

$\phi = (A/Q)w$
$= [3,840/(41,800/60)]\ 0.605$
$= 5.512 \times 0.605$
$= 3.335$

The efficiency may now be calculated by

$\eta = 1 - e^{-3.335}$
$= 0.9644 = 96.44\%$

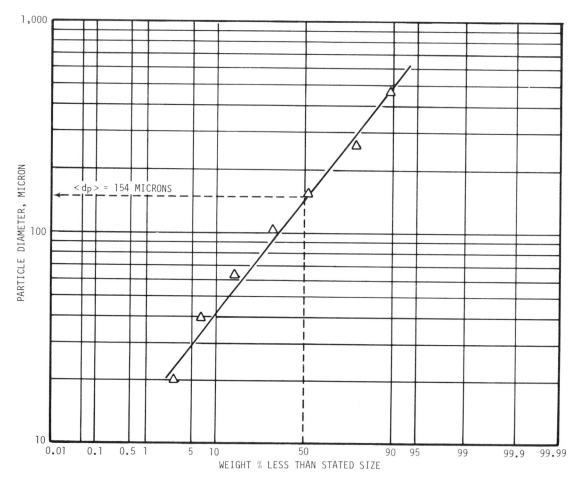

EXAMPLE 5.6.3.   Fly ash particle-size distribution.

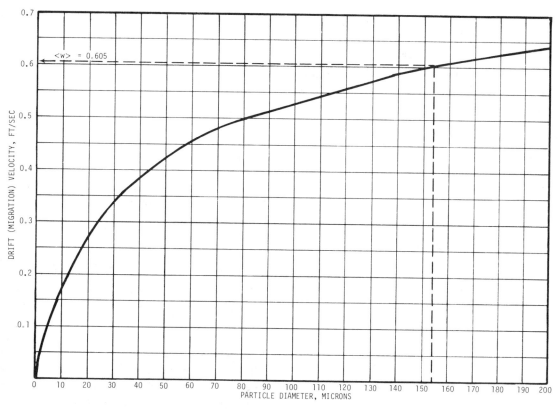

<w> = 0.605

DRIFT (MIGRATION) VELOCITY, FT/SEC

PARTICLE DIAMETER, MICRONS

EXAMPLE 5.6.3.   Drift velocity (w) vs. particle diameter (d_p) for fly ash-air system.

Example 5.6.4

Obtain the collection efficiency for the unit described in Example 5.6.3 if the particle-size distribution and drift velocity data are employed.

Solution

Using both figures cited previously, we can develop the following data:

Wt % < d_p	d_p, μm	w, ft/sec
20	58	0.45
40	106	0.54
60	210	0.6425
80	320	0.68
99.9	900	0.70

For this type of situation, the efficiency is given by

$$\eta = 1 - \Sigma\, x_i e^{-(A/Q)w_i}$$

Substituting the data gives

$$\eta = 1 - 0.2[e^{-5.512 \times 0.45} + e^{-5.512 \times 0.54}$$
$$+ e^{-5.512 \times 0.6425}$$
$$+ e^{-5.512 \times 0.68}$$
$$+ e^{-5.512 \times 0.70}\,]$$

$$= 0.9583 = 95.83\,\%$$

Example 5.6.5

Obtain the collection efficiency for the unit described in Example 5.6.3 if both particle-size distribution data and drift velocity variation from theory are employed in the calculation.

Solution

According to theory, the drift velocity variation is given by

$$w = 0.058\, E_c E_p d_p / 2\, \mu$$

For this system we may write

$w = K^* d_p$

where K^* is a constant. In order to obtain a crude comparison, the value of K^* is arbitrarily determined from average-value data in the previous examples.

$0.605 = K^* (154)$

$K^* = 0.0039$

Therefore, we have

$w = 0.0039 \, d_p$

The resulting particle size drift velocity variation is

Wt % $<d_p$	d_p, μm	w, ft/sec
20	58	0.2262
40	106	0.4134
60	210	0.819
80	320	1.248
99.9	900	3.51

The collection efficiency is given by

$\eta = 1 - 0.2 \, \Sigma \, e^{-(A/Q)w_i}$
$= 0.9196 = 91.96\%$

Example 5.6.6

Due to a rapid expansion just before the inlet to the precipitator, the velocity profile is not fully developed; the result of this is a volume rate of flow in the inner ducts that is twice that of the outer ducts. Calculate a revised collection efficiency for the unit described in Example 5.6.3 under these conditions. Use the same average particle size and drift velocity.

Solution

If the flow rates through the four passages are labeled Q1, Q2, Q3, and Q4, we have

$Q1 = Q4 = Q2/2 = Q3/2$

Since the total flow rate is known, we may determine the individual flow rates by

$Q = Q1 + Q2 + Q3 + Q4 = 41,800$
$6(Q1) = 41,800$

so that

$Q1 = Q4 = 6,967 \, ft^3/min$

and

$Q2 = Q3 = 13,933 \, ft^3/min$

Assuming that the loading is still uniform, the weight fraction of particulates in the outer ducts, x_o, is given by

$x_o = (Q1 + Q4)/Q = 13,933/41,800$
$= 0.333$

Therefore, the weight fraction in the inner ducts is 0.667. The plate area of two passages is

$A = 3,840/2 = 1,920 \, ft^2$

The efficiency may now be calculated by

$\eta = 1 - 0.333 \, e^{-(1,920/2 \times 6,967)36.3}$
$\quad - 0.667 \, e^{-(1,920/2 \times 13,933)36.3}$
$= 0.9431 = 94.31\%$

Example 5.6.7

Further complications are introduced to the calculations in Example 5.6.3 because of variations in the particle-size distribution at the inlet to the precipitator. Due to inertial effects, none of the particles larger than 50 μm enter the outer passages. The remaining (smaller) particles, however, are uniformly distributed. Calculate a revised collection efficiency for the unit described in Example 5.6.3 under these conditions. Use an appropriate average drift velocity for each passage.

Solution

The solution to this example is similar to the previous one; now, however, all the particles larger than 50 μm which were entering the two outer passages are entering the inner passages. From the particle diameter distribution curve, 85% of the particles are greater than 50μm. Therefore, the weight percent in the outer ducts will be

$x_o = 0.15 \times 0.333 = 0.05$

The weight percent in the inner ducts, x_i, is then

$x_i = 1 - 0.05 = 0.95$

For the outer passages (see figure below)

$\langle d_p \rangle = 35.5 \, \mu$m

and

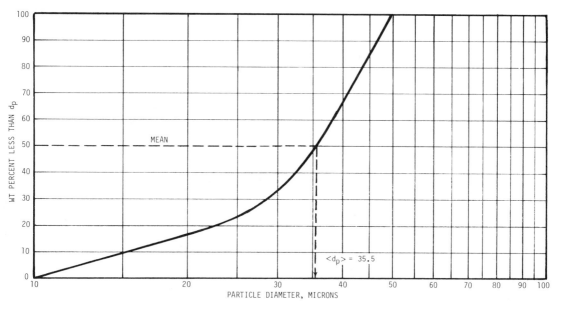

EXAMPLE 5.6.7.   Fines distribution.

$\langle w \rangle = 0.366$ ft/sec $= 22$ ft/min

For the inner passages we use (as a first approximation) the same values employed earlier, i.e.,

$d_p = 154$ μm
$w = 36.3$ ft/min

The efficiency is given by

$\eta = 1 - 0.05\ e^{-(1,920/2\ \times\ 6,967)22}$
$\qquad - 0.95\ e^{-(1,920/2\ \times\ 13,933)36.3}$
$\quad = 0.9197 = 91.97\%$

Example 5.6.8

An electrostatic precipitator operates at an overall efficiency of 97% when the gas temperature is 300°F. Estimate the new overall efficiency when the gas temperature is increased to 400°F. Assume that the precipitator handles the same mass flow rate of gas, and all other operating parameters remain constant.

Solution

$\eta = 1 - e^{-\phi}$
$0.97 = 1 - e^{-\phi}$
$\phi = 3.52$ (see figure in Example 5.6.2)

The increase in temperature will increase the flow rate by a factor of 1.13.

$Q_{300°\text{F}} \propto \left(\dfrac{300 + 460}{460} \right) = 1.65$

$Q_{400°\text{F}} \propto \left(\dfrac{400 + 460}{460} \right) = 1.87$

$Q_{400°\text{F}}/Q_{300°\text{F}} = 1.87/1.65 = 1.13$

If one assumes that all other operating parameters remain constant, the new overall efficiency will be

$\phi = 3.52\ (1/1.13) = 3.11$
and
$\eta = 95.5\%$

Example 5.6.9

As a recently hired engineer for an equipment vending company, you have been assigned the job of submitting a preliminary (process) design of an electrostatic precipitator to treat 180,000 ACFM of gas laden with solids from an incinerator burning dry sewage sludge. The inlet loading of 3.47 grains/ft³ is to be reduced to 0.07. Submit your design.

Solution

The volumetric flow rate is

$Q = 180,000$ ft³/min $= 3,000$ ft³/sec

The efficiency can be calculated from the outlet loading requirement.

$\eta = (3.47 - 0.07)/3.47$
  $= 0.98 = 98\%$

Using the Deutsch-Anderson model we have

$\eta = 1 - e^{-\phi}$

Substituting the data gives

$0.98 = 1 - e^{-\phi}$

and solving for ϕ

$\phi = 3.91 = (Q/A)w$

The drift velocity, w, for fly ash is set at 0.2 ft/sec (based on past experience for a similar application). Therefore,

$Q/A = 19.6$ sec/ft

Solving for A gives

$A = 58,800$ ft^2

From previous design sizing data we have

Z = 3; number of electrical fields
H = 30 ft; electrode height
v = 4.0 ft/sec; bulk gas velocity

The area available for bulk flow is

$A_c = 3,000/4 = 750$ ft^2

The number of passages, N, now can be calculated (assuming a plate-to-plate spacing of 10 in.) by

$N = A_c/0.833$ H

Substituting the data gives

$N = 750/0.833 \times 30 = 30$

The total collection area is given by

$A = (2NHZ)l$

Substituting the data gives

$58,800 = 2 \times 30 \times 30 \times 3 \times 1$

Solving for l provides the length of the passage in each field.

$l = 10.9$ ft

The total length, L, is given by

$TL = 1 \times Z = 10.9 (3)$
    $= 32.7$ ft

The total residence time, θ, is

$\theta = L/v = 32.7/4.0$
  $= 8.17$ sec

A representative sketch of the design is shown below.

The above constitutes the approach a typical design company would take in preparing a preliminary process design for this unit. Note that *four* design variables were specified. This information is usually available in company files.

Example 5.6.10

An electrostatic precipitator is to be used for fly ash removal from a 500,000 ACFM gas stream at 300°F. The coal fired contains 1.8% sulfur (by weight). The fly ash resistivity has been determined to be approximately 6×10^{10} Ω-cm. Estimate the precipitator design parameters to achieve 99% efficiency.

Solution

From Figure 5.5.1, for a resistivity of 6×10^{10} Ω-cm, a precipitation parameter of 0.34 ft/sec is estimated.

$\eta = 1 - \exp(-Aw/Q)$
$0.99 = 1 - \exp(-\phi)$

From the graph in Example 5.6.2,

$\phi = 4.6$
$4.6 = Aw/Q$
$A = 4.6 (500,000/60)/0.34$
$A = 112,750$ ft^2

The total power requirements can be determined from Figure 5.5.4. For 99% efficiency, the power required is approximately 140 W/1,000 ACFM Thus, for 500,000 ACFM,

Total Power = (140/1,000) (500,000) = 70,000 W

The number of bus sections is determined from Figure 5.5.6. For 99% collection efficiency, the

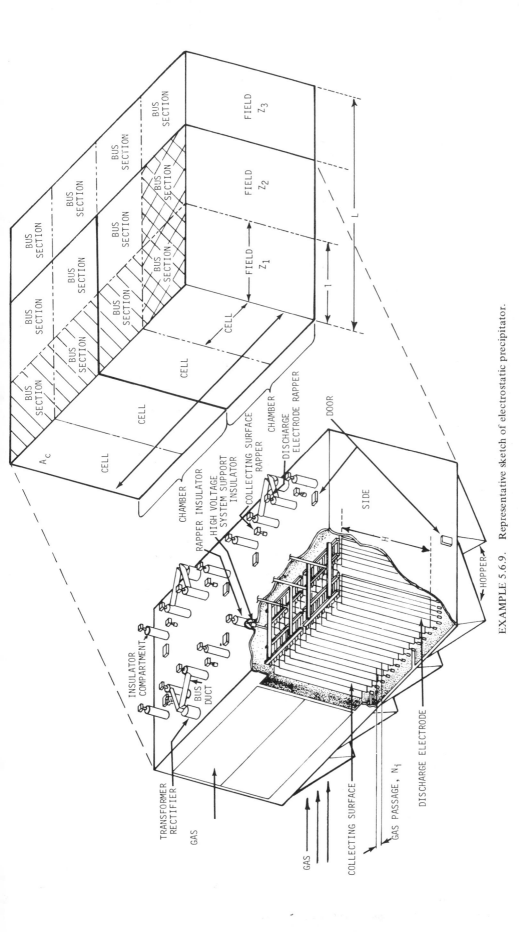

EXAMPLE 5.6.9.   Representative sketch of electrostatic precipitator.

187

number of bus sections required is 3.5/100,000 ACFM or approximately

$5 \times 3.5 \approx 18$ bus sections

Note that the collection surface area required could also have been obtained from Figure 5.5.5. For 99% efficiency and 1.8% sulfur coal, approximately 225 ft²/1,000 ACFM is required, or

$(225)(500) = 112,500$ ft²

Figure 5.5.3 could also have been used to determine collection electrode area. For a precipitation parameter of 0.34 ft/sec, a power density of 0.625 W/ft² is selected. Hence, the area is given by

$(70,000)(1/0.625) = 112,000$ ft²

Since the curves relating the various factors are mutually compatible, it makes little difference which approach is finally chosen to arrive at a design estimate.

NOMENCLATURE

A	Total collecting surface area		s	Distance
A_c	Tubular precipitator cross section		S	Tubular precipitator perimeter
b	Ion mobility, m²/V-sec		t	Time, sec
e	Electric charge, C		T	Temperature, °K
E_c	Charging electric field, V/m		v	Gas velocity
E_p	Collection field intensity, V/m		$\bar{v}$	Mean thermal velocity of ions, m/sec
F	Resultant force		V	Applied potential
F_D	Drag force		w	Particle migration velocity or precipitation rate parameter
F_E	Electrostatic force		W	Work
I	Current		y	Distance traveled
k	Boltzmann's constant, J/°k		Δz	Differential length
K	Dielectric constant of particle		α	Particle acceleration
L	Precipitator length		δ	Boundary region thickness
m	Particle mass		ϵ_o	Permittivity of free space, C²/N-m²
n	Number of sections		ρ	Particle density
N_o	Free ion density, number/m³		η	Particle collection efficiency
P	Power		μ	Gas viscosity
q	Charge, C		τ	Particle charging time constant
Q	Gas volumetric flow rate			
r	Particle radius			

PROBLEMS

1. A fly ash particle receives a 3.73×10^{-7} esu charge in a 2.2 kV/in. electron field. It is moving at a velocity of 4.2 cm/sec. Calculate the diameter of the particle.

2. A horizontal parallel-plate electrostatic precipitator consists of a single duct 16 ft high $\times$ 20 ft deep, with a 12-in. plate-to-plate spacing. A collection efficiency of 94.4% is obtained with a flow rate of 3,350 ACFM. The inlet loading is 4.07 grains/ft^3. Calculate the following.
   a. The bulk velocity of the gas (assume a uniform distribution).
   b. The outlet loading.
   c. The drift velocity for this system.
   d. A revised collection efficiency if the flow rate is increased to 5,400 ACFM.
   e. A revised collection efficiency if the plate spacing is decreased to 9 in.

3. The following experimental data have been obtained for the carbon black air system in an electrostatic precipitator.

Particle diameter, μm	Drift velocity, cm/sec	Weight %, $< d_p$
5	2.2	–
10	5.9	10
20	8.3	50
40	11.2	90
80	13.8	99.6
150	14.1	–
200	13.9	–

Generate a particle diameter-drift velocity (ft/sec) graph for this system.

4. A horizontal parallel-plate electrostatic precipitator consisting of three gas passages 16 ft high $\times$ 16 ft deep with a 12-in. plate spacing is to treat 19,200 ACFM of air containing 2.2 grains/ft^3 of carbon black. Using an average drift velocity for the system, calculate the collection efficiency of the unit. Assume the carbon black particle-size distribution may be represented by an average particle diameter of 20 μm.

5. Obtain the collection efficiency for the unit described in Problem 4 if the particle-size distribution and drift velocity data are employed.

6. Obtain the collection efficiency for the unit described in Problem 4 if both particle-size distribution data and drift velocity variation from theory are employed in the calculation.

7. Due to a rapid expansion just before the inlet to the precipitator, the velocity profile is not fully developed. The result of this is a volume rate of flow in the middle duct twice that of the outer duct. Calculate a revised collection efficiency for the unit described in Problem 4 under these conditions. Use the same average particle size and drift velocity.

8. Further complications are introduced to the calculations because of variations in the particle-size distribution at the inlet to the precipitator. Due to the inertial effects, none of the particles larger than 40 μm enter the outer passages. The remaining (smaller) particles, however, are uniformly distributed. Calculate a revised collection efficiency for the unit described in Problem 4 under these conditions. Use an appropriate average drift velocity for each passage.

9. Outline a method to calculate the collection efficiency for the above unit if particle-size and flow rate variations exist in both the horizontal and vertical direction.

10. As a recently hired engineer for an equipment vending company, you have been assigned the job of submitting a preliminary (process) design of an electrostatic precipitator to treat 78,000 ACFM of gas laden with solids from a gypsum plant operation. The inlet loading of 33.46 grains/ft^3 is to be reduced to 0.50. Submit your design.

11. An industrial installation has two electrostatic precipitators each designed to handle 100,000 ACFM. The collecting surface per precipitator is 15,500 ft^2. For a migration velocity of 0.45 ft/sec, calculate the efficiency of each precipitator. If one precipitator is shut down and it is decided to treat the total gas volume in the other precipitator, calculate the new efficiency.

12. An electrostatic precipitator is to be used for particulate removal at a municipal incinerator. The effluent gas stream flow rate is 100,000 ACFM. Estimate the precipitator design parameters to achieve 96% collection efficiency.

REFERENCES

1. White, H. J., *J. Air Pollut. Control Assoc.,* 7, 166, 1957.
2. Magill, P. L., Holden, F. R., and Ackley, C., Eds., *Air Pollution Handbook,* McGraw-Hill, New York, 1956.
3. Carlton-Jones, D., *J. Air Pollut. Control Assoc.,* 24(11), 1035, 1974.
4. Oglesby, S. and Nichols, G., *A Manual of Electrostatic Precipitator Technology,* Southern Research Institute, Birmingham, Alabama, prepared for Environmental Protection Agency, NTIS, PB-196, August 1970, 380.
5. Strauss, W., *Industrial Gas Cleaning,* Pergamon Press, New York, 1966.
6. White, H. J., *Industrial Electrostatic Precipitation,* Addison-Wesley, Reading, Massachusetts, 1963.
7. Rose, H. E. and Wood, A. J., *An Introduction to Electrostatic Precipitation in Theory and Practice,* Constable and Company Ltd., London, 1956.
8. Craggs, J. M. and Meek, J. D., *Electrical Breakdown in Gases,* Clarendon Press, Oxford, 1953.
9. Gooch, J. P. and Francis, N. L., *J. Air Pollut. Control Assoc.,* 25, 108, 1975.
10. Robinson, M., Electrostatic precipitation, in *Air Pollution Control. Part I,* Strauss, W., Ed., Interscience, New York, 1971.
11. Theodore, L. and Pardini, J., 64th Annu. APCA Meet. Atlantic City, New Jersey, Paper No. 71-124, June 1971.
12. APTD-1101, U.S. Environmental Protection Agency.
13. Penny, G. W. et al., *Eng. Dig.,* 29(12), 61, 1968.
14. Department of Health, Education, and Welfare, Public Health Safety, Control of Particle Emissions, Office of Manpower Development, Air Pollution Training Institute, Research Triangle Park, North Carolina, 1969.
15. Petroll, J., *Staub,* 29(9), 22, 1969.
16. Seman, G. W. and Penny, G. W., *IEEE, Trans. Power Appar. Syst.,* 86(3), 365, 1967.
17. Theodore, L., Proc. Annu. Northeast Regional Antipollution Conf., July 1969, 89.
18. Theodore, L. and Eastment, T., 65th Annu. APCA Meet., Miami Beach, Paper No. 72-108, June 1972.
19. Theodore, L., Reynolds, J., and Navarette, R., 66th Annu. APCA Meet., Chicago, Paper No. 73-292, June 1973.
20. Buonicore, A. J., Reynolds, J., and Theodore, L., Proc. 4th Annu. Pittsburgh Modeling and Simulation Conf., Pittsburgh, April 1–5, 1973.
21. Reynolds, J., Theodore, L., and Marino, J., *J. Air Pollut. Control. Assoc.,* 25(6), 610, 1975.
22. Ramsdell, R. G., *Proc. Am. Power Conf.,* 30, 129, 1968.
23. Barrett, A. A., Tech. Note BD/7, Part 2, Central Electricity Generating Board, England, August 1967.
24. Sproull, W. T. and Nakada, Y., *Ind. Eng. Chem.,* 43, 1350, 1951.
25. Environmental Elements Corporation, Ductwork Arrangement Criteria for Electrostatic Precipitators Without Model Study, bulletin based on information presented at the 62nd Annu. APCA Meet., New York City, June 22–26, 1969.
26. Soo, S. L., *Environ. Sci. Technol.,* 7, 63, 1973.
27. Vatavuk, W. M. and Theodore, L., Proc. 2nd Natl. Conf. on Energy and the Environment, AIChE and APCA, November 1974, 181.
28. Sundberg, R. E., *J. Air Pollut. Control Assoc.,* 24(8), 758, 1974.

Chapter 6

WET SCRUBBERS

6.1. INTRODUCTION

Wet scrubbers have found widespread use in cleaning contaminated gas streams because of their ability to remove effectively both particulate and gaseous pollutants. Specifically, wet scrubbing describes the technique of bringing a contaminated gas stream into intimate contact with a liquid. Wet scrubbers include all the various types of gas absorption equipment. In this book, however, the term "scrubber" will be restricted to those systems which utilize a liquid, usually water, to achieve or assist in the removal of particulate matter from a carrier gas stream. The use of wet scrubbers to remove gaseous pollutants from contaminated streams is not considered here, but information is available in the literature.[1]

Wet scrubbers are constructed with such a multiplicity of designs that no single type can be considered representative of the category as a whole. Some units simply consist of an existing dry-type collector modified by the introduction of a liquid phase to assist in particulate removal and to prevent particulate reentrainment; other units are specifically designed to operate as wet collectors. Wet collectors can increase particulate removal efficiency by conditioning fine particles so that their effective size is increased. This enables the particles to be collected more easily. Reentrainment of the collected particles is minimized by trapping them in the liquid film. The effective particle size may also be increased by promoting condensation on fine particles which act as nuclei when the vapor passes through its dew point. Nevertheless, the most prominent mechanism of particle collection on liquid droplets is accomplished by impaction, which takes advantage of inertial forces.

The particulate collection mechanisms involved in the wet scrubbing operation may include some or all of the following.

1. Inertial impaction.
2. Direct interception.
3. Diffusion (Brownian movement).
4. Electrostatic forces.
5. Gravitational forces.
6. Condensation.
7. Thermal gradients.

Inertial impaction occurs when an object (the droplet), placed in the path of a particulate-laden gas stream, causes the gas to diverge and flow around it. Larger particles, however, tend to continue in a straight path because of their inertia; they may impinge on the obstacle and be collected (as in Figure 6.1.1.a). Since the trajectories of particle centers can be calculated, it is possible to theoretically determine the probability of collision. Direct interception also depends on inertia and is merely a secondary form of impaction. As previously stated, the trajectory of a particle center can be calculated; however, even though the center may bypass the target object, a collision might occur since the particle has finite size (see Figure 6.1.1.b). A collision occurs due to direct interception if the dust particle's center misses the target object by some dimension less than the particle's radius. Direct interception is, therefore, not a separate principle, but only an extension of inertial impaction. Diffusion is another extension of the impaction principle. Very small particles (submicron) suspended in a gas stream have an individual oscillatory motion known as Brownian movement (see Figure 6.1.1.c). In this case, particle and target collide as a result of relative motion within limited space. As in all diffusional processes, the rate of diffusion is favored by large areas for diffusion, thereby necessitating small liquid droplets with high surface-to-volume ratios for high collection efficiencies. While collision or impaction may be the result of either inertia or Brownian movement, the results are the same. Inertial impaction, direct interception, and diffusion are usually considered to be the dominant collection mechanisms in wet scrubbers.

The remaining collection mechanisms are secondary in nature and should be considered as such. Gravitation forces can cause a particle, as it passes an obstacle, to fall from the streamline and settle on the surface of the obstacle (see Figure 6.1.1.d). Such forces come into play only when dealing with the larger size particles (usually greater than 40 μm). Electrostatic forces result when particles and liquid droplets become electrically charged (see Figure 6.1.1.e). In addition, when only the particle or obstacle is charged, a charge may be induced on the uncharged component, resulting in a polarization force that can also effect particle

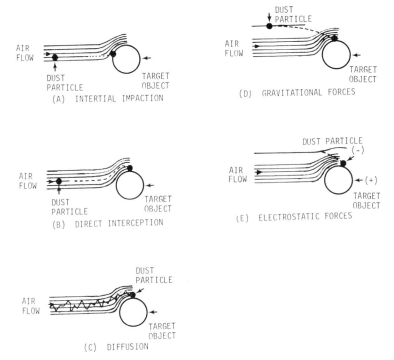

FIGURE 6.1.1. Principal collection mechanisms in wet scrubbers.

removal. The electrostatic charge may be acquired, for example, by liquid droplets during their formation. An electrical charge also may be induced by flame ionization, friction, or the presence of charged matter. The effect of the electrostatic mechanism may be significant when the charge on the particle or obstacle is high and when gas velocity is low. The significance of particle size and obstacle size varies, depending on whether the electrical attraction originates from Coulomb or polarization forces. Condensation effects, as mentioned previously, may also come into play. Condensation occurs if the gas or air is rapidly cooled below its dew point. When moisture is condensed out of the gas stream, fogging occurs, and the dust particles can serve as condensation nuclei. The dust particles can become larger as a result of the condensed liquid, and the probability of removal by impaction is increased. Condensation, however, generally removes only a relatively small amount of the particles, primarily because the amount of condensation required to remove high concentrations is usually greater than can be readily achieved. Particle collection may also be affected by thermal gradients. Such forces can drive particles from hotter to colder regions. The motion can be caused by unequal gas molecular collision energy on the surfaces of the hot and cold sides of the particle; it is directly proportional to the temperature gradient. In wet scrubbers the effect of thermal gradients is usually negligible; significant particle collection is seldom attributed to this mechanism.

6.2. TYPES OF WET SCRUBBERS

Due to the large variety of wet scrubbers currently on the market, it is difficult to generalize about relationships among operating parameters such as pressure drop and liquid flow rate. It is also difficult to classify wet scrubbers according to particle collection mechanisms since the usual case finds many of the collection mechanisms working simultaneously in each type of scrubber. However, in a very general sense, wet scrubbers may be loosely categorized by pressure drop (or energy consumption). Low-energy scrubbers are those with typical pressure drops less than 5 in. of water; medium-energy scrubbers are those with typical pressure drops from 5 to 15 in. of water; and high-energy scrubbers are those with typical pressure drops greater than 15 in. of water. Spray chambers and spray towers, for example, provide the lowest pressure drop and, correspondingly, the lowest collection efficiencies; they would be classified as low-energy scrubbers. The medium pressure drop group could include centrifugal fan wet scrubbers, atomizing impingement collectors, and certain packed-bed scrubbers. The most familiar of the high-pressure-drop (high-energy) group would be the venturi-type collector. While the venturi scrubber is capable of providing high collection efficiencies, the high pressure drop can represent a significant cost item, i.e., pumps or fans must be purchased, operated, and maintained to keep the gas flowing through the system. Since many collectors could conceivably be listed in more than one of the above categories, in this section each type of collector will be considered individually, with its eventual application determining whether it will be classified as a low-, medium-, or high-energy scrubber.

Spray Towers

The most common low-energy scrubbers are gravity spray towers in which liquid droplets are made to fall through rising exhaust gases and are drained at the bottom of the chamber (see Figure 6.2.1). The droplets are usually formed by liquid atomized in spray nozzles. The spray is directed into a chamber shaped to conduct the gas through the finely divided liquid. In a vertical tower the relative velocity between the droplets and the gas is eventually the terminal settling velocity of the droplets. However, to avoid spray droplet re-entrainment, the terminal settling velocity of the droplets must be greater than the velocity of the rising gas stream. In practice, the vertical gas velocity typically ranges from 2 to 5 ft/sec. For higher velocities, a mist eliminator must be used in the top of the tower.

For high collection efficiency to occur by impaction, there must be both a high relative velocity difference between the droplets and the particles, and small-sized scrubbing droplets. In gravitational spray towers, however, these conditions tend to be mutually incompatible, i.e., small droplets have low free-falling (terminal) velocities. Consequently, there is an optimum droplet size (for a given particle size) for maximum collection efficiency by impaction. Stairmand[2] has shown (see Figure 6.2.2) that as droplet size diminishes to the 500- to 1,000-μm range, the impaction efficiency increases. However, a further decrease in droplet size decreases the impaction efficiency. Figure 6.2.2 shows that the maximum theoretical efficiency for the smaller particle sizes (less than 5 μm) occurs for droplet sizes of about

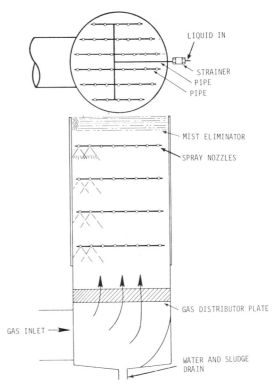

FIGURE 6.2.1. Gravity spray tower.

800 μm. For larger particle sizes, the efficiency varies little over the range of droplet sizes 500 to 1000 μm. Hence, in gravitational spray towers there is little point in using very fine spray nozzles.

Spray towers are suited for both particle collection and mass transfer (gas absorption), as are all wet scrubbers. Operating characteristics include low pressure drop (typically less than 1 to 2 in. of water, exclusive of mist eliminator and gas distribution plate), ability to handle spray liquids having a high solids content, and liquid requirements ranging from 3 to 20 gal/1,000 ft³ of gas treated. Spray towers are capable of handling large gas volumes and are often used as precoolers to reduce gas stream temperatures. Gas rates from 800 to 2,500 lb/hr ft² are typical. Gas retention times within the tower typically range from 20 to 30 sec. The chief disadvantage of spray towers is their relatively low scrubbing efficiency for dust particles in the 0- to 5-μm range. Particles larger than 10 μm can typically be removed with efficiencies up to about 70%. The efficiency can be improved by the addition of high-pressure sprays, ranging from 100 to 400 psig. Depending on the spray pressure utilized, efficiencies can be increased by

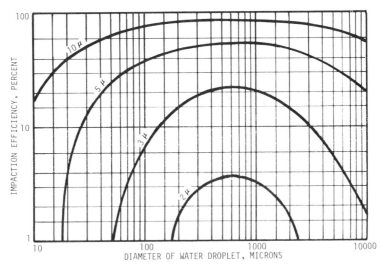

FIGURE 6.2.2. Relation between collection efficiency and droplet size for a gravitational spray tower.

as much as 20%. The use of baffles can also increase collection efficiency. An important advantage of spray towers is their capability to treat relatively high dust concentrations without fear of any plugging. Although the units have a relatively large space requirement, they are inexpensive and, are used in practice primarily for the collection of coarse dusts (greater than approximately 25 μm) and a precoolers.

Centrifugal Collectors

Particulate collection efficiency is improved by increasing the relative velocity between the droplets and the gas stream. The particulates are assumed to travel at the same velocity as the gas stream. An increase in this relative velocity may be achieved by utilizing the centrifugal force of a spinning gas. The spin may come from introducing gases to the scrubber tangentially or by directing the gas stream against stationary swirl vanes. Although normally designed for specific installations, cyclonic spray scrubbers can accommodate gas entrance velocities up to 200 ft/sec. In the centrifugal systems shown in Figures 6.2.3 to 6.2.5, the principal benefit is derived from the wetted walls hindering reentrainment of collected particulates. Water rates of 2 to 5 gal/1,000 ft^3 of gas and pressure drops from 2 to 6 in. of water are typical. In Figure 6.2.6 the liquid spray is directed outward from sprays set in a central pipe manifold. Sprays in this fashion enhance collection efficiency by increasing particle impaction on the spray droplets. Sprays directed in from the walls,

as in Figure 6.2.7, are more easily serviced. However, since they can be made accessible from the outside of the scrubber, an unsprayed section is usually provided to give liquid droplets containing collected particles sufficient time to reach the walls of the collector and prevent them from exiting the unit in the cleaned gas stream. Figure 6.2.8 is an example of the rotating motion given to the gas stream by fixed vanes and impellers, with the scrubbing liquid introduced centrally either as a spray or liquid stream.

Dynamic Collectors

Dynamic collectors, as depicted in Figure 6.2.9, serve primarily as air movers (centrifugal blowers). Spray nozzles at the inlet offer an opportunity for impaction. Liquid droplets from the nozzles and uncaptured dust must pass through the many specially shaped blades of the rotating fan wheel. Centrifugal force and impingement on the blades are utilized for further collection and water separation. Problems have arisen, however, due to instability attributed to sludge build-up on the fan wheel. Slurry is removed and discharged separately from the cleaned air. Design pressure drop is about 6 in. of water with a maximum pressure drop of 9 in. Water requirements typically range from 0.5 to 1.5 gal/1,000 ft^3 of gas, and power requirements range from 1 to 2 hp/1,000 ACFM of gas treated. The collection efficiency is similar to other scrubbers with a 6-in. pressure drop. The chief advantages are compactness, moderate power requirements, and low water consumption.

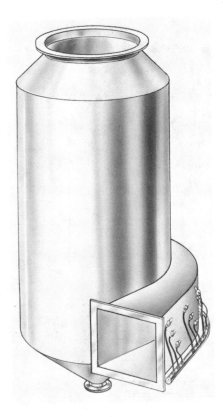

FIGURE 6.2.3. PolyCon cyclone spray scrubber. (Courtesy of Poly Con Corporation.)

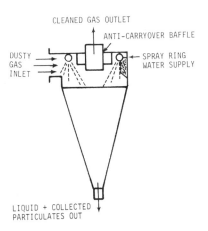

FIGURE 6.2.4. Large-diameter irrigated cyclone.

Packed-bed Scrubbers

Packed-bed scrubbers find normal application in the removal of pollutant gases and vapors. They are considered in depth in a companion text.[1] Within the last few years, however, such systems have also been considered for the removal of particulate matter. There are four general ways in which

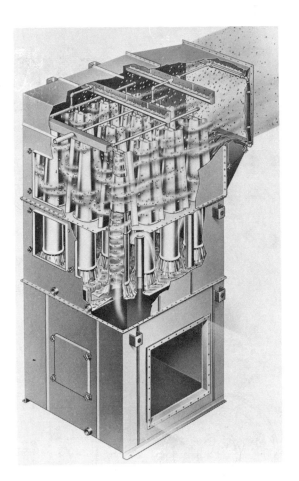

FIGURE 6.2.5. Tubular-type centrifugal wet collector. (Courtesy of American Filter Company, Inc.)

these beds may be operated to effect particulate removal (see Figure 6.2.10). Cross-flow scrubbers will efficiently remove the relatively large-size particulates; they are also used for the removal of liquid particulates. The co current flow scrubber is somewhat more efficient than the cross flow and is effective in removing both solid and liquid particulates. For the collection of particulates as small as 3 to 5 μm, packed-countercurrent scrubbers have been found to be most efficient. These scrubbers operate at much higher liquid rates than either the cross-flow or the cocurrent-flow types; because of this, they are capable of handling heavier particulate loadings. Bed depth in packed countercurrent scrubbers is typically 3 to 10 ft, which is greater than that in cross-flow or cocurrent-flow scrubbers. Gas velocities typically range between 3 and 6 ft/sec. Cross-flow beds are usually less than 2 ft in depth (with a maximum of about 6 ft).

The difficulty of removal of particulate

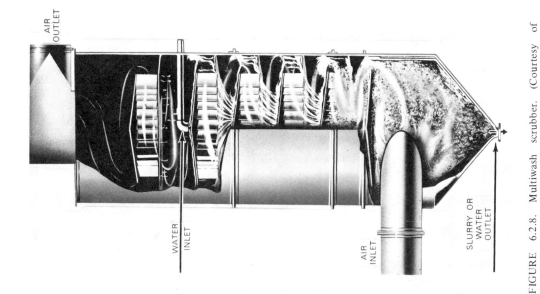

FIGURE 6.2.8. Multiwash scrubber. (Courtesy of Claude B. Schneible Company.)

AIR OUTLET

WATER INLET

SLURRY OR WATER OUTLET

AIR INLET

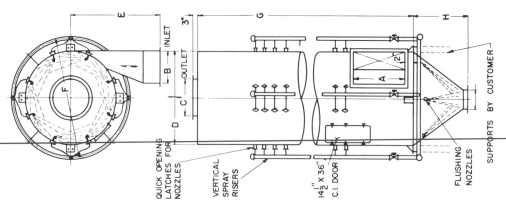

FIGURE 6.2.7. Cyclonic spray scrubber. (Courtesy of Buffalo Forge Company.)

QUICK OPENING LATCHES FOR NOZZLES

VERTICAL SPRAY RISERS

$14\frac{1}{2}$" X 36" C.I. DOOR

FLUSHING NOZZLES

SUPPORTS BY CUSTOMER

INLET

OUTLET

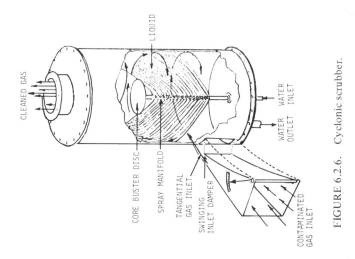

FIGURE 6.2.6. Cyclonic scrubber.

CLEANED GAS

LIQUID

CORE BUSTER DISC

SPRAY MANIFOLD

TANGENTIAL GAS INLET

SWINGING INLET DAMPER

CONTAMINATED GAS INLET

WATER OUTLET

WATER INLET

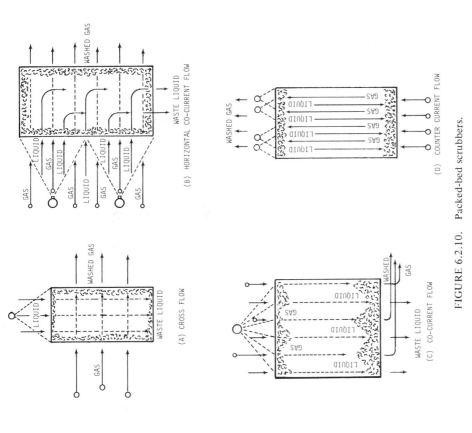

FIGURE 6.2.10. Packed-bed scrubbers.

(A) CROSS FLOW

(B) HORIZONTAL CO-CURRENT FLOW

(C) CO-CURRENT FLOW

(D) COUNTER CURRENT FLOW

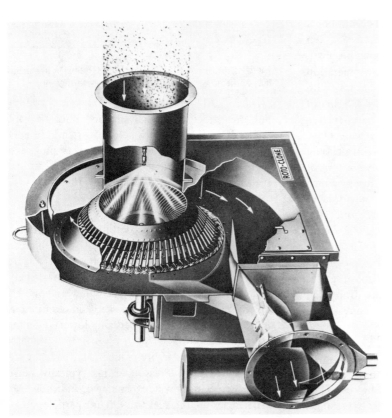

FIGURE 6.2.9. Centrifugal fan wet scrubber. (Courtesy of American Air Filter Company.)

material increases rapidly with a decrease in particulate size. A 1-μm particle is only 10 times larger in diameter than a 0.1-μm particle, but it will have 100 times more surface area and 1,000 times more weight. As particle size decreases, the surface area-to-mass ratio increases so rapidly that eventually the surface properties can dominate over the mass properties. When this happens, higher velocities and more acute changes in direction are required to permit the particle to be separated from the gas stream by impingement. Cross-flow, cocurrent-flow, and countercurrent-flow packed scrubbers are not capable of achieving a high enough gas velocity to effectively remove particulates smaller than 3 to 5 μm in diameter. To remove particles in this small size range (down to about 0.25 μm), much more energy must be used to attain the velocities needed and, to avoid flooding, the liquid must be moved in the same direction as the gas, i.e., the bed is operated in cocurrent flow.

To date, the major problems in using packed-bed scrubbers for particulate removal are plugging of the packing and the maintenance problems subsequently incurred. A general rule of thumb is to allow a maximum of 0.2 grains per standard cubic foot of dust to enter a packed tower. However, the application of moving-bed scrubbers (discussed below) to particulate removal often minimizes, if not eliminates, the plugging problem.

Liquid requirements for cross-flow operation range from 1 to 4 gal/1,000 ft^3 of gas, with pressure drops typically from 0.2 to 0.5 in. of water per foot of bed depth. Liquid requirements for countercurrent-packed scrubbers usually range from 10 to 20 gal/1,000 ft^3 of gas, with pressure drops typically 0.5 to 1.0 in. of water per foot of bed depth. However, some adaptations, which make use of a highly efficient turbulent layer above the bed (see Figure 6.2.11), require considerably less scrubbing liquid, typically 2 to 2.5 gal/1,000 ft^3 of gas at a pressure drop ranging from 4 to 6 in. of water. In cocurrent flow a liquid requirement of 7 to 15 gal/1,000 ft^3 of gas is fairly common. The operating pressure drop is on the order of 1 to 4 in. of water per foot of bed depth.

Coarsely packed beds are used for removing coarse dusts and mists 10 μm and larger, with velocities through the bed on the order of 400 ft/min. Finely packed beds may be used for removing contaminants in the smaller size range,

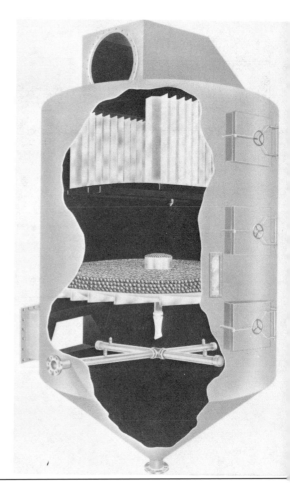

FIGURE 6.2.11. Flooded-bed wet scrubber with turbulent contact layer. (Courtesy of Riley-Environeering, Inc.)

but the velocity through the bed must be kept relatively low, preferably below 50 ft/min. Finely packed beds have a greater tendency to plug, and their applications are generally limited to gas streams with relatively low grain loadings.

Moving-bed Scrubbers

Moving-bed (fluid-bed) scrubbers incorporate a zone of movable packing where gas and liquid can intimately mix. The system shown in Figure 6.2.12 uses packing consisting of low-density polyethylene or polypropylene spheres about 1½ in. in diameter; these are kept in continuous motion between the upper and lower retaining grids. Such action keeps the spheres continually cleaned and considerably reduces any tendency for the bed to plug. Pressure drops typically range from 3 to 5 in. of water (per stage), and collection efficiencies are in excess of 99% for particles down

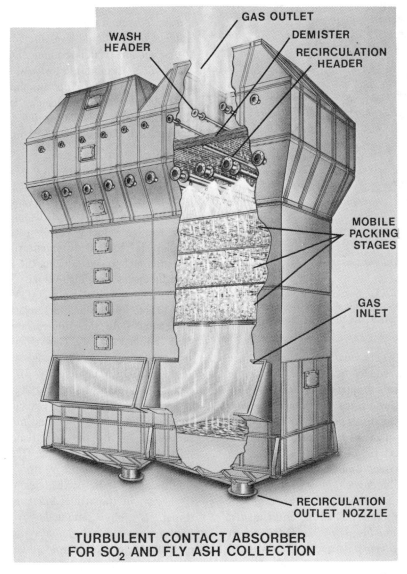

WASH HEADER

GAS OUTLET

DEMISTER

RECIRCULATION HEADER

MOBILE PACKING STAGES

GAS INLET

RECIRCULATION OUTLET NOZZLE

TURBULENT CONTACT ABSORBER FOR SO₂ AND FLY ASH COLLECTION

FIGURE 6.2.12. Moving-bed scrubber. (Courtesy of UOP Air Correction Division.)

to 2 μm. Particle collection may be enhanced by using several moving-bed stages in series.

Atomizing-inertial Scrubbers

The atomizing-inertial category of wet scrubbers probably represents the largest grouping of commercial dust collectors. Available designs vary more than in any other category. For the sake of convenience, this category will be further divided into those which utilize the kinetic energy of the gas stream to fragment or atomize the liquid on which the particle impacts (orifice and venturi scrubbers) and those which utilize a perforated

plate with an impingement baffle over each perforation.

Orifice-type Wet Scrubbers

In orifice-type wet scrubbers (sometimes referred to as self-induced spray scrubbers), the gas stream comes into contact with a pool of liquid at the entrance to a constriction (submerged orifice). Liquid is entrained and carried into the restriction where greater liquid-particulate interaction occurs, resulting in a high frequency of particulate impaction on the droplets (see Figure 6.2.13). Upon leaving the restriction, most of the water droplets

FIGURE 6.2.13. Swirl-orifice scrubber. (Courtesy of United Swirl Orifice Scrubbers, United McGill Corporation.)

(those large enough) are separated by gravity since the gas velocity is reduced from what it was in the restriction. Smaller droplets are subsequently removed by centrifugal force and impingement on baffles located in the upper part of the unit. Water rate in motion through the restriction ranges from 10 to 25 gal/1,000 ft^3 of gas. At a typical gas velocity of 50 ft/sec, droplets in the 300- to 400-μm range can be created. Most of the water is recirculated from the pool (hence this does not contribute to the scrubbers' water requirements, which typically range from 1 to 3 gal/1,000 ft^3 of gas). Pressure drop typically ranges from 3 to 10 in. of water, with collection efficiencies often in the 90 to 95% range. The chief advantage of these systems is their ability to handle high dust concentration (no fine clearances to cause plugging) and high solids-content slurries.

A slight modification of this system is the combined venturi-impingement scrubber. The scrubber section contains a liquid reservoir just below the throat section of a venturi. An adjustable weir is provided to maintain a constant liquid level. The scrubbing liquid is recycled (recirculation is normally 3 to 7 gal/1,000 ft^3 of saturated gas) through nozzles near the top of the scrubber tube. The scrubbing liquid flows down the inside of the tube and into the throat section of the venturi where it is deflected and atomized by the high-velocity gases. The particulates impact with the droplets formed by the high-velocity gas stream. A second scrubbing occurs when the gases impinge on the liquid level immediately below the throat section. Water requirements are limited to make-up for evaporation loss and slurry bleed-off; for most conditions, this amounts to about 0.5 gal/1,000 ft^3 of gas. Efficiency is relatively high for particulates as small as 0.5 μm in diameter. Pressure drop usually ranges from 8 to 15 in. of water.

Venturi Scrubbers

To achieve high collection efficiency of particulates by impaction, a small droplet diameter and high relative velocity between the particle and droplet are required. In a venturi scrubber this is accomplished by introducing the scrubbing liquid at right angles to a high-velocity gas flow in the venturi throat (vena contracta). Very small water droplets are formed, and high relative velocities are maintained until the droplets are accelerated to their terminal velocity. Gas velocities through the venturi throat typically range from 12,000 to 24,000 ft/min. The velocity of the gases alone causes the atomization of the liquid. The energy expended in the scrubber (except for the small amount used in the sprays and mist eliminator) is accounted for by the gas stream pressure drop through the scrubber. Another factor important to the effectiveness of the venturi scrubber is the conditioning of the particulates by condensation. If the gas in the reduced-pressure region in the throat is fully saturated, or supersaturated (preferably), some condensation will occur on the particulates in the throat due to the Joule-Thompson effect. Condensation will be more pronounced if the gas is hot, due to the cooling effect of the scrubbing liquid.

The venturi itself is only a gas conditioner and must be followed by a separating section for the elimination of entrained droplets (see Figures 6.2.14 and 6.2.15). Water is injected into the venturi in quantities ranging from 6 to 10 gal/1,000 ft^3 of gas. Very high collection efficiencies are achievable with operating pressure drops ranging from 6 to 70 in. of water. Pressure drops of 25 to 30 in. are not at all uncommon. For example, a 10-in. pressure-drop venturi can typically remove particles as small as a couple of microns with virtually 100% efficiency, while a 60-in. pressure-drop venturi is often required to remove particles as small as 0.3 to 0.4 μm. Since collection efficiency is directly related to pressure

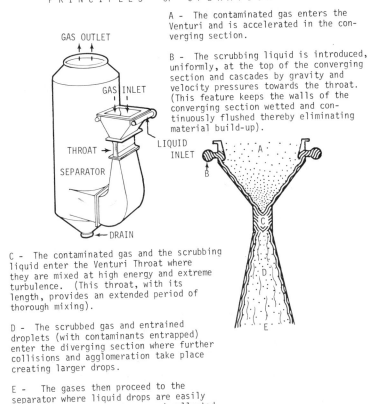

GAS OUTLET

GAS INLET

THROAT

SEPARATOR

LIQUID INLET

← DRAIN

A - The contaminated gas enters the Venturi and is accelerated in the converging section.

B - The scrubbing liquid is introduced, uniformly, at the top of the converging section and cascades by gravity and velocity pressures towards the throat. (This feature keeps the walls of the converging section wetted and continuously flushed thereby eliminating material build-up).

C - The contaminated gas and the scrubbing liquid enter the Venturi Throat where they are mixed at high energy and extreme turbulence. (This throat, with its length, provides an extended period of thorough mixing).

D - The scrubbed gas and entrained droplets (with contaminants entrapped) enter the diverging section where further collisions and agglomeration take place creating larger drops.

E - The gases then proceed to the separator where liquid drops are easily removed from the gas stream and collected.

FIGURE 6.2.14.   Venturi scrubber with cyclone separator.

drop, variable-throat venturi scrubbers have been introduced (see Figure 6.2.16) to maintain pressure drop with varying gas flows. In these systems the scrubbing efficiency and pressure drop may be adjusted by changing the position of a disk located in the venturi throat.

As indicated previously, a major drawback in utilizing the venturi scrubber for fine particulate control is the relatively large pressure drop and, therefore, the high power requirement. For example, a 6,000-ACFM venturi scrubber operated at a 65- to 70-in. pressure drop would require a fan motor of 125 hp. The "rule of thumb" for calculating motor operating costs is $50 per brake horsepower per year. Thus, if 125 hp is needed, operating costs for that fan would be $6,250 over a 1-year period.

A recent development, the surface intensive venturi (see Figure 6.2.17), shows promise in achieving the expected high collection efficiency characteristic of the venturi scrubber without the usual accompanying high pressure loss. In the surface-intensive venturi, the flow channel is not restricted; instead, the flow to the throat is gradually restricted and then derestricted. At the same time the fluid channel contact area is gradually increased and then decreased with an enormous effective area in the throat. Pressure drops of 12 to 15 in. of water are often able to achieve extremely high collection efficiencies. The manufacturer claims that the channel spacing at the throat is 80 μm. This obviously will create fabrication problems. However, the small spacing may produce laminar flow in this region, which may account for the low pressure drop.

Another offshoot of the venturi scrubber is the two-phase jet scrubber, which finds primary application in treating high-temperature exhaust streams. Power to operate the equipment is derived from this high-temperature stream (it typically must be above 800°F). One such system is shown in Figure 6.2.18. Heat is transferred to the water from the gas, thus increasing the temperature of the water to the required level — usually between 300 to 400°F. By expanding through the nozzle of the two-phase jet, partial flashing occurs, and the

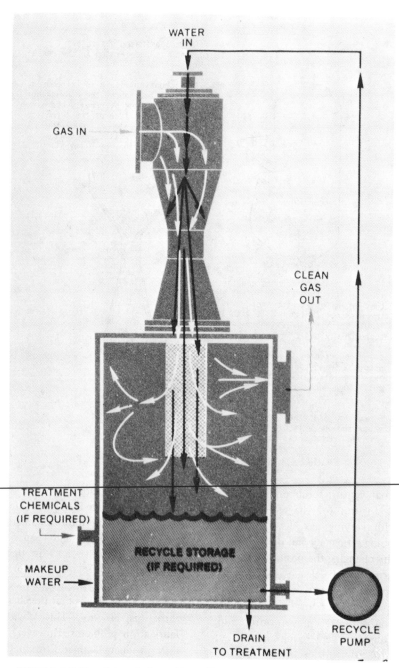

WATER IN

GAS IN

CLEAN GAS OUT

TREATMENT CHEMICALS (IF REQUIRED)

MAKEUP WATER

RECYCLE STORAGE (IF REQUIRED)

DRAIN TO TREATMENT

RECYCLE PUMP

FIGURE 6.2.15.   Jet-venturi scrubber. (Courtesy of Croll-Reynolds Company, Inc.)

remaining liquid is atomized. Thus, a two-phase mixture of steam and small water droplets leaves the nozzle at high velocity. The system produces a differential velocity between the particulates and water droplets in excess of 800 ft/sec. The gas is entrained by this high-velocity two-phase mixture; in the ensuing mixing with the gas, cleaning occurs by scrubbing. Extremely high removal efficiencies are achieved on particulates smaller than 0.1 μm. At the same time, the transfer of momentum to the gas results in a pressure rise across the mixing section. This pressure rise provides the driving force which moves the gas through the system; hence, no exhaust fans and motors are required. For example, a 14-in. pressure loss in the ducting and heat exchanger and an 8-in. loss in the separator can be made up by utilizing a water temperature of approximately 360°F. Since the operating energy is obtained from process waste heat, the operating cost is reported to be about half that of comparable equipment.

Another recent development in the atomization and acceleration of scrubbing liquor to achieve high particle-removal efficiencies similar to those experienced in venturi scrubbers, only at considerably lower pressure drop, is the centripetal vortex contactor (see Figures 6.2.19 and 6.2.20). Based on the much-researched centripetal vortex principle,[66] the contaminant-laden gases are forced to pass through a high-velocity, high-intensity droplet cloud formed by the aerodynamic motion of the gas stream passing through

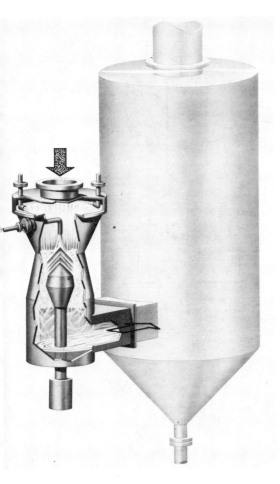

FIGURE 6.2.16. Variable-throat venturi scrubber. (Courtesy of Koch Engineering Company, Inc.)

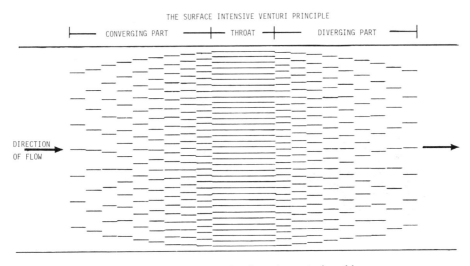

FIGURE 6.2.17. The surface intensive venturi scrubber.

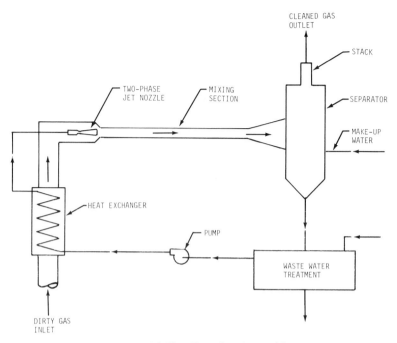

FIGURE 6.2.18.   Two-phase jet scrubber.

FIGURE 6.2.19.   Centripetal vortex contactor wet scrubbers on a coal-fired boiler for simultaneous fly ash and sulfur dioxide removal. (Courtesy of Entoleter, Inc.)

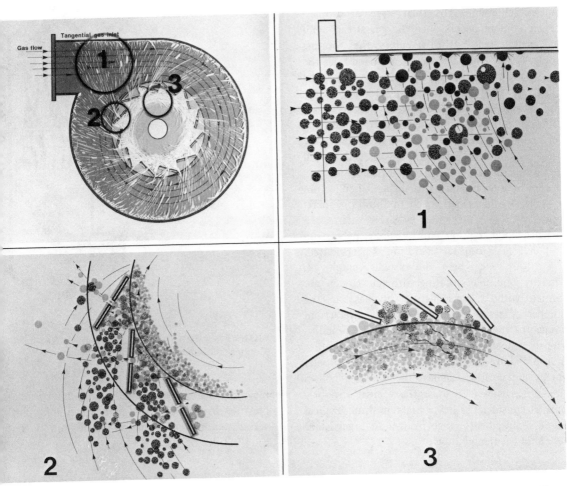

FIGURE 6.2.20. Particle collection mechanisms experienced in the single-vane cage centripetal vortex scrubber (1) at scrubber inlet, (2) at entrance into cloud, and (3) in cloud. (Courtesy of Entoleter, Inc.)

a stationary circular vane cage. The scrubbing liquor, which is fed through an open pipe with no nozzles or restrictions, assumes a fog-mist-droplet phase and forms a tornado-like cloud within the vane cage. Rotation is initiated and sustained by using only the energy in the moving gas stream. There are no moving parts in the unit. The rotating cloud is maintained by the ability of the vane cage to stabilize it axially within the contact area. The cloud is relieved of scrubbing liquor at a rate equal to that at which it is fed. The multiple stages of droplet-particle interaction in the contact area enable the centripetal vortex scrubber to achieve efficiencies comparable to venturi scrubbers, but at lower pressure drop. As the gases enter the centripetal vortex contactor, they are bombarded by the larger size droplets flushed from the rotating droplet cloud. The centrifugal-centripetal

force balance on a droplet in the cloud insures a relatively small equilibrium droplet diameter, i.e., should a droplet be enlarged in any way (size or mass) by agglomeration with other droplets or particle impaction, the centrifugal force on it will overcome the centripetal force and cause the droplet to be flushed. The droplet-particle interaction, resulting from this continual flushing of the gas stream as it enters the contactor and makes its way toward the vane cage, serves two purposes: (1) removal of a substantial portion of the larger size particles and (2) prequenching/ preconditioning of the gas stream. The next stage of contact occurs just as the gas-particle stream interacts (almost cocurrently) with the high-velocity, rotating droplet cloud. Just as in the venturi scrubber, the high relative velocity difference between the droplets and the particles at this point accounts for the high particle collection efficiencies achievable. The final stage of droplet-particle contact occurs once the gas stream with any uncollected particles enters the rotating droplet cloud. Once the gas stream penetrates the cloud, any particles still entrained assume the velocity of the droplets in the cloud, i.e., the relative velocity difference goes to zero. Yet, as a result of both a pressure and concentration driving force, the particle tends to migrate through the droplet cloud. Its path through the cloud will usually insure contact with and, subsequently, capture by a droplet. This final stage of collection is similar to that experienced in filtration operations.

When code requirements are extremely stringent or a mass transfer operation is necessitated, concentric vane cages are usually employed, whereby multiple rotating droplet clouds are formed with a consequential increase in the number of stages of droplet-particle interaction. Numerous successful installations in the foundry, asphalt, phosphate, coal preparation, and other industries have demonstrated that the centripetal vortex contactor can achieve the same high collection efficiencies (99+%) as the venturi scrubber, only at considerably lower pressure drop. Typical liquid requirements range from 2 to 5 gal/1,000 ACFM of gas treated.

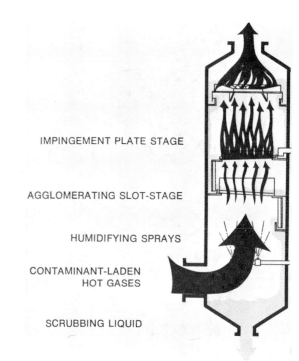

IMPINGEMENT PLATE STAGE

AGGLOMERATING SLOT-STAGE

HUMIDIFYING SPRAYS

CONTAMINANT-LADEN HOT GASES

SCRUBBING LIQUID

FIGURE 6.2.21. Impingement plate scrubbers. (Courtesy of Peabody Engineering Corporation.)

may range from 90 to 98% for 1-μm particles; pressure drops from 1 to 8 in. of water are typical. Water requirements usually range from 3 to 5 gal/1,000 ft^3 of gas.

Impingement Plate Scrubbers

Impingement plate scrubbers (see Figure 6.2.21) utilize perforated plates with an impingement baffle over each perforation. The intention here is to expand the surface area of the liquid through use of the gas stream's kinetic energy. Gas flowing upward is divided into thousands of jets by the orifices. Gas velocities of 15 to 20 ft/sec through the orifices are common. Each jet aspirates liquid from the blanket and creates a wetted surface on the baffle, located at the point of maximum jet velocity. The directed impingement on a wetted target dynamically precipitates particles and entraps them in the scrubbing liquid. On impingement, each jet forms minute gas bubbles which rise through and create turbulence in the liquid blanket. This provides extremely close gas-liquid contact for maximum cleaning. Continuous violent agitation of the blanket by the bubbles prevents settling of entrapped particles and flushes them away in the scrubbing liquid.

Overall collection efficiencies for a single plate

Atomizing-mechanical Scrubbers

In mechanically induced scrubbers, high-velocity sprays are generated at right angles to the direction of gas flow by a partially submerged rotor (see Figure 6.2.22). The dirty gas stream passes through the area of the collector that contains the mechanically produced droplets. Scrubbing is achieved by impaction because of both high radial-droplet velocity and vertical gas velocity. Liquid atomization occurs at the rotor and the outer wall.

Power and liquid requirements range from 3 to 10 hp and from 4 to 5 gal/1,000 ft^3 of gas, respectively, for the high-velocity design (see Figure 6.2.22), depending on particle size and the desired collection efficiency. The chief advantages of these scrubbers are relatively low liquid and small space requirements, high scrubbing efficiency, and high dust-load capacity. The rotor, however, is susceptible to erosion from large particles and abrasive dusts. In addition, high-energy scrubbing applications usually require a mist eliminator.

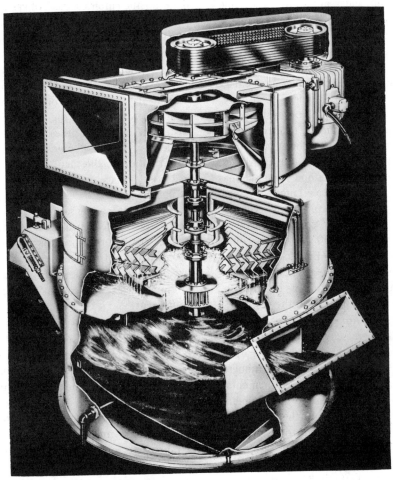

FIGURE 6.2.22.   Center spray high-velocity scrubber. (Courtesy of Centri-Spray Corporation.)

Disintegrator Scrubbers

To collect submicron particles, a very finely dispersed liquid is required. One method of providing these fine-liquid droplets is by shearing the liquid between a stator and a rapidly moving rotor and permitting the gas to pass through the unit, i.e., in a disintegrator scrubber. Disintegrator scrubbers consist of an outer casing containing alternate rows of stator and rotor bars; the relative velocity between adjacent bars is on the order of 200 to 300 ft/sec. Water is injected axially and is effectively atomized into fine droplets by the rapidly rotating vanes. The dust-laden gas also enters axially and passes through the dense spray zone where the particles are subjected to intense bombardment by the water droplets. Water and power requirements typically range from 4 to 9 gal and 10 to 20 hp, respectively, per 1,000 ft^3 of gas treated. This power is largely expended in atomizing and accelerating the water. Although disintegrator scrubbers are efficient on submicron particles, they have a high operating cost due to the energy required to drive the impeller. These scrubbers are also usually preceded by conventional collectors, such as cyclones, to insure that only low concentrations, on the order of 0.25 to 0.50 grains/ft^3, are allowed to enter the unit. These precautions are necessary to avoid build-up in the disintegrator which, when running at high speed with fine clearance, is particularly susceptible to trouble if operated under unstable conditions. Larger particles (greater than about 10 μm) also tend to erode the vanes of the scrubber if they are not removed upstream.

6.3. LITERATURE REVIEW

Although particulate scrubbers have been in use

for a long time, their wider application was long hampered by the noticeable lack of any systematic procedure for designing and selecting units for a specific application and duty. A number of investigators noted that scrubber collection efficiency was generally a function of the power consumed, with the higher collection efficiencies usually coinciding with the higher pressure drops. Lapple and Kamack[17] recognized that the relationship of scrubber collection efficiency to power consumption was actually a functional one, thus providing a highly useful, if empirical, method for designing scrubbers for a given service. Later development[18-20] of this method for correlating scrubber performance data led to the "contacting power concept" which over the past 20 years has become a widely accepted basis for practical scrubber design. Contact power theory assumes that the collection efficiency of a scrubber is solely a function of the total pressure loss for the unit.

The current demand for higher collection efficiencies has led to increased interest in possible additional particle collection mechanisms that might accentuate the efficiencies of scrubbers without further raising the power requirements. The use of water vapor condensation phenomena was suggested many years ago, but there has been very little information presented to assess the magnitude of such effects in practical scrubbing systems. At least two rather different mechanisms are involved.[18,21] One is the build-up of particles that act as nuclei for the condensation of water vapor into droplets; this action increases the effective size of the particles, facilitating their deposition by the inertial mechanism. The inertial mechanism has probably received the most attention from research workers and others. The other mechanisms, diffusional in nature, have received appreciable attention only recently.

Up to 1962, the available literature on scrubbers was reviewed from the standpoint of the contacting power correlation of Semrau et al.,[18-20] following the pioneering paper by Lapple and Kamack.[17] Walker[22] and Walker and Hall[23] also used the contacting power basis, as well as some data from the literature, in correlating their own experimental data on scrubber efficiency. Since 1963 most of the papers on scrubbers (other than those that were purely descriptive) have fallen into two classes.[24] The first consists of those papers that treat applications and present some efficiency data, or correlations of efficiency

data, on the empirical basis of gas pressure drop or some other expression of contacting power. A few empirical or semiempirical studies have attempted more systematic approaches and have reported either general agreement with the contacting power concept or some exceptions to it. The second class of papers consists mostly of theoretical approaches to the problem of scrubber operation and design; these are not usually accompanied by much, if any, experimental data for confirmation of the theory. Most of these theoretical studies have treated the case of the venturi scrubber.

Studies of condensation effects to date have been largely theoretical or speculative in nature, but a number of laboratory investigations have been carried out in recent years. Most of the latter have dealt with basic phenomena and did not attempt to treat applications to practical scrubbing equipment.

A number of investigators have made theoretical analyses of the venturi scrubber, but few of them have attempted experimental verification of the theoretical models. Boll[40] developed a model for the venturi scrubber and attempted to fit the data of Guntheroth,[41] but acknowledged that the agreement was only fair. Behie and Beeckmans[42] developed a mathematical model of venturi scrubber performance and attempted an experimental verification, but without attempting to correlate efficiency as a function of gas pressure drop. Calvert et al.[21,43] also developed a mathematical model for the operation of venturi and other atomizing scrubbers. The analysis was extended to present the efficiency of the scrubber as a function of the gas pressure drop.[4] The model developed by Bakke et al.[51] permitted the economic optimization of a venturi scrubber with a cyclonic water separator by balancing the fixed charges against the power consumption costs. By utilizing existing theory and experimental data on scrubber collection efficiency, the mathematical model was able to describe the scrubbing action, the liquid drop separation, and the pressure losses through the unit. The mathematical model developed by Taheri and Sheih[67] for predicting particle collection efficiency solves the diffusion equations for both droplets and particles. The results of the mathematical prediction seem to agree well with data reported in the literature.

The possibilities of using condensation phenomena to assist in scrubbing of particulates have long been considered and were discussed at length by Harmon[44] with specific reference to the cleaning of blast furnace gas. The earlier suggestions were made almost entirely with reference to the build-up of aerosol particle size by using the aerosols as nuclei for the condensation of water vapor. More recent theoretical and experimental studies[45-49] have treated the phenomena of diffusiophoresis and Stefan flow. Although many studies have been entirely theoretical, there have been a number of laboratory investigations[45-48] clearly demonstrating the existence and nature of these phenomena. However, there has been very little information to indicate the magnitude of possible effects in practical or conventional scrubbing equipment. Apparently, the first data of this sort were published by Semrau et al.,[20] who found different relationships between contacting power and collection efficiency in the scrubbing of Kraft recovery furnace fume with hot and cold water. West et al.[50] later obtained very similar data, although they did not ascribe the differences in scrubber performance to condensation phenomena. Other reports of the improvement of industrial scrubber performance by scrubbing with cold water have been qualitative. A more comprehensive review of the literature is already available[4] and, hence, will not be attempted here.

6.4. FUNDAMENTALS

The venturi scrubber can be examined at the macroscopic, microscopic, or molecular level. At the "macroscopic" level, interest lies in determining changes occurring at the inlet and outlet of the unit. The resultant equation (usually algebraic) describes the overall changes occurring *to* the system, without regard for internal variations *within* the system. This is the design engineer's approach and is considered in the next section. The "microscopic" approach is employed when detailed information concerning the behavior *within* the system is required. The describing equation is differential and is then expanded, via an integration, to describe the behavior of the entire system. The "molecular" approach requires an examination of the behavior of individual molecules. This leads to a study of statistical and quantum mechanics — both of which are beyond the scope of this text. The microscopic approach is adopted in this section, while the macroscopic approach is considered in the next section.

There are many process units that involve the simultaneous transport of gas, liquid, and solid phases. The venturi is one such example and is unquestionably a complex and difficult unit to model. The gas-liquid-solid flow phenomenon has yet to be satisfactorily described from fundamental principles. Industry has relied primarily on empirical formulas obtained from pilot plant models and existing equipment to predict the collection efficiency and pressure drop of (new) scrubbers. The major drawback of this method is that venturi scrubbers are of fixed configuration and usually operate within a limited range of conditions; therefore, the extension of these formulas to a venturi with a different configuration, aerosol, and operating conditions is questionable. Stricter particulate emission standards make the present method inadequate and costly.

The purpose of this section is, then, to develop a satisfactory mathematical model which can be used to describe both particle collection efficiency as a function of power consumption and venturi scrubber performance *a priori*. This will permit evaluation of the effects of new and/or different scrubber geometries, other aerosol properties, and varying operating conditions, as well as lead to improved design procedures. Finally, it can be used to find the most economical scrubber for a given application without recourse to experimental data.

The primary mechanisms involved in the capture of particles in a venturi scrubber are diffusion, direct interception, inertial impaction, and gravity settling. Electrical and thermal effects may also appear, but generally these effects are negligible and need not be considered. Figure 6.4.1 illustrates the collection of an aerosol particle by a spherical droplet collector.

Deposition by diffusion is caused by the Brownian motion of the aerosol particle, resulting in a deviation from its normal flow and subsequent deposition onto the liquid collector. This effect is prevalent at low velocities and for small particles. In analyzing collection by this mechanism, it is customary to consider the particles as points with no mass or size. The aerosol particle velocity, upon which the Brownian velocity is superimposed, is assumed to be equal to the fluid velocity.

Deposition by direct interception occurs when the particles, moving along streamlines of a fluid,

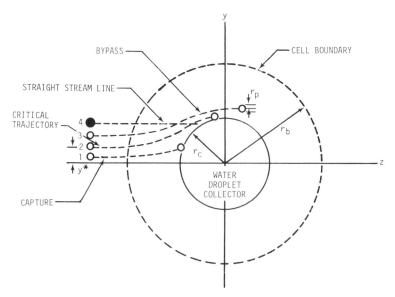

FIGURE 6.4.1.   Particulate collection by a spherical collector.

approach the collector within a distance equal to the radius of the impinging particle. From Figure 6.4.1, it is apparent that particle 2 will be captured by this mechanism; particle 3 will not be captured. This mechanism is independent of the fluid velocity, but increases with the size of the aerosol particle and decreases as the size of the collector increases. In analyzing collection by this mechanism, the particles are considered to have a length dimension but no mass.

The mechanism of removal by inertial impaction occurs when the size or velocity of the particle is so large that the particle does not follow the streamline of the fluid, but resists the directional change imposed by the collector and subsequently impacts upon it. Particles 1 and 4 illustrate typical deposition by this mechanism. An increase in velocity and mass of the impinging particle increases the effect of this mechanism. In analyzing deposition by inertial impaction, the particles are considered to be point masses in the calculation of the collection efficiency. However, their size is accounted for in evaluation of the fluid's resistance to the particles' motion.

Deposition by gravity settling can be considered as a removal mechanism superimposed on any of the above. It is most prevalent at lower velocities and for the relatively larger particles.

The above description applies to each of the mechanisms acting independently of one another. Unfortunately, for the purpose of mathematical

analysis of the capture process, these mechanisms usually are superimposed on one another. The overall collection efficiency is usually assumed to be composed of some combination of the collection efficiencies of the individual mechanisms.

Once a particle reaches and touches a collector, it is assumed to adhere to it. While this is undoubtedly true in most instances, it is certainly not always the case. The usual procedure is to multiply the overall collection efficiency by a retention or adhesive efficiency to account for possible reentrainment.

The primary particle collection mechanism in venturi scrubbers is inertial impaction; therefore this mechanism alone is considered below. It is assumed that there is 100% retention efficiency for particles striking collectors.

We begin our microscopic analysis of venturi scrubbers by examining the mechanics of fluid-particle-collector behavior. A somewhat unique and different approach is employed to represent the capture of a single particle by a collector. The physical system is represented by a geometric model that is ideally suited for analytical study; it has been used successfully in the past to describe the behavior of other, but somewhat analogous and similar, systems.

The mechanics of solid capture by the liquid phase are of major importance in predicting the performance of a venturi scrubber. A prerequisite to a model of particle capture is a description of the flow field in the vicinity of the liquid droplet. However, the flow is so complex in this system that it can only realistically be represented by a simplified model. One of the simplest is the "free surface" or "cellular" model originally proposed by Happel[25,26] in his study of the rate of sedimentation and pressure drop in packed beds and flow relative to arrays of cylinders. Happel's model is developed on the basis that two concentric spheres will describe a typical cell in a random assemblage which is considered to consist of many cells, each of which contains a droplet surrounded by a fluid envelope. The ratio of fluid volume to droplet volume per cell is the same as that in the entire assemblage. In reality, these fluid envelopes will be distorted, but it can be assumed that a typical cell is spherical. In addition, the outside surface of each cell is assumed to be frictionless or having a free surface. Thus, the entire disturbance to the flow field due to each particle is confined to the cell of the fluid with which it is associated. This approach has been used with reasonable success to describe heat and mass transfer in multiparticle systems,[27] pressure drop and sedimentation studies,[25,26] and collection efficiencies in fibrous filters[28] and granular beds.[29] One disadvantage of the model is that the effect of the other cells on the flow pattern is not taken into account; it does, however, represent an improvement on previous approaches which obtained the flow pattern around a sphere located in an infinite medium.

The application of the "free surface model" to particle capture in a venturi scrubber should now be apparent. The idealized cellular model is assumed to consist of two concentric spheres; the outer sphere represents a fluid envelope having a "free surface" and containing the aerosol, and the inner sphere contains the droplet. The "free surface model" can then be used to predict particle capture. This is accomplished by computing the trajectory of an aerosol particle as the fluid flows around the inner sphere (the liquid collector) in the two-concentric-sphere model. The details of this development are presented below.

It is assumed that the mechanism of operation in a venturi scrubber is such that:

1. The liquid (usually water) is atomized by a moving gas (usually air) stream in the throat of the scrubber.

2. The particles impact and are collected by the slower moving liquid droplets.

As stated above, the "free surface model" is to be used to predict particle capture by inertial impaction. This is accomplished by computing the trajectory of the aerosol particle as the fluid flows around the inner sphere (the droplet collector) in the two-concentric-sphere model. The flow field in spherical coordinates is two dimensional with respect to r and θ and symmetric with respect to ϕ. The velocity profile of a single particle may, therefore, be described in a two-dimensional rectangular coordinate system (see Figure 6.4.1). If the droplet collector is moving relative to the fluid, it sweeps out a tube of fluid of cross section equal to the projected area of the sphere. If the particle is moving in a straight line, it will collide with the spherical collector, provided that it was originally within this tube. This is regarded as a collision efficiency of unity. On the other hand, if the smaller particle is following the stream lines of the main fluid pattern, it will be carried out of the tube, giving a collision efficiency of zero. (As the particle is influenced by both the fluid forces and its inertia, the expected collision efficiency will be somewhere between unity and zero, depending on various parameters and initial conditions.) The single-collector inertial impaction efficiency, η, is therefore defined as the square of the ratio of the ordinate of the starting point of the critical trajectory at the cell boundary (y*) to the collector radius, i.e.,

$$\eta = \pi (y^*)^2 / \pi (r_c)^2 = (y^*/r_c)^2 \qquad (6.4.1)$$

The critical trajectory is defined as the trajectory of an aerosol particle starting at the cell boundary and just missing capture by the collector as it flows around it. Thus, complete collection (100%) arises if the particle(s) moves in a straight line (see particle 4 in Figure 6.4.1). The effect of interception may be included by increasing the radius of the collector by an amount equal to the radius of the aerosol particle.

The particle is assumed to be a point mass which does not affect the fluid velocity flow field; it is assumed to be traveling in the z direction with the undisturbed stream velocity at the cell boundary. It is also assumed that the concentration of particles in the aerosol is small enough so that each particle can be treated individually in the flow system. It is further assumed that the solid particles and liquid collector can be represented as spherical in shape. The problem now reduces to one of determining the trajectory of the solid particles as they either flow around the sphere or are captured. Paretsky et al.,[29] in a granular bed study, obtained particle trajectories for aerosol flow past a solid stationary spherical collectory. The development, with appropriate modifications for application to a venturi scrubber, is given below.

A force balance on the aerosol particle results in the following vector equation

$$m_p dV/dt = \pi C_D (r_p)^2 \rho_p (v - V)^2 / 2 \qquad (6.4.2)$$

where

    V = particle velocity vector;
    v = gas velocity vector.

The y and z components of Equation 6.4.2 in the Stokes' regime are given by

$$\left(\frac{m_p}{6\pi\mu_G r_p} \right) \frac{dV_y}{dt} + V_y - v_y = 0 \qquad (6.4.3)$$

$$\left(\frac{m_p}{6\pi\mu_G r_p} \right) \frac{dV_z}{dt} + V_z - v_z = 0 \qquad (6.4.4)$$

Equations 6.4.3 and 6.4.4 can be written in dimensionless form:

$$N_I \frac{dV_y^+}{dt^+} + V_y^+ - v_y^+ = 0 \qquad (6.4.5)$$

$$N_I \frac{dV_z^+}{dt^+} + V_z^+ - v_z^+ = 0 \qquad (6.4.6)$$

The v_y^+ and v_z^+ terms represent the velocities of the fluid in the y and z directions, respectively. V_y^+ and V_z^+ or their corresponding derivatives $(dy^+/dt^+, dz^+/dt^+)$ represent the particle velocities. The dimensionless group N_I is defined as the inertial parameter and is given by

$$N_I = 2r_p^2 \rho_p v / 9 \mu_G r_c \qquad (6.4.7)$$

The Cunningham correction factor should be included in the above equation for particle sizes below 1.0 μm. To solve the system given in Equations 6.4.5 and 6.4.6, information on the fluid velocities must be made available.

Using the creeping motion equations,[30] Happel obtained a solution for the v_r and v_θ fluid velocity components.[25] The stream function ψ' was given by

$$\psi' = \frac{v \sin^2 \theta}{2\omega} \left[(2+3\gamma^5)r^2 + \left(\frac{r_c^3}{r}\right) - (3+2\gamma^5)r_c r - \gamma^5 \left(\frac{r^4}{r_c^2}\right) \right]$$

so that

$$v_r = -(1/r^2 \sin \theta)(\delta\psi'/\delta\theta)$$
$$v_\theta = (1/r \sin \theta)(\delta\psi'/\delta r)$$

and where

$$\omega = 2 - 3\gamma + 3\gamma^5 - 2\gamma^6$$
$$\gamma = r_c / r_b$$

If we now set

$$A = (2 + 3\gamma^5/2\omega)$$
$$B = (r_c^3/2\omega)$$
$$C = -r_c(3 + 2\gamma^5/2\omega)$$
$$D = -(\gamma^5/2\omega r_c^2)$$

then

$$\psi' = \sin^2 \theta \ [Ar^2 + (B/r) + Cr + Dr^4] v$$

and

$$v_r = -2 \cos \theta \ [A + (B/r^3) + (C/r) + Dr^2] v$$
$$v_\theta = \sin \theta \ [2A - (B/r^3) + (C/r) + 4Dr^2] v$$

Some modest manipulation of these results produces the dimensionless rectangular components of the fluid velocity.

$$v_y^+ = -\frac{2y^+ z^+}{r^{+2}} \left[A + \frac{B}{r^{+3}} + \frac{C}{r^+} + Dr^{+2} \right]$$
$$+ \frac{y^+ z^+}{r^{+2}} \left[2A - \frac{B}{r^{+3}} + \frac{C}{r^+} + 4Dr^{+2} \right] \qquad (6.4.8)$$

$$v_z^+ = -\frac{2z^{+2}}{r^{+2}} \left[A + \frac{B}{r^{+3}} + \frac{C}{r^+} + Dr^{+2} \right]$$
$$- \frac{y^{+2}}{r^{+2}} \left[2A - \frac{B}{r^{+3}} + \frac{C}{r^+} + 4Dr^{+2} \right] \qquad (6.4.9)$$

where the dimensionless constants A, B, C, and D are dependent only on the void volume.

The two second-order differential equations (6.4.5 and 6.4.6) are now converted to four first-order differential equations as shown below

$$dV_y^+/dt^+ = (v_y^+ - V_y^+)/N_I$$
$$dy^+/dt^+ = V_y^+$$
$$dV_z^+/dt^+ = (v_z^+ - V_z^+)/N_I$$
$$dz^+/dt^+ = V_z^+ \qquad (6.4.10)$$

with IC (initial conditions)

$$V_y^+ = 0 \text{ at } t^+ = 0$$
$$y^+ = y_0^+ \text{ at } t^+ = 0$$
$$V_z^+ = -1 \text{ at } t^+ = 0$$
$$z^+ = z_0^+ \text{ at } t^+ = 0 \qquad (6.4.11)$$

where

y_0^+ and $z_0^+ =$ the dimensionless initial position of the particle at the cell boundary.

Although the cell (with the liquid collector) is moving, we have assumed that the cell is stationary in the venturi scrubber model. The velocities and position variables in Equations 6.4.10 and 6.4.11 are, therefore, relative quantities. In essence, the analysis applies to a reference coordinate system moving with the liquid collector velocity. Equation 6.4.10 (in conjunction with Equations 6.4.8 and 6.4.9 and the IC) constitutes the mathematical model to predict the particle trajectory. Equation 6.4.1 is employed to calculate the single-collector collection efficiency.

The solution to the system in Equation 6.4.10 is an initial value problem and has been solved numerically using a fourth-order Runge-Kutta forward integration method. An initial position y_0^+ for the particle at the outer cell is first chosen. The Runge-Kutta calculation proceeds (generating the particle's trajectory (y^+, z^+) at succeeding time intervals) until the particle either is captured by or bypasses the liquid collector. The initial guess on y_0^+ is then updated, and the calculation is repeated until the critical initial position is obtained.

The single-particle efficiency, η, for the cellular model, as obtained by Paretsky et al.,[29] is plotted in Figure 6.4.2 against the inertial impaction parameter, N_I, for three values of the void volume:

$\epsilon = 0.38$, $\epsilon = 0.66$, and $\epsilon = 0.90$. Results for $\epsilon = 1.0$ (a single spherical collector) are included in the figure for both the creeping motion and potential flow regimes. The data of Walton and Woolcock[31] are also presented in the graph.

A word of interpretation for Figure 6.4.2 is in order. The results for a single spherical collector ($\epsilon = 1.0$) are in excellent agreement with those obtained previously by Herne,[32] thus presenting a reasonable check on the validity of the numerical calculations for the cellular model. As can be seen in the figure, the shape of the curves for the various values of ϵ are quite similar, with η approaching unity as N_I goes to infinity. For the single collector, Herne found that there is a limiting value of the inertial parameter. It is intuitively felt that a minimum value of the inertial parameter is a requisite for the particle capture model. Since the velocity of the aerosol approaches zero at the surface of the collector, a particle may not possess sufficient inertia in its approach to the collector. Thus, for a particles initially positioned at $(y_0 z_0)$ if it does not possess this minimum inertia, it will either never reach or bypass the collector — and the numerical calculations confirm this. An examination of the results in Figure 6.4.2 indicates that over the entire range of N_I, an increase in N_I results in an increase in the single-particle collection efficiency. A decrease in the gas viscosity or an increase in droplet diameter, particle velocity, and particle density results in an increase in the single-particle collection efficiency. In addition, the results clearly show that a decrease in the void volume produces an increase in the collection efficiency.

This particle collection model is valid at low Reynolds numbers. At these conditions the viscous forces tend to overshadow the effect of inertia and, therefore, reduce the chances of a particle impacting on the collector. At high Reynolds numbers the streamlines do not begin to diverge until they are in the immediate vicinity of the collector, thus increasing the probability of particle capture. This model is, therefore, viewed as a lower or conservative limit for collection efficiency. Interestingly, theory and experimental results for a single collector in the high Reynolds-number range are bounded by the viscous cellular model calculations for $\epsilon = 0.66$ and 0.90. The above results are applicable where the droplet diameter is very small and/or the relative velocity of the droplet with respect to the fluid is also

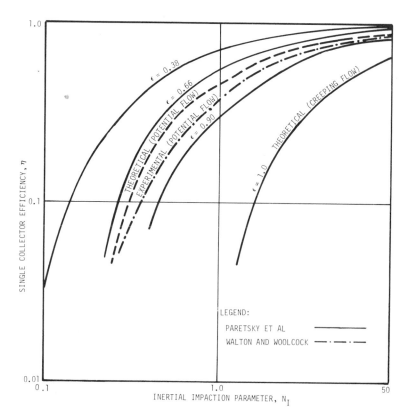

FIGURE 6.4.2. Single-particle collection efficiency vs. the inertial impaction parameter.

small, i.e., for Reynolds numbers approaching zero. We now proceed to calculate single collector efficiencies when the Reynolds number approaches infinity — a condition that more closely approximates venturi scrubber behavior.

In order to obtain particle collection efficiency at high Reynolds-number flow, the model must use a fluid velocity equation derived for the potential flow regime. By applying the solution for potential flow past a sphere located in an infinite medium[33] to the "free surface" model, the fluid velocity streamlines may be evaluated. The describing equation for incompressible potential flow is

$$\nabla^2 \Phi = 0 \qquad (6.4.12)$$

where

Φ = the velocity potential for this flow.

The corresponding velocity vector is given by

$$\mathbf{v} = -\nabla \Phi$$

Noting that the flow is axially symmetric, then

$$v_r = v_r (r, \theta)$$
$$v_\theta = v_\theta (r, \theta)$$
$$v_\phi = 0$$

Therefore,

$$\Phi = \Phi (r, \theta)$$

The expansion of Equation 6.4.12 in spherical coordinates is

$$\frac{\delta}{\delta r} \left(r^2 \frac{\delta \Phi}{\delta r} \right) + \frac{1}{\sin \theta} \frac{\delta}{\delta \theta} \left(\sin \theta \frac{\delta \Phi}{\delta \theta} \right) = 0 \qquad (6.4.13)$$

By use of the method of separation of variables, one can easily show that Equation 6.4.13 has a solution of the form

$$\Phi = \Sigma \, r^n \, [A_n \, P_n(\cos \theta) + B_n \, Q_n(\cos \theta)] \qquad (6.4.14)$$
$$+ \, r^{-(n+1)} \, [C_n \, P_n(\cos \theta) + D_n \, Q_n(\cos \theta)]$$

where

$P_n(\cos\theta)$ = Legendre polynomial of the first kind;

$Q_n(\cos\theta)$ = Legendre polynomial of the second kind.

A_n, B_n, C_n, and D_n are constants. The solution of Equation 6.4.14 requires two boundary conditions for the cellular model.

These are given by

$$v_r = -\frac{\delta\Phi}{\delta r} = 0 \text{ at } r = r_c$$

$$v_r = -\frac{\delta\Phi}{\delta r} = -v\cos\theta \text{ at } r = r_b$$

The solution of Equation 6.4.14, in conjunction with the required boundary conditions, yields the following velocity potential for the fluid within the "free surface" model under potential flow conditions.

$$\Phi = v\left(\frac{r}{\epsilon} + \frac{r_c^3}{2\epsilon r^2}\right)\cos\theta \qquad (6.4.15)$$

where

ϵ = void volume = $1 - \gamma^3$;

γ = r_c/r_b.

Since the corresponding components of the velocity are given by

$v_r = -\delta\Phi/\delta r$
$v_\theta = -(1/r)(\delta\Phi/\delta\theta)$

then

$$v_r = \frac{v}{\epsilon}\left(\frac{r_c^3}{r^3} - 1\right)\cos\theta$$

and

$$v_\theta = \frac{v}{\epsilon}\left(\frac{r_c^3}{2r^3} + 1\right)\sin\theta$$

Some modest manipulation of the above two equations yields the dimensionless rectangular components of the fluid velocity in potential flow.

$$v_y^+ = \frac{3}{2\epsilon r^{+3}}\left(\frac{y^+ z^+}{r^{+2}}\right)$$

$$v_z^+ = \frac{1}{\epsilon}\left[\frac{1}{r^{+3}} - 1\right]\left(\frac{z^{+2}}{r^{+2}}\right) - \frac{1}{\epsilon}\left[\frac{1}{2r^{+3}} + 1\right]\left(\frac{y^{+2}}{r^{+2}}\right)$$

$$(6.4.16)$$

The trajectory equations and initial conditions, Equations 6.4.10 and 6.4.11, have been solved in a manner similar to that described earlier, but using the potential flow fluid velocity profiles given in Equation 6.4.16. Calculated results for single collector efficiency vs. inertial impaction number for various void volumes are presented in Figure 6.4.3.

This model and these results are valid at high Reynolds numbers. At these conditions the viscous effects are negligible, and the effect of particle inertia predominates. In potential flow the streamlines do not begin to diverge until they are in the immediate vicinity of the collector, thus increasing particle capture. This model should then be considered as the upper limit of particle capture. Under conditions of low Reynolds-number flow, note that viscous forces tend to overshadow the effect of inertia, and higher divergence of the velocity streamlines is noted within close proximity of the collector. The results for the potential flow and creeping motion flow regimes should then represent the upper and lower limits, respectively, on particle collection predictions. Examination of Figure 6.4.3 confirms this for a single collector (ϵ = 1.0) in both the creeping motion and potential flow regimes. Also, a comparison of the calculated results for the cellular model with the limited experimental data shows the two to be in excellent agreement. At this time, a study to obtain particle collection efficiencies for the intermediate Reynolds-number flow regime is under investigation.[35]

Traditionally, the mass or weight efficiency of this unit is obtained by extending the single-particle collection efficiency η to an overall collection efficiency η_T by summing up the contribution to the entire assemblage of eligible collector cells. The equation for η_T is generated by applying a particle-mass balance across a differential length dz of the venturi (see Figure 6.4.4).

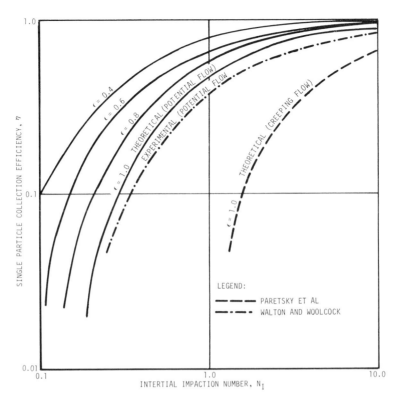

FIGURE 6.4.3. Single-particle collection efficiency vs. inertial impaction number in the potential flow regime.

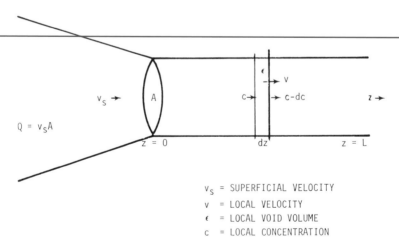

v_s = SUPERFICIAL VELOCITY
v = LOCAL VELOCITY
ϵ = LOCAL VOID VOLUME
c = LOCAL CONCENTRATION

FIGURE 6.4.4. Mass balance across a differential length of the venturi.

$$\left\{\begin{matrix}\text{rate of}\\\text{particles}\\\text{in}\end{matrix}\right\} - \left\{\begin{matrix}\text{rate of}\\\text{particles}\\\text{out}\end{matrix}\right\} = \left\{\begin{matrix}\text{rate of}\\\text{particles}\\\text{accumulated}\end{matrix}\right\}$$

A   B   C

(6.4.17)

The terms in the above equation are now examined. Terms A and B are given by

$$Qc - Q(c - dc) = Qdc$$

which may also be written as

$$Qdc = Av_s dc \qquad (6.4.18)$$

Term C is an inventory term which requires some development. If ϵ is the void volume, $(1 - \epsilon)$ represents the volume of collectors per unit volume. The volume of collectors in Adz is then $(1 - \epsilon)$Adz. The ratio of a collector cross-sectional area to its volume is

$$\pi r_c^2/(4/3) \pi r_c^3 = 3/4 r_c$$

Therefore, the cross-sectional area available for capture in Adz is

$$(1 - \epsilon) \, Adz \, (3/4 \, r_c) = [3(1 - \epsilon) \, A/4 \, r_c] \, dz$$

The volume rate of flow of gas approaching the area available for capture in dz is given by the local velocity, v, in the venturi (not the superficial velocity) times the area available for capture, i.e.,

$$[3(1 - \epsilon) \, A/4 \, r_c] \, vdz \qquad (6.4.19)$$

The particle-mass flow rate eligible for capture in dz is then the product of the local concentration, c, and Equation 6.4.19.

$$[3(1 - \epsilon) \, A/4 \, r_c] \, v \, c \, dz \qquad (6.4.20)$$

We then multiply by the single-collector efficiency η to obtain the rate of particles collected.

$$[3(1 - \epsilon) \, A/4 \, r_c] \, v \, c \, \eta \, dz$$

Inserting Equations 6.4.18 and 6.4.21 into Equation 6.4.17 gives

$$Av_s dc = [3(1 - \epsilon) \, A/4 \, r_c] \, vc \, \eta \, dz \qquad (6.4.21)$$

Rearranging and noting that

$$v_s/v = \epsilon \qquad (6.4.22)$$

gives

$$dc/dz = (3/4 \, r_c) \, [(1 - \epsilon)/\epsilon] \, c \, \eta \qquad (6.4.23)$$

If both η and c are constant across the effective length of capture, L, the above equation may be integrated subject to the IC

$$c = c_i \text{ at } z = 0$$
$$c = c_o \text{ at } z = L$$

The following equation results

$$\ln (c_o/c_i) = -\Phi'L \qquad (6.4.24)$$

where

$$\Phi' = (3/4 \, r_c) \, [(1 - \epsilon)/\epsilon] \, \eta \qquad (6.4.25)$$

The total collection efficiency is then given by

$$\eta_T = (1 - e^{-\Phi'L}) \, 100 \qquad (6.4.26)$$

An alternate form of Equation 6.4.25, omitting the voidage in the denominator, has been presented by other investigators. They claim that this difference is due to a difference in the definition of η. However, the discrepancy arises because the total projected area A is considered to be the area available for capture, rather than Aϵ. We caution the reader that this alternate form is incorrect; it should only be used in the limit where $\epsilon \rightarrow 1.0$.

The extension of single-collector collection efficiency calculations to include the effect of all the collectors in the system presents additional problems. The usual approach (see Equation 6.4.26) assumes that the approach velocity and void volume are constant during the residence collection period. Both quantities, however, are very definite functions of position in the scrubber. Information on simultaneous local velocities of both the particle and collector, as well as the void volume, is required. Information on these variables can be obtained from basic momentum considerations, which are now considered.

The major cause of pressure loss through a venturi scrubber is due to the transfer of momentum from the gas to the liquid in the throat. The high-velocity gas entering the throat of the venturi scrubber encounters, for all practical purposes, a stationary liquid. The gas impacts the liquid and immediately atomizes it. The liquid, which is very nearly completely atomized, is assumed to be equally distributed across the venturi throat. The surrounding gas exerts a drag force on the liquid droplets and accelerates them.

In this analysis it is assumed that all the liquid droplets are of the same mean diameter, d_o, where d_o is given in the next section by Equation 6.5.1. The effect of droplet size distribution is also discussed later. Newton's first law of motion for these droplets is

$$F_D = \left(\frac{m_l}{g_c}\right)(dv_l/dt) \qquad (6.4.27)$$

The drag force, F_D, exerted by the gas on the liquid droplets is given as

$$F_D = C_D A_d \rho_G v_r^2/2 g_c \qquad (6.4.28)$$

where

v_r = local relative velocity between liquid and gas.

The drag coefficient, C_D, relates the force on the droplet to the relative velocity between the droplet and the gas. The drag coefficient equations for a particle in two-phase flow are chosen as

$$C_D = (24/Re)(1 + 0.15\,Re^{0.687}) \text{ for } Re \leqslant 1,000 \quad (6.4.29)$$

$$C_D = 0.44 \qquad \text{for } Re > 1,000 \qquad (6.4.30)$$

Combining Equations 6.4.27 to 6.4.30 and simplifying,

$$\frac{dv_l}{dt} = \frac{18\,v_r\,\mu_G}{d_o'^2\,\rho_L}\left[1 + 0.15\left(\frac{d_o'\,v_r\,\rho_G}{\mu_G}\right)^{0.687}\right]; Re \leqslant 1,000$$
$$(6.4.31)$$

and

$$\frac{dv_l}{dt} = 0.33\,\rho_L\,v_r^2/\rho_L\,d_o'; Re > 1,000 \qquad (6.4.32)$$

Noting that the droplets are moving in the z direction,

$$dt = dz/v_l$$

Substituting this into Equations 6.4.31 and 6.4.32 gives

$$\frac{dv_l}{dz} = \frac{18\,v_r\,\mu_G}{d_o'^2\,v_l\,\rho_L}\left[1 + 0.15\left(\frac{d_o'\,v_r\,\rho_G}{\mu_G}\right)^{0.687}\right]; Re \leqslant 1,000$$
$$(6.4.33)$$

and

$$\frac{dv_l}{dz} = 0.33\,\rho_G\,v_r^2/\rho_L\,d_o'\,v_l; Re > 1,000 \qquad (6.4.34)$$

If it is assumed that there is no evaporation from the droplets, the momentum equation for a control volume of differential length dz is

$$A dp + \frac{\dot{m}_G}{g_c}\,dv_G + \frac{\dot{m}_l}{g_c}\,dv_l + dF = 0 \qquad (6.4.35)$$

where

p = pressure;
$\dot{m}$ = mass flow rate;
F = friction.

The gas and liquid flow rates are generally known so we can obtain from the continuity equation

$$\dot{m}_G = Q\,\rho_G \qquad (6.4.36)$$

or

$$\dot{m}_G = \rho_G\,A\,\epsilon\,v_G \qquad (6.4.37)$$

and

$$\dot{m}_l = R\,Q\,\rho_L/7480 \qquad (6.4.38)$$

where

R = gal $H_2O/1,000$ ft^3 air.

Combining Equations 6.4.36, 6.4.37, and 6.4.38 yields

$$\dot{m}_l = R' \, v_G \, A \, \epsilon \, \rho_L \qquad (6.4.39)$$

where

$$R' = \frac{R}{7,480} \, ; \text{ft}^3/\text{ft}^3 .$$

Combining Equations 6.4.35, 6.4.37, and 6.4.39 and simplifying gives

$$-dp = \frac{\rho_G \, \epsilon \, v_G}{g_c} \, d\,v_G + \frac{\rho_L \, R' \, v_G \, \epsilon}{g_c} \, d\,v_l + \left(\frac{d\,F}{A}\right) \quad (6.4.40)$$

The pressure loss due to wall friction, dF, is given as

$$dF = \frac{2 \, f v_G{}^2 \, \rho_G \, A}{g_c \, d_e} \, dz \qquad (6.4.41)$$

where

d_e = an equivalent diameter term assumed to be equal to the diameter of the throat in this analysis.

Combining Equations 6.4.40 and 6.4.41 and rearranging,

$$-\frac{dp}{dz} = \frac{\rho_G \, \epsilon \, v_G}{g_c} \, \frac{d\,v_G}{dz} + \frac{\rho_L \, R' \, v_G \, \epsilon}{g_c} \, \frac{d\,v_l}{dz} + \frac{2 \, f v_G{}^2 \, \rho_G}{g_c \, d_e}$$

$$(6.4.42)$$

The liquid velocity (v_l), the gas velocity (v_G), and the void fraction (ϵ), do not remain constant throughout the venturi, but are functions of z and are related to each other from the continuity equation.

$$v_G = Q/A\epsilon$$

Differentiating this with respect to the spatial position variable, z, gives

$$\frac{d\,v_G}{dz} = -Q\left[\frac{1}{A\epsilon^2} \, \frac{d\epsilon}{dz} + \frac{1}{A^2 \, \epsilon} \, \frac{dA}{dz}\right] \qquad (6.4.43)$$

An expression for the void fraction is obtained by differentiating the continuity equation for the liquid

$$\dot{m}_l = \rho_L \, A(1 - \epsilon)v_l$$

giving

$$\frac{d\epsilon}{dz} = \frac{A(1 - \epsilon)^2}{Q_L} \, \frac{d\,v_l}{dz} + \frac{(1 - \epsilon)}{A} \, \frac{dA}{dz} \qquad (6.4.44)$$

Equations 6.4.33, 6.4.34, and 6.4.42 to 6.4.44 represent the final equations for the model of the pressure drop through a venturi scrubber. The solution to this system of equations represents an initial value problem. These equations have been solved numerically using a fourth-order Runge-Kutta forward integration method.

Overall pressure drops have been calculated for various system conditions, and several pressure profiles have been generated.[37] The results were consistent with theory. In the nozzle of the venturi, the conversion of the pressure head of the gas to kinetic energy and the frictional effects of the wall cause a rather large pressure drop. The conversion of the kinetic energy of the gas to a pressure head in the diffuser yields an incomplete recovery of the initial pressure because of frictional effects. While the profiles predicted by the model for the nozzle and the diffuser are essentially the same as those presented by Boll,[38] the predicted profiles differ substantially in the throat.

The gas entering the throat of the venturi encounters, essentially, a stationary sheet of liquid. The gas impacts the liquid and atomizes it into relatively slow moving droplets without substantially reducing its own velocity. These conditions — the liquid concentrated near the entrance to the throat and the large relative velocity — result in a very low initial void fraction. Once the liquid is atomized, however, the droplets are rapidly accelerated by the surrounding gas stream to a velocity close to that of the gas stream. This acceleration of the droplets causes a sharp increase in the void fraction and, consequently, a reduction in the gas velocity. A partial pressure recovery is obtained from this rapid reduction in gas velocity. As the relative velocity between the gas and the droplets decreases, the increase in the void fraction tapers off; the pressure loss due to frictional effects from the walls of the throat becomes more significant than the pressure recovery caused by the expanding gas. A small pressure loss is incurred due to wall friction through the remainder of the throat.

The above model can be used to predict

pressure profiles and overall pressure drops for venturi scrubbers. It can be extended to include particle collection efficiency by adding Equation 6.4.23, in conjunction with single-collector efficiency data, to the four pressure-drop equations.[39] A stepwise numerical integration for the five describing equations across the effective length of capture is then dictated, subject to the appropriate IC. This length should be given by the critical value of the inertial number – below which no collection can occur. The effect of particle-size and droplet-size distribution must also be considered. At present, the authors are not aware of a satisfactory correlation to predict liquid (droplet) size distribution in a venturi. Once this information is available, the effect of these two variables can be treated by application of a Monte Carlo technique – similar to that presented in the earlier chapters. This aspect of the fundamentals is currently under study.[39] While this research is being completed, it is hoped that the objectives set forth at the beginning of this section will be achieved.

6.5. DESIGN PRINCIPLES

The design of wet scrubbers usually focuses on those parameters affecting collection efficiency and pressure drop. In most cases the scrubber must be designed to guarantee a specified collection efficiency, which, in turn, is strongly dependent upon pressure drop (among other parameters). The system pressure drop also dictates the power requirements and the size of auxiliary equipment such as the fans. The development which follows considers those parameters important in scrubber design.

Droplet Size

The size of the droplets generated in scrubber units affects both the collection efficiency and pressure drop, i.e., small droplet sizes requiring high-pressure atomization give greater collection efficiencies. Various correlations are available in the literature to estimate the mean liquid drop diameter from different types of atomizers under different operating conditions. These correlations are applicable to fluids within a certain range of operating conditions and properties such as the volume ratio of gas to liquid, the relative velocity of gas to liquid, the type of nozzle, the surface tension of the liquid, etc. In using one of these correlations to estimate droplet diameter, it is important to select a correlation which takes these factors into consideration.

The empirical relationship of Nukiyama and Tanasawa (N-T) is probably the best known and the most widely used to predict the average droplet size in pneumatic (gas-atomized) sprays.[3] In this type of spray the stream of liquid is broken up or atomized by contact with a high-velocity gas stream. The N-T relationship is given by

$$d_o = \frac{1,920}{v_r}\left(\frac{\sigma}{\rho_L'}\right)^{0.5} + 597\left(\frac{\mu_L'}{\sqrt{\sigma \rho_L'}}\right)^{0.45}\left(1,000\frac{L'}{G'}\right)^{1.5}$$

$$(6.5.1)$$

where

d_o = average surface volume mean droplet diameter, μm;
v_r = relative velocity of gas to liquid, ft/sec;
σ = liquid surface tension, dyne/cm;
ρ_L' = liquid density, g/cm^3;
μ_L' = liquid viscosity, p;
L'/G' = ratio of liquid-to-gas volumetric flow rates at the venturi throat.

Equation 6.5.1 reduces to the following expression for standard air and water in a venturi scrubber:

$$d_o = (16,400/v_G) + 1.45(R)^{1.5} \qquad (6.5.2)$$

where

v_G = gas velocity at venturi throat, ft/sec;
R = ratio of liquid-to-gas flow rate, gal/1,000 actual ft^3.

The correlation should not be used outside the range of variables for which it was developed (see Table 6.5.1). Its predicted drop size is subject to an uncertainty of about a factor of two.

The more recently developed correlation of Kim and Marshall[52] covers a much wider mass ratio of gas to liquid (0.06 to 40). Their correlation has a form similar to the N-T equation, but predicts smaller droplet sizes under similar operating conditions.

TABLE 6.5.1

Applicability Range of N-T Equation as Compared to Typical Commercial Operation

Parameter	Units	Symbol	Applicable range for N-T equation	Typical commercial venturi scrubber
Atomizing velocity	ft/sec	v_r	240–750	150–350
Liquid-to-gas ratio	gal/1,000 ft³	R	0.6–7.5	5–30
Mass ratio of gas to liquid	lb/lb	G/L	1.8–15	
Liquid viscosity	cp	μ_L	0.3–50	1+
Liquid surface tension	dyne/cm	σ	19–73	70
Liquid density	g/cm³	ρ'_L	0.7–1.2	1.0

$$d_m = 249 \left(\frac{\sigma^{0.41} \mu_L^{0.32}}{(v_r^2 \rho_G)^{0.57} S^{0.36} \rho_L^{0.16}} \right)$$

$$+ 1{,}260 \, (\mu_L^2/\rho_L \sigma)^{0.71}$$

$$(1/v_r^{0.54}) \, (G/L)^m \qquad (6.5.3)$$

where

d_m = mass median diameter of droplet, μm;

μ_L = liquid viscosity, cp;

ρ_G = gas density, lb/ft³;

ρ_L = liquid density, lb/ft³;

S = cross-sectional area of venturi, ft²;

G = mass flow rate of gas, lb/sec;

L = mass flow rate of liquid, lb/sec;

m = dimensionless constant, for G/L < 3, m = -1 and for G/L > 3, m = -0.5.

For gas-atomizing nozzles, the power can be calculated from the gas isothermal expansion. If M moles of air are used to atomize 1 ft³ liquid from pressure p_1 to p_2, the energy used is

$$P'' = 24.8(M)T \, \ln \, (p_1/p_2) \qquad (6.5.4)$$

where

P'' = energy used, ft lb$_f$/lb of water;

M = lb$_m$ air used to atomize 1 ft³ of liquid, lb$_m$/ft³;

T = absolute temperature, °R.

Gas-atomizing nozzles are typically used when relatively small droplet sizes are desired. Since this condition is desirable in a wet scrubber, i.e., to obtain higher collection efficiencies, gas-atomizing nozzles have found widespread use in scrubber systems.

Other spray nozzles finding use in scrubber systems include pressure nozzles, in which the fluid is under pressure and is broken up by its inherent instability and impact on the atmosphere or by its impact on another jet or a fixed plate; rotating nozzles (spinning atomizers), in which the fluid is fed at low pressure to the center of a rapidly rotating disk or cup (centrifugal force causes the fluid to be broken up into drops); and sonic nozzles, in which sound waves are used to produce the droplets.

Pressure nozzles are relatively simple, small, and inexpensive; they usually consume less power than the other types. They may be used with fluids of a kinematic viscosity less than 1 cm/sec, which do not contain solid particles larger than the passage in that nozzle. The most common pressure nozzle is the hollow-cone nozzle, in which fluid is fed into a whirl chamber through tangential passages or through a fixed spiral so that it acquires a rapid rotation. The orifice is placed on the axis of the whirl chamber, and the fluid exits in the form of a hollow conical sheet which then breaks up into drops. The capacity of a given nozzle is nearly proportional to the square root of the pressure, except at extremely high pressures where friction limits the discharge. Operating pressures do not usually exceed 300 psi. The spray angle typically varies from 15 to 135°. For a full cone nozzle injecting into a fast moving gas stream, Orr[5] recommends

$$d_m = 0.61 \left(\frac{v'_r \mu_L}{\sigma} \right)^{2/3} \left(1 + \frac{1{,}000 \, \rho'_G}{\rho'_L} \right)$$

$$\left(\frac{D_o \, \rho'_L \, \sqrt{\mu''_G \, v_L}}{\mu_L^2} \right) \left(\frac{\sigma}{\rho'_G \, v_r'^2} \right) \qquad (6.5.5)$$

where

ρ'_G = gas density, g/cm^3;
v'_r = relative velocity between gas and liquid, m/sec;
D_o = orifice diameter, cm;
μ''_G = gas viscosity, cp;
v_L = liquid injection velocity, m/sec.

The approximate range of variables covered by the correlation is

$60 \text{ m/sec} < v'_r < 300 \text{ m/sec}$
$0.00074 \text{ g/cm}^3 < \rho'_G < 0.0042 \text{ g/cm}^3$
$1.2 \text{ m/sec} < v_L < 30 \text{ m/sec}$
$3.3 \text{ cp} < \mu_L < 11.3 \text{ cp}$
$19 \ \mu m < d_m < 118 \ \mu m$
$0.12 \text{ cm} < D_o < 0.5 \text{ cm}$

Another form of pressure nozzle is the fan nozzle which sprays the liquid in the form of a flat fan-shaped fluid sheet which then breaks up into drops. The included angle of the fan is from 10 to 130° in standard nozzles. For fan nozzles spraying water, Fraser et al.[6] found the surface mean droplet diameter,

$$\ln d_o = 1.823 + (0.3/\Delta P'') + (0.695 \ \overline{Q}_L/(\Delta P'')^{0.5})$$

$$(6.5.6)$$

where

$\Delta P''$ = pressure drop through the nozzle, atm;
$\overline{Q}_L$ = liquid volume flow rate, l/min.

The impact nozzle is another type of pressure nozzle. A solid stream of fluid under pressure is caused to strike a fixed surface or another similar stream. By proper orientation and shape of the plate, or by varying the size and direction of the two fluid streams, it is possible to obtain a hollow cone-, fan-, or disk-shaped fluid sheet. If laminar flow is maintained, it is possible to produce drops of more uniform size with an impact nozzle than with other types of pressure nozzles. Fraser et al.[6] reported that for an impact nozzle with water striking a flat plate tilted 30° to the nozzle axis, the mass median droplet diameter can be estimated from:

$$d_m = 13,400 \ \overline{Q}_L^{1/3} (\Delta P'')^{0.5} \qquad (6.5.7)$$

Pressure nozzles are commonly furnished in cast iron, cast brass, or bronze in the larger sizes

and in steel, brass, or bronze in the smaller sizes. When corrosion or erosion is important, the nozzles may be formed from any material that can be machined, cast, or molded. Some of the more common specific materials are stainless steel, monel metal, hard lead, ceramics, hard rubber, and glass. When erosion is an important consideration, tips of stellite or other hard alloys may be used. Monel metal nozzles are particularly useful for high-temperature applications.

The power required to pump liquid through a pressure nozzle is calculated from

$$P = 5.82 \times 10^{-4} \ Q'_L \Delta p \qquad (6.5.8)$$

where

P = power consumed at the nozzle, hp;
Δp = pressure drop across nozzle, psi;
Q'_L = volumetric flow rate of liquid through nozzle, gal/min.

Unlike pressure nozzles, in rotating nozzles (spinning atomizers) the liquid to be sprayed attains its velocity with little or no pressure increase. Thus, the feed is brought to the disk at low pressure at or near its center, and the feed rate can be controlled independently with respect to the atomizer operating conditions. The atomizer may be smooth with peripheral vanes or it may be hollow with equispaced radial vanes or channels in its interior, along which the liquid to be dispersed is directed by the centrifugal head developed. From the viewpoint of droplet formation, the only difference between a rotating nozzle and a pressure nozzle is that in a rotating nozzle the liquid is formed into a thin sheet by centrifugal forces instead of by direct fluid pressure. Friedman et al.[7] found a correlation for rotating nozzles based on studies of a variety of vaned, cupped, and shrouded disks.

$$d_o = 0.4 \ r_o \left(\frac{L_w}{\rho'_L \ P_w \ N \ r_o} \right)^{0.6} \left(\frac{\mu_L}{L_w} \right)^{0.2} \left(\frac{\sigma \ \rho'_L \ P_w}{L_w^2} \right)^{0.1}$$

$$(6.5.9)$$

where

L_w = liquid feed rate based on wetted perimeter, g/(cm)(sec);
P_w = wetted perimeter of disk, cm;

N = number of revolutions per second;

r_o = disk radius, cm.

The correlation covers the following range of parameters:

$60 < N < 220$

$1 \text{ cp} < \mu_L < 90 \text{ cp}$

$1 \text{ g/cm}^3 < \rho'_L < 1.4 \text{ g/cm}^3$

$73 \text{ dyne/cm} < \sigma < 99 \text{ dyne/cm}$

The distribution of the droplet diameters follows the log-normal distribution with the log standard deviation given by

$$\sigma_g \approx 3.3 \, d_o^{0.1} \qquad (6.5.10)$$

The power required by a spinning atomizer is the sum of the requirement to pump the liquid, the losses to mechanical inefficiency in the drive and bearing systems, and the losses due to interaction between the disk and its gaseous environment. The liquid pumping power can be calculated for its maximum (assuming no slip) condition:

$$P' = 1.33 \times 10^{-11} \, [L''] \, n^2 \, [(D_d^2 - D_{df}^2)/2] \qquad (6.5.11)$$

where

P' = power, kW;

L'' = mass rate of liquid flow, lb/min;

n = disk rotation rate, rev/min;

D_d = disk diameter, in.;

D_{df} = diameter at which feed is applied to disk, in.

In the last type of spray nozzle (sonic spray nozzles), the liquid flows out of an annular chamber through holes under low pressure (less than an atmosphere). The liquid filaments are shattered by sound waves (produced by the impingement of a jet of compressed air or steam of 1 to 4 atm) impinging on a resonator centrally located between the holes. Sonic spray nozzles are capable of producing small and very uniform droplets.

Although the preceding development, with the exception of rotating nozzles, said little of the droplet-size distribution, this distribution is extremely important. As already noted, the smallest range of droplet size at a given pressure and capacity will be formed by an impact nozzle designed to produce a laminar fluid sheet. For applications requiring the smallest possible range of droplet sizes, a large number of small nozzles is preferable to a few nozzles of large capacity. If a maximum number of small drops is required, nozzles of the smallest size practicable should be used and operated at the highest possible pressure. However, the smallest size nozzles can experience considerable plugging problems from entrained contaminants. A few typical droplet-size distributions which illustrate the effect of pressure variations and of nozzle size are given in Table 6.5.2.

For a graphical representation of droplet-size distribution, it is convenient to make use of the Rosin-Rammler[53] equation:

$$F_d = e^{-bd^n} \qquad (6.5.12)$$

where

F_d = fraction of the mass of sample contained in droplets of diameter greater than d;

b, n = constants.

Most size distributions appear to follow this equation, which yields a straight line if log d is plotted against $\log \log(1/F_d)$. The slope of the line is a measure of the breadth of the distribution. Normal and log probability plots also are often used, as are a number of other distribution functions. There is little or no theoretical justification for selecting one over another, and the simplest and most consistent for a given case should be selected.

In addition to the droplet-size distribution, another parameter worth mentioning is the droplet stability. Lane[54] noted that the maximum size of a water droplet than can be projected through air without disruption can be determined from the following relationship:

$$v_d^2 r_d' = 306 \qquad (6.5.13)$$

where

v_d = velocity of the droplet, m/sec;

r_d' = droplet radius, mm.

Goldshmid,[55] in another method of predicting the stable droplet size for a given gas velocity, used the

TABLE 6.5.2

Droplet Size Distribution Produced by Three Hollow-cone Nozzles of the Same
Design

Nominal droplet diameter, μm	Number of drops in each size group				
	0.063-in. orifice diameter			0.086-in. orifice diameter	
	50 psi	100 psi	200 psi	100 psi	200 psi
10	375	800	1700	100	300
25	200	280	580	60	150
50	160	180	260	41	100
100	50	60	70	26	34
150	27	31	35	14	18
200	19	23	27	9	12
300	8	9	11	5	8
400	2	4	4	4	7
500	1	1		2	1
600	1			1	

fact that droplets will shatter at a critical value of the Weber number:

$$N_W = \rho_G v^2 r_d / g_c \sigma' \text{ (dimensionless)} \qquad (6.5.14)$$

where

ρ_G = gas density lb/ft^3 ;
v = velocity, ft/sec;
r_d = radius of drop, ft;
σ = surface tension, lb_f/ft ;
g_c = conversion constant.

Experiments on the drop shatter of several liquids gave critical values of the Weber number, ranging from 5 to 12. Using the properties of standard air and water with a critical Weber number of 6, for example, and a droplet radius of 2 mm (raindrop size), Equation 6.5.14 estimates that it would take an air velocity of about 42 ft/sec to shatter the drop.

The primary objective of much of the published literature on scrubber design involves evaluating the overall particulate collection efficiency and pressure drop and relating these to system parameters. Such data are considered below for some typical wet scrubber types.

Venturi Scrubbers

Collection efficiency in venturi scrubbers typically approaches 100% for particles larger

than 5 μm. Johnstone and Roberts[8] found that the specific surface, S_d, of droplets formed by atomization

$$S_d = 244 \, R/d_o \qquad (6.5.15)$$

correlated satisfactorily with the particle collection efficiency (see Figure 6.5.1). Further investigation by Johnstone et al.[9] showed that the inertial impaction collection mechanism predominated in conventional venturi scrubbers. They correlated collection efficiency data with a dimensionless inertial impaction parameter, ψ_I, given by

$$\psi_I = C \, \rho_p \, v_G \, d_p{}^2 / 18 \, d_o' \, \mu_G \qquad (6.5.16)$$

where

C = Cunningham correction factor;
v_G = gas velocity at venturi throat, ft/sec;
d_p = particle diameter, ft;
d_o' = droplet diameter, ft;
μ_G = gas viscosity, lb/(ft)(sec).

(Note that this dimensionless inertial parameter differs from that given in Equation 6.4.7 by a factor of 2.0.) Their results are shown in Figure 6.5.2. These experimental data are compared with the efficiency predicted by Equation 6.5.17 which correlates the experimental results.

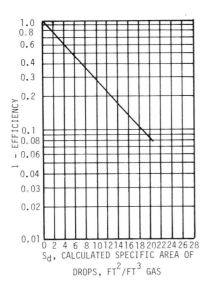

FIGURE 6.5.1. Collection efficiency as a function of the specific area of the droplets in venturi scrubbers.

$$\eta = 1 - \exp (\delta\, c_d \sqrt{\psi_I}) \qquad (6.5.17)$$

where

δ = the droplet concentration;

c_d = a constant and a function of the effective path length and droplet specific surface area.

More recently, Calvert[4] developed an equation for predicting particle penetration, defined as $(1 - \eta)$, based on an analysis of particle and droplet motion in the venturi throat. In his development Calvert made several assumptions related to the collection mechanism, slip, drag, droplet size, and uniformity. His final equation is given by

$$1 - \eta = \exp \left\{ \frac{2\, R''\, v_G'\, \rho_L'\, d_o''}{55\, \mu_G'}\ F(\psi_I, f) \right\} \qquad (6.5.18)$$

where

R'' = liquid-to-gas ratio, l/m^3;

v_G' = gas throat velocity, cm/sec;

d_o'' = diameter of atomized liquid droplet, cm;

μ_G' = gas viscosity, g/(cm)(sec).

The $F(\psi_I, f)$ term is given by

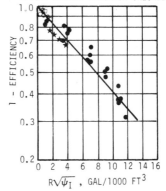

- 10-MICRON DIBUTYL PHTHALATE (ECKMAN).
- ★ 1.22-MICRON AMMONIUM SULPHITE.
- ○ 0.58-MICRON DIBUTYL PHTHALATE.
- □ 0.27-MICRON AMMONIUM CHLORIDE

FIGURE 6.5.2. Collection efficiency of venturi scrubber as a function of system parameters.

$$F(\psi_I, f) = \frac{2}{\psi_I} \left[-0.7 - 0.5\, \psi_I f + 1.4 \ln \left(\frac{0.5\, \psi_I f + 0.7}{0.7} \right) + \left(\frac{0.49}{0.7 + 0.5\, \psi_I f} \right) \right]$$

where

f = 0.1 to 0.3 for hydrophobic aerosols or 0.4 to 0.5 for hydrophilic aerosols (or an average value of 0.25 may be used).

Perhaps the most popular and widely used collection efficiency equation is that originally suggested by Johnstone[8,9]

$$\eta = 1 - e^{-kR\sqrt{\psi_I}} \qquad (6.5.19)$$

where

η = efficiency;

ψ_I = inertial impaction parameter;

R = liquid rate, gal/1,000 ACFM

k = correlation coefficient whose value depends on the system geometry and operating conditions, typically 0.1 to 0.2 gal/ACFM.

The pressure drop for gas flowing through a venturi scrubber can be estimated from knowledge of liquid acceleration and frictional effects along the wall of the equipment. Frictional losses depend largely on the scrubber geometry and usually are determined experimentally. The effect of liquid acceleration is, however, predictable. Calvert's equation[4] for estimating pressure drop through venturi scrubbers is given as a function of throat gas velocity and liquid-to-gas ratio and assumes that all the energy is used to accelerate the liquid droplets to the throat velocity of the gas.

$$\Delta P' = 5 \times 10^{-5} \, v_G^2 \, R \qquad (6.5.20)$$

where

$\Delta P'$ = pressure drop, in. water.

Studies by Hesketh[10] showed that the pressure drop predictions obtained from throat velocity measurements may be subject to error at low velocities if Equation 6.5.20 is applied for all ranges of velocities. Hesketh's equation for venturi scrubbers that have liquid injected before the throat[11] is given by

$$\Delta P' = \frac{v_G^2 \, \rho_G \, A_t^{0.133} \, (0.56 + 0.125 \, R + 2.3 \times 10^{-3} \, R^2)}{507}$$
$$(6.5.21)$$

or

$$\Delta P' = \frac{v_G^2 \, \rho_G \, A_t^{0.133} \, R^{0.78}}{1,270} \qquad (6.5.22)$$

where

A_t = throat cross-sectional area, ft^2.

When the same amount of liquid is injected at the throat, available data indicate that the pressure drop can be up to 10% higher. Hesketh[10] also related the penetration to the pressure drop for particles smaller than 5 μm (since collection efficiency in venturi scrubbers is virtually 100% for particles larger than this):

$$1 - \eta = 3.47 \, (\Delta P')^{-1.43} \qquad (6.5.23)$$

Combining Equations 6.5.22 and 6.5.23, Hesketh obtained an equation suitable for predicting the collection efficiency of fine, noncharged particles.

$$1 - \eta = 9.52 \times 10^4 / (v_G^{2.86} \, \rho_G^{1.43} \, A_t^{0.190} \, R^{1.12}) \qquad (6.5.24)$$

When charged particles are to be collected in the venturi scrubber, i.e., when the venturi is located downstream of an electrostatic precipitator, Hesketh found that these charged particles are collected more efficiently. The penetration can be determined from

$$1 - \eta \approx 3.45 \times 10^{-7} \, v_G^{3.56} \, A_t^{0.145} \, (\rho_G/\Delta P')^{1.78} \qquad (6.5.25)$$

Some other pressure drop correlations available in the literature for venturi scrubbers are summarized in Table 6.5.3.

Although Calvert's equation does not take into account frictional loss on the wall of the venturi scrubber (which becomes negligibly small at high liquid rates), it is recommended in lieu of experimental data and usually gives conservative results. The work of Theodore et al. is also recommended. Their results compared most favorably with the limited experimental data available and over a wide range of operating conditions.

Flooded-bed Scrubbers

Flooded-bed wet scrubbers (see Figure 6.2.11) have become popular recently, primarily because of their ability to simultaneously remove both particulates and gaseous contaminants (i.e., sulfur dioxide) effectively. Based on work by Leva[12] and Ergun,[13] Epstein et al.[14] presented a correlation

TABLE 6.5.3

Pressure Drop Correlations for Venturi Scrubbers

Equation		Reference
Δp	$= \Delta p_f + 26.1 \times 10^{-4} \, v_G^{1.08} \, W^{0.63}$	56
Δp	$= 3.158 \times 10^{-5} \, v_G^2 \, q^{0.26} \, t_L^{0.143}$	57
Δp	$= 1.756 \times 10^{-7} \, v_G^2 \, (Q_L' + 73.8)$	58
$\Delta p'$	$= 0.8 + 0.12R$	59

Note: Δp = pressure drop, psi; Δp_f = friction loss, psi; $\Delta p'$ = dimensionless pressure drop, pressure drop/velocity head; v_G = gas velocity at throat, ft/sec; W = specific wetting, ft^3 liquid/ft^3 gas; Q_L' = liquid rate, gal/min; q = liquid rate, l/m^3; t_L = throat length, mm; R = liquid-to-gas ratio, gal/1,000 ft^3.

for pressure drop through the glass-sphere region of the flooded-bed scrubbers,

$$\frac{\Delta P'}{z} = \frac{1.75 \, C_f \overline{G}^2}{12 \, g_c' \rho_G} \exp[\beta(R) \, \overline{G}^2] \qquad (6.5.26)$$

where

$\Delta P'/z$ = pressure drop, in. water, per ft of bed (glass spheres);
$\overline{G}$ = gas flow rate, lb/(hr)(ft^2);
C_f = characterization factor, $6(1 - \epsilon)/\epsilon^3 d_g$;
g_c' = gravitational constant, ft/hr^2;
ρ_G = gas density, lb/ft^3;
ϵ = void fraction;
d_g = diameter of glass spheres, ft;
R = liquid-to-gas ratio, gal/1,000 ft^3;
β = constant depending on the type of packing (for glass spheres use 1.5×10^{-8}).

The pressure drop due to the turbulent layer above the spheres can be estimated from[15]

$$\Delta P' = 0.75 + 0.375 \, H_t \qquad (6.5.27)$$

where

H_t = height of turbulent layer, ft.

This height can be estimated from a correlation presented by Lowry and Van Winkle[60]

$$H_t = 1.1 + 7.5 \times 10^{-7} \, (\overline{G}/\rho_G)^2 \, [\rho_G/(\rho_L - \rho_G)] \quad (6.5.28)$$

The total pressure drop is simply the sum of the pressure drop through the glass-sphere bed and the turbulent layer.

The collection efficiency of particulates of size d_p within each stage (glass-sphere bed and turbulent layer region) of a flooded-bed scrubber can be obtained from[14]

$$\eta(d_p) = 1 - [1 - \eta_G(d_p)] \, [1 - \eta_{TL}(d_p)] \qquad (6.5.29)$$

where

$\eta_G(d_p)$ = collection efficiency for particulates of size d_p in the glass-sphere bed;

$\eta_{TL}(d_p)$ = collection efficiency for particulates of size d_p in the turbulent layer region.

The particulate collection efficiency in the glass-sphere bed can be estimated from the following equation:

$$\eta_G(d_p) = 1 - \exp[-0.2 \, (R) \, \psi'' \, H_g/d_g] \qquad (6.5.30)$$

where

ψ'' = inertial impaction parameter given by $1.29 \times 10^{-10} \, \overline{G} \rho_p (d_p)_i^2 / 9 \rho_G \mu_G d_g$;
ρ_p = particulate density, lb/ft^3;
$(d_p)_i$ = diameter of particulate of size i, μm;
H_g = height of glass sphere bed, ft;
d_g = diameter of glass spheres, ft.

The particulate collection efficiency in the turbulent layer region can be estimated from the following equation:

$$\eta_{TL}(d_p) = 1 - \exp[-6.3 \, F^2 \, \psi'' \, H_t/d_g] \qquad (6.5.31)$$

where

F = specific gravity of turbulent layer.

The flooded-bed wet scrubber is often operated in either a single-stage or double-stage (two glass-sphere beds and turbulent layers) configuration. For the double-stage configuration, the particulate removal is given by

$$\eta(d_p)_{2 \, stages} = 1 - [1 - \eta(d_p)_{1st \, stage}] \, [1 - \eta(d_p)_{2nd \, stage}] \qquad (6.5.32)$$

Moving-bed Scrubbers

For reasons similar to the attractiveness of flooded-bed scrubbers (i.e., simultaneous removal of both particulates and gases), moving-bed scrubbers (see Figure 6.2.12) are also becoming popular. Pressure drop data have been correlated by Epstein et al.[14] and can be estimated from

$$\Delta P'_{MB} = 1.52 \times 10^{-8} \frac{n_s H_{ps} \overline{G}^2}{d_{ps}} \exp[8 \times 10^{-3} R^{0.9} \overline{G}^{0.17}] \qquad (6.5.33)$$

and

$$\Delta P'_D = 1.35 \times 10^{-7} \; \bar{G}^2 \qquad\qquad (6.5.34)$$

where

$\Delta P'_{MB}$ = pressure drop through the moving-bed section, in. water;

n_s = number of stages (moving beds) in scrubber;

H_{ps} = static height of packing for a single-stage moving-bed scrubber, ft;

d_{ps} = diameter of plastic spheres in moving bed, ft;

$\Delta P'_D$ = pressure drop through the demister section (to remove entrained liquid droplets) usually located at the top of the scrubber, in. water.

Typically, the pressure drop through the demister section is less than 15% of the total pressure drop.

The collection efficiency of particulates of size d_p, within each stage of the moving-bed scrubber can be estimated from[14]

$$\eta \, (d_p) = 1 - \exp \, [-5 \times 10^{-17} \; R^{3.3} \; \bar{G}^{3.66} \; \psi'' \; n_s \; H_{ps}/d_{ps}]$$
$$(6.5.35)$$

For packed-bed scrubbers (see Figure 6.2.10), Eckert[16] determined that the pressure drop can be estimated by

$$\Delta P'/z = (a + b \; \bar{L}^\alpha)(\bar{G}^{c+d \; \bar{L}}) \qquad (6.5.36)$$

where

$\Delta P'/z$ = pressure drop per foot of packing, in. water/ft;

$\bar{L}$ = liquid rate, lb/hr ft$^2 \times 10^{-3}$;

$\bar{G}$ = gas rate, lb/hr ft$^2 \times 10^{-4}$;

a,b,c,d,α = constants given in Table 6.5.4.

Particulate removal in packed-bed scrubbers is usually greater than 95% by weight. The performance of a cocurrent scrubber on clay particles with an average size of 0.5 μm is presented in Table 6.5.5. The scrubber removed 98% by weight of the particulate matter in the gas stream.[16] The cocurrent (vertical downflow) packed-bed scrubber used a 3-ft bed of 1-in. Intalox® saddles. The gas flow rate used in the test was 5,000 lb/(hr)(ft^2). The water rate was 960 lb/(hr)(ft^2).

Other Approaches

Contact power theory was alluded to briefly in Section 6.3 as an empirical approach relating particulate collection efficiency and pressure drop in wet scrubber systems. The concept is an outgrowth of the observation by Lapple and Kamack[17] that particulate collection efficiency in spray-type scrubbers was mainly determined by pressure drop for the gas plus any power expended in atomizing the liquid. Contact power theory assumes that the particulate collection efficiency in a scrubber is solely a function of the total pressure loss for the unit. The total pressure loss,

TABLE 6.5.4

Constants for Pressure Drop Correlation in Packed-bed Scrubbers

Packing	Size, in.	a	b	α	c	d	Liquid rate, lb/hr ft^2
Polypropylene	2.0	0.0868	0.04531	1.0833	1.960	−0.054	<25,000
pall rings		0.0868	0.03023	1.8940	1.910	−0.1086	>25,000
Carbon steel	1.5	0.132	0.080	1.5261	1.890	−0.132	<25,000
pall rings		0.132	0.06427	1.7667	1.825	−0.14505	>25,000
Carbon steel	2.0	0.1925	0.14865	1.1084	1.940	−0.14783	<25,000
Raschig rings		0.1925	0.10442	1.5916	1.704	−0.09505	>25,000
Polypropylene	2.0	0.105	0.03190	1.2910	1.900	−0.040	<25,000
Intalox® saddles		0.105	0.01235	2.0749	2.012	−0.08533	>25,000
Porcelain	1.5	0.15	0.091	1.5982	2.06	−0.192	<25,000
Intalox saddles		0.15	0.093	1.6156	1.81	−0.13364	>25,000
Porcelain	1.0	0.88	1.38	1.1227	1.83	−0.396	<25,000
Raschig rings							

Courtesy of Norton Company, Chemical Process Products Division, Akron, Ohio.

TABLE 6.5.5

Performance Characteristics of Cocurrent Scrubber on Clay with Average Particle Size of 0.5 μm

Particle size, μm	Wt, g	In			Out	
		No. of particles[a]	Sample wt,[b] g	Actual wt,[b] g	No. of particles[a]	% of particles removed
10 and over	0.07	2.8×10^7	0.00	0.00	0	100
5–10	0.03	2.8×10^7	0.00	0.00	0	100
2–5	0.09	8.4×10^8	0.03	0.0006	5.6×10^6	99.3
1–2	0.22	2.6×10^{10}	0.14	0.0028	3.3×10^8	98.7
0.5–1	0.26	2.46×10^{11}	0.40	0.0080	7.58×10^9	97.0
0.25–0.5	0.18	1.37×10^{12}	0.28	0.0056	4.31×10^{10}	96.9
0.10–0.25	0.15	1.12×10^{13}	0.15	0.0030	2.24×10^{11}	98.0
	1.00			0.02		

[a]Assumed specific gravity for 1-g sample = 2.5. $1 \ \mu m = 1 \times 10^{-6}$ m; $1 \ \mu m^3 = 1 \times 10^{-12}$ cm³.

[b]Overall wt% removal was 98; thus, wt out = (wt % out) (1.00 −0.98).

P_T, is assumed to be composed of two parts: the pressure drop of the gas passing through the scrubber, P_G, and the pressure drop of the spray liquid during atomization, P_L. These two terms can be estimated by[18,20]

$$P_G = 0.157 \ \Delta P' \qquad (6.5.37)$$

where

P_G = contacting power based on gas stream energy input, hp/1,000 ACFM;
$\Delta P'$ = pressure drop across the scrubber, in. water.

and

$$P_L = 0.583 \ p_L \ (Q_L'/Q_G') \qquad (6.5.38)$$

where

P_L = contacting power based on liquid stream energy input, hp/1,000 ACFM;
p_L = liquid inlet pressure, psi;
Q_L' = liquid feed rate, gal/min;
Q_G' = gas flow rate, ft³/min.

Then,

$$P_T = P_G + P_L \qquad (6.5.39)$$

To correlate contacting power with scrubber collection efficiency, the latter is best expressed as the number of transfer units. The number of transfer units is defined by analogy to mass transfer and given by

$$N_t = \ln \ [1/(1 - \eta)] \qquad (6.5.40)$$

where

N_t = number of transfer units, dimensionless;
η = fractional collection efficiency, dimensionless.

The relationship between the number of transfer units and collection efficiency is by no means unique. The number of transfer units for a given value of contacting power (hp/1,000 ACFM) or vice versa varies over nearly an order of magnitude. For example, at 2.5 transfer units ($\eta = 0.918$), the contacting power ranges from approximately 0.8 to 10.0 hp/1,000 ACFM, depending on the scrubber and the particulate.

For a given scrubber and particulate properties, there will usually be a very distinct relationship between the number of transfer units and the contacting power. Semrau[18,20] plotted the number of transfer units for a series of scrubbers and particulates against total power consumption; a linear relation, independent of the type of scrubber, on a log-log plot was obtained. The relationship could be expressed by

$$N_t = \alpha \, P_T^{\beta} \qquad (6.5.41)$$

where

α, β = characteristic parameters for the type particulates being collected (see Table 6.5.6).

While the power function relationship can represent what has been observed, it cannot be used to predict what will happen — except for identical conditions. In order to predict collection efficiency for any particulate size and various scrubber configurations and operating conditions, it is necessary to use the more accurate relationships discussed previously for the particular type of scrubber in question.

The simplified method of Vatavuk et al.,[63] as introduced in Section 3.5 of Chapter 3, can also be applied to venturi scrubbers to predict collection efficiency from the particle-size distribution of the dust in the inlet gas stream and equipment operating parameters. The combined work of Ranz and Wong[64] has resulted in a theoretical size efficiency function, similar in form to that of the cyclone:

$$\eta \, (d_p) = 1 - \exp \left[-m \, R' \, d_p \sqrt{\frac{v_G \, \rho_p \, C}{18 \, d_o' \, \mu_G''}} \right] \qquad (6.5.42)$$

where

m = experimental factor determined by throat geometry and other factors (varies from 0.1 to 2.0);

R' = liquid injection rate, ft^3/1,000 ft^3;

d_p = particle diameter, ft;

v_G = gas stream velocity through venturi throat, ft/sec;

TABLE 6.5.6

Parameters for Equation 6.5.41

Aerosol	Scrubber type	α	β
Raw gas (lime dust and soda fume)	Venturi and cyclonic spray	1.47	1.05
Prewashed gas (soda fume)	Venturi, pipe line, and cyclonic spray	0.915	1.05
Talc dust	Venturi	2.97	0.362
	Orifice and pipe line	2.70	0.362
Black liquor recovery furnace fume	Venturi and cyclonic spray	1.75	0.620
Cold scrubbing water humid gases			
Hot fume solution for scrubbing (humid gases)	Venturi, pipeline, and cyclonic spray	0.740	0.861
Hot black liquor for scrubbing (dry gases)	Venturi evaporator	0.522	0.861
Phosphoric acid mist	Venturi	1.33	0.647
Foundry cupola dust	Venturi	1.35	0.621
Open-hearth steel furnace fume	Venturi	1.26	0.569
Talc dust	Cyclone	1.16	0.655
Copper sulfate	Solivore (A) with mechanical spray generator	0.390	1.14
	(B) with hydraulic nozzles	0.562	1.06
Ferrosilicon furnace fume	Venturi and cyclonic spray	0.870	0.459
Odorous mist	Venturi	0.363	1.41

From Strauss, W., *Industrial Gas Cleaning*, Pergamon Press, New York, 1966. (With permission.)

ρ_p = particle density, lb/ft³;
d_o = average liquid droplet diameter, ft;
μ_G = gas viscosity, lb/ft sec;
C = Cunningham correction factor.

For a given venturi, all of the terms above become constants, except d_p, so that Equation 6.5.42 can be simplified to

$$\eta (d_p) = 1 - e^{-\gamma d_p} \qquad (6.5.43)$$

where

$$\gamma = m\,R'\sqrt{\frac{v_G\,\rho_p}{18\,d_o'\,\mu_G}} \qquad (6.5.44)$$

Substitution into Equation 3.5.10 results in an expression for overall efficiency identical in form to that of the cyclone:

$$\eta = \frac{\gamma}{\gamma + \beta} = \frac{1}{1 + (\beta/\gamma)} \qquad (6.5.45)$$

The terms in Equation 6.5.45 have been defined previously in Chapter 4, Section 4.5. Equation 6.5.45 is graphically represented in Figure 6.5.3. An example of its use is presented in Section 6.6.

The other simplified technique mentioned previously is that of Sundberg,[65] previously developed in Chapter 3. Sundberg suggests that the collection efficiency can be determined from the mass median diameter and geometric standard

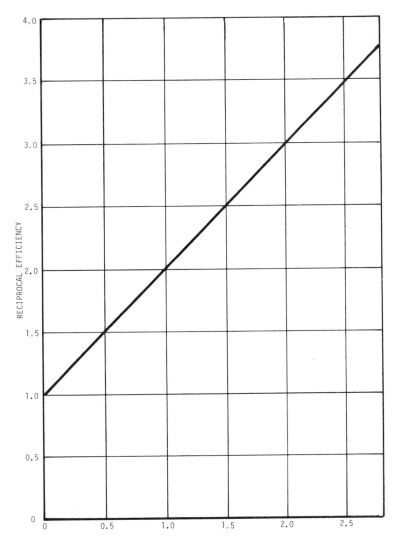

FIGURE 6.5.3.   Reciprocal efficiency vs. β/α for venturi scrubber.

deviation of the particle size distribution curve, and the cut size and geometric standard deviation of the fractional efficiency curve. The latter two parameters are a function of the air pollution control device under consideration. The application of this technique to venturi scrubbers is demonstrated in Section 6.6.

Scrubber Selection

Some of the more important conditions which indicate a potential scrubber application are presented below.[61]

1. Introduction of liquid to the gas is permissible to the process.

2. The liquid can be purged from the process without causing a water pollution problem. Water quality requirements of the receiving water must be considered, and a satisfactory effluent treatment system must be provided.

3. The gas must be cooled in any event.

4. Combustible particles or gases must be treated with minimum risk.

5. The particulate matter is rather fine (predominantly under 20 μm in diameter).

6. A high collection efficiency is required.

7. Vapors or gaseous matter must also be removed from the gas.

Table 6.5.7 lists some of the advantages and disadvantages of utilizing wet scrubbers.

There are a number of additional factors to consider in selecting a scrubber. In general, they can be grouped into three categories: economic, environmental, and engineering. These are outlined in Table 6.5.8. Proper selection of the particular type of wet scrubber for a particular application can often be difficult. It is in the best interest of the prospective user to review the literature, request performance information available from the scrubber manufacturers and, if possible, visit an installation(s) with a similar type of application. In the final analysis, one should rely on previous experience.

Miscellaneous Considerations

As mentioned previously, venturi scrubbers are rapidly gaining widespread popularity, especially in view of the current emphasis on the collection of submicron particulates. The venturi's basic construction and principles of operation are non-complex in nature. Since there are no internals, workings are accessible from the unit's exterior. As a result of the equipment's simplicity, designers can choose from a full range of construction materials to handle problems of corrosion and/or abrasion, depending on the nature of the emission. Among materials frequently specified are stainless steel or Hastelloy. Rubber linings may be employed for protection against concentrations of sulfuric acid and can also provide protection against fluorine and phosphoric acid fume emissions. Brick (ceramic) linings are often used for protection against high temperatures and/or excessively abrasive particles. To minimize deterioration and reduce maintenance, current designs frequently specify plastics such as fiberglass and PVC when temperature conditions permit.

TABLE 6.5.7

Advantages and Disadvantages of Wet Scrubbers

Advantages		Disadvantages	
1.	No secondary dust sources	1.	May create water disposal problem
2.	Small space requirements	2.	Product is collected wet
3.	Ability to collect gases as well as particulates (especially "sticky" ones)	3.	Corrosion problems are more severe than with dry systems
4.	Ability to handle high-temperature high-humidity gas streams	4.	Steam plume opacity may be objectionable
5.	First cost is low	5.	Pressure drop and horsepower requirements may be high
6.	For some processes, the gas stream is already at high pressures	6.	Solids build-up at the wet-dry interface may be a problem

TABLE 6.5.8

Factors Involved in Scrubber Selection

Environmental factors	Engineering factors	Economic factors
1. Equipment location	1. Characteristics of the dust, fume, mist, or fog to be collected	1. First cost
2. Space available	a. Particulate-size distribution	a. Equipment
3. Ambient conditions	b. Concentration or loading	b. Installation
4. Availability of adequate water and power utilities and sludge disposal facilities	c. Chemical reactivity	2. Operating cost
	d. Physical and chemical properties (e.g., density, solubility in scrubbing liquid, agglomeration tendencies, shape, explosiveness, stickiness, etc.)	a. Utilities
5. Maximum allowable emission (air pollution codes)		b. Maintenance
	e. Corrosiveness and abrasiveness	c. Savings (when recovering valuable products) or disposal costs
6. Visible water vapor or steam plume	f. Toxicity	
	2. Characteristics of the gas stream (e.g., temperature, pressure, humidity, volume, composition, etc.)	3. Expected equipment lifetime
7. Equipment noise levels (i.e., in case of high-energy scrubbers, the noise level of high tip speed fans may be objectionable)	3. Characteristics of the scrubbing liquid (e.g., density, viscosity, corrosiveness, foaming tendencies, etc.)	
	4. Design characteristics of the scrubber	
	a. Size and weight	
	b. Fractional efficiency curve (i.e., collection efficiency vs. particle size)	
	c. Pressure drop	
	d. Reliability and dependability	
	e. Method of disposal	
	f. Materials of construction	
	g. Effect of air volume changes (efficiency, pressure drop)	
	h. Power requirements other than fan	
	i. Utility requirements	
	j. Temperature limitations	
	k. Maintenance requirements	

As a general rule for atomizing scrubbers, the ideal operating range of liquid injected into the system varies from 5 to 8 gal/1,000 ft^3. A higher liquid rate is usually more advantageous than a higher gas velocity. To provide some insight into the reasoning behind the ideal operating range of liquid injected into the venturi, consider the following circumstances. Assume, for example, that 2 gal/1,000 ft^3 can be considered an extremely low liquid rate. The combination of high velocity and low liquid rate would probably create an unwetted void space through the middle of the venturi. In other words, if one were to look down the venturi, there would be an area in the middle of the venturi where wetting action (liquid droplet-particulate contact) does not take place.

Hence, it is always preferable to lean toward a higher liquid rate to be sure of a proper liquid-to-gas impaction level. On the other hand, however, a problem can occur where a low gas velocity exists with too high a liquid rate (for example, assume 12 gal/1,000 ft^3). Under these conditions, liquid shattering may be reduced to such a point that the scrubber begins to operate like an ejector. This means very poor collection efficiencies are achieved. Using 5 to 8 gal liquid/1,000 ft^3 should minimize these problems.

The basic high-energy venturi scrubber configuration is illustrated in Figure 6.5.4 (see also Figure 6.2.15). In practice the overall dimensions of the scrubber are sized to achieve the desired gas velocities within the various parts. Although there

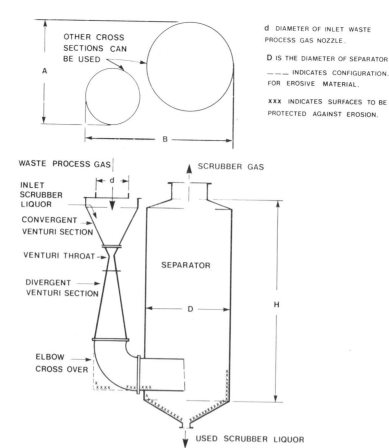

WASTE PROCESS GAS
SCRUBBER GAS

d DIAMETER OF INLET WASTE PROCESS GAS NOZZLE.

D IS THE DIAMETER OF SEPARATOR

——— INDICATES CONFIGURATION. FOR EROSIVE MATERIAL.

xxx INDICATES SURFACES TO BE PROTECTED AGAINST EROSION.

OTHER CROSS SECTIONS CAN BE USED

INLET SCRUBBER LIQUOR

CONVERGENT VENTURI SECTION

VENTURI THROAT

DIVERGENT VENTURI SECTION

SEPARATOR

ELBOW CROSS OVER

USED SCRUBBER LIQUOR

FIGURE 6.5.4. Basic components of a high-energy venturi scrubber. (From Busch, J. S., MacMath, W. E., and Lin, M. S., *Pollut. Eng.*, p. 28, January 1973; p. 32, February 1973; p. 34, March 1973. With permission.)

are variations among the scrubber manufacturers, the typical inlet gas velocity of high-energy orifice scrubbers ranges from 3,300 to 3,700 ft/min. The superficial gas velocity in the separator is approximately 600 ft/min. The typical H/D (height to diameter) ratio of the separator is approximately 2:1. Figure 6.5.4, from Busch et al.,[62] shows the relationship of the various scrubber dimensions as a function of inlet ACFM. For example, a scrubber designed to handle 100,000 ACFM would have the following dimensions: d = 6 ft, D = 13.5 ft, A = 15.3 ft, B = 23.5 ft, H = 28 ft, and an internal surface area of 1,500 ft^2.

Busch et al.[62] also describe the next step in sizing the scrubber. This involves determining the required thickness of the metal. This thickness value is fixed by the buckling load on the separator section. In the design of the separator, operating experience has established that the scrubber liquor outlet at the bottom of the

separator should be large enough to preclude liquid flooding of this section. In addition, the scrubber is normally installed so that it is not subjected to axial loading. Because of these factors, the sole design basis for establishing the metal thickness of the separator is the external pressure acting on the separator wall. This external pressure, which acts to buckle the separator, is related to the separator dimensions and material properties by the following equation:

$$W = 55.416 \, bt/SD \qquad (6.5.46)$$

where

b = the critical buckling stress given by

$$b = 26.21 \times 10^6 \, K \, (t/H)^2 \qquad (6.5.47)$$

and

W = net external pressure, in. of water;
t = separator wall thickness, in.;
S = design safety factor (use a minimum of 2);
D = separator diameter, in.;
K = buckling coefficient, defined in terms of z;
H = separator height, in.;
z = buckling correlation coefficient, $H^2 \sqrt{1 - M^2}/0.5\,tD$;
M = Poisson's ratio (say 0.3).

Figure 6.5.5 shows the required metal thickness plotted as a function of the ACFM into the scrubber. The calculations used to develop this graph were based on the separator dimensions given in Figure 6.5.6 and on a design safety factor of 2. No corrosion or erosion allowance, however, is included. Thus, for example, when 100,000 ACFM enters the scrubber, a ¼-in. thick wall would be adequate (safety factor of 2) for a total pressure drop (scrubber plus demister plus internal cooler) of 42 in. of water. The internal gas cooler installed within the separator housing consists of a water spray countercurrent to the scrubbed gas flow, some form of extended gas-water contact

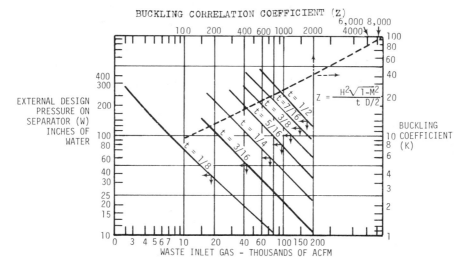

FIGURE 6.5.5. Metal thickness required in a scrubber as a function of the amount of gas treated. (From Busch, J. S., MacMath, W. E., and Lin, M. S., *Pollut. Eng.*, p. 28, January 1973; p. 32, February 1973; p. 34, March 1973. With permission.)

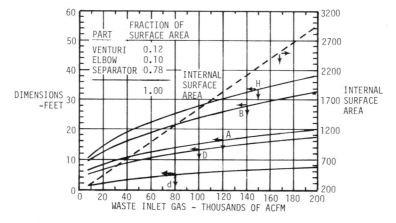

FIGURE 6.5.6. Relationship of scrubber dimensions to the quantity of contaminated gas treated. (From Busch, J. S., MacMath, W. E., and Lin, M. S., *Pollut. Eng.*, p. 28, January 1973; p. 32, February 1973; p. 34, March 1973. With permission.)

surface, and a collection device so that water spray used for cooling can be collected separately from the scrubber liquor.

In general, the initial cost for wet scrubbers in the 100,000-ACFM capacity range is approximately $0.35 to 0.50 per ACFM in mild steel to $0.90 to $1.30 in stainless steel. Installation cost for low- and medium-energy scrubbers is typically 0.5 to 2.0 times the initial purchase cost; for high-energy scrubbers the installation cost is typically 1 to 4 times the initial purchase cost. Operating cost is relatively high, primarily due to the required energy input to collect the smaller sized particles. Operating cost typically ranges from $0.35 to 1.00 per year per ACFM, depending on the circumstances. Maintenance cost is usually low, ranging from $0.02 to $0.06 per year per ACFM capacity.

The theoretical annual cost of operation and maintenance for wet scrubbers can be expressed as follows:

$$\$ = ACFM \left[0.7457 \, t \, E \left[1{,}000 \, P_T + (Lh/1{,}980) \right] + \right.$$
$$\left. WtL_c + M \right] \tag{6.5.48}$$

where

t = annual operating time, hr (maximum 8,760 hr);

E = power cost, $/kW-hr (typically $0.01 to 0.02/kW-hr);

P_T = total power input required for a specific scrubbing efficiency, hp/1,000 ACFM (see Equation 6.5.39);

L = water circulation, gal/ACFM;

h = elevation of pumping liquor in circulating system for collector, ft;

W = make-up liquid rate, gal/hr/ACFM;

L_c = cost of liquid, $/ACFM;

M = maintenance cost, $/ACFM.

It is best to consult the manufacturer directly to obtain cost information on specific systems.

Suppressing Scrubber Steam Plume

Water scrubber systems removing pollutants from high-temperature processes (i.e., combustion) can generate a supersaturated water vapor which becomes a visible white plume as it leaves the stack. Although not strictly an air pollution problem, such a plume may be objectionable for aesthetic reasons. Regardless, there are several ways to avoid or eliminate the steam plume. The most obvious way is to specify control equipment which does not use water in contact with the high-temperature gas stream (i.e., electrostatic precipitators, cyclones, or fabric filters). Should this not be possible or practical, a number of suppression methods are available.

1. Mixing with Heated and Relatively Dry Air — Low moisture content ambient air may be reheated and mixed with the saturated scrubber exhaust (see Figure 6.5.7). Exhaust high-temperature gases are first cooled by mixing with ambient air to limit the temperature of the gases entering the heat exchanger and thus prevent damage to the exchanger system metal. In the exchanger heat is transferred to the ambient air, which subsequently is mixed with the scrubber effluent gas stream.

2. Condensation of Moisture by Direct Contact with Water, then Mixing with Heated Ambient Air — This suppression method uses a medium-energy scrubber with an excess of cold water for cooling. The wet-bulb temperature of the scrubber exhaust gases can be reduced by direct contact with the water (see Figure 6.5.8). The already 100% saturated gases are further cooled with the cold water. Sufficient "coolness" is required to dehumidify or condense water vapor down to the desirable lower saturation.

3. Condensation of Moisture by Direct Contact with Water, then Reheating Scrubber Exhaust Gases — In this method (see Figure 6.5.9) moist combustion gases are dehydrated in the scrubber by direct contact with cooling water, followed by reheating to suppress the steam plume. Gases

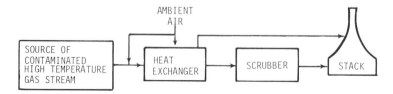

FIGURE 6.5.7. Steam plume suppression by transferring heat from a high-temperature exhaust gas stream and mixing with heated ambient air.

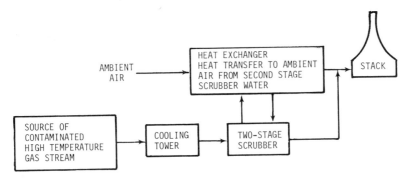

FIGURE 6.5.8. Steam plume suppression by dehydrating the effluent and mixing it with heated ambient air.

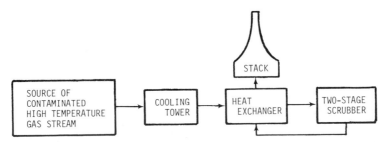

FIGURE 6.5.9. Steam plume suppression by condensing the moisture in the exhaust gases with cool water, then reheating the effluent before exhausting it.

leaving the high-temperature source are cooled in a conditioning spray tower to reduce and control the temperature of the gas entering the heat exchanger. The gases are then scrubbed and cooled in the two stages of the scrubber. Leaving the scrubber, gases are reheated in the heat exchanger by heat transferred from the gases during cooling.

4. Indirect Cooling of Hot Gases – Since saturation is dependent on both the initial moisture content and the initial hot gas temperature, reduction of either or both of these conditions ultimately decreases the saturation temperature. Cooling of the hot gas stream is usually affected within specially shaped ducts with sufficient surface exposure for radiation and cooling by atmospheric air surrounding the ducts.

5. Cooling by Mixing with Atmospheric Air – In some special cases sensible cooling may be obtained by the addition of atmospheric air having a low dew point temperature. However, this method becomes impractical where already large saturated volumes of gas with high saturation temperatures are involved.

6. Direct Heating – In those cases where a high-temperature source is not available, it frequently becomes necessary to install a gas-fired (or oil-fired) reheater downstream of the scrubber to heat the gas stream approximately 50°F above its dew point. Although costs for any of the systems to suppress the steam plume are higher than for a basic scrubber system, operating costs are not proportionally higher. Operating costs of a scrubber include water which is lost by evaporation and any auxilliary fuel required. Methods 1 and 2 will not require significant amounts of make-up water, even though they have larger power costs. Method 3 requires large amounts of cooling water for the conditions shown. Normally, the cost of this water would be prohibitive, unless it could be reprocessed in a cooling tower. Method 4 usually involves the addition of ductwork which can be both expensive and undesirable if the space is not available. Method 6 requires the use of an auxiliary fuel source, such as natural gas, which, if available, considerably increases operating costs.

6.6. ILLUSTRATIVE EXAMPLES

The design procedures and equations presented in the previous discussion are now applied to demonstrate their use in scrubber analysis.

Example 6.6.1

Show that the gas horsepower requirement for a venturi unit can be determined from

$$P_B = Q'_G (\Delta P')/6{,}356$$

where

$$
\begin{aligned}
Q'_G &= \text{gas flow rate, } ft^3/\text{min;} \\
\Delta P' &= \text{pressure drop, in. } H_2O; \\
P_B &= \text{energy required, hp.}
\end{aligned}
$$

Solution

The developed pressure head is given by the following equation

$$(P_1 - P_2)/\rho_G = -W_n, \text{ (ft) (lb}_f)/\text{lb}$$

and

$$\Delta P/\rho_G = 550\, P_B/\dot{m}_G$$

where

$$
\begin{aligned}
\Delta P &= \text{pressure drop, lb}_f/ft^2; \\
\rho_G &= \text{average gas density, lb}/ft^3; \\
P_B &= \text{horsepower;} \\
\dot{m}_G &= \text{gas mass flow rate, lb/sec.}
\end{aligned}
$$

Since

$$Q = \dot{m}_G/\rho_G \ \ ft^3/\text{sec}$$

substitution gives

$$\Delta P = 550\, P_B/Q$$

Converting to the proper units results in

$$\Delta P' = 6{,}356\, P_G/Q'_G$$

where

$$
\begin{aligned}
\Delta P' &= \text{pressure drop, in. } H_2O; \\
Q_G{}' &= \text{flow rate, } ft^3/\text{min.}
\end{aligned}
$$

Then

$$P_G = Q'_G\, \Delta P'/6{,}356$$

Example 6.6.2

Calculate the gas power requirement of a venturi scrubber treating 220,000 ACFM of gas and operating at a pressure drop of 48 in. H_2O.

Solution

Using the equation developed in Example 6.6.1, the gas power is given by

$$
\begin{aligned}
P_B &= Q'_G (\Delta P')/6{,}356 \\
&= 1{,}660 \text{ hp}
\end{aligned}
$$

Or, alternately, using Equation 6.5.37,

$$
\begin{aligned}
P_G &= 0.157\, \Delta P' \\
&= 0.157\,(48) \\
&= 7.56 \text{ hp/1,000 ACFM}
\end{aligned}
$$

Thus, the power would be

$$(7.56 \text{ hp/1,000 ACFM}) (220{,}000 \text{ ACFM}) = 1{,}663 \text{ hp}$$

To determine the brake horsepower, the gas horsepower must be divided by the fan efficiency. Assuming a fan efficiency of 65%, the operating brake horsepower would be

Brake hp = 1,663/0.65 = 2,559

Example 6.6.3

A venturi scrubber is employed to reduce the discharge of particulates from a certain source to the atmosphere. The unit is presently treating 80,000 ACFM of gas with a concentration of 8.2 grains/ft^3 of particulates and operating at a pressure drop of 5 in. H_2O. Experimental studies have yielded the following particle-size collection efficiency data:

Particle diameter, μm	Collection efficiency, %
20	58
30	76
50	91
75	94
100	98.9
150	99.4
200	99.9+

Determine the overall collection efficiency of the venturi scrubber assuming the following particle-size distribution: 2% by weight of 20-μm particles; 3%, 30 μm; 7%, 50 μm; 10%, 75 μm; 13%, 100 μm; 19%, 150 μm; 46%, 200 μm.

Solution

The results are presented in tabular form.

Particle diameter, μm	Weight fraction, w_i	Size range collection efficiency, η_i	$w_i \times \eta_i$
20	0.02	58	1.16
30	0.03	76	2.28
50	0.07	91	6.37
75	0.10	94	9.40
100	0.13	98.9	12.85
150	0.19	99.4	18.89
200	0.46	99.9	46.00
			$\eta = 96.95\%$

The overall collection efficiency is 96.95%.

Example 6.6.4

Calculate the daily mass (in tons) of particulates collected by the scrubbing liquid and discharged to the atmosphere in the Example 6.6.3.

Solution

The total mass entering the unit is

(8.2 grains/ft^3) (80,000 ft^3/min) (60 min/hr)
(24 hr/day)/(1.4 × 10^7 grains/ton)
= 67.5 ton/day

The mass collected daily is

67.5(0.9695) = 65.4 ton/day

The mass discharged to the atmosphere is then

67.5 − 65.4 = 2.1 ton/day

Example 6.6.5

Obtain the particle-size distribution of the carbon black collected and discharged to the atmosphere in Example 6.6.3. Comment on the results.

Solution

The solution is again presented in tabular form.

Particle diameter, μm	w_i	η_i	Mass entering, tons	Mass collected, tons	Mass discharged, tons
20	0.02	58	1.35	0.783	0.567
30	0.03	76	2.03	1.54	0.49
50	0.07	91	4.73	4.30	0.43
75	0.10	94	6.75	6.35	0.40
100	0.13	98.9	8.78	8.68	0.10
150	0.19	99.4	12.83	12.75	0.08
200	0.46	99.9	31.03	31.00	0.03
			67.50	65.4	2.1

The weight fractions for the collected and discharged streams appear below.

Particle diameter, μm	w_i collected, mass	w_i discharged, mass
20	0.012	0.270
30	0.024	0.233
50	0.066	0.205
75	0.097	0.190
100	0.133	0.048
150	0.195	0.038
200	0.474	0.014
	1.007	0.998

The collector works reasonably well for the larger size particles. The weight fraction of emitted particles is concentrated in the smaller particle size ranges.

Example 6.6.6

Using the N-T correlation, calculate the average water droplet diameter in a venturi scrubber under the following operating conditions:

Gas flow rate = 120,000 ACFM
Liquid flow rate = 600 gal/min
Throat area = 6.04 ft²

Repeat the calculation using the simplified equation.

Solution

The Nukiyama and Tanasawa correlation for droplet diameter is

$$d_o = (1,920/v_r)(\sigma/\rho'_L)^{0.5} + 597 \, [\mu'_L/(\sigma\rho'_L)^{0.5}]^{0.45}$$
$$(1,000 \, L'/G')^{1.5}$$

The gas velocity is

$$v_G = 120,000/6.04 \, (60 \, \text{sec/min})$$
$$= 331 \, \text{ft/sec}$$

The liquid velocity is

$$v_l = 120/6.04 \, (60) \, (7.48 \, \text{gal/ft}^3)$$
$$= 0.0442 \, \text{ft/sec}$$

The relative velocity is

$$v_r \approx 331 \, \text{ft/sec}$$

The gas volumetric flow rate is

$$G' = 120,000/60$$
$$= 2,000 \, \text{ft}^3/\text{sec}$$

The liquid rate is

$$L' = 600/7.48 \times 60$$
$$= 1.335 \, \text{ft}^3/\text{sec}$$

Therefore, the droplet size is

$$d_o = (1,920/331) \, (72/1)^{0.5} + 597 \, [0.00982/(72)^{0.5}]^{0.45}$$
$$(1,000 \times 1.335/2,000)^{1.5}$$

or

$$d_o = 64.75 \, \mu m$$

Using the simplified equation gives

$$d_o = (16,400/v_G) + 1.45 \, (R)^{1.5}$$
$$= (16,400/331) + 1.45 \, (5)^{1.5}$$
$$d_o = 65.76 \, \mu m$$

Example 6.6.7

Estimate the pressure drop across the unit in Example 6.6.6.

Solution

The describing equation is

$$\Delta P' = 5 \times 10^{-5} \, (v_G - v_l)^2 \, R$$

Substituting the data gives

$$\Delta P' = 5 \times 10^{-5} \, (331)^2 \, (5)$$
$$= 27.4 \, \text{in. H}_2\text{O}$$

Example 6.6.8

Calculate the inertial impaction parameter for particles of 5-μm diameter and a specific gravity of 1.1 in an air stream at ambient conditions. The aerosol is flowing past a 256-μm diameter spherical droplet collector at a velocity of 170 ft/sec.

Solution

The inertial impaction parameter is given by

$$N_I = 2 \, v_G r_p^2 \, \rho_p/9 \, \mu_G \, r_c$$

Substituting the data gives

$$N_I = 2 \times 170 \times (2.5 \times 3.28 \times 10^{-6})^2 \times (1.1 \times$$
$$62.4)/9 \times 1.21 \times 10^{-5} \times (128 \times 3.28 \times 10^{-6})$$

Solving gives

$$N_I = 34.3$$

Example 6.6.9

Obtain the single-droplet collection efficiency for the system in Example 6.6.8 for potential flow.

Solution

The collector efficiency is obtained from Figure

6.4.2. This value is 96% at an inertial impaction number of 34.3.

Example 6.6.10

Estimate the single-droplet collection efficiency for the system in Example 6.6.8 if the interception effect is included.

Solution

From Equation 6.4.1,

$$\eta = (y^*/r_c)^2$$

we may back-calculate y^* from

$$y^* = r_c (\eta)^{0.5}$$

Substituting the data

$$y^* = 128 (0.96)^{0.5} = 125.4 \ \mu m$$

The efficiency with the interception effect is

$$\eta = 100 (125.4 + r_p)/r_c$$
$$= 100 (125.4 + 2.5)/128$$
$$= 99.9\%$$

Example 6.6.11

A fly ash-laden gas stream is to be cleaned by a venturi scrubber using a liquid-to-gas ratio of 8.5 gal/1,000 ft^3. The fly ash has a particle density of 0.7 g/cm^3. Use a throat velocity of 272 ft/sec, a liquid-to-gas ratio of 8.5 gal/1,000 ft^3, and a gas viscosity of 1.5×10^{-5} lb/ft sec. The particle size distribution is

Particle size range, μm	% by wt
<0.10	0.01
0.10–0.50	0.21
0.60–1.00	0.78
1.10–5.00	13.00
6.00–10.00	16.00
11.00–15.00	12.00
16.00–20.00	8.00
>20.00	50.00

Assume the N-T relationship to be applicable and a correlation coefficient, k, of 200 ft^3/gal. Determine the overall collection efficiency.

Solution

Equation 6.5.19 is used. For the sake of simplicity, the Cunningham correction factor will be neglected.

Mean droplet diameter — from the Nukiyama-Tanasawa correlation:

$$d_o = \frac{16,400}{v_G} + 1.45 \ (R)^{1.5}$$

$$= \frac{16,400}{272 \ \text{ft/sec}} + 1.45 \ (8.5)^{1.5}$$

$$d_o = 96.23 \ \mu m$$

Inertial impaction parameter, ψ_I

$$\psi_I = \frac{d_p^2 \ \rho_p \ v_G}{18 \ \mu_G \ d_o'}$$

$$= \frac{d_p^2 \ (0.7 \times 62.4 \ \text{lb/ft}^3) \ (272 \ \text{ft/sec})}{18(1.5 \times 10^{-5} \text{lb/ft sec})(96.23 \ \mu m)(25,400 \ \mu m/\text{in.})(12 \ \text{in./ft})}$$

$$\psi_I = 1.500 \ d_p^2$$

Individual efficiencies, η_i

$$\eta_i = 1 - \exp \ [-k \ R \ \sqrt{\psi_I}]$$

$$= 1 - \exp \left[-\left(0.2 \times \frac{1,000 \ \text{ft}^3}{\text{gal}} \right) \left(8.5 \ \frac{\text{gal}}{1,000 \ \text{ft}^3} \right) \sqrt{\psi_I} \right]$$

$$\eta_i = 1 - \exp \ [-2.082 \ d_p]$$

Overall efficiency

d_p (μm)	η_i	$w_i(\%)$	$\eta_i w_i$
0.05	0.0989	0.01	9.886×10^{-6}
0.30	0.4645	0.21	9.755×10^{-4}
0.80	0.8109	0.78	6.325×10^{-3}
3.0	0.9981	13.0	1.298×10^{-1}
8.0	1.0000	16.0	0.16
13.0	1.0000	12.0	0.12
18.0	1.0000	8.0	0.08
80.0	1.0000	50.0	0.50
		100.0	$\eta_T = 0.9971$

The overall collection efficiency is therefore 99.71%.

Example 6.6.12

The velocity in the throat of a venturi scrubber is 328 ft/sec. The temperature of the carrier gas is 86°F, and the density of the dust particles to be collected is 187 lb/ft^3. The liquid to gas rate is

12.36 gal/1,000 ft^3 of gas. What is the minimum size particle in microns that can be removed with 98% efficiency?

Solution
Calculate the average droplet diameter:

$d_o = (16,400/328) + 1.45 (12.36)^{1.5} = 113 \, \mu m$

or

3.71×10^{-4} ft.

The describing equation for the collection efficiency is given by

$\eta = 1 - \exp [-m \, R' \, d_p \sqrt{v_G \, \rho_p \, C/18 \, d_o' \, \mu_G}]$

Assume m = 0.2; then the term in brackets as a function of the particle diameter is

$[-0.2 \, (12.36/7.48)$
$\qquad d_p \sqrt{(328) \, (187)/18 \, (3.7 \times 10^{-4}) \, (1.24 \times 10^{-5})}] =$
$[-2.84 \times 10^5 \, d_p] ; d_p$ in ft

The minimum size particle (in microns) which can be removed with 98% efficiency is

$0.98 = 1 - \exp [-2.84 \times 10^5 \, d_p]$

and solving for d_p,

$d_p = -3.9/-2.84 \times 10^5 = 1.373 \times 10^{-5}$ ft

or

$4.18 \, \mu m$.

Example 6.6.13

A vendor proposes to use a spray tower on a lime kiln operation to reduce the discharge of solids to the atmosphere. The inlet loading of the gas stream from the kiln is 5.0 grains/ft^3 and is to be reduced to 0.05 in order to meet state regulations. The vendor's design calls for a water pressure drop of 80 psi and a pressure drop across the tower of 5.0 in. H$_2$O. The gas flow rate is 10,000 ACFM, and a water rate of 50 gal/min is proposed. Assume the contact power theory to apply.

1. Will the spray tower meet regulations?

2. What total pressure loss is required to meet regulations?

3. Propose a set of operating conditions that will meet the standard. The maximum gas and water pressure drop across the unit are 15 in. H$_2$O and 100 psi, respectively.

4. What conclusions can be drawn concerning the use of a spray tower for this application.

Solution
For part 1, the collection efficiency is calculated from Equation 6.5.40

$N_t = \ln [1/(1 - \eta)]$

Also

$N_t = \alpha \, P_T^\beta$

P_T is calculated as follows

$P_T = P_G + P_L$

$P_G = 0.157 \, \Delta P'$
$\quad = 0.157 \, (5) = 0.785$
$P_L = 0.583 p_L \, (Q_L'/Q_G')$
$\quad = 0.583 \, (80) \, (50/10,000) = 0.233$
$P_T = 1.018$ hp/1,000 ACFM

For a lime kiln dust and/or fume, $\alpha = 1.47$ and $\beta = 1.05$ (Table 6.5.6). Thus,

$N_t = 1.47 \, (1.018)^{1.05} = 1.50$

Substitution into Equation 6.5.40

$1.5 = \ln [1/(1 - \eta)]$
$\eta \quad = 77.7\%$

Since the regulations require $(5.0 - 0.05)/5.0 = 99\%$, the spray tower will not meet the regulations.
For part 2, calculate P_T for $\eta = 0.99$.

$N_t \quad = \ln [1/(1 - 0.99)] = 4.605$
$4.605 = 1.47 \, (P_T)^{1.05}$
$P_T \quad = 2.96$ hp/1,000 ACFM

For part 3, assume the maximum gas and water pressure drop across the unit to be 15 in. H$_2$O and 100 psi, respectively. Calculate P_G and P_L.

$P_G = 2.36$
$P_L = 0.60$

alculate (Q_L'/Q_G') in gallons per 1,000 ACFM.

$Q_L'/Q_G' = P_L/0.583\, p_L = 0.6\,(1,000)/0.583\,(100)$

$\qquad = 10.3\ gal/1,000\ ACFM$

etermine new water flow rate.

$0.3\ gal/1,000\ ACFM)\,(10,000\ ACFM) = 103\ gal/min$

For part 4, the unit has limited, at best, pplicability for high collection efficiency operaons.

xample 6.6.14

The installation of a venturi scrubber is proposed to reduce the discharge of particulates from n open-hearth steel furnace operation. Preliminry design information suggests a water and gas ressure drop across the scrubber of 5.0 psi and 36 n. H_2O, respectively. A liquid-to-gas ratio of 6.0 al/min/1,000 ACFM is usually employed in this pplication. Estimate the collection efficiency of he proposed venturi scrubber. Assume contact ower theory to apply.

Solution
Due to the low water pressure drop, it can be assumed that

$P_G >>> P_L; P_T \approx P_G$

with

$P_G = 0.157\,(\Delta P')$

Solving for P_G gives

$P_G = 0.157\,(36)$
$\qquad = 5.65\ hp/1,000\ ACFM$

The number of transfer units is calculated from

$N_t = \alpha\, P_T^{\beta}$

where α and β are 1.26 and 0.57, respectively, for this industry (Table 6.5.6). Thus,

$N_t = 1.26\,(5.65)^{0.57}$
$\qquad = 3.38$

The collection efficiency can now be calculated.

$N_t = \ln\,[1/(1-\eta)]$
$\eta\ = 0.966 = 96.6\%$

Example 6.6.15

A venturi scrubber is to be installed to clean the contaminated gas stream in Example 3.6.13. The operating parameters of the scrubber are

$m\ = 1.4$
$R'\ = 1.5\ ft^3/1,000\ ft^3$
$v_G = 250\ ft/sec$
$d_o = 100\ \mu m$

Estimate the collection efficiency.

Solution
From Equation 6.5.44

$\gamma = m\,R'\,\sqrt{v_G\,\rho_p/18\,d_o\,\mu_G}$
$= 1.4(1.5)\sqrt{(250)(150)/(18)(100)(30.48\times10^4\ \mu m/ft)\,1.68\times10^{-5}}$
$\gamma = 4.2\ \mu m^{-1}$

The overall efficiency for the venturi is determined from Equation 6.5.45

$\eta = 1/[1 + (\beta/\gamma)] = 1/[1 + (0.025/4.2)] = 99.4\%$

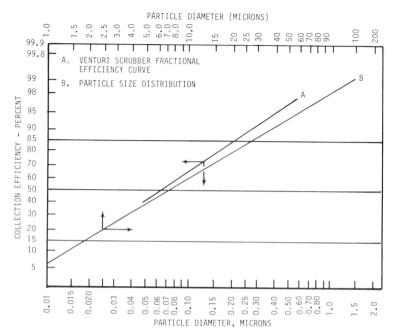

PARTICLE DIAMETER (MICRONS)

A. VENTURI SCRUBBER FRACTIONAL
   EFFICIENCY CURVE
B. PARTICLE SIZE DISTRIBUTION

PARTICLE DIAMETER, MICRONS

FIGURE 6.6.15. Venturi scrubber fractional efficiency and particle size distribution curves.

Example 6.6.16

Using the particulate-laden gas stream with the size distribution shown above, determine the collection efficiency of a venturi scrubber. The fractional efficiency curve of the venturi scrubber is also given above. Use Sundberg's method.

Solution

As in Example 3.6.14,

$d_{p\,50} = 7.2\ \mu m$

$\sigma_g = 25/7.2 = 3.472$

From the scrubber fractional efficiency curve

$d'_{p\,50} = 0.063\ \mu m$

$\sigma'_g = 0.19/0.063 = 3.016\ \mu m$

$\eta_T = \text{erf}\ [\ln (7.2/0.063)/(\ln^2\ 3.472 + \ln^2\ 3.016)^{1/2}\ ]$

$\quad = \text{erf}\ (2.85)$

From Table 3.4.2, $\eta_T = 0.9978$ or 99.78%.

Example 6.6.17

A venturi scrubber with a cyclonic separator (as in Figure 6.5.4) is to be designed to treat a 50,000 ACFM steam from a boiler exhaust at 550°F and atmospheric pressure. A pressure drop of 45 in. of water is required to achieve the desired

particulate collection efficiency. Estimate the scrubber dimensions.

Solution

With reference to Figures 6.5.4 and 6.5.5, the basic dimensions of the scrubber to treat 50,000 ACFM are

Separator height (H) = 21 ft
Separator diameter (D) = 10 ft
Diameter of inlet gas nozzle (d) = 4 ft
   Distance (A) = 12 ft
   Distance (B) = 17 ft
Total internal surface area = 900 ft²
   Venturi surface area = 108 ft²
   Elbow surface area = 90 ft²
   Separator surface area = 702 ft²

Assuming a safety factor of 2, Figure 6.5.6 shows that for 50,000 ACFM and 45 in. of water pressure drop, the wall thickness should be 3/16 in.

Example 6.6.18

A venturi scrubber, with a throat velocity of 300 ft/sec, is selected to treat 200,000 ACFM of fly ash-laden gases at 150°C from a pulverized coal-fired furnace. The size distribution for particles emitted is as follows.

Particle size range (μm)	% of total weight
0–5	25
5–10	20
10–20	15
20–30	15
30–40	10
40+	15

Assume the fly ash has a density of 0.7 g/cm^3, and 10 gal of water are utilized in the scrubber per 1,000 ACFM of gas treated. Determine the scrubber efficiency and pressure drop.

Solution

The efficiency as a function of particle size can be estimated using Equation 6.5.42 with m = 0.2.

$$\eta\,(d_p) = 1 - \exp\,[-m\,R'\,d_p\,\sqrt{v_G\,\rho_p\,C/18\,d'_o\,\mu_G}]$$

where

R' = $(10\ \text{gal}/1{,}000\ \text{ft}^3)/7.48\ \text{gal/ft}^3$ = 1.34 ft^3/1000 ft^3;

v_G = 300 ft/sec;

d_o' = 1.45 $(10)^{1.5}$ + (16,400/300) = 100 μm;

C $\approx$ 1.0;

μ_G = (2.38 $\times$ 10^{-4} p for air at 150°C) $\times$ (6.72 $\times$ 10^{-2} lb/ft-sec/p)
= 1.6 $\times$ 10^{-5} lb/ft-sec;

ρ_p = 0.7 g/cm^3 (62.4) = 43.7 lb/ft^3.

Then

$$\eta\,(d_p) = 1 - \exp\,[-0.2\,(1.34)$$

$$d_p\sqrt{(300)(43.7)(1)/18(100)(1.6\times10^{-5})(30.48\times10^4)}$$

$$\eta\,(d_p) = 1 - \exp\,[-0.328\,d_p]$$

where d_p is in microns. From the particle-size distribution curve, the following table can be generated.

Particle size range (μm)	Percent of total weight (%)	Average particle size for range (μm)	$\eta(d_p)$ (%)	(% by wt) $\eta(d_p)$
0–5	25	2.5	55.85	0.1396
5–10	20	7.5	91.45	0.1829
10–20	15	15	99.28	0.1489
20–30	15	25	99.97	0.1500
30–40	10	35	100.00	0.1000
40+	15		100.00	0.1500

$$\eta_T = 0.8714$$

The pressure drop can be estimated from Equation 6.5.20.

$$\Delta P' = 5 \times 10^{-5} \; v_G{}^2 \; R$$
$$= 5 \times 10^{-5} \; (300)^2 \; 10$$
$$= 45 \text{ in. water}$$

Note here that the efficiency is approximately 87% with a pressure drop of 45 in. water. The efficiency is relatively low primarily due to the large weight percentage of fine particles. Increasing the efficiency requires smaller liquid droplet sizes, a greater relative velocity between the gas and the liquid, or a larger amount of water. This would considerably increase the power requirement.

NOMENCLATURE

A	Projected area available for capture, ft^2
A_d	Projected area of droplet, ft^2
A_t	Throat cross-sectional area, ft^2
c	Local particle concentration, lb/ft^3
C	Cunningham correction factor
C_D	Drag coefficient
d	Diameter of droplet, μm
D_d	Disk diameter, in.
d_e	Equivalent diameter, ft
d_g	Diameter of glass spheres, ft
d_m	Mass median droplet diameter, μm
d_o	Average surface-volume mean droplet diameter, μm
D_o	Orifice diameter, cm
$d_o{}'$	Droplet diameter, ft
$d_o{}''$	Diameter of atomized liquid droplet, cm
d_p	Particle diameter, ft
F	Specific gravity of turbulent layer
F_d	Fraction of the mass of sample contained in droplets of diameter greater than d
F_D	Drag force, lb$_f$
G	Mass flow rate of gas, lb/sec
$\bar{G}$	Gas flow rate, lb/hr ft^2
G'	Gas volumetric flow rate, ft^3/sec
g_c	Gravitational constant
H_t	Height of turbulent layer, ft
L	Mass flow rate of liquid, lb/sec (or effective length of capture, where indicated)
$\bar{L}$	Liquid rate, lb/(hr)(ft^2)
L'	Liquid volumetric flow rate, ft^3/sec
L''	Mass flow rate of liquid, lb/min
L_W	Liquid feed rate based on wetted perimeter, g/(cm)(sec)
$\dot{m}_G$	Mass flow rate of gas, lb/sec
m_l	Mass of liquid droplet, lb
$\dot{m}_l$	Mass flow rate of liquid, lb/sec
m_p	Particle mass, lb
n	Disk rotation rate, rev/min
N	Number of revolutions per second
N_I	Inertial parameter
N_t	Number of transfer units
N_W	Weber number
p	Pressure, lb$_f$/ft^2
P	Power, hp
P'	Power, kW
P''	Energy, (ft)(lb$_f$)/lb
P_G	Contacting power based on gas stream energy input, hp/1,000 ACFM
P_L	Contacting power based on liquid stream energy input, hp/1,000 ACFM

P_T	Total pressure loss, hp/1,000 ACFM
P_W	Wetted perimeter of disk, cm
Δp	Pressure drop, $lb_f/in.^2$
$\Delta p'$	Dimensionless pressure drop
$\Delta P'$	Pressure drop, in. H_2O
$\Delta P''$	Pressure drop, atm
q	Liquid rate, l/m^3
Q	Gas volumetric flow rate, ft^3/sec
Q'_G	Gas volumetric flow rate, ft^3/min
Q_L'	Liquid volumetric flow rate, ft^3/sec
Q_L'	Volumetric flow rate of liquid, gal/min
$\bar{Q}_L''$	Liquid volume flow rate, l/min
R	Ratio of liquid-to-gas flow rate, gal/1,000 actual ft^3
R'	Liquid-to-gas ratio, ft^3/ft^3
R''	Liquid-to-gas ratio, l/m^3
r_b	Radius of
r_c	Collector radius, ft
r_d'	Droplet radius, mm
Re	Reynolds number
r_o	Disk radius, cm
r_p	Radius of the particle, ft
S	Cross-sectional area of venturi, ft^2
S_d	Specific surface of droplets, ft^2/ft^3
t	Time, sec
T	Absolute temperature
t_L	Throat length, mm
v	Velocity, ft/sec
V	Gas flow rate, ft^3/min
v_d	Droplet velocity, m/sec
v_G	Velocity of gas, ft/sec
v_G'	Gas throat velocity, cm/sec
v_l	Droplet velocity, ft/sec
v_L	Liquid injection velocity, m/sec
v_r	Relative velocity between gas and liquid, ft/sec
v_r'	Relative velocity between gas and liquid, m/sec
v_s	Superficial gas velocity
y^*	Ordinate of the starting point of the critical trajectory at the cell boundary
δ	Droplet concentration
ϵ	Void volume
η	Single-particle inertial impaction efficiency
η_T	Overall collection efficiency
ρ_G	Gas density, lb/ft^3
ρ_G'	Gas density, g/cm^3
ρ_L	Liquid density, lb/ft^3
ρ_L'	Liquid density, g/cm^3
ρ_p	Particle density, lb/ft^3
μ_G	Gas viscosity, lb/(ft)(sec)
μ_G'	Gas viscosity, g/(cm)(sec)
μ_G''	Gas viscosity, cP
μ_L	Liquid viscosity, cP
μ_L'	Liquid viscosity, P
σ	Liquid surface tension, dyn/cm
ψ_I	Inertial parameter

PROBLEMS

1. Calculate the power requirement of a venturi scrubber treating 380,000 ACFM of gas and operating at a pressure drop of 60 in. H_2O.

2. A venturi scrubber is employed to reduce the discharge of fly ash to the atmosphere. The unit is presently treating 215,000 ACFM of gas, with a concentration of 4.25 grains/ft^3, and operating at a pressure drop of 32 in. H_2O. Experimental studies have yielded the following particle-size collection efficiency data.

Particle diameter, μm	Collection efficiency, %
5	30
10	42
20	86
30	93
50	97
75	98.7
100	99.9+

Estimate the overall collection efficiency of the unit.

3. Calculate the daily mass (in tons) of fly ash collected by the scrubbing liquid and discharged to the atmosphere.

4. Obtain the particle-size distribution of the fly ash collected and discharged to the atmosphere. Comment on the results.

5. The following data were collected using a bench-scale venturi scrubber:

Gas rate = 1.56 ft^3/sec
Liquid rate = 0.078 gal/min
Throat area = 1.04 in^2

Estimate the average liquid droplet in the scrubber. Repeat the calculation using the simplified equation.

6. Estimate the pressure drop across the above unit.

7. Calculate the inertial impaction number for particles of 10 μm in diameter and with a specific gravity of 1.87 in an air stream at ambient conditions. The aerosol is flowing past a 325 μm diameter spherical collector at a velocity of 210 ft/sec.

8. Obtain the single-droplet collection efficiency for the above system.

9. Estimate the single-droplet collection efficiency for the same system if the interception effect is included.

10. Design a venturi scrubber (calculate the throat area) to operate at 98% collection efficiency. The flow rate of the process gas stream is 11,040 ACFM (68°F) and the density of the dust is 187 lb/ft^3. A liquid-to-gas rate of 2 gal/min/1,000 ft^3 is suggested. The average particle size and water droplet diameter have been previously determined to be 3.2 and 48 μm, respectively.

11. A venturi scrubber with a cyclonic separator is to be designed to treat a 150,000-ACFM stream from a boiler exhaust at 460°F and 1 atm. A pressure drop of 60 in. of water is required to achieve the desired collection efficiency. Estimate the scrubber dimensions.

REFERENCES

1. **Theodore, L. and Buonicore, A. J.,** *Industrial Control Equipment for Gaseous Pollutants,* CRC Press, Cleveland, 1975.
2. **Stairmond, C. J.,** Dust Collection by Impingement and Diffusion, presented at the Inaugural Meeting of the Midland Branch of A. Inst. P., Birmingham, England, October 14, 1950.
3. **Nukiyama, S. and Tanasawa, Y.,** *Trans. Soc. Mech. Eng.* (Japan), 5(18), 68, 1939.
4. **Calvert, S., Goldshmid, J., Leith, D., and Mehta, D.,** Wet Scrubber System Study, Vol. 1, Scrubber Handbook, PB-213 016; Vol 2, Final Report and Bibliography, PB-213 017 U.S. Environmental Protection Agency, July 1972.
5. **Orr, C., Jr.,** *Particulate Technology,* MacMillan, New York, 1966.
6. **Fraser, R. P., Eisenklam, P., and Dombrowski, N.,** *Br. Chem. Eng.,* 2, 417, 1957.
7. **Friedman, S. J., Gluckert, F. A., and Marshall, W. R., Jr.,** *Chem. Eng. Prog.,* 48, 181, 1952.
8. **Johnstone, H. F. and Roberts, M. H.,** *Ind. Eng. Chem,* 41, 2417, 1949.
9. **Johnstone, H. F., Feild, R. B., and Tassler, M. C.,** *Ind. Eng. Chem.,* 46, 1601, 1954.
10. **Hesketh, H. E.,** *J. Air Pollut. Control Assoc.,* 24(10), 939, 1974.
11. **Hesketh, H. E.,** Atomization and Cloud Behavior in Wet Scrubbers, U.S.-U.S.S.R. Symp. on Control of Fine Particulate Emissions, January 15–18, 1974.
12. **Leva, M.,** *Chem. Eng. Prog.,* 50(10), 51, 1954.
13. **Ergun, S.,** *Chem. Eng. Prog.,* 48(2), 89, 1952.
14. **Epstein, M., Leivo, C. C., and Rowland, C. H.,** Mathematical Models for Pressure Drop, Particulate Removal and SO_2 Removal In Venturi, TCA and Hydro-Filter Scrubbers, presented at the 2nd Int. Lime, Limestone Wet Scrubbing Symp., New Orleans, November 8–12, 1971.
15. **Ludwig, E. E.,** *Applied Process Design for Chemical and Petrochemical Plants,* Gulf Publishing, Houston, 1960.
16. **Eckert, J. S. and Strigle, R. F., Jr.,** *J. Air Pollut. Control Assoc.,* 24(10), 961, 1974.
17. **Lapple, C. E. and Kamack, H. J.,** *Chem. Eng. Prog.,* 51(3), 110, 1955.
18. **Semrau, K. T.,** *J. Air Pollut. Control Assoc.,* 10(3), 200, 1960.
19. **Semrau, K. T.,** *J. Air Pollut. Control Assoc.,* 13(12), 587, 1963.
20. **Semrau, K. T., Marynowski, C. W., Lunde, K. E., and Lapple, C. E.,** *Ind. Eng. Chem.,* 50(11), 1615, 1958.
21. **Calvert, S., Goldshmid, J., and Leith, D.,** *AIChE Symp. Ser.,* 70(137), 357, 1974.
22. **Walker, A. B.,** *J. Air Pollut. Control Assoc.,* 13(12), 622, 1963.
23. **Walker, A. B. and Hall, R. M.,** *J. Air Pollut. Control Assoc.,* 18(5), 319, 1968.
24. **Semrau, K. and Witham, C. L.,** Wet Scrubber Liquid Utilization, EPA-650/2-74-108, October 1974.
25. **Happel, J.,** *AIChE J.,* 4, 197, 1958.
26. **Happel, J.,** *AIChE J.,* 5, 174, 1959.
27. **Pfeffer, R. and Happel, J.,** *AIChE J.,* 10, 605, 1964.
28. **Harrop, J. A. and Stenhouse, J. I. T.,** *Chem. Eng. Sci.,* 24, 1475, 1969.
29. **Paretsky, L., Theodore, L., Pfeffer, R., Squires, A. M.,** *J. Air Pollut. Control Assoc.,* 21, 204, 1971.
30. **Theodore, L.,** *Transport Phenomena for Engineers,* International Textbook, Scranton, 1971.
31. **Walton, W. H. and Woolcock, A.,** in *Aerodynamic Capture of Particles,* Richardson, E. G., Ed., Pergamon Press, 1960.
32. **Herne, H.,** in *The Classical Computations of the Aerodynamic Capture of Particles by Spheres,* Richardson, E. G., Ed., Pergamon Press, 1960.
33. **Slattery, J.,** *Momentum, Energy and Mass Transfer in Continua,* McGraw-Hill, New York, 1972.
34. **Theodore, L., Gergerich, E., and Buonicore, A. J.,** unpublished work.
35. **Theodore, L. and Buonicore, A. J.,** ongoing research.
36. **Nukiyama, S. and Tanasawa, Y.,** *Trans. Soc. Mech. Eng.* (Japan), 4, 86, 1938.
37. **Theodore, L., Byrne, P., and Murtha, S.,** Pressure drop in venturi scrubbers: I. Describing equations, Proc. 4th Environ. and Eng. Conf., University of Louisville, 1974.
38. **Boll, R. H.,** Particle Collection and Pressure Drop in Venturi Scrubbers, presented at 69th Nat. AIChE Meet., Cincinnati, 1971.
39. **Theodore, L. and Buonicore, A. J.,** unpublished research.
40. **Boll, R. H.,** *Ind. Eng. Chem. Fundam.,* 12(1), 40, 1973.
41. **Guntheroth, H.,** *Fortschr. Ber. VDI Z.,* Series 3, Issue 13, 1966.
42. **Behie, S. W. and Beeckmans, J. M.,** *Can. J. Chem. Eng.,* 51(4), 430, 1973.
43. **Calvert, S.,** *AIChE J.,* 16(3), 392, 1970.
44. **Harmon, R.,** *J. Inst. Fuel,* 11(60), 514, 1938.
45. **Fuchs, N. and Kirsch, A.,** *Chem. Eng. Sci.,* 20, 181, 1965.
46. **Goldsmith, P. and May, F. G.,** in *Aerosol Science,* Davies, C. N., Ed., Academic Press, New York, 1966, 163.
47. **Melandri, C., Prodi, V., Rimondi, O., and Tarroni, G.,** Proc. Symp. Treatment of Airborne Radioactive Wastes, 1968, 541.
48. **Reiss, L.,** *Ind. Eng. Chem. Process Des. Dev.,* 6(4), 486, 1967.
49. **Sparks, L. E. and Pilat, M. J.,** *Atmos. Environ.,* 4, 651, 1970.

50. West, P. H., Markant, H. P., and Coulter, J. H., *Tappi,* 44(10), 710, 1961.
51. Bakke, E. and Reiter, S. H., 63rd Annu. Meet. Air Pollution Control Assoc., Paper 70-7, St. Louis, June 14—18, 1970.
52. Kim, K. Y. and Marshall, W. R., *AIChE J.,* 17(3), 575, 1971.
53. Rosin, P. and Rammler, J., *J. Inst. Fuel,* 7, 29, 1933.
54. Lane, W. R., *Ind. Eng. Chem.,* 43, 1312, 1951.
55. Goldshmid, Y. and Calvert, S., *AIChE J.,* 9, 352, 1963.
56. Matrozov, V. I., *Soobshch. Nauchno Tekh. Rab. Resp.,* 6, 152, 1958.
57. Volgin, B. P., Efimova, T. F., and Gofman, M. S., *Int. Chem. Eng.,* 8(1), 113, 1968.
58. Gleason, R. J. and McKenna, J. D., AIChE 69th Nat. Meet., Cincinnati, May 16—19, 1971.
59. Theodore, L., LoPinto, C., Llama, L., and Murray, C., *Proc. Environ. Eng. Sci. Conf.,* 4, 365, 1974.
60. Lowrey, R. P. and Van Winkle, M., *AIChE J.,* 15(5), 665, 1969.
61. Krockta, H. and Lucas, R. L., *J. Air Pollut. Control Assoc.,* 22(6), 459, 1972.
62. Busch, J. S., MacMath, W. E., and Lin, M. S., *Pollut. Eng.,* p. 28, January 1973; p. 32, February 1973; p. 34, March 1973.
63. Vatavuk, W. and Theodore, L., Proc. Energy-Environmental Interactions Conf. Hueston Woods, Ohio, 1974.
64. Ranz, W. E. and Wong, J. B., *Ind. Eng. Chem.,* 44, 1371, 1952.
65. Sundberg, R. E., *J. Air Pollut. Control Assoc.,* 24(8), 758, 1974.
66. Walling, J. C., *J. Air Pollut. Control Assoc.,* 22(11), 891, 1972.
67. Taheri, M. and Sheih, C. M., *AIChE J.,* 21(1), 153, 1975.
68. Strauss, W., *Industrial Gas Cleaning,* Pergamon Press, New York, 1966.

Chapter 7

FABRIC FILTERS

7.1. INTRODUCTION

One of the oldest, simplest, and most efficient methods for removing solid particulate contaminants from gas streams is by filtration through fabric media. The fabric filter is capable of providing high collection efficiencies for particles as small as 0.5 μm and will remove a substantial quantity of those particles as small as 0.01 of a micron. In its simplest form the industrial fabric filter consists of a woven or felted fabric through which dust-laden gases are forced. A combination of factors results in the collection of particles on the fabric fibers. When woven fabrics are used, a dust cake eventually forms; this, in turn, acts predominantly as a sieving mechanism. When felted fabrics are used, this dust cake is minimal or nonexistent. Instead, the primary filtering mechanisms are a combination of inertial forces, impingement, etc., as related to individual particle collection on single fibers. These are essentially the same mechanisms which are applied to particle collection in wet scrubbers, wherein the collection media is in the form of liquid droplets rather than solid fibers.

As particles are collected, the pressure drop across the fabric filtering media increases. Due in part to fan limitations, the filter must be cleaned at predetermined intervals. Dust is removed from the fabric by gravity and/or mechanical means. The fabric filters or bags are usually tubular or flat. The structure in which the bags hang is frequently referred to as a baghouse. The number of bags in a baghouse may vary from a couple to several thousand. Quite often when great numbers of bags are involved the baghouse is compartmentalized so that one compartment may be cleaned while others are still in service.

All the various aspects mentioned above are considered in some detail in the sections to follow. In the first section the various types of fabric filters are presented, including the various methods of cleaning the filters and the types of filter media. A review of the more pertinent literature follows. The remaining sections concentrate on filtration fundamentals, design procedures, costs, and operation and maintenance practices.

7.2. TYPES OF FABRIC FILTERS

The basic filtration process may be conducted in many different types of fabric filters in which the physical arrangement of hardware and the method of removing collected material from the filter media will vary. The essential differences may be related, in general, to:

1. Type of fabric.
2. Cleaning mechanism.
3. Equipment geometry.
4. Mode of operation.

Depending on the above factors, equipment will follow one of three systems, as shown in Figure 7.2.1. Bottom-feed units are characterized by the dust-laden gas introduced through the baghouse hopper and then to the interior of the filter tube. In top-feed units dust-laden gas enters the top of the filter tubes. In exterior filtration the gas passes from the outside of the filters to the interior or clean-air side. When the gas flow is from inside the bag to outside, by virtue of the pressure differential, the internal area of the filter element will be open and self-supporting. The unsupported filter elements are tubular. When the filtration process is reversed, with the gas flow from outside the bag to inside, it is necessary to support the media against the developed pressures so that the degree of collapse is controlled. Supported filter elements are either of the tubular or envelope shape.

Gases to be cleaned can be either "pushed" or "pulled" through the baghouse. In the pressure system (push through) the gases may enter through the cleanout hopper in the bottom or through the top of the bags. In the suction type (pull through) the dirty gases are forced through the inside of the bag and exit through the outside. Figures 7.2.2 through 7.2.4 depict these flows.

Baghouse collectors are available for either intermittent or continuous operation. Intermittent operation is employed where the operational schedule of the dust-generating source permits halting the gas cleaning function at periodic intervals (regularly defined by time or by pressure differential) for removal of collected material from

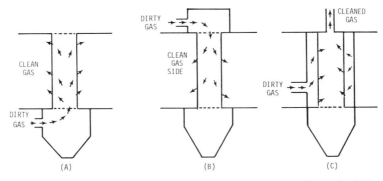

FIGURE 7.2.1. Types of filtering systems: (a) bottom feed; (b) top feed; (c) exterior filtration.

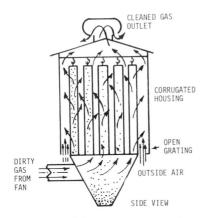

FIGURE 7.2.2. Open pressure baghouse.

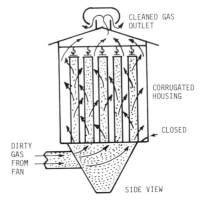

FIGURE 7.2.3. Closed pressure baghouse.

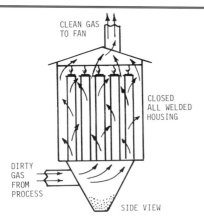

FIGURE 7.2.4. Closed suction baghouse.

the filter media (cleaning). Collectors of this type are primarily utilized for the control of small-volume operations such as grinding, polishing, etc, and for aerosols of a very coarse nature. For most air pollution control installations and major dust control problems, however, it is desirable to use collectors which allow for continuous operation. This is accomplished by arranging several filter areas in a parallel flow system and cleaning one area at a time according to some preset mode of operation (see Figures 7.2.5 and 7.2.6).

Baghouses may also be characterized and identified according to the method used to remove collected material from the bags. Particle removal can be accomplished in a variety of ways, including shaking the bags, reversing the direction of air flow through the bags, blowing a jet of air on the bags from a reciprocating manifold, or rapidly expanding the bags by a pulse of compressed air. Table 7.2.1 lists the standard cleaning methods along with a number of characteristics frequently associated with the various methods. In general, the various types of bag cleaning methods can be divided into those involving fabric flexing and those involving a reverse flow of clean air.

Fabric flexing methods include mechanical shaking and rapping, sonic cleaning, collapse cleaning, and pressure-jet and pulse-jet cleaning. Mech-

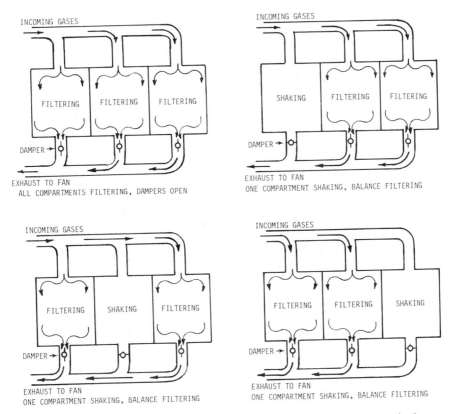

INCOMING GASES

FILTERING FILTERING FILTERING

DAMPER →

EXHAUST TO FAN
ALL COMPARTMENTS FILTERING, DAMPERS OPEN

INCOMING GASES

SHAKING FILTERING FILTERING

DAMPER →

EXHAUST TO FAN
ONE COMPARTMENT SHAKING, BALANCE FILTERING

INCOMING GASES

FILTERING SHAKING FILTERING

DAMPER →

EXHAUST TO FAN
ONE COMPARTMENT SHAKING, BALANCE FILTERING

INCOMING GASES

FILTERING FILTERING SHAKING

DAMPER →

EXHAUST TO FAN
ONE COMPARTMENT SHAKING, BALANCE FILTERING

FIGURE 7.2.5. Typical parallel flow system for a conventional multicompartment baghouse.

anical shaking and rapping involve the use of a rocker arm-lever assembly to produce a motion at the top of the filter tubes. The motion may be generally horizontal (sometimes concave upwards, sometimes concave downwards), vertical, or cover a 90° arc from the bottom to the top of the swing. Vertical motion is sometimes accomplished by rapping. A variation which provides a more gentle "shake" than mechanical shaking is inducement of an oscillating flexing motion. The top of each bag is moved back and forth in a relatively flat arc, causing ripples in the filter bags to dislodge the dust. This type of cleaning is best used with light, flocculent dusts. Sonic cleaning employs sound generators which produce a low-frequency sound, causing the bags to vibrate gently. These vibrations, frequently combined with reverse air, gently loosen dust particles from the inner surface of the bags. Noise level is barely discernible outside the filter compartment. Sonic cleaning is often recommended for use with heavy, dense, and carbonaceous dusts. To clean filter bags by the collapsing technique, small reversals in pressure are created such that the pressure drop

from the dirty air side to the clean air side is slightly negative. This causes the filter bag to deflate and, hopefully, discharge the dust cake. In some cases the bag is slowly collapsed and "popped" open. In pressure-jet cleaning a momentary burst of compressed air is introduced through a tube or nozzle attached to the top of the bag. A bubble of air flows down the bag, causing bag walls to collapse behind it. In the pulse-jet bag cleaning method a momentary burst of compressed air is introduced in the discharge nozzle of a filter bag, which inflates the bag in the opposite direction. Figure 7.2.7 illustrates some of these fabric flexing filter bag cleaning methods.

Reverse-air bag cleaning methods include reverse-jet and reverse-flow cleaning. The reverse-jet cleaning mechanism employs a high-velocity (small volume) jet of compressed air, blown back through the fabric, to dislodge collected dust. Reverse-jet baghouses incorporate a jet case or manifold that surrounds each bag. The manifold travels the length of the bag in a constantly repeating cycle. As it passes over the surface of the bags, a jet of high-pressure air issues from orifices in the mani-

FIGURE 7.2.6. Continuous operating compartmentalized baghouse collector. (Courtesy of Dustex Division, American Precision Industries, Inc.)

fold and blow the dust cake off the bags. Reverse-air cleaning collapses the filter bag by the differential air pressure. Reverse-flow baghouses are equipped with an auxiliary fan that forces air through the bags in the direction of filtration. This backwash action collapses the bag and fractures the dust cake. When the bag is reinflated by being brought back on line, the fractured dust cake is dislodged into the hopper. If the unit operates under suction (the main fan located on the clean side of the baghouse), reducing the pressure in the baghouse may eliminate the need for an auxiliary fan. The reverse-jet and reverse-flow cleaning methods are illustrated in Figures 7.2.8 and 7.2.9, respectively.

There are two basic types of filtration that occur in commercial fabric filters. The first is referred to as "media" or fiber filtration, and the second is layer or "cake" filtration. In fiber filtration the dust is retained on the fibers themselves by settling, impaction, interception, and diffusion. In cake filtration the fiber acts as a support on which a layer of dust is deposited to form a microporous layer capable of removing

additional particles by sieving as well as other basic filtration mechanisms (impaction, interception, diffusion, settling, and electrostatic attraction). In practical industrial cloth filters, both methods occur, but cake filtration is the more important process after the new filter cloth becomes thoroughly impregnated with dust.

A wide variety of woven and felted fabrics is used in fabric filters. Clean felted fabrics are more efficient dust collectors than woven fabrics, but woven materials are capable of giving equal filtration efficiency after a dust layer accumulates on the surface. When a new woven fabric is placed in service, visible penetration of dust may occur until build-up of the cake or dust layer. This normally takes from a few hours to a few days for industrial applications, depending on dust loadings and the nature of the particles. For extremely low grain loadings and especially fine dusts, fabrics are often precoated. Fabrics may be precoated with asbestos or similar materials to form an artificial filter cake to prevent dust penetration. Another method of reducing dust penetration in fabrics is based on the use of electrostatics. These forces not only assist

TABLE 7.2.1

Comparison of Bag Cleaning Methods[2]

Cleaning method	Uniformity of cleaning	Bag attrition	Equipment ruggedness	Type fabric	Filter velocity	Apparatus cost	Power cost	Dust loading	Submicron efficiency
Shake	A	A	A	Woven	A	A	L	A	G
Reverse flow, no flexing	G	L	G	Woven	A	A	M-L	A	G
Reverse flow, with collapse	A	H	G	Woven	A	A	M-L	A	G
Pulse – compartment	G	L	G	Felt, woven	H	H	M	H	H
Pulse – bags	A	A	G	Felt, woven	H	H	H	VH	H
Reverse – jet	VG	A-H	L	Felt, woven	VH	H	H	H	VH
Vibration, rapping	G	A	L	Woven	A	A	M-L	A	G
Sonic assist	A	L	L	Woven	A	A	M	–	G
Manual Flexing	G	H	–	Felt, woven	A	L	–	L	G

Note: A = average; G = good; H = high; L = low; M = medium; VG = very good; VH = very high.

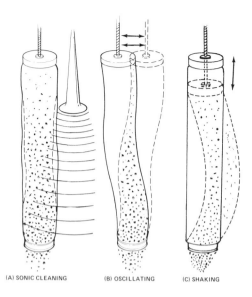

(A) SONIC CLEANING   (B) OSCILLATING   (C) SHAKING

AIR NOZZLE

BUBBLE

(D) PRESSURE-JET CLEANING

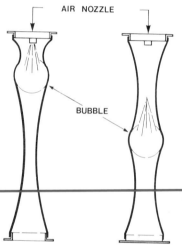

FIGURE 7.2.7. Some typical fabric flexing bag cleaning methods.

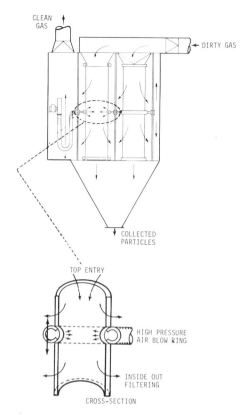

FIGURE 7.2.8. Reverse-jet (traveling ring-type) baghouse filter.

filtration by providing an attraction between the dust and fabric, but also may affect particle agglomeration, fabric cleanability, and collection efficiency. Electrostatic charges may be induced in both fabrics and dusts by friction. Agglomeration of some charged dusts may be aided by selection of a fabric with an opposite charge. Thus, for example, a negatively charged dust would agglomerate with a positively charged fabric.

When using woven fabrics care must be exercised to prevent overcleaning so as not to completely dislodge the filter cake; otherwise, efficiency will drop. Overcleaning of felted fabrics is generally impossible because they always retain substantial dust deposits within the fabric. Felted fabrics require more thorough cleaning methods than woven materials. For the same cleaning efficiency, felted fabrics are often capable of higher air-to-cloth ratios (i.e., cubic feet per minute per square foot of cloth) than woven fabrics, thereby requiring less filter cloth area and, consequently, less space for a given air or gas volume. Woven fabrics in conventional baghouses usually have air-to-cloth ratios of 1:1 to 5:1; felted fabrics usually have ratios of 3:1 to 16:1, or ratios several times those of woven fabrics. This is balanced, though, by the higher cost of the felt fabrics and the cleaning method employed. If felted fabrics are used, filter cleaning is limited to the pressure-jet and reverse-jet methods. When woven fabrics are employed, any cleaning technique may be used. Woven fabrics are available in a greater range of temperature and corrosion-resistant materials than felts and, therefore, cover a wider range of applications.

Textile materials used as filtering media can be woven or felted and made from a large variety of

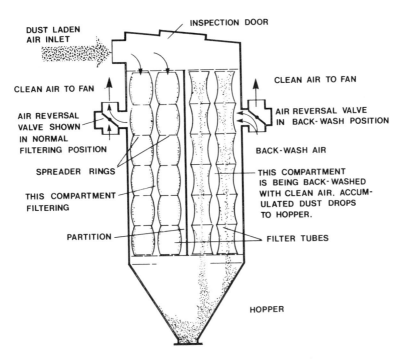

FIGURE 7.2.9. Typical reverse-flow cleaning baghouse.

materials. Until recently natural fibers such as cotton and wool were used. The introduction of synthetic fibers (see Table 7.2.2) as filter media has produced greater efficiency and durability.

Synthetic fiber yarns are manufactured in three forms.

1. Continuous multifilament consists of several fibers of unlimited length twisted tightly together to produce a smooth yarn. The greater the number of filaments, the bulkier and stronger the yarn.

2. Staplefiber consists of extended continuous fiber which is cut into short lengths. This must then be carded and spun into a yarn similar to the processing of natural fibers such as cotton and wool.

3. Monofilament consists of unbroken lengths extruded in a coarse diameter of a single fiber.

Cloth can be produced from any of these basic yarns, either singly or in combination. In conventional fabric dust collectors, the filtering media is often woven cloth; the permeability is restricted largely to the open pores in the weave; very little air movement can take place through the twisted

fibers in the yarn. The weave employed must produce a stable cloth in which the threads cannot be easily pushed about and where the pores between the threads remain relatively constant. Twill or satin weaves are much more stable than plain ones. Cotton satin makes a satisfactory filter media for general purposes and is slightly cheaper than the synthetics, although synthetic materials usually possess advantages over cotton. This is true when handling plain harmless noncorrosive and nonabrasive dust particles at normal temperature, but the advantages are more apparent when the gas stream is hot, moist, corrosive, abrasive, or sticky or with a combination of these difficulties. Wool makes an excellent filter cloth, but it is heavy and expensive. Cloth which employs synthetic continuous-filament yarn has a completely smooth surface which results in advantages such as excellent cake release, good moisture resistance, and easy cleaning. The regularity and smoothness of the filament yarn permits the construction of very closely woven lightweight cloth which is capable of retaining the particles. The continuous form of the fiber results in high tensile strength.

Cloth made from staple fiber yarns has a lower tensile strength than that of the continuous filament; because of its greater resilience, how-

TABLE 7.2.2
Typical Properties of Common Filter Media

Fabric	Generic name	Type yarn	Maximum temperature range, °F — Long periods of time (months)	Maximum temperature range, °F — Short periods of time (min)	Melting temperature °F	Acid resistance	Fluoride resistance	Alkali resistance	Flex and abrasion resistance	Relative cost (approximate)	Supports combustion
Cotton[a]	Natural fiber cellulose	Staple	180°	225°	302° decomposes	Poor	Poor	Fair-good	Fair-good	1.0	Yes
Wool[b]	Natural fiber protein	Staple	200°	250°	572° chars	Very good	Poor-fair	Poor-fair	Fair	2.75	No
Nylon[c]	Nylon polyamide	Filament spun	200°	250°	480°	Fair	Poor	Very good-excellent	Very good-excellent	2.5	Yes
Dynel[®d]	Modacrylic	Filament spun	180°	240°	325° softens	Good-very good	Poor	Good-very good	Fair-good	3.2	No
Polypropylene[e]	Polyolefin	Filament spun	200°	250°	333°	Excellent	Poor	Excellent	Very good-excellent	1.75	Yes
Orlon[®f]	Acrylic	Spun	240°	275°	482° softens	Good-excellent	Poor-fair	Fair	Fair	2.75	Yes
Dacron[®g]	Polyester	Filament spun	275°	325°	482°	Good	Poor-fair	Fair-good	Very good	2.8	Yes
Nomex[®h]	Nylon aromatic	Filament spun	425°	500°	700° decomposes	Fair	Good	Excellent	Very good-excellent	8.0	No
Teflon[®i]	Fluorocarbon	Filament spun	450°	500°	750° decomposes	Excellent	Poor-fair	Excellent	Fair	30.0	No
Fiberglass[j]	Glass	Filament spun bulked	500°	600°	1,470°	Fair-good	Poor	Fair	Poor	5.5	No
Polyethylene	Polyolefin	Filament spun	200°	—	—	Very good-excellent	Poor-fair	Very good-excellent	Good	2.0	Yes
Stainless steel[k] (type 304)	—	—	1,400–1,500°	—	2,550–2,650°	Excellent	—	Excellent	—	100.0	No

[a] Poor resistance to mildew and fungi; excellent selection in ventilation-type collector.
[b] Similar to those of cotton; good filterability.
[c] High tensile strength, good elasticity; unaffected by mildew and fungi; rugged fiber with excellent resistance to abrasion and alkalies; fair to poor resistance for most sodium salts.
[d] Good chemical and abrasion resistance and excellent dimensional stability; attacked by concentrated nitric acid, sodium hydroxide, and affected by most halogens; adversely affected by ketones, amines, cyclohexanone, and acetone.
[e] Chemically resistant to acids and alkalies; strong fiber, low moisture absorption; attacked at elevated temperatures by nitric acid and chlorosulfuric acid; has poor resistance to sodium and potassium hydroxide at high temperatures; not to be used with aromatics and chlorinated hydrocarbons.
[f] Resistance to moisture; not harmed by common solvents; not recommended for sulfuric acid (generally fair in environments above acid dewpoint); attacked by zinc chloride; good at elevated temperatures in acid conditions.
[g] High tensile strength, good dimensional stability, and excellent temperature resistance.
[h] Outstanding temperature resistance, high tensile strength, good resistance to abrasion.
[i] Can be used at elevated temperatures and possesses excellent chemical resistance.
[j] Low mechanical strength, hence vulnerable to abrasion; can be used at high temperatures and has high tensile strength.
[k] For extremely high temperatures.

ever, it has excellent resistance to abrasion and mechanical damage. It cannot be produced as closely woven as filament cloth, but the hairy nature of the yarns assists fine-particle filtration. Cake release is not as efficient, but this can be improved by surface treatment. Staple fiber may be spun either to the cotton or the wool systems. The former is fine and tightly twisted. Usually, it is necessary to twist yarns together to produce bulk for a filter cloth. In the case of woolen spun yarns, sufficient bulk can be achieved by spinning and twisting a single thread. This is because of the more delicate way in which woolen spinning is effected. Cloth made from monofilament is completely smooth and has good mechanical resistance, but it cannot be produced in close or even moderately close weave; therefore, it is not well suited to dust collection from a gas stream.

A successful filter cloth is based on filament and spun yarn, doubled together in warp and weft. This type of material combines high tensile strength with resilience, good filtering properties, and good cake discharge characteristics.

In contrast to the woven cloth, there are various types of nonwoven materials. Felted wool has been known and used for hundreds of years; its origins are lost in antiquity. One story relates that the inventor was a monk who, on one of his long pilgrimages, eased his sore feet by putting wool into his sandals. When he arrived in the monastery he found, to his great surprise, that he had made the first woolen felt insole. Heat, moisture, pressure, and the motion of the feet had activated the felting properties of wool. The same four factors are used in pressed felt manufacture today.

Wool or hair felt was the first real nonwoven material used for dust collection. No spinning, weaving, or knowtting is required because the element of felt is the single fiber, not a manufactured thread or yarn. The fibers are randomly oriented with spaces between them. Felts have a three-dimensional structure.

At present the most important felts for dust collection are needle felts. The needle felting process produces tough strong fabrics by mechanical interlocking, without recourse to the use of bonding agents. In manufacture the fiber is laid out on traveling aprons to form a bat, a thick layer of fibers laid in different directions. The bat is then pressed down with boards containing needles with barbs which vibrate through the bat to intermingle the fibers and produce a complex interlocking. The final fabric varies in thickness from 1 to 8 mm. Using an assortment of natural and synthetic fibers, sometimes in blends, a comprehensive range of needle felts can be produced.

All filter media, both woven and nonwoven, should have the right finish. Cotton and wool fabrics should be preshrunk. Sometimes other finishes (such as moisture proofing or fire-retarding) are desirable, but in applying these care should be taken not to affect the permeability of the filter cloth.

Synthetic materials should be heat set; they are sometimes silicone treated for better heat resistance. Some of the synthetic fibers can have a strong static charge, and these should receive antistatic treatment. In applications where the static charge could cause explosions, ground wire strips must be used.[1]

Natural fiber felts are not presently used to any great extent. Needle felts combine the useful properties of both felt and woven fabrics. They have remarkable pore volume and, therefore, good permeability to air; yet, the fine-pore felt achieves an efficient dust separation, even if dusts are of very small particle size. For equal efficiency, felts require a smaller filtration area, as they can be used at higher air velocities. By special callender treatment, the surface of the needle felt can be rendered smoother, thereby providing easier cake release.

The choice of fabric is usually dependent on the following.

1. Temperature of the gas stream.
2. Physical and chemical characteristics of the particles to be collected.
3. Chemical composition of the gas carrier.
4. Moisture content of the carrier gas.

Certain filter media are commonly associated with applications in some industries because of temperature considerations and methods of cleaning. For example, a baghouse handling a low-temperature gas stream could use a fabric made of cotton; because of the strength of this type of media, a shaker mechanism could be used to clean the baghouse. On the other hand, for high-temperature applications it might be necessary to use fiberglass bags, which are structurally weak. A very gentle cleaning technique would then be required so that the bags would not rupture. Quite often there is an economic trade-off between the type of material and the cleaning mechanism which must be considered for a specific type of process.

7.3. LITERATURE REVIEW

A comprehensive review of the literature is already available;[2] hence, only certain aspects of filtation theory will be highlighted here. In fabric filtration, particulate matter is removed from gas streams by impinging on or adhering to the fibers. The filter fibers are usually woven with relatively large open spaces, sometimes 100 μm or larger. The filtration process is not simple fabric sieving, as is evident from the fact that high collection efficiency has been achieved for dust particles 1 μm in diameter or less. Small particles are initially captured and retained on the fiber of the fabric by direct interception, inertial impaction, diffusion, electrostatic attraction, and gravitational settling. These mechanisms are illustrated in Figure 7.3.1, and their relative importance is compared in Table 7.3.1. Once a mat or cake of dust is accumulated, further collection is accomplished by mat or cake sieving, as well as by the above mechanisms. Periodically the accumulated dust is removed; however, some residual dust usually remains and serves as an aid to further filtration.

As the gas stream with the entrained particulates approaches the fiber obstacle, elements of the gas stream accelerate and diverge to pass around the object. The suspended particle may not immediately be able to accommodate the local fluid acceleration, and a difference in velocity between the gas stream and particle may develop. Inertia tends to maintain the forward motion of the particle while the diverging fluid tends to drag the particle aside. Subsequent motion of the particle is the result of the inertial projection and the fluid (gas stream) drag. From dimensional considerations, it can be shown that the solutions to the equation of particle motion depend on an inertial impaction parameter, N_I, defined as

$$N_I = 2\, m_p v / d_p F_D \qquad (7.3.1)$$

where

m_p = particle mass;
v = undisturbed stream velocity approaching the obstacle;
d_p = particle diameter;
F_D = fluid resistance to particle motion.

Assuming that the fluid resistance can be given by Stokes' law and that the Cunningham correction factor, C, is used for small particles (less than 1.0 μm), the impaction parameter becomes

$$N_I = C\, \rho_p d_p{}^2\, v/9\, \mu_G d_c \qquad (7.3.2)$$

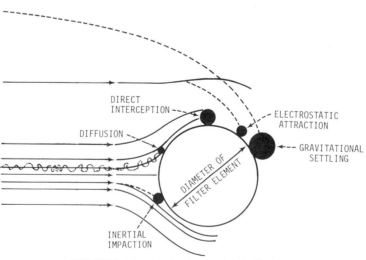

FIGURE 7.3.1.   Mechanisms of fabric filtration.

where

ρ_p = particle density;
μ_G = fluid (gas) viscosity;
d_c = diameter of the collecting obstacle.

This parameter also represents the ratio of the distance a particle will travel in a still fluid when projected with an initial velocity of v to the characteristic dimension of the obstacle (stopping distance/d_c). Strauss[3] has compiled an excellent overview of the most important inertial impaction literature. In general, the particle inertial impaction collection efficiency is determined as a function of the impaction parameter and the Reynolds number (Re_c) based on the obstacle (fiber collector) size. Langmuir and Blodgett[4] have theoretically determined the impaction efficiency for the collection of spherical particles by cylindrical fibers, spherical fibers, and flat ribbons. Their results are presented in Figure 7.3.2 and compared with the experimental results of Ranz and Wong[5] and Jarman[6] in Figure 7.3.3. Strauss notes that while practical values for the Reynolds number in

fiber filtration are about 0.2, the usual Reynolds number values for the inertial impaction efficiency are much higher. Hence, impaction efficiencies estimated from the above data tend to be on the high side.

Particles in the submicron range do not follow the gas streamlines surrounding the collecting body (fibers). Such small particles collide with gas molecules, resulting in a random Brownian motion that increases the chance of contact between the particles and the collecting body. In a still gas, small particles move freely and distribute themselves evenly throughout the gas; if an obstacle were placed in the gas, some of the particles would settle on it, thus being removed from the gas. In a flowing gas only limited time is available for the process of removal by diffusion, i.e., while the gas remains sufficiently close to the collector.[3] Lower air velocity, then, increases the chances for collection by increasing the time available for collision, therefore increasing the chances of contacting a collecting body.

The transport of suspended particles to a collecting body under the combined effects of diffusion and fluid motion can be determined from solutions to the equation of convective diffusion. From dimensional considerations, the solutions can be shown to be a function of the Peclet number, Pe, defined as

$$Pe = d_c v/D \tag{7.3.3}$$

D is the particle diffusion coefficient and is given by

$$D = kTC/F_D \tag{7.3.4}$$

TABLE 7.3.1

Primary Control Mechanisms for Particle-size Collection

Primary collection mechanism	Particle diameter (μm)
Direct interception	>1.0
Inertial impaction	>1.0
Diffusion	0.001–0.5
Electrostatic	0.01–5.0
Gravity settling	>40.0

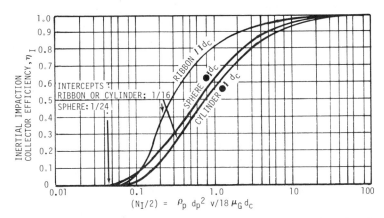

FIGURE 7.3.2.   Impaction efficiency for circular particles and various obstacles in potential flow.

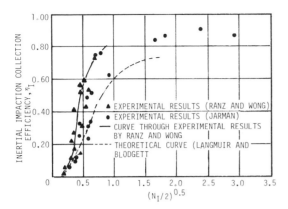

FIGURE 7.3.3. Comparison of theoretical results of Langmuir and Blodgett[4] with experimental results for inertial impaction of spherical particles on spherical collector.

where

k	=	Boltzmann's constant;
T	=	absolute temperature;
C	=	Cunningham correction factor;
F_D	=	fluid resistance to particle motion ($3\pi\mu_G vd_p$ for Stokes' law).

The Peclet number is the characteristic parameter for the relative magnitude of the effects of convection and diffusion in particle transport.

Strauss,[3] from Langmuir's[7] work, introduces a diffusion parameter, N_D, for viscous flow around a cylinder. It is given by

$$N_D = [(4.48 - 2.24 \ln Re_c)/Pe]^{1/3} \qquad (7.3.5)$$

The efficiency of collection by diffusion could then be calculated by

$$\eta_D = \frac{1}{2.002 - \ln Re_c}$$
$$\left[(1 + N_D)\ln(1 + N_D) - \frac{N_D(2 + N_D)}{2(1 + N_D)}\right] \qquad (7.3.6)$$

Bosanquet[8] determined that the collection efficiency by diffusion for flow around a cylinder should be given by

$$\eta_D = (8/Pe)^{1/2} \qquad (7.3.7)$$

and for flow around a sphere by

$$\eta_D = (8/Pe\ d_c)^{1/2} \qquad (7.3.8)$$

Other theories for the collection efficiency by diffusion are based on the theory of mass transfer and follow the established concentration gradient. Johnstone and Roberts[9] correlated the collection efficiency by diffusion for a spherical collector with the Peclet number, Reynolds number, and Schmidt number ($Sc = \mu_G/\rho_G D$).

$$\eta_D = \frac{4}{Pe}(2 + 0.557\ Re_c^{1/2}Sc^{3/8}) \qquad (7.3.9)$$

A similar equation for flow around cylindrical collectors was given by Ranz.[10]

$$\eta_D = \frac{\pi}{Pe}\left[\frac{1}{\pi} + 0.55\ Re_c^{1/2}Sc^{1/3}\right] \qquad (7.3.10)$$

Equation 7.3.10 was used for $0.1 < Re_c < 10,000$ and Sc less than 100.

More recent work on the collection efficiency by diffusion attempts to incorporate other filter characteristics into the development. Experiments by Stern et al.[11] used an equation by Torgeson to determine the collection efficiency (by diffusion) of submicron polystyrene particles. The describing equation was given by

$$\eta_D = 0.775\ Pe^{-0.6}(C_{DC}Re_c/2)^{0.4} \qquad (7.3.11)$$

where

C_{DC}	=	fiber (collector) drag coefficient;
Re_c	=	fiber (collector) Reynolds number.

$(C_{DC}Re_c/2)$ is determined experimentally from the pressure drop, (Δp), the filter density (α, defined as the fiber volume fraction or fraction of volume of filter occupied by the fibers, usually less than 0.10) and the filter thickness (w). From Chen,[12]

$$(C_{DC}Re_c/2) = \frac{\pi}{4}\frac{\Delta p}{v}\left[\frac{1 - \alpha}{\alpha}\right]\frac{d_c^2}{\mu_G} \qquad (7.3.12)$$

Using the "free surface" model, Pfeffer[13] solved the diffusion equation to obtain an expression for the average Sherwood number around a solid particle as a function of the Peclet number and bed porosity.

$$Sh_{avg} = 1.26\ \psi^{-1/3}\ Pe^{1/3} \qquad (7.3.13)$$

where

$$\psi = \text{function of the bed porosity } (\epsilon);$$

$$\frac{2 - 3(1 - \epsilon)^{1/3} + 3(1 - \epsilon)^{5/3} - 2(1 - \epsilon)^2}{1 - (1 - \epsilon)^{5/3}}$$

The single-particle collection efficiency due to diffusion is related to the Sh_{avg} and is given by

$$\eta_D = \frac{4\,Sh_{avg}}{Pe} = 5.04\, \psi^{-1/3}\, Pe^{-2/3} \qquad (7.3.14)$$

Equation 7.3.14 predicts collection by diffusion to decline as collector particle size and gas superficial velocity increase. The equation also predicts collection to increase with decreasing bed porosity. Figure 7.3.4 gives a plot of the single-particle collection efficiency vs. the Peclet number in the range of Peclet number where diffusion is the dominant mechanism of aerosol capture.[14] The experimental data of Thomas and Yoder[15] and Paretsky et al.[14] are also plotted for comparison with data theoretically predicted from Equation 7.3.14. The agreement of data and theory is best at a low Peclet number, i.e., low velocity.

Particle capture arising from diffusion or inertial impaction can be determined by assuming that the particle is a mathematical point having the property of random molecular motion or inertia. If a particle of finite size passes near an obstacle as a result of diffusion, inertia, or fluid motion alone, contact can occur if the path of the center of the particle comes within a distance of one particle radius of the surface. The effect of finite particle size on capture is referred to as direct interception. Collection efficiency can be shown to be a function of the direct interception parameter, N_{DI}, where

$$N_{DI} = d_p / d_c \qquad (7.3.15)$$

It is then possible to treat the effect of direct interception as a boundary condition in the solutions for collection efficiency by diffusion and inertial impaction. If the particle passes near a fiber surface as a result of fluid motion alone, fiber efficiency because of direct interception is[2]

$$\eta_{DI} \sim N^2_{DI} \qquad (7.3.16)$$

for $N_{DI} < 1$ and $Re_c < 1$.

Ranz and Wong[16] calculated the collection efficiency by direct interception for cylindrical collectors, assuming potential flow, as

$$\eta_{DI} = 1 + N_{DI} - [1/(1 + N_{DI})] \qquad (7.3.17)$$

and for spherical collectors,

$$\eta_{DI} = (1 + N_{DI})^2 - [1/(1 + N_{DI})] \qquad (7.3.18)$$

For viscous flow, Ranz and Wong used Langmuir's equation[7] and obtained the interception collection efficiency of a cylindrical collector as

$$\eta_{DI} = \frac{1}{2.002 - \ln Re_c}\left[(1 + N_{DI})\ln(1 + N_{DI}) - \left(\frac{N_{DI}(2 + N_{DI})}{2(1 + N_{DI})}\right)\right] \qquad (7.3.19)$$

Strauss[3] emphasizes that a much better estimate of combined interception and impaction efficiency is obtained when an allowance is made for those particles whose centers lie on trajectories closer to the collecting body than their radius. This, however, requires the stepwise calculation of particle trajectories for different values of N_{DI} and Re_c. Davies[17] carried out this calculation for $Re_c = 0.2$ (typical for fibrous filters) and obtained an equation for the combined efficiency due to impaction and interception

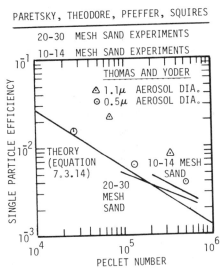

FIGURE 7.3.4. Comparison of Equation 7.3.14 with experimental data of Thomas and Yoder[15] and Paretsky et al.[14] for the single-particle efficiency due to diffusion.

$$\eta_{I-DI} = 0.16 [N_{DI} + (0.5 + 0.8 N_{DI})(N_I/2) -$$

$$0.1052 N_{DI}(N_I/2)^2] \qquad (7.3.20)$$

Strauss[3] suggests that as an approximation for impaction and interception, the combined collection efficiency be given by

$$\eta_{I-DI} = 1 - (1 - \eta_{DI})(1 - \eta_I) \qquad (7.3.21)$$

which allows for the fact that a particle caught by one mechanism cannot be captured again. In a similar fashion, Strauss[3] further recommends that the combined collection efficiency for interception, impaction, and diffusion be given by

$$\eta_{I-D-DI} = 1 - (1 - \eta_{DI})(1 - \eta_I)(1 - \eta_D) \qquad (7.3.22)$$

Additional effects can be taken into consideration by expanding Equation 7.3.22 in an analogous fashion. The validity and applicability of this equation have yet to be shown.

Gravity settling of particles as a method of collection in fabric filters is usually assumed to be negligible. However, at very low velocities and for large-size particles, the effect should be taken into consideration. Anderson and Silverman[18] and Thomas and Yoder[15] suggest that the efficiency of separation by gravity settling can be obtained from[2]

$$\eta_G = C \rho_p g d_p^2 /18 \mu_G v \qquad (7.3.23)$$

More recently, Thomas et al.[45] used a unique and novel approach to obtain information on this collection mechanism.

Electrostatic collection will result from electrostatic forces drawing particles and collecting bodies together whenever either or both possess a static charge. These forces may be either direct, as when both particle and collector are charged, or induced, as when only one is charged. Such charges are usually not present unless deliberately introduced during the manufacture of the fiber. The effect of the electrostatic mechanism may be significant when the charge on the particle or collecting body is high and when gas velocity is low. The significance of particle and collector size varies, depending on whether the electrical attraction originates from Coulomb or polarization forces. Most small particles have naturally acquired charges due to electron transfer during contact and separation or free ion diffusion. An excellent review

of capture resulting from electrostatic forces may be found in Strauss.[3] In most cases substantial improvements in collection efficiency may result from the added effects of electrostatic charge.[21-24]

Although it is obvious that more than one type of collecting action will usually take place, it is common practice to assume that collection can be attributed entirely to that mechanism which predominates over all others. More often than not, the collection of particles by inertial impaction is much greater than by any other mechanisms; hence, collection in fabric filters is usually attributed entirely to this mechanism.

In addition to particle collection efficiency, another important consideration is pressure drop in fabric filters. The resistance of a *clean* fabric filter prior to filtration is determined by fabric design and construction and is reported by fabric manufactures as air flow permeability, equal to the air flow through the fabric in ACFM/ft² at a 0.5-in. water pressure drop. In general, gas flow through fabrics is viscous at low velocities and pressure drop is directly proportional to flow,

$$\Delta p = K'v = K'\left(\frac{Q}{A}\right) \qquad (7.3.24)$$

where

Δp	=	pressure drop, in water;
K'	=	fabric resistance (experimentally determined), in water/ft/min;
v	=	filtration velocity, ft/min;
Q	=	volumetric flow rate, ACFM;
A	=	area of filter presented to gas stream, ft².

Pressure drop through a clean filter has also been predicted theoretically where no experimental data are available either by regarding the filter as a packed bed and using equations such as the Kozeny-Carman[36] or Ergun[26] equations (based upon Darcy's law of laminar flow) or by summing the drag effect of the gas on all of the filter elements.[25]

During filtration a layer of dust deposits on the fabric and produces an additional resistance to flow which is proportional to the properties of the granular layer. Fair and Hatch[19] determined this resistance to be given by

$$\frac{h}{L} = \frac{k'}{g_c} \frac{\mu_G}{\rho_G} v \left(\frac{A_p}{V_p}\right)^2 \frac{(1 - \epsilon)^2}{\epsilon^3} \qquad (7.3.25)$$

where

h = dust layer resistance, centimeters of fluid flowing;

L = depth of dust deposit on filter, cm;

k' = Kozeny-Carman coefficient;

g_c = acceleration constant, 980 cm/sec^2; cm/sec^2;

μ_G = gas viscosity, g/cm-sec;

ρ_G = gas density, g/cm^3;

v = average filtration velocity, cm/sec (total flow rate divided by the effective filter area);

(A_p/V_p) = surface area-to-volume ratio of the dust particles, cm^{-1};

ϵ = porosity (void fraction) of the dust layer.

Williams, et al.[20] modified Equation 7.3.25 by expressing bed depth (L) in terms of dust weight per unit of cloth area and the density and porosity of the dust,

$$L = W/\rho_p (1 - \epsilon) \tag{7.3.26}$$

where

W = dust weight on the filter per unit of cloth area, g/cm^2;

ρ_p = true density of dust, g/cm^3.

This expression can be further modified to include time.[2]

$$W = c_i v t \, \overline{E} \tag{7.3.27}$$

where

c_i = dust loading to the filter, g/cm^3;

t = elapsed time of filter operation at above loading, sec;

$\overline{E}$ = function of W (assume $\overline{E} \approx 1$).

With these substitutions, the filter pressure equation becomes

$$\Delta p(t) = \rho_G g h(t) = \left[\frac{k' \mu_G}{\rho_p} \left(\frac{A_p}{V_p} \right) 2 \frac{(1-\epsilon)}{\epsilon^3} \right] c_i v^2 t \tag{7.3.28}$$

where

$\Delta p(t)$ = pressure drop as a function of time, dyne/cm^2.

Equation 7.3.28 is a steady state approximation, i.e., the flux ($c_i v$) is assumed constant through the time interval, t. The bracketed term is the specific dust-fabric resistance coefficient. Williams et al.[20] suggest that this bracketed term, and some of the conversion constants to convert to engineering units, be lumped into a specific dust-fabric filter resistance coefficient, K_2.

$$\Delta p(t) = K_2 \left(\frac{c_i v^2 t}{7000} \right) \tag{7.3.29}$$

In Equation 7.3.29 c_i is expressed in grains per cubic foot, v in feet per minute, and t in minutes. The pressure drop is then expressed in units of inches of water. The resistance coefficient is then evaluated from

$$K_2 = \left[\frac{k' \mu_G}{\rho_p} \left(\frac{A_p}{V_p} \right)^2 \frac{(1-\epsilon)}{\epsilon^3} \left(\frac{1 \text{ in. H}_2\text{O}}{5.2 \text{ lb/ft}^2} \right) \left(\frac{1 \text{ min}^2}{3{,}600 \text{ sec}^2} \right) \right] \tag{7.3.30}$$

Measured values of K_2 for certain industrial dusts are given in Table 7.3.2.[20] These data were obtained by laboratory experiments using an air flow of 2 ft^3/min through 0.2 ft^2 cloth area (equivalent to a filtering velocity of 10 ft/min). The tests were terminated at a maximum pressure differential of 8 in. of water column. Such theoretical approaches to pressure drop determination in fabric filters have proven valuable in the absence of experimental data.

7.4. FUNDAMENTALS

As with wet scrubbers, one can examine a fabric filter at the macroscopic, microscopic, or molecular level (see first paragraph in Section 6.4). Little practical information has been obtained from the molecular approach. The microscopic approach, which will be considered in this section, has attempted to predict the performance and design of a fabric filter from fundamental principles — *a priori*, i.e., without recourse to experi-

TABLE 7.3.2

Filter Resistance Coefficient (K_2) for Certain Industrial Dusts[a]

	Particle size						
	Coarse			Medium		Fine	
Material	<20 mesh (~800 μm)	<140 mesh (~100 μm)	<375 mesh (~44 μm)	<90 μm	<45 μm	<20 μm	<2 μm
Granite	1.58	2.20	–	–	–	19.8	–
Foundry dust	0.62	1.58	3.78	–	–	–	–
Gypsum	–	–	~6.30	–	–	18.9	–
Feldspar	–	–	6.30	–	–	27.3	–
Stone	0.96	–	–	6.30	–	–	–
Lamp black	–	–	–	–	–	–	47.2
Zinc oxide	–	–	–	–	–	–	15.7[b]
Wood	–	–	–	6.30	–	–	–
Resin (cold)	–	0.62	–	–	–	25.2	–
Oats	1.58	–	–	9.60	11.80	–	–

[a]K_2 in inches, water gauge per pound of dust per square foot per foot per minute filtering velocity.
[b]Flocculated material not dispersed, size actually larger.

mental data. However, the problem of constructing an adequate and/or useful model is complicated by the number of system variables. It is unlikely that it will ever be possible to develop a model from fundamentals of the filtration process. Present theories at this level are incomplete. Notwithstanding this criticism, valuable and substantial information can be gained by the study of this process at the microscopic level. In this section, describing equations are developed for particle capture by single and multifiber collectors and pressure drop equations from fundamentals. However, industry still relies primarily on empirical formulas obtained from pilot plant data and existing equipment to predict the performance and design of (new) filter units. This subject is treated in the next section.

Filtration is a complex process and depends on many variables. A conventional filter consists of fibers in a porous layer. The spaces (two dimensional) or voids (three dimensional) between the fibers are usually larger than the particle(s) to be captured. Particles larger than the pores are captured. Particles may also be captured if the size and shape of the voids in the filter do not correspond with the particles'. For many dust/fabric combinations, particles greater than 0.1 the fabric pore diameter tend to bridge the pores and be captured. In filtration operations the particulate-laden gas passes through the filter perpendicular to the filter medium. At the start of filtration, the particles may impinge on, and (hopefully) adhere to, individual fibers. The particles then continue to deposit at the outer surface of the filter. The deposit of particles thus collected becomes, in turn, the filtering medium for succeeding particles. As the process continues, the spaces or voids between the fibers and particles become smaller and smaller. This basic collection mechanism is shown in Figure 7.4.1. Figure 7.4.1.a portrays the filter fibers and flow at initial conditions. As the filter cake increases with time, one encounters the situation illustrated in Figure 7.4.1.b. Although this pictorial representation is oversimplified (small particles deposit within the tortuous pores of the cake), it is here that one can see the role of the deposited cake in filtration. Thus, the filtration process is a transient operation that can basically be considered to occur in two separate stages.

1. Filtration by the filter medium.
2. Filtration by the particles deposited on and in the medium.

The so-called filter "resistance" is comprised of the resistance to flow presented by the filtering medium plus the layer of particles deposited on the surface of the fabric. The latter resistance may be the major contributor to particle capture and overall pressure drop across the filter. (Although the term "resistance" is usually used to describe

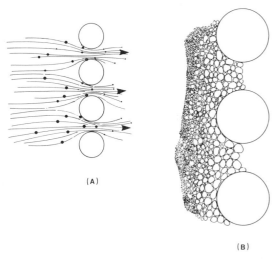

(A)

(B)

FIGURE 7.4.1. Pictorial representation of particle collection on a fabric filter. (A) Filter fibers and flow at initial conditions. (B) Build-up of filter cake.

the pressure drop across a filter, the same term is also employed to describe the capture process.)

Nonwoven fabrics (felts or mats) primarily filter particles *within* the filter. *Woven* fabrics primarily filter particles *onto* the surface. Most of the theories developed so far, and the theory presented below, apply directly to mat filtration. However, the development can also be applied to woven fabrics by simple, but appropriate, modification of the describing equations.

Present theories are, for the most part, based on considerations of the flow around a single cylinder lying transverse to the direction of flow and (preceded by) the flow around a single sphere deposited on the (cylindrical) filter medium. These single-collector filtration models can then be expanded to one which will fit multiple-target filtration data, as in a fibrous filter. Thus, the effect of all the cylindrical filter collectors and all the deposited spherical particles can be included in the analysis. Although the analysis below applies to this type of (fabric) filter medium, it can be extended to include sand and granular bed filters by the appropriate combination of the material presented in this section and Section 6.4.

As pointed out in the previous section, the primary mechanisms involved in the filtration of dust-laden gas are inertial impaction, diffusion, direct interception, and gravity settling. Although these mechanisms were defined and described earlier, this material will again be presented as applied to cylindrical fibrous collectors. There is

also the additional certainty (or at least strong probability) of electrostatic effects. Depending on the electrostatic charge on both the particle and the filter, they may either be mutually attracted or repelled. Thermal and humidity effects may also appear, but these are not treated here.

Figure 7.4.2 illustrates the collection of an aerosol particle by a cylindrical collector. Deposition by diffusion is caused by the Brownian motion of the aerosol particle which results in a deviation from its normal flow and subsequent deposition and adherence to the filter media. As mentioned previously, this effect is prevalent at low velocities or long residence times and for small particles. In analyzing collection by this mechanism, it is customary to consider the particles as points with no mass or size. The aerosol particle velocity, upon which the Brownian velocity is superimposed, is assumed to be equal to the fluid velocity.

Deposition by direct interception occurs when the particles moving along streamlines of a fluid approach the collector within a distance equal to the radius of the impinging particle. From Figure 7.4.2 it is seen that particle 2 will be filtered by this mechanism; particle 3 will not be captured. This mechanism is independent of the fluid velocity, but increases with the size of the aerosol particle and decreases as the size of the collector increases. In analyzing filtration by this mechanism, the particles are considered to have a length dimension but no mass. The mechanism of removal by inertial impaction occurs when the size or velocity of the particle is so large that the particle does not follow the streamline of the fluid, but resists the directional change imposed by the collector and strikes it. Particles 1 and 4 illustrate typical deposition by this mechanism. An increase in velocity and mass of the impinging particle increases the effect of this mechanism. In analyzing deposition by inertial impaction, the particles are considered to be point masses in the calculation of the collection efficiency. However, their size is accounted for in evaluation of the fluid's resistance to the particles' motion. Deposition by gravity settling can be considered as a removal mechanism superimposed on any of the above. It is most prevalent at lower velocities and for larger particles. The above description applies for each of the mechanisms acting independently of one another. Unfortunately, for the purpose of mathematical analysis of the filtration process, the

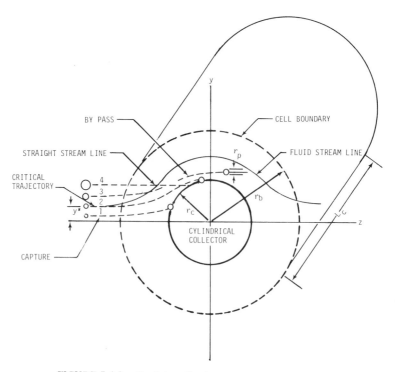

FIGURE 7.4.2. Particle collection on a cylindrical collector.

overall collection efficiency will depend on some appropriate combination of the collection mechanisms. One possibility suggested in the literature is to assume that the overall efficiency is composed of the sum of the collection efficiencies associated with each individual mechanism. This approach is criticized because it is possible to calculate overall efficiencies in excess of 100%. Strauss[3] (as discussed earlier), in an apparent attempt to remove this shortcoming, suggests that a simple method of combining effects is to set the overall term, η_T, equal to

$$\eta_T = 1 - (1 - \eta_1)(1 - \eta_2)(1 - \eta_3) \dots$$

where

η_1 represents the collection efficiency associated with mechanism 1.

Obviously, more than one collecting action takes place in the filter capture process. However, as in wet scrubber theory, it is assumed that the primary particle collection mechanism is inertial impaction. In the development below, the filtration collection process (on a mass basis) is assumed

to be attributed entirely to this one mechanism that predominates. The reader is again referred to the work of Billings,[2] Strauss,[3] and Davies[27] for complete details on the remaining collecting actions.

It will be assumed, as it is in most theories of filtration, that if a particle comes into contact with a fiber during its passage through the filter, it is retained by adhesive forces.[46,47] These may be "weak" van der Waals, surface tension, or electrostatic forces. Opposing these are rebound and/or drag forces. The former force arises due to the elastic rebound of particles colliding with the collector. The latter effect appears when the particle(s) peel or slip off the collector due to aerodynamic drag. The particle is retained only if the adhesive force exceeds the removal force. A lack of sound particle-adhesion theory may account for some of the discrepancies that exist between experimental and calculated collection efficiencies. Although the usual procedure is to multiply the overall collection efficiency by a retention or adhesion efficiency to account for possible reentrainment, 100% retention efficiency is assumed in the following development.

In addition to the "retention" effect described above, certain other assumptions must be postulated before proceeding to the theory of fabric filtration. These include the following.

1. The direction of air flow is perpendicular to the filter surface. The fiber in the filter is cylindrical, and the particles are spherical. The different degrees of orientation of the cylindrical fibers, as well as the size distribution of both the cylindrical and spherical collectors, are not included. Various interaction effects are also not considered.

2. Filtration occurs in two separate stages: filtration on the filter medium and filtration by the deposited solids. For purposes of calculating collection efficiencies and pressure drop, flow is assumed to occur past deposited equidiameter spheres followed by a parallel array of identical cylinders lying transverse to the direction of flow.

3. There is an initial period of poorer performance in a new filter as the particles bridge and fill the openings between the fibers. Once deposited, most of the embedded particles become a permanent part of the filter medium and are not removed when the bulk of the deposited cake is dislodged in cleaning. Eventually, the amount and location of the deposited dust in the filter remains relatively constant. As a rule of thumb, the mass of the retained dust is approximately equal to the fabric mass. Thus, after the filter has been used, the resistance of the clean new fabric will certainly never be attained again. Note that the resistance of the filter embedded with particles may be an order of magnitude higher than that for the clean medium. Preconditioning or start-up effects are not considered; the resistance of the filter is assumed to be constant during operation.

Much of the theoretical work done in the field of fibrous filters has been concerned with the prediction of the pressure drop and the single-fiber collection efficiency. A prerequisite for a model of particle capture and pressure drop is a description of the flow field in the vicinity of the collector. However, the flow is so complex in this system that it can only realistically be represented by a simplified model. The three main models considered are those of Brinkman,[28] Happel,[29] and Kuwabara.[30] The Brinkman model predicts pressure drop for several different internal arrangements of fibers. The essence of this model is that, on the average, the fluid in proximity to an obstacle embedded in a filter experiences, in addition to the usual force terms, a body-damping force proportional to the local velocity; this accounts for the influence of neighboring objects on the flow. The Happel and Kuwabara models are somewhat similar in that their prediction of the pressure drop and filtration efficiency is based on a cellular model. The details of the Happel model have already been presented in Chapter 6. Kuwabara's approach involves the idea of zero vorticity, as opposed to zero tangential stress, at the outer surface of the cell. It is still impossible to state which assumption gives rise to more accurate results. The essential difference between the cell models and the Brinkman hypothesis is that the cell models account for the neighboring collector influence by means of a microscopic envelope around the central collector, with the characteristic envelope size depending on the void volume. The Brinkman hypothesis implies that the neighboring collectors damp the microscopic flow near the central collector in precisely the same manner that the collectors of the medium damp local flow through the medium when averaged over all conceivable collector arrangements. From this latter consideration, the validity of Brinkman's hypothesis may be expected to be limited to conditions where the neighboring collectors are distributed about the central collector in much the same manner as they are distributed in the filter medium. Because the effect of many solid boundaries in immediate proximity to the central object cannot be well described by a simple damping coefficient, the hypothesis breaks down when applied to media of sufficiently low porosity (void volume). However, the Brinkman model possesses the advantage of immediate applicability to filters composed of collectors with nonuniform diameters and distributed orientations with respect to the direction of flow. It may also be applied to mixtures of geometrical collectors, such as spheres and fibers, and thereby provide a treatment of transient filtration. Thus, the models of Happel and Kuwabara apply where the collectors are all identical and act independently of one another, while in Brinkman's approach size, orientation, and interference effects are considered to some extent. It is concluded that the cellular model presents a simple and uniform method for handling creeping and potential flow past assemblages of collectors. This approach has further application in examining more complicated systems, such as that involving the simultaneous flow past beds of spherical particles and arrays of cylinders. Due to some of the limitations of the Brinkman model, the cellular model is employed (as with wet scrubber theory in Chapter 6), and the results are applied in the presentation below.

The model for collection in a fabric filter is first considered. An analysis of the pressure drop will follow. Relatively speaking, little is available in the literature on this subject, perhaps due to the fact that efficiencies in industrial applications typically approach 100%. Particle capture can occur with either a cylindrical or spherical collector. The cylindrical (fiber) capture process is now examined. As stated above, the cellular model is used to predict particle capture by inertial impaction. This is accomplished by computing the trajectory of a particle as the fluid flows around the inner cylinder (the collector) in the two-concentric-cylinder model. The flow field in cylindrical coordinates is two dimensional with respect to r and ϕ. The velocity profile of a single particle may, therefore, be described in a two-dimensional rectangular coordinate system (see Figure 7.4.2). If the radius and length of the cylindrical collector are r_c and L_c, respectively, the single-collector inertial impaction efficiency, η, may be defined as the ratio of the particles captured by the cylindrical collector to those particles eligible for capture (see Figure 7.4.3.). This ratio is given by the ordinate of the starting point of the critical trajectory at the cell boundary (y^*) to the collector radius, i.e.,

$$\eta = (2L_c y^*/2L_c r_c) = (y^*/r_c) \tag{7.4.1}$$

The critical trajectory is defined as the trajectory of an aerosol particle starting at the cell boundary and just missing capture by the collector as it flows around it. Thus, complete collection (100%) arises if the particle(s) moves in a straight line (see particle 4 in Figure 7.4.2). The effect of interception may be included by increasing the radius of the collector by an amount equal to the radius of the aerosol particle.

The particle is assumed to be a point mass which does not affect the fluid velocity flow field; it is also assumed to be traveling in the z direction, with the undisturbed stream velocity at the cell boundary. It is further assumed that the concentration of particles in the aerosol is small enough that each particle can be treated individually in the flow system. Also, the solid particles and fiber

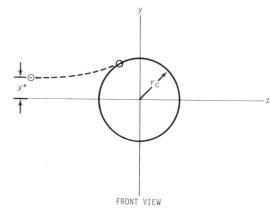

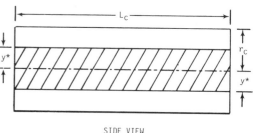

FIGURE 7.4.3. Nomenclature for a cylindrical collector.

collector can be represented as spherical and cylindrical, respectively, in shape. The problem now reduces to one of determining the trajectory of the solid particles as they either flow around the fiber or are captured.

A force balance on the aerosol particle results in the following vector equation:

$$m_p \frac{d\mathbf{V}}{dt} = C_D \pi r_p^2 \rho_p \frac{(\mathbf{v} - \mathbf{V})^2}{2} \tag{7.4.2}$$

where

$\mathbf{V}$ = particle velocity vector;
$\mathbf{v}$ = gas velocity vector.

The y and z components of Equation 7.4.2 in the Stokes' regime are given by

$$\left(\frac{m_p}{6\pi\mu_G r_p}\right)\frac{dV_y}{dt} + V_y - v_y = 0 \tag{7.4.3}$$

$$\left(\frac{m_p}{6\pi\mu_G r_p}\right)\frac{dV_z}{dt} + V_z - v_z = 0 \tag{7.4.4}$$

Equations 7.4.3 and 7.4.4 may be written in dimensionless form:

$$N_I \frac{dV_y^+}{dt^+} + V_y^+ - v_y^+ = 0 \qquad (7.4.5)$$

$$N_I \frac{dV_z^+}{dt^+} + V_z^+ - v_z^+ = 0 \qquad (7.4.6)$$

The v_y^+ and v_z^+ terms represent the velocities of the fluid in the y and z directions, respectively, and V_y^+ and V_z^+ or their corresponding derivatives $(dy^+/dt^+, dz^+/dt^+)$ represent the particle velocities. The dimensionless group N_I is defined as the inertial parameter and is given by

$$N_I = 2r_p^2 \, \rho_p \, v/9 \, \mu_G r_c \qquad (7.4.7)$$

The Cunningham correction factor should be included in the above analysis for particle sizes below 1.0 μm. In order to solve Equations 7.4.5 and 7.4.6, information on the fluid velocities must be made available. Using the creeping motion equations,[28] Happel[29] obtained a solution for the v_r and v_ϕ fluid velocity components in cylindrical coordinates. The stream function ψ' was given by

$$\psi' = [(A/r) + Br + Cr \ln r + Dr^3] \sin \theta$$

where

$$v_r = (1/r)(\delta\psi'/\delta\phi)$$
$$v_\phi = -(\delta\psi'/\delta r)$$

with A, B, C, and D as dimensionless constants dependent only on the void volume. After converting to rectangular coordinates, Harrop and Stenhouse[32] solved the above system of equations in a manner similar to that described in Section 6.4 for venturi scrubbers. Their results for the single-collector efficiency for the cylindrical cellular model are given in terms of the inertial impaction number for various void volumes. (The creeping motion results for a cylinder of diameter d_c, as well as those for a sphere of diameter d_c and a flat plate of width d_c, are presented in Figure 7.4.4.) This particle collection model is valid at low Reynolds numbers — a condition filter operation approaches. At these conditions, the viscous forces tend to overshadow the effect of inertia

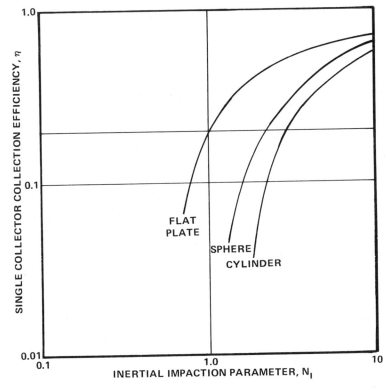

FIGURE 7.4.4. Single-collector collection efficiency vs. inertial impaction parameter.

and, therefore, reduce the chances of a particle impacting on the collector. At high Reynolds numbers, the streamlines do not begin to diverge until they are in the immediate vicinity of the collector, thus increasing the probability of particle capture. This model is, therefore, viewed as a lower or conservative limit for collection efficiency. Work in the potential (high Reynolds-number) flow regime is currently under study.[33]

Traditionally, the mass or weight efficiency of the filter medium is obtained by extending this single-collector collection efficiency η to an overall collection efficiency η_T by summing up the contribution to the entire assemblage of eligible collector cells. The equation for η_T is generated by applying a particle-mass balance across a differential length, dz, of the filter (see Figure 7.4.5).

$$\left\{\begin{array}{c}\text{rate of}\\\text{particles}\\\text{in}\end{array}\right\} - \left\{\begin{array}{c}\text{rate of}\\\text{particles}\\\text{out}\end{array}\right\} = \left\{\begin{array}{c}\text{rate of}\\\text{particles}\\\text{accumulated}\end{array}\right\}$$

$$\qquad\ \ \text{A} \qquad\qquad\quad \text{B} \qquad\qquad\quad \text{C} \qquad (7.4.8)$$

The terms in the above equation are examined below.

Terms A and B are given by $Qc - Q(c - dc) = Qdc$, which may be rewritten as

$$Qdc = Av_s dc \qquad (7.4.9)$$

Term C is an inventory term requiring some development. If ϵ is the void volume, $(1 - \epsilon)$ represents the volume of collectors per unit volume. The volume of collectors in Adz is then $(1 - \epsilon)$Adz. The ratio of a collector cross-sectional area to its volume is

$$2 r_c L_c / \pi\, r_c^2\, L_c = 2/\pi\, r_c$$

Therefore, the cross-sectional area available for capture in Adz is

$$(1 - \epsilon)Adz\, (2/\pi\, r_c) = [2(1 - \epsilon)A/\pi\, r_c]dz$$

The volume rate of flow of gas approaching the area available for capture in dz is given by the local velocity, v, in the filter (not the superficial velocity, v_s) times the area available for capture, i.e.,

$$[2(1 - \epsilon)A/\pi\, r_c]\,vdz \qquad (7.4.10)$$

The particle-mass flow rate eligible for capture in dz is then the product of the local concentration, c, and Equation 7.4.10.

$$[2(1 - \epsilon)A/\pi\, r_c]\,vcdz \qquad (7.4.11)$$

Multiplying by the single-collector efficiency η gives the rate of particles collected.

$$[2(1 - \epsilon)A/\pi\, r_c]\,vc\eta dz \qquad (7.4.12)$$

Inserting Equations 7.4.9 and 7.4.12 into Equation 7.4.8 gives

$$Av_s dc = [2(1 - \epsilon)A/\pi\, r_c]\,vc\eta dz \qquad (7.4.13)$$

Rearranging and noting that

$$v_s/v = \epsilon \qquad (7.4.14)$$

gives

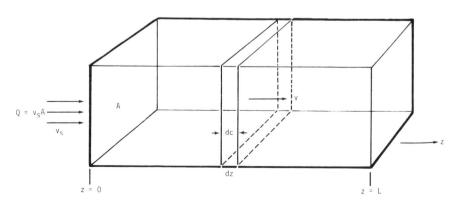

FIGURE 7.4.5.   Nomenclature for particle-mass balance across differential length of filter.

$$dc/dz = (2/\pi \, r_c) \, [(1 - \epsilon)/\epsilon] \, c\eta \tag{7.4.15}$$

If both η and c are constant across the effective length of capture, L the above equation may be integrated subject to the initial conditions

$c = c_i$ at $z = 0$

$c = c_o$ at $z = L$

The following equation results

$$\ln \left(\frac{c_o}{c_i} \right) = -\psi L \tag{7.4.16}$$

where

$$\psi = \left(\frac{2}{\pi \, r_c} \right) \left(\frac{1 - \epsilon}{\epsilon} \right) \eta \tag{7.4.17}$$

The collection efficiency is then given by

$$\eta = (1 - e^{-\psi L}) \tag{7.4.18}$$

An alternate form of Equation 7.4.17, omitting the voidage in the denominator, has been presented by other investigators. They claim that this difference is due to a difference in the definition of η. However, the discrepancy arises because the total projected area A is considered to be the area available for capture — rather than Aϵ. The reader is cautioned that this alternate form is *incorrect;* it should only be used in the limit where $\epsilon \to 1.0$.

The second stage of filtration — that by the deposited particles — will now be treated. The cellular model work of Paretsky et al.[14] can be employed for low Reynolds-number capture by a spherical collector. (Potential flow capture results are also available.)[34] These results, with appropriate modification, can be applied to the deposited cake on a filter. Much of the developmental work, discussion, and suggestions for future work presented in the wet scrubber section is again applicable here. One of the results given in Section 6.4 for the collection efficiency is Equation 6.4.26. This is the integrated form of Equation 6.4.23,

$$\eta = 1 - e^{-\Phi L} \tag{6.4.26}$$

where L is the effective length of capture. In filtration operation, L is the thickness of the deposited particles. This cake thickness is a vari-able, increasing with time until cleaning is initiated. Thus, Equation 6.4.23 applies.

$$dc/dz = (3/4 \, r_c) \, [(1 - \epsilon)/\epsilon] \, c\eta \tag{7.4.19}$$

The differential width of the cake in the above equation can be expressed in terms of the time of operation. The mass of particles passing the filter in time t is

$Qc_i t$

The corresponding bulk volume of deposited particles is

$Qc_i t/\rho_B$

where

ρ_B = the bulk density of cake.

The thickness of the cake becomes

$Qc_i t/\rho_B A$

so that

$$dz = (Qc_i/\rho_B A)dt \tag{7.4.20}$$

Substituting into Equation 7.4.19 gives

$$dc/c = (3/4 \, r_c) \, [(1 - \epsilon)/\epsilon] \, (Qc_i/\rho_B A)\eta dt \tag{7.4.21}$$

If the terms on the right-hand side of the above equation are constant, it may be integrated subject to the initial conditions

$c = c_i$ at $t = 0$

$c = c_o$ at $t = t$

The following equation results

$$\ln (c_o/c_i) = -\Phi t \tag{7.4.22}$$

where we now have

$$\Phi = (3/4 \, r_c) \, [(1 - \epsilon)/\epsilon] \, (Qc_i/\rho_B A)\eta \tag{7.4.23}$$

The collection efficiency is then given by

$$\eta = (1 - e^{-\Phi t}) \tag{7.4.24}$$

This represents the collection efficiency associated with the cake at time, t. The overall efficiency, η_T, due to both the deposited particles and the filter medium, is then

$$\eta_T = 1 - (1 - \eta_1)(1 - \eta_2) \qquad (7.4.25)$$

where

η_1 = collection efficiency given in Equation 7.4.18;

η_2 = collection efficiency given in Equation 7.4.24.

The exit concentration, c_e, for the combined resistance system becomes

$$c_e = c_i e^{-\Phi t} e^{-\psi L} \qquad (7.4.26)$$

The average discharge concentration, $\langle c_e \rangle$, over the the time interval $(t_1 - t_0)$ is, in accordance with the definition of average values,

$$\langle c_e \rangle = \int_{t_0}^{t_1} c_i e^{-\Phi t} e^{-\psi L}\, dt \bigg/ \int_{t_0}^{t_1} dt$$

$$\langle c_e \rangle = -\frac{c_i e^{-\psi L} (e^{-\Phi t_1} - e^{-\Phi t_0})}{\Phi (t_1 - t_0)} \qquad (7.4.27)$$

This analysis applies to a rather simplified system. The effect of particle-size and fiber-size distributions must also be considered. At present, the authors are not aware of data and/or a satisfactory correlation that exists for collector-size distribution. Once this information is available, the effect of these two variables can be treated by application of a Monte Carlo technique — similar to that presented in the earlier chapters — in conjunction with a stepwise numerical integration across the effective length of capture. This aspect of the fundamentals is currently under study by the authors.[35]

Pressure Drop

Starting with the Navier-Stokes equations, and using the cellular model, Happel[29] was also able to derive equations for the pressure drop for flow past arrays of cylinders and beds of spherical particles. Equations were presented for flow parallel perpendicular to cylinders. For the latter case, Happel obtained

$$\Delta p_f = v_s \mu_G L_f/K_f \qquad (7.4.28)$$

where

$$K_f = (1/8r_b{}^2) [4r_c{}^2 r_b{}^2 - r_c{}^4 - 3r_b{}^4 \ln(r_b/r_c)] ;$$

L_f = the thickness of the filter medium.

For flow through a bed of spherical particles (the deposited cake), he derived

$$\Delta p_p = v_s \mu_G L_p/K_p \qquad (7.4.29)$$

where

K_p = $[(3 + 2\gamma^5)/(3 - 4.5\gamma + 4.5\gamma^5 - 3\gamma^6)]$ $(4.5\,\gamma^3/r_c{}^2)$;

γ = r_c/r_b;

L_p = the width of the deposited particles.

Since this length varies with time (see Equation 7.4.20),

$$L_p = (Qc_i/\rho_B A)t \qquad (7.4.30)$$

so that

$$\Delta p_p = (Qc_i/\rho_B A)(v_s \mu_G/K_p)t \qquad (7.4.31)$$

The above equation thus provides the pressure drop across the deposited solids. The overall pressure drop across the entire filter system, Δp_o, is then the sum of Equation 7.4.28 and either Equation 7.4.29 or 7.4.31.

$$\Delta p_o = \Delta p_f + \Delta p_p$$

Happel also compared this theory with other relationships and data reported in the literature. Of special interest is the close agreement with the well-known Carman-Kozeny equation (to be discussed in the next section) which has been widely used to correlate data on packed beds. This is somewhat remarkable in view of the fact that the force on each collector in a packed assemblage of collectors can be up to several hundred times that exerted on a single collector in an undisturbed infinite medium. Scattered statements in the literature indicate that the proposed model overestimates the pressure drop by 25 to 50%.

Despite some of the mathematical sophistication above, the theory rarely works in actual practice and probably has never been used by industry. There are many drawbacks. For the filter medium, the first step in the capture process, it is to be noted that:

1. The filter is not a perfect cylinder.
2. The size distribution of the fiber is not treated.
3. The void volume distribution effect is not included in the analysis, i.e., the fibers are not equally spaced.
4. Flow is not exactly perpendicular to the filter.
5. The filter is not incompressible.
6. Preconditioning, i.e., particles embedded in the filter, effects are not treated.

For the deposited solids, the second stage in the filtration process, the questionable assumptions include:

1. The particle is not a perfect sphere.
2. The size distribution of the particle is not treated.
3. Particle-size distribution variation within the deposited cake is not included in the analysis.
4. The cake may be compressible.
5. Void volume variations are not treated.
6. Agglomeration effects are not considered.

The authors strongly feel that distribution effects, and distribution variations, are parameters that should and can be included in a fundamental analysis of the filtration process.[35] At this point in time, the application of modeling techniques to a description of pressure drop and collection efficiency from basic principles remains incomplete. The simple, basic reason that there is so much divergence between theory and practice is that many of the assumptions necessary to develop the describing equations are absolutely false. However, it has been possible to draw many qualitative and a few quantitative conclusions of practical importance. Limited research, lack of meaningful data, and industry's attitude toward proprietary information have severely limited the ultimate application of theory to design.

7.5. DESIGN PRINCIPLES

It should be evident at this point that the number of variables necessary to design a fabric filter is very large. Since fundamentals cannot treat all of these factors in the design and/or prediction of performance of a filter, this determination is basically left up to the experience and judgment of the design engineer. In addition, there is no one formula that can determine whether or not a fabric filter application is feasible. A qualitative description of the filtration process is possible, although quantitatively the theories are far less successful. Theory, coupled with some experimental data, can help predict the performance and design of the unit. The state-of-the-art of engineering process design is selection of filter medium, superficial velocity, and cleaning method that will yield the best economic compromise. Industry relies on certain simple guides and calculations, which are usually considered proprietary information, to achieve the above.

The objective of this section is to examine the filtration process at the macroscopic level. Semi-empirical models are presented to predict pressure drop. A more practical equation is developed to describe this system for constant pressure and constant rate operation. Optimum cleaning cycles are reviewed, including that for a variable parallel resistance in a compartmentalized unit. The calculation of collection efficiency is also considered. Energy and horsepower requirements for different operating conditions are presented. The section concludes with a fairly detailed discussion of equipment design considerations in order to illustrate how a fabric filter fits into an overall process scheme and how to determine whether the application of a fabric filter is technically and economically feasible.

Despite the progress in developing pure filtration theory, and in view of the complexity of the phenomena, the most common methods of correlation are based on predicting a form of a final equation that can be verified by experiment.

Pressure Drop

Pressure drop will be considered first. The pressure drop equation for a fluid flowing through a circular duct of diameter D_d and length L_d is given by

$$\Delta p = 4 f_f L_d v^2 \rho_G / D_d g_c$$

where

f_f = the Fanning friction factor.

A similar form of this equation may be applied to a bed of collectors.

$$\Delta p = 4 f L_d v_s^2 \, \rho_G / 2 g_c d_c'$$

where

f = friction factor for this system;
v_s = superficial velocity in the bed;
d_c' = equivalent diameter of the collector.

Although briefly discussed in Section 7.3, there are at present several well-recognized correlations which permit reasonable accurate prediction of the friction factor and/or pressure drop through a bed of spherical or nonspherical material. Ergun[26] expressed the above equation in the following form:

$$\Delta p / L_d = f \rho_G L_d v_s^2 \, (1 - \epsilon) / d_c' \epsilon^3 \qquad (7.5.1)$$

The Reynolds number was given as

$$Re_p = d_c' v_s \rho_G / \mu_G (1 - \epsilon) \qquad (7.5.2)$$

After correlating a mass of experimental data over a wide range of Reynolds numbers, he obtained an equation for the friction factor which can be shown to take the form

$$f = 150 / Re_p + 1.75 \qquad (7.5.3)$$

At low Reynolds numbers, the second term on the right-hand side of Equation 7.5.3 is negligible in comparison with the first term. The equation can be written for this case as

$$f = 150 / Re_p \qquad (7.5.4)$$

so that

$$\Delta p / L_d = 150 \, \mu_G v_s (1 - \epsilon)^2 / (d_c')^2 \, \epsilon^3 \qquad (7.5.5)$$

If the volume and surface area of a collector are v_p and s_p, respectively, the specific surface, S, is defined as

$$S = s_p / v_p \qquad (7.5.6)$$

Thus, for a spherical particle

$$S = 6 / d_c' \qquad (7.5.7)$$

In considering collectors in general, d_c' can be used as the equivalent diameter of a spherical particle so that

$$d_c' = 6/S \qquad (7.5.8)$$

Equation 7.5.5 may then be written as

$$\Delta p / L_d = k [(1 - \epsilon)^2 S^2 / \epsilon^3] \, \mu_G v_s \qquad (7.5.9)$$

where

$k = 4.167.$

The coefficient k in the above equation has come to be defined as the Kozeny-Carman constant. Carman[36] concluded that the best correlation corresponds to a value of k equal to 4.8 with a range of variation, due to experimental uncertainty, of 4.5 to 5.1. Other data on beds consisting of a number of shapes of collectors, some rather extreme, indicate that k may be taken as equal to approximately 5.0 and independent of shape and void volume from $\epsilon = 0.26$ to $\epsilon = 0.8$.[29]

Perhaps the most convenient starting point to describe flow through porous media is with the classic D'Arcy equation

$$dp/dz = -\mu_G v_s / K \qquad (7.5.10)$$

which may be integrated (for constant coefficients) to give

$$\Delta p / L_d = \mu_G v_s / K$$

The term K is defined as the permeability coefficient for the filtering medium. If Equation 7.5.10 is compared with Equation 7.5.9, it can be seen that

$$K = \epsilon^3 / kS^2 (1 - \epsilon)^2 \qquad (7.5.11)$$

with k = 4.8 from the work of Carman and k = 4.167 from Ergun's results. Sullivan and Hertel[37] suggested a value of 5.5 for the numerical constant for a fibrous filter in the above equation. Several other empirical correlations for the permeability coefficient K have been suggested in the literature.[3] Interestingly, the theoretical results of Happel (see Equations 7.4.27 and 28) can be directly related to the calculation of the permeability coefficient and/or the Carman-Kozeny constant through the equation

$$K = \epsilon \, r_h^2 / k \qquad (7.5.12)$$

where

r_h = the hydraulic radius of the collector.

For example, in the cellular model for cylinders,

$$r_h = (r_b^2 - r_c^2)/2 \, r_c \qquad (7.5.13)$$

Happel's results for k were in excellent agreement with the values obtained above from experiment.

The same criticisms leveled at the theory can be applied concerning the use of these equations. There are two main problems. First, the collector diameter, d_c, is not one value, but a distribution of values. It may be represented by a mean value such as a diameter based on the collector with the average volume or, perhaps more correctly, a diameter based on a collector with mean specific surface. Thus, for a particle-size distribution, the mean specific surface, $\langle S \rangle$, can be defined as

$$\langle S \rangle = \Sigma \, x_i S_i \qquad (7.5.14)$$

where

x_i = volume fraction of collectors with specific surface S_i.

The mean effective diameter, $\langle \, d_c \, \rangle$, is then

$$\begin{aligned} \langle d_c \rangle \quad &= 6/\langle S \rangle \\ &= 6/\Sigma \, x_i(6/d_{c,i}) \\ &= 1/\Sigma \, (x_i/d_{c,i}) \end{aligned} \qquad (7.5.15)$$

For example, the mean diameter for a mixture containing equal volumes of $10\text{-}\mu$ and $20\text{-}\mu\text{m}$ deposited spherical particles is 13.3 μm, rather than 15.0 μm as given by a simple arithmetic average. Second, the void volume, ϵ, is not known theoretically, and it is difficult to measure experimentally. The void can be a function of several variables, including particle-size distribution. When the cake being formed is compressible, the void will also vary with time of operation. There have been attempts to correlate data to arrive at a value of ϵ; however, the possible number of variables in baghouse filtration is so high that most of the industry relies on bench-scale tests that have been conducted with the particular dust to be collected. This data is used to calculate the empirical constants that are used in design equations. Thus, the above approach for determining pressure drop rarely works in a real filter application. One cannot calculate, *a priori*, a usable value for the permeability coefficient, K. The following more practical empirical approach is instead employed to predict pressure drop.

D'Arcy's equation may be rewritten as

$$v_s = -(K/\mu_G)(dp/dz)$$

Multiplying both sides of this equation by the approach (face) area of the filter, A, gives

$$\begin{aligned} v_s A &= -(KA/\mu_G)(dp/dz) \\ Q &= -(KA/\mu_G)(dp/dz) \end{aligned} \qquad (7.5.16)$$

where

Q = the volumetric flow rate of the dust-laden gas passing A.

Integrating yields

$$\Delta p = [\mu_G(\Delta z)/KA] \, Q \qquad (7.5.17)$$

The bracketed term represents the resistance to flow. It is a constant for the fabric since Δz is simply the filter thickness, L_f. The pressure drop across the fabric medium is then

$$\Delta p_f = [\mu_G L_f / KA] \, Q \qquad (7.5.18)$$

The development for the pressure drop across the filter cake is similar to that for the fabric. The bracketed term in Equation 7.5.17 is not a constant for the deposited particles since Δz is a variable. If the collection efficiency is close to 100%, which is usually the case in an industrial operation, then

$$\begin{aligned} \Delta z &= V_G c/\rho_p (1 - \epsilon) A \\ &= V_G c/\rho_B A \end{aligned} \qquad (7.5.19)$$

where

V_G = volume of gas filtered for deposited thickness Δz;

c = inlet particulate loading or concentration; mass/volume;

ρ_p = true density of the particle;
ρ_B = bulk density of the cake of deposited particles.

Substituting Equation 7.5.19 into Equation 7.5.17 yields an equation for the pressure drop across the cake.

$$\Delta p_c = [\mu_G c/\rho_B KA^2] V_G Q \qquad (7.5.20)$$

If it is assumed that Equations 7.5.18 and 7.5.20 are additive (i.e., the dust and fabric do not interact), the total or overall pressure drop across the filter system is obtained by combining Equations 7.5.18 and 7.5.20.

$$\Delta p = [\mu_G c/\rho_B KA^2] V_G Q + [\mu_G L_f/KA] Q \qquad (7.5.21)$$

Setting

$$B = [\mu_G c/\rho_B KA^2]$$
$$C = [\mu_G L_f/KA]$$

then

$$\Delta p = (BV_G + C)Q \qquad (7.5.22)$$

Note that BV_G is the resistance to flow due to the filter cake where V_G is the net volumetric throughput of the gas. C is the resistance of the filter media, usually a cloth bag. This resistance term can take on two values. First, if a cloth is brand new, it will have a resistance to flow when clean air is passed through it. A second value of C can be measured if air with a dust loading is allowed to pass through it. When the dust cake builds up, the cloth will be cleaned. If clean air is passed through the cloth now, it will have a higher value than the original resistance. This happens because the cloth has not been completely cleaned. Some dirt will remain entrained on the fabric fibers causing a higher resistance. Eventually, the resistance will level off to a constant value due to the permanently trapped particles in the filter. (In actual practice, C may gradually change over the life of the bag.) When Equation 7.5.22 is used as a design equation, it is more accurate to use the second value of C since this higher value will predominate during the operation of this unit. Thus, an empirical equation for the pressure drop has been developed. It consists of two functional terms: one associated with the resistance of the filter medium and another with the deposited solids. Also, it applies to either a single- or multiple-bag filter system.

Constant Pressure Operation

During a constant (overall) pressure (drop) operation, the flowrate (Q) is a function of time.

$$Q(t) = dV_G/dt$$

Substituting Q(t) into Equation 7.5.22 yields

$$\Delta p = (BV_G + C) dV_G/dt$$
$$(\Delta p)dt = (BV_G + C)dV_G$$

Integrating this from 0 to t and from 0 to V_G and solving for t,

$$t = [BV_G^2/2 \Delta p] + [CV_G/\Delta p] \qquad (7.5.23)$$

This equation can be rearranged so that V_G is an explicit function of t.

$$V_G = \sqrt{[2\Delta pt/B] + (C/B)^2} - [C/B] \qquad (7.5.24)$$

Also, V_G can be shown to be related to an instantaneous value of Q(t) by rearrangment of Equation 7.5.22.

$$V_G = [\Delta p/BQ] - [C/B] \qquad (7.5.25)$$

Equating Equations 7.5.24 and 7.5.25 and solving for Q yields,

$$Q = \Delta p/(B \sqrt{(2\Delta pt/B) + (C/B)^2}) \qquad (7.5.26)$$

Numerical values for design coefficients B and C are usually obtained from experimental data. If Equation 7.5.23 is rewritten as

$$t/V_G = (B/2\Delta p)V_G + (C/\Delta p) \qquad (7.5.27)$$

a plot of t/V_G vs. V_G will yield a straight line of slope $(B/2 \Delta p)$ and an intercept $(C/\Delta p)$. Note that only two (V_G, t) data points are necessary to provide a first approximation to B and C.

Constant Rate Operation

Most industrial filter operations are conducted in a manner approaching constant rate. For this condition,

$dQ/dt = 0$

and

$Q = dV_G/dt = $ constant

so that

$V_G = Qt$

Equation 7.5.22 now becomes

$$\Delta p = BQ^2 t + CQ \qquad (7.5.28)$$

Thus, a plot of Δp vs. t yields a straight line of slope BQ^2 and intercept CQ. At $t = 0$, the only resistance to flow is that of the filter medium; the pressure drop, however, is a linear function of time (see Figure 7.5.1), and as time increases, the resistance due to the dust cake may predominate. Figure 7.5.2 presents the relationship for a typical industrial system.

Some filter operations have both a constant pressure and constant rate period. At the beginning of a normal cycle, the pressure drop is held constant until the flow rate increases to a maximum value that is obtained by experiment. The flow rate is then maintained constant until the

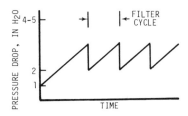

FIGURE 7.5.1. Pressure drop as a function of time.

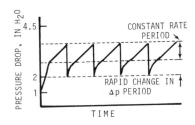

FIGURE 7.5.2. Pressure drop as a function of time in a typical industrial system.

pressure drop increases above an economical limit.

Optimizing the Cleaning Cycle

As time increases in constant rate operation, pressure drop increases to the point where it must be reduced because either the flow capacity of the system is reduced or the bag ruptures. At this point, the filter is cleaned by a variety of means — mechanical shaking, collapsing, pneumatic pulses, etc. The cleaning operation is destructive to the fabric media — particularly those used at high temperature which, at this point in time, are fiberglass; it will eventually, after a repeated number of cycles, cause it to fail and necessitate its replacement. Thus, a great deal of effort has been devoted to the development of many cleaning methods to increase the bag life — mechanical, pneumatic, shock wave, pressure pulse, etc. In fact, since all fabric filter suppliers generally utilize the same fabric filter media, the principal distinction between the fabric filters of different manufacturers is the method of cleaning and the cleaning cycle employed. Optimizing this cleaning cycle is an important design consideration. Consider now two cases: the first, a somewhat idealized situation and the second, one that might readily apply to an industrial application.

Constant Pressure

A constant pressure operation may be designed to allow a maximum volumetric throughput. If, for instance, the bags are to be cleaned by shaking, all flow through the compartment must be stopped during the cleaning cycle. The time period (t_p) for one cycle is equal to the filtering time (t_f) plus the cleaning time (t_c).

$$t_p = t_f + t_c$$

The maximum throughput for the cycle is

$$V_G/(t_f + t_c) = \text{maximum}$$

The cleaning time can be determined by considering just how completely the bags are to be cleaned; for our purposes, t_c shall be considered to be a constant value. The volume of gas processed, from Equation 7.5.24, is

$$V_G = \sqrt{(2 \Delta p/B)t + (C/B)^2} - C/B \qquad (7.5.29)$$

This can be written as

$$V_G = \sqrt{Yt + Z^2} - Z$$

where

$$Y = 2\Delta p/B;$$
$$Z = C/B.$$

In order to maximize the cyclic throughput, the first derivative of $V_G/(t_f + t_c)$ can be taken with respect to t_f and set equal to zero.

$$d/dt_f[V_G/(t_f + t_c)] = 0 \qquad (7.5.30)$$

Substituting V_G from Equation 7.5.29 into Equation 7.5.30 yields

$$d/dt_f[((Yt_f + Z^2)^{1/2} - Z)/(t_f + t_c)] = 0$$

Upon taking the derivative,

$$\frac{(t_f + t_c)[0.5(Yt_f + Z^2)^{-1/2}Y] - [(Yt_f + Z^2)^{1/2} - B]}{(t_f + t_c)^2} = 0$$

and solving this expression for t_f yields

$$t_f = t_c + 2B\sqrt{t_c/A} \qquad (7.5.31)$$

The second term on the right-hand side of Equation 7.5.31 is usually very small and can be neglected. Therefore,

$$t_f \approx t_c \qquad (7.5.32)$$

As a rule of thumb, then, when the cleaning cycle takes an appreciable amount of time during a constant pressure filtration process, the cyclic throughput can be maximized by setting the filtering time equal to the cleaning time. However, in normal practice the shake time is usually a small fraction of the total cycle time. Care should be taken if, for example, a pulsed-air cleaning system is used. The cleaning intervals would be so small that the operation, as dictated by Equation 7.5.32, may be impractical and uneconomical.

Variable Parallel Resistance – Constant Rate

Most common industrial situations require a baghouse filter to operate at a constant rate. The filter consists of a compartment with many bag filters arranged in rows and columns. Air flows continuously through the compartment. The bags can be cleaned by pulsed air, one row at a time. With this type of process, the compartment does not need to be shut down for the cleaning period. The problem that must be confronted, however, is that of calculating the pressure drop through a system in which the resistance to flow in each row is different.

At any given time, it is known that the pressure drop across each row is the same. Yet this overall value (Δp) changes with time. The overall flowrate (Q_T) is the summation of the flows from each row of bags (Q_i, where $i = 1, 2, 3, \ldots$). Q_i (from Equation 7.5.22) is equal to

$$Q_i = \Delta p/(BV_{G,i} + C) \qquad (7.5.33)$$

where Δp and $V_{G,i}$ are time dependent. Since at any instant of time, Δp is the same for each row,

$$Q_T = \sum_i \Delta p[1/(BV_{G,i} + C)] \qquad i = 1,2,3, \ldots \quad (7.5.34)$$

$V_{G,i}$ can be expressed as a function of the flow rate through row i and time. From the definition of the flow rate

$$dV_{G,i} = Q_i(t)dt_i \qquad (7.5.35)$$

so that

$$dV_{G,i}/dt_i = Q_i(t) = Q_i$$

where

t_i = the elapsed time from the most recent cleaning interval of row i.

Since, from Equation 7.5.33,

$$Q_i = \Delta p/(BV_{G,i} + C)$$

Q_i may be substituted into Equation 7.5.35 to give the following equation in differential form:

$$dV_{G,i}/dt_i = \Delta p/(BV_{G,i} + C) \qquad (7.5.36)$$

Δp is known from Equation 7.5.34 in this form:

$$\Delta p = Q_T \sum_i [1/(BV_{G,i} + C)]^{-1} \qquad i = 1,2,3, \ldots (7.5.37)$$

Equations 7.5.36 and 7.5.37 may be solved

simultaneously to yield Δp as a function of elapsed time and cleaning intervals. It is suggested that Equation 7.5.36 be solved by using a numerical method such as the fourth order, forward progression Runge-Kutta technique.[38]

For example, the operation of a baghouse filter with one compartment, that has four rows and operates at constant rate, may be represented by five equations.

$$\Delta p = \frac{Q_T}{\dfrac{1}{BV_{G,1} + C} + \dfrac{1}{BV_{G,2} + C} + \dfrac{1}{BV_{G,3} + C} + \dfrac{1}{BV_{G,4} + C}}$$

$$dV_{G,1}/dt_1 = \Delta p/(BV_{G,1} + C)$$
$$dV_{G,2}/dt_2 = \Delta p/(BV_{G,2} + C)$$
$$dV_{G,3}/dt_3 = \Delta p/(BV_{G,3} + C)$$
$$dV_{G,4}/dt_4 = \Delta p/(BV_{G,4} + C)$$

The simulation can start with clean bags in each row, therefore,

$$\Delta p_{(t = 0)} = Q_T C/4$$

Since no dust has been collected as this point,

$$V_{G,1 (t = 0)} = 0$$
$$V_{G,2 (t = 0)} = 0$$
$$V_{G,3 (t = 0)} = 0$$
$$V_{G,4 (t = 0)} = 0$$

If each row is to be cleaned at 4-min intervals, row 1 is first cleaned at $t = 1$, row 2 at $t = 2$, row 3 at $t = 3$, and row 4 at $t = 4$. Whenever the cleaning time for row i is reached, $V_{G,i}$ and t_i will be set to zero and the simulation can proceed from there.

By varying the cleaning intervals, it is possible to determine the maximum operating conditions, with respect to operating pressure and pressure variation, which can be related to the cost of controlling the unit. The elapsed time necessary to clean a row, using pulsed air, may be ignored since it usually takes on the order of 100 msec to clean a row during the valve open-time period.

If the bags are cleaned by shaking, as opposed to pulsed air, the entire compartment must be shut off during the cleaning cycle; there is no variable parallel resistance. If, however, a shaking process is used in a number of compartments which are connected in parallel, these equations can be modified to handle the situation. Instead of speaking in terms of row i, reference can be made to compartment i. When compartment i is being cleaned, the $1/(BV_{G,i} + C)$ term of Equation 7.5.37 must be set to zero. When the filtering cycle is started again in compartment i, $V_{G,i}$ is set to zero, and the simulation can proceed as normal.

Collection Efficiency

Perhaps the outstanding characteristic of fabric filters is their capability for very high efficiency on even the finest particles. In considering fabric filters from a macroscopic (engineering) point of view, one is rarely concerned with prediction of efficiency, for these units usually have the capability of 99+% almost automatically — provided they are properly constructed and maintained in satisfactory operating condition. (In the future, however, industry is expected to be very much concerned with efficiency, especially on a particle-size basis.)

An equation has been proposed to describe collection efficiency

$$\eta = (G - 1)/G \qquad (7.5.38)$$

with

$$G = (E)L^a \rho_G{}^b v_s{}^c$$

This calculation suffers in that the above is a four- (E, a, b, c) coefficient equation. Empirical constants that have been determined experimentally are available for various fiber classifications.[3,39]

Energy and Horsepower Requirements

Information on energy and horsepower requirements are two important considerations in any optimization study for filters. For constant pressure operation, the pumping (fan) work, W_p, is

$$W_p = V_G \Delta p \qquad (7.5.39)$$

The gas horsepower requirement is

$$HP = Q_o \Delta p \qquad (7.5.40)$$

where

Q_o = the maximum flow rate through the filter.

This occurs at initial conditions, i.e., when $t = 0$.

For constant rate operation, the energy expended in fan work is

$$W_p = \int_0^{V_G} (\Delta p) dV_G \qquad (7.5.41)$$

Note that Δp is a variable in the above integration. The horsepower requirement is simply

$$HP = Q\Delta p_m \qquad (7.5.42)$$

where

Δp_m = the maximum or final pressure drop achieved before cleaning.

In engineering units, the actual energy requirement for filtration operations can be estimated from

$$E = 1.173 \, QR_f/10,000 \, \eta_B\eta_M \qquad (7.5.43)$$

where

E = electrical energy required, kW;
Q = quantity of air to be filtered, ft^3/min;
R_f = filter resistance, in. of water;
η_B = blower efficiency;
η_M = motor efficiency.

Typically, the energy requirements of fabric filter baghouses range from 0.1 to 1.0 kW/1,000 SCFM of gas treated.

Design Practice

The design of industrial dust-collection equipment requires consideration of many factors. Figure 7.5.3 illustrates the complex nature of the final selection of a fabric collector.[40] The most important design considerations include the operational pressure drop, cloth area, cleaning mechanism, fabric and fabric life, baghouse configuration, and costs. Exhaust volume through the usual single-compartment fabric collector will not be constant because of the increasing resistance to air flow as the dust cake accumulates. The reduction in flow rate will be a function of the system pressure relationships, the exhaust fan characteristics, and the point of rating. Drop-off of exhaust volume is usually not severe in practice because pressure losses for the system of ducts and hoods usually equal or exceed that of the fabric collector; therefore reduction in exhaust volume will cause a corresponding reduction in the pressure needs for that portion of the system. Most fabric collectors have the centrifugal fan on the clean-air side of the collector, where the more efficient backward-curved blade fan can be applied. This fan construction has a steeply rising pressure-volume characteristic, providing a significant increase in available static pressure as exhaust volume is reduced. This fan characteristic prevents overloading when collectors with new, clean media

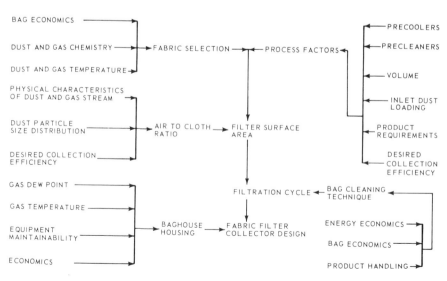

FIGURE 7.5.3.   System analysis for fabric filter collector design.

are first placed in service and where, for a short time, the pressure loss through the clean fabric is low. When fabric collectors are designed for continuous operation, pressure relationships become more complex, but approach a constant value. The smaller the fraction of the elements taken out of service at any one time for dust-cake removal, the more uniform the pressure drop of the fabric collector. Typical pressure diagrams for four-and six-compartment, continuous fabric collectors with mechanical shakers or reverse-flow cleaning are shown in Figure 7.5.4. For reverse-jet types of continuous collectors, minor pressure variations occur, depending on the position and direction of travel of the blow-back device. Pressure variations are minimal in pulse-jet designs because the cleaning cycle is extremely short and relatively few elements are taken out of service at any one time. Typical pressure drops for woven cloths range between 3 to 6 in. of water. However, the use of high-velocity filtration, felted fabrics, or the presence of a sticky or low-porosity dust cake often requires pressure drops on the order of 6 to 10 in. of water.

The size of a filter plant is primarily determined by the area of filter cloth required to filter the gases. The choice of a filtration velocity (or its equivalent, the air-to-cloth ratio in cubic feet per minute of gas filtered per square foot of filter area) must take certain factors into consideration. Although the higher velocities are usually associated with the greater pressure drops, they also reduce the filter area required. Practical experience has led to the use of a series of air-to-cloth ratios for various materials collected and types of equipment. Ratios in current use range from less than 1:1 to more than 20:1. The choice depends on cleaning method, fabric, and characteristics of the particles. The rule of thumb for air-to-cloth ratios for conventional fabric filter baghouses with

woven cloth is 1.5 to 3.0 ft^3/min/ft^2 for dusts and 1.0 to 2.0 ft^3/min/ft^2 for fumes. Typical ratios for a number of materials in various situations are listed in Tables 7.5.1 through 7.5.4. Remember that during the cleaning cycle, the air-to-cloth ratio (ACR) is increased if compartmentalization is used with one compartment always offstream. This increased value is then given by (ACR) (N − 1)/N, where N is the total number of compartments. When dust is fine or loadings are high, it is recommended that the filtering velocity stay less than 3 ACFM/ft^2. Experience has also demonstrated that more cloth is required with increased temperature. Typical industrial data are presented in Table 7.5.5.

It is best to select the cleaning mechanism and the filter fabric together, since both items are closely related (see Section 7.2). For example, felted fabrics are almost exclusively cleaned by pulse or reverse-jet air, whereas most woven fabrics are cleaned by other means. By the process of elimination, a review of past successful filtering operations will usually show that only a few cleaning mechanism/fabric combinations are compatible and sufficiently attractive to warrant economic evaluation. The time required for cleaning also determines the choice of cleaning mechanism. This time should be a small fraction of the time required for dust deposition; otherwise, too large a fraction of the fabric will be out of service for cleaning at any given time. It is fairly common with shake cleaning equipment, for example, to have a cleaning-to-deposition time ratio on the order of 0.1 or less. Applying this criterion to a ten-compartment baghouse would mean that one compartment is out of service at all times.

Fabric deterioration often results from the combined assault of several factors, rather than from any single effect such as thermal erosion, mechanical stress through repeated flexing, chemical attack, abrasion, etc. All possible modes of failure should be considered and, again, previous experience is usually the best guide. Extrapolating from experience, one might estimate that the reduction in fiber life through thermal erosion might double for a 20°F rise in temperature or that the mechanical attrition rate might double when the frequency of cleaning is doubled.

With shaker mechanisms, bags are usually 5 in. in diameter and 8- to 10-ft high, occasionally extended to 14 ft. Reverse-flow economics dictate

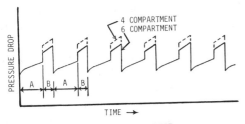

A - ALL COMPARTMENTS IN SERVICE

B - ONE COMPARTMENT OUT OF SERVICE FOR CLEANING

FIGURE 7.5.4. Compartmented collector cycles.

TABLE 7.5.1

Recommended Maximum Filtering Velocities for Various Dusts and Fumes in Conventional Shaker Baghouses with Woven Fabrics[40]

Dust or fumes	Maximum filtering ratio, ACFM/ft² cloth area	Dust or fumes	Maximum filtering ratio ACFM/ft² cloth area
Abrasives	3.0	Flint	2.5
Alumina	2.25	Flour	2.5
Aluminum oxide	2.0	Glass	2.5
Asbestos	2.75	Granite	2.5
Baking powder	2.5	Graphite	2.0
Batch sprouts for grains	3.0	Grinding and separating	2.25
Bauxite	2.5	Gypsum	2.5
Bronze powder	2.0	Iron ore	2.0
Brunswick clay	2.25	Iron oxide	2.0
Buffing wheel operations	3.25	Lamp black	2.0
		Lead oxide	2.25
Carbon	2.0	Leather	3.5
Cement crushing and grinding	1.5	Lime	2.0
		Limestone	2.75
Cement kiln (wet process)	1.5	Manganese	2.25
		Marble	3.0
Ceramics	2.5	Mica	2.25
Charcoal	2.25	Oyster shell	3.0
Chocolate	2.25	Packing machines	2.75
Chrome ore	2.5	Paint pigments	2.0
Clay	2.25	Paper	3.5
Cleanser	2.25	Plastics	2.5
Cocoa	2.25	Quartz	2.75
Coke	2.25	Rock	3.25
Conveying	2.5	Sanding machines	3.25
Cork	3.0	Silica	2.75
Cosmetics	2.0	Soap	2.25
Cotton	3.5	Soapstone	2.25
Feeds and grain	3.25	Starch	2.25
Feldspar	2.5	Sugar	2.25
Fertilizer (bagging)	2.4	Talc	2.25
Fertilizer (cooler, dryer)	2.0	Tobacco	3.5
		Wood	3.5

taller bags, usually 20- to 30-ft high, with bag diameters in the 11- to 12-in. range. Consequently, space requirements are favorable for the reverse flow unit. Yet for the usual application using fabrics other than glass cloth (reverse-flow cleaning is the usual selection for fabrics like glass cloth where fiber damage can occur from the flexing and snapping action of conventional shaker collectors), the shaker cleaning mechanism is the most frequently selected. Reverse-jet economics also dictate tall bags, often 20 ft or taller, because the jet mechanism becomes a major cost factor as bag

length is reduced. Bag diameters are in the 8- to 12-in. range. Most pulse-jet designs, on the other hand, use 6- to 8-ft long bags; difficulty often arises in cleaning the bottom of taller bags.

Selecting the number of compartments for a fabric filter installation requires information such as the allowable variation in gas flow, the availability of sizes of commercial units, and the expected frequency of maintenance. A single-compartment unit is the most foolproof and predictable and least expensive fabric collector design. It may be necessary, however, to provide

TABLE 7.5.2

Recommended Maximum Filtering Velocities and Fabric for Dust and Fume Collection in Reverse-jet Baghouses[40]

Dust or fumes	Fabric	Filtering ratio, ACFM/ft²	Dust or fumes	Fabric	Filtering ratio, ACFM/ft²
Aluminum oxide	Napped cotton	11	Mica	Napped cotton	11
Bauxite	Cotton sateen	10	Paint pigments	Cotton sateen	10
Carbon, calcined	Napped cotton, wool felt	8[a]	Phenolic molding powders	Cotton sateen	10
Carbon, green	Orlon® felt	7	Polyvinyl chloride (PVC)	Wool felt	10[a]
Carbon, banbury mixer	Wool felt	8	Refractory brick sizing (after firing)	Napped cotton	12
Cement, raw	Cotton sateen	9	Sandblasting	Napped cotton, wool felt	6–8[a]
Cement, finished	Cotton sateen	10			
Cement, milling	Cotton sateen	8	Silicon carbide	Cotton sateen	9–11
Chrome, (ferro) crushing	Cotton sateen	10	Soap and detergent powder	Dacron® felt, Orlon felt	12[a]
Clay, green	Cotton sateen	10	Soy bean	Cotton sateen	14
Clay, vitrified silicious	Cotton sateen	12	Starch	Cotton sateen	10
Enamel, (porcelain)	Napped cotton	12	Sugar	Cotton sateen, wool felt	10[a]
Flour	Cotton sateen	14[a]			
Grain	Wool felt, cotton sateen	16	Talc	Cotton sateen	11
			Tantalum fluoride	Orlon felt	6[a]
Graphite	Wool felt	7[a]	Tobacco	Cotton sateen	12
Gypsum	Cotton sateen, orlon felt	10	Wood flour	Cotton sateen	10
			Wood sawing operations	Cotton sateen	12
Lead oxide fume	Orlon felt, wool felt	8[a]	Zinc, metallic	Orlon felt, Dacron felt	11
Lime	Napped cotton	10			
Limestone (crushing)	Cotton sateen	10	Zinc oxide	Orlon felt	8[a]
Metallurgical fumes	Orlon felt, wool felt	10[a]	Zirconium oxide	Orlon felt	8

[a]Decrease 1.0 ACFM/ft² if dust concentration is high or particle size is relatively small.

additional compartments for emergency, extended maintenance, or unexpected increases in process effluent.

Gas Preconditioning

Successful operation of fabric collectors in filtering high-temperature gases requires that the gases be properly cooled prior to filtration; otherwise, the bags are liable to be destroyed (or at least suffer a decrease in life). In addition to extending fabric life, lowering the temperature will reduce the flow volume which, in turn, decreases the filter-fabric area requirement. The three basic methods used for the cooling of high-temperature gases are dilution, radiation, and evaporative cooling.

The simplest method of cooling exhaust gases is to dilute them with ambient air. This is generally added near the baghouse, provided good mixing of

air and gases can be assured. Cooling by dilution has the lowest installation cost, especially at very high initial temperatures, and precise control of the temperature is possible. On the other hand, dilution is almost always uneconomical because the volume of ambient air required to achieve the desired cooling is so great that a substantially larger baghouse is required to handle it. Figure 7.5.5 graphically illustrates the added capacity needed in the baghouse when hot gases are diluted with ambient air at 70°F.[41] Furthermore, the greatly increased volume means increased power requirements to pull the additional air through the filter. A further disadvantage is the uncontrollable intake of ambient moisture, dust, and other contaminants without prior conditioning of the dilution air.

Radiation cooling transfers heat from the gas stream to the atmosphere via the duct walls, as the

TABLE 7.5.3

Typical Filtering Velocities for Various Dusts and Fumes in Pulse-jet Baghouses[a]

Dusts or fumes	Filtering ratio, ACFM/ft²	Dusts or fumes	Filtering ratio, ACFM/ft²
Alumina	8–10	Leather dust	12–15
Asbestos	10–12	Lime	10–12
Bauxite	8–10	Limestone	8–10
Carbon black	5–6	Mica	9–11
Coal	8–10	Paint pigments	7–8
Cocoa, chocolate	12–15	Paper	10–12
Clay	9–10	Plastics	7–9
Cement	8–10	Quartz	9–11
Cosmetics	10–12	Rock dust	9–10
Enamel frit	9–10	Sand	10–12
Feeds, grain	14–15	Sawdust (wood)	12–15
Feldspar	9–10	Silica	7–9
Fertilizer	8–9	Slate	12–14
Flour	12–15	Soap, detergents	5–6
Graphite	5–6	Spices	10–12
Gypsum	10–12	Starch	8–9
Iron ore	11–12	Sugar	7–10
Iron oxide	7–8	Talc	10–12
Iron sulfate	6–8	Tobacco	13–15
Lead oxide	6–8	Zinc oxide	5–6

[a]Light to moderate dust loadings.

TABLE 7.5.4

Recommended Filtering Velocities for Glass-cloth Collectors

Material	Filtering ratio, ACFM/ft²
Carbon black generator furnace and channel black	1.1–1.3
Electric furnace and ferro alloy furnaces; most metallurgical fume	1.5–1.8
Cement and lime kilns, wet and dry process; open-hearth and oxygen-lanced open-hearth furnaces and smelters	1.8–2.0
Clinker coolers, refractory kilns and furnaces; coal-fired boilers (power plant)	2.0–2.3

gas travels towards the baghouse through long, uninsulated ducts. As a rule of thumb, radiation cooling provided by 100 ft of duct conveying 1,600°F gases to the baghouse can take care of one third to one half of the total cooling requirements. Since 100 ft is an average distance between the hot-gas source and the baghouse, substantial cooling is economically accomplished. When further radiation cooling is desired, additional lengths of duct are calculated on the basis of heat to be removed from the gas under regional weather conditions. Radiation-cooling ducts may also be in the form of vertical U's that may be 40 ft or more high. Although radiation cooling does not require an enlarged baghouse, it does have economic limitations. Radiation cooling of gases below 1,000°F requires substantial surface areas, lengthy duct runs, and increased fan horsepower, which quickly offset the economic advantages of a minimum-size baghouse (see Figure 7.5.6).[41] Precise temperature control is usually difficult to maintain, and there is the possibility of duct plugging by sedimentation.

TABLE 7.5.5

Typical Industrial Data for Reverse-air Baghouse Collectors[4] [1]

Type industry	Process or operation	Dust handled	Dust loading gr/ft³	Volume ACFM	Temperature °F	Collector Data		
						Air/cloth ratio	ΔP in. water	Bag material
Mineral products	Transfer point ventilation	Gypsum	8–10	2,500	160	6.4 to 1	6	11 oz Dacron®
Food processing	Material handling	Corn Oats Sugar	4–5	3,000	70	8.9 to 1	6	16 oz Dacron
Food processing	Bin vent	Sugar	4–5	675	70	3 to 1	4	Polypropylene
Metal products	Abrasive blast cleaning	Flint	10–15	12,000	70	16 to 1	2.5	16 oz Dacron
Grain processing	Entoleter ventilation	Starch	4–5	5,000	70	6.7 to 1	6	11 oz Acrylic®
Building products	Plastic fabrication	Formica	5	7,500	70	10 to 1	4	11 oz Dacron
Aluminum production	Materials handling	Alumina	8–10	4,000	70	6.6 to 1	6	11 oz Acrylic
Chemical	Conveyor ventilation	Soda ash	6–8	800	300	3.5 to 1	4	14 oz Nomex®
Ceramic	Crusher	Ferro-silicon	15	10,000	70	10 to 1	6	11 oz Dacron
Food processing	Rotary dryer material handling	Dehydrated onion and garlic	8	2,600	70	6 to 1	6	14 oz Acrylic
Mineral products	Conveyor	Hydrate lime	3–4	1,700	100	3.4 to 1	3	14 oz Acrylic
Food processing	Spray dryer	Dried blood	4	11,000	190	8 to 1	6	11 oz Dacron
Chemical	Fluid energy mill	Barium and calcium	1	1,600	150	4.4 to 1	6	11 oz Acrylic
Electronics	Printed circuit production	Copper and epoxy	3	7,500	70	10 to 1	6	Polypropylene
Food processing	Hammermill	Miscellaneous grain	8–10	2,400	70	10 to 1	5	11 oz Acrylic

TABLE 7.5.5 (continued)

Typical Industrial Data for Reverse-air Baghouse Collectors[41]

Type industry	Process or operation	Dust handled	Dust loading gr/ft³	Volume ACFM	Temperature °F	Collector data		
						Air/cloth ratio	ΔP in. water	Bag material
Glue manufacturing	Ventilation	Animal glue	2–3	3,000	70	6.7 to 1	6	Polypropylene
Chewing gum manufacturing	Ventilation	Sugar	3–5	4,000	70	6 to 1	5	Polypropylene
Grain milling	Counter flow dryer	Wheat Flour	200	5,400	125	9 to 1	5	16 oz wool
Agricultural chemical	Materials handling	DDT and clay	50–60	1,000	70	3.4 to 1	6	11 oz Acrylic
Food processing	Ventilation	Cereal	3–4	5,500	75	10.5 to 1	4	11 oz Dacron
Agricultural chemical	Dryer	2-4 D weed killer	10–15	600	100	2 to 1	4	16 oz Dacron
Chemical	Dryer	Fumeric acid	1–3	2,900	200	4.8 to 1	4	11 oz Dacron
Grain milling	Ventilation	Flour	3–5	1,000	70	6 to 1	4	10 oz cotton

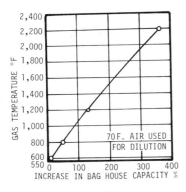

FIGURE 7.5.5. Additional capacity required in baghouse when hot gases are cooled by dilution with ambient air.

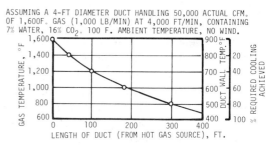

FIGURE 7.5.6. Radiation effectiveness in cooling hot gases.

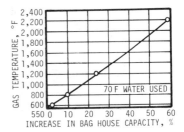

FIGURE 7.5.7. Additional capacity required in baghouse when hot gases are cooled by means of evaporative cooling.

To avoid material build-up along the bottoms of straight runs, a minimum gas velocity should always be maintained, typically ranging from 3,500 to 6,000 ft/min.

Evaporative cooling is accomplished by injecting fine water droplets into the gas stream; the droplets evaporate, absorbing heat from the gas. Spray nozzles are located either in a quench chamber or in ducting that precedes the baghouse. The gas is cooled quickly and in a relatively small space. Greater baghouse capacity is needed than for radiation cooling because of the added volume of the evaporated (gaseous) water. On the other hand, 90% less baghouse capacity is required for evaporative cooling than would be required for dilution cooling (see Figure 7.5.7).[41] Evaporative cooling also gives the greatest amount of cooling at low installation cost. Temperature control can be flexible and precise. However, this method of cooling increases the danger of exceeding the dew point of the gas which, in turn, increases the possibility of chemical attack of the filter fabric. All the water injected into the gas stream must be evaporated before the gases reach the baghouse; otherwise, metal parts may become corroded, and gas passages in the bag fabric may become plugged as dry dust being collected is turned to sludge.

Auxiliary Equipment Considerations

The selection and design of filter system auxiliary equipment also requires consideration when planning to install a fabric filtration system. The principal trade-off area is between the pressure drop through the ducting and stack systems and the fan size and cost. Often it is the pressure drop through the fabric filter alone which largely determines fan size. The positioning and amount of ducting are determined mainly by the expected locations of the effluent source, collector, fan, and venting point. The usual case is to minimize duct lengths and diameters unless ducting will be used to provide radiant cooling of the hot gases. The distance from the collector to both the dust generating source and the point of discharge of the filtered effluent must be considered with regard to duct costs and space availability. The cost of plant floor space may be a reason for locating the collector outside the plant, other possible limitations being ceiling limitations and safety. On the other hand, the outdoor collector must usually be protected against weather and insulated against temperature changes. A common problem with fabric filters located outdoors has been condensation due to improper insulation.

It is also important to minimize the use of horizontal ducting and select diameters which allow for complete transport of the dust load to the collector. Sharp bends and abrupt changes in dimension should also be avoided to prevent dust accumulation and erosion. In the case of fluctuating flow, the ducting should be sized for an intermediate flow between the average and peak loads. Standard steel ducting is normally used, unless there is danger of corrosion, abrasion, adhesion, high temperature, thermal distortion, insulation requirements, or unusual surges in pressure or temperature. Aluminum, fiberglass, etc., can sometimes be used as substitutes for steel.

The total-system pressure drop is that of the combined losses in the ducting and the fabric filter unit. Ducting losses vary approximately as the square of the gas velocity and can readily be calculated by standard formulas.[2] Ordinarily, the total pressure drop associated with the ducting alone will be in the range of 3 to 6 in. of water. The pressure drop through the ductwork is then added to the collector pressure drop and that of any other component of the system (e.g., a centrifugal collector) to obtain the total pressure drop of the complete system. This result will be the net pressure to be supplied by the fan when ambient pressures are the same at the system inlet and outlet. Centrifugal fans are most often chosen for the primary flow in industrial fabric filtration systems. A maximum-rated fan capacity of approximately 20% greater than the required capacity is usually specified.

Operation and Maintenance Practices

A properly attended fabric filter system is usually capable of operating satisfactorily for up to 15 years and possibly longer. Certain practices are essential for successful operation, including:

1. Selection of the most suitable equipment in the planning stages (e.g., if a process is characterized by variations in gas flow and/or dust loading, the equipment must operate at peak loads without media plugging, as well as reduced flows where condensation may occur).
2. Familiarity with the operating, instrumentation, equipment, and maintenance manuals.
3. Knowledge of the contaminated gas stream to be treated.
4. Proper care of the fabric media.
5. Minimizing the temperature into the filter, limited only by the danger of reaching the dew point. This can considerably minimize operating and maintenance costs.
6. Establishing and following a preventive maintenance program.

The primary operating problems associated with fabric filters have been bag caking and pluggage, leakage, and short bag life. To avoid plugging, because of condensation, the gas temperature should be 50 to 75°F above the dew point. In some installations a small auxiliary heater is used to prevent condensation in the baghouse when it is shut down. An unusually heavy grain loading may also cause excessive wear or blinding. As a rule of thumb, dust loadings above 10 grains/ft^3 are often handled by a precleaner such as a medium- or low-efficiency cyclone. Leakage through the filter is perhaps the most important service problem. Each bag must be regularly inspected for holes or tears. Chemical deterioration has also been mentioned as one of the factors that can add to the maintenance costs. The rate at which a fabric media will deteriorate is generally related to the weight of the fabric and the gas stream composition. The heavier the fabric weight, the greater the initial and replacement cost of the filters. Bag spacing is also important. Sufficient clearance must be provided so that one bag does not contact another. A minimum of 2 in., for example, is needed between bags 10- to 12-ft long, while longer bags require greater clearance distances. Whenever the dust is a combustible material, the principal hazards in the operation of fabric collectors are explosion and fire. Precoating the bags with an inert material before start-up can provide a noncombustible surface on the surface of the bags. This can prevent sparks which might trigger combustion.

Advantages and Limitations of Fabric Filter Systems

The principal advantages of fabric filter systems include:

1. Particle collection efficiency is very high and can be maintained at consistently high levels (usually greater than 99%).
2. Efficiency and pressure drop are relatively unaffected by large changes in inlet dust loadings for continuously cleaned filters.
3. Filter outlet air may be recirculated within the plant in many cases.
4. The collected material is recovered dry for subsequent processing or disposal.
5. There are no problems of liquid waste disposal, water pollution, or liquid freezing.
6. Corrosion and rusting of components are usually not problems.

7. There is no hazard of high voltage, simplifying maintenance and repair and permitting collection of flammable dusts.

8. Use of selected fibrous or granular filter aids (precoating) permits the high-efficiency collection of submicron smokes and gaseous contaminants.

9. Filter collectors are available in a large number of configurations, resulting in a range of dimensions and inlet and outlet flange locations to suit installation requirements.

Some limitations in the use of fabric filters include:

1. Fabric life may be shortened at elevated temperatures and in the presence of acid or alkaline particle or gas constituents.

2. Temperatures much in excess of 500°F require special refractory mineral or metallic fabrics that are still in the developmental stage and can be very expensive.

3. Hygroscopic materials, condensation of moisture, or tarry adhesive components may cause crusty caking or plugging of the fabric or require special additives.

4. Certain dusts may require fabric treatments to reduce seeping of the dust or, in other cases, assist in the removal of the collected dust.

5. Concentrations of some dusts in the collector ($\sim$ 50 g/m^3) may represent a fire or explosion hazard if spark or flame is admitted by accident. Fabrics can burn if readily oxidizable dust is being collected.

6. Replacement of fabric may require respiratory protection for maintenance personnel.

The principal competitors of the high-efficiency fabric filter are the high-efficiency electrostatic precipitator and the high-efficiency, high-energy wet scrubber. Fabric filters have been designed and installed to handle from 100 to 4.5 million ACFM in a single installation. A well-designed (and properly maintained) baghouse is capable of handling the entire range of gas-borne stack emission particles, fine or coarse in size, light or heavy in grain loading. Its efficiency is approximately constant, regardless of varying moisture, temperature, particle size, or gas flow. On applications where the dust resistivity is high, the electrostatic precipitator can become large and expensive and the first cost of a fabric filter can

become comparatively attractive. For example, fabric filters compete in certain situations with electrostatic precipitators in the control of particulates from coal-fired power plants. Primarily due to the nature of this resistivity problem (high resistivity often associated with low-sulfur coals), it is becoming readily apparent that with coals having sulfur contents below 1.5 to 2.0%, the baghouse can offer a substantial reduction in capital costs over a high-efficiency (99.5 to 99.8%) electrostatic precipitator.[43] Another example is the filtration of iron oxide fume from the melting operations of ferrous scrap in the steel and foundry industries. Due to the lack of moisture, fume resistivity is high, making it especially difficult to separate particles through the use of electrostatic precipitators. Furthermore, because of the extremely small particle size, the energy requirements of a high-energy wet scrubber would be very high (as high as 70 in. of water), resulting again in a preference for the fabric filter.[44]

Economics

As a general rule of thumb, the equipment purchase cost of typical fabric-filter collectors constructed with standard mild steel (for relatively low-temperature operation) ranges between \$0.50 to 1.25/ACFM. Erection costs generally fall between \$0.25 to 0.50/ACFM (typically 75% of the equipment purchase cost). Total installed costs (equipment purchase cost plus erection) of medium-temperature baghouses (250°F) typically range from \$0.75 to 1.50/ACFM, and high-temperature baghouses (500°F) range from \$1.50 to 3.00/ACFM.

The theoretical annual operating and maintenance costs associated with fabric filters can be calculated from

$$\$ = ACFM [(1.173 (10^{-4}) (\Delta P) tE/\eta_f) + M]$$

where

ACFM	=	design capacity of the fabric filter, ACFM;
ΔP	=	pressure drop, in. of water;
t	=	annual operating time, hr;
E	=	power cost, \$/(kW)(hr);
η_f	=	fan efficiency;
M	=	maintenance costs, \$/ACFM.

Annual maintenance costs vary from \$0.02 to

0.08/ACFM and are typically $0.05/ACFM. The overall efficiency for fan and motor is typically 0.55. Power costs at present average about $0.015/(kW)(hr). Using these typical values and a fabric filter pressure drop of 5 in. of water (common) with operation 24 hr/day, 365 days/year, the annual operation and maintenance costs can be estimated from

$$\$ \approx 0.20 \ (ACFM)$$

In comparison with other particulate control devices, fabric filters usually have the highest maintenance costs. However, on the other hand, they are capable of demonstrating the highest efficiencies. In general, only electrostatic precipitators require a greater capital investment.

7.6. ILLUSTRATIVE EXAMPLES

The following example problems demonstrate the application of some of the more important material in this chapter. They are intended as a guide to assist the reader in solving typical fabric-filtration problems.

Example 7.6.1
Calculate the inertial impaction number for particles 10 μm in diameter with a specific gravity of 2.3 in an air stream at ambient conditions. The aerosol is flowing past a cylindrical collector 1,000 μm diameter at a velocity of 6.5 ft/sec.

Solution
The equation used for calculating the inertial impaction number is

$$N_I = 2 \ vr_p^2 \ \rho_p/9 \ \mu_G r_c$$

Substituting the data gives

$$N_I = 2 \times 6.5 \times (5 \times 3.28 \times 10^{-6})^2 \times 2.3 \times 62.4/9 \times$$
$$1.21 \times 10^{-5} \times 500 \times 3.28 \times 10^{-6}$$
$$= 2.81$$

Example 7.6.2
Obtain the single-collector collection efficiency for the above system.

Solution
The collector efficiency is obtained from Figure 7.3.2. This value is 64% for an inertial impaction number of 2.81 and a cylindrical collector.

Example 7.6.3
Estimate the single-collector collection efficiency for the same system if the interception effect is included.

Solution
Since $\eta = (y^*/r_c)100$, we may back-calculate y^* by

$$64 = (y^*/r_c)100$$
$$y^* = 320 \ \mu m$$

We also know that the interception effect can be included by setting

$$\eta = [(y^* + r_p)/r_c] \ 100$$

Substituting the data

$$\eta = [(320 + 5)/500] \ 100$$
$$= 65\%$$

We see that, as expected, interception has a small effect on the collection efficiency.

Example 7.6.4
The dimensions of a bag in a filter unit are 11 3/4 in. in diameter and 18-ft long. Calculate the filtering area of the bag.

Solution
We assume the bag to be cylindrical in shape with diameter D and height h. The area of the curved surface, neglecting the flat top surface for the time being, is

$$A = \pi \ (bag \ diameter)(bag \ height)$$

Substituting the data

$$A = \pi \ (11.75/12)18$$
$$A = 55.4 \ ft^2$$

The area of the top surface is 0.752 ft^2, which is negligible when compared to the total area.

Example 7.6.5
If the filtering unit in the previous example consists of 24 such bags and is to treat 545,000 ACFH of gas from a smelter operation, calculate the "effective" filter velocity in feet per minute and ACFM per square foot of filter area.

Solution

The total area for 24 bags is

$$A = 24(55.4) = 1,330 \text{ ft}^2$$

The filter velocity is then

$$v = 545,000/60 \times 1,330$$
$$= 6.83 \text{ ft/min}$$

The calculation for ACFM per square foot of filter area is the same.

Example 7.6.6

The filter unit in the previous example operates at 99.99+% collection efficiency. Calculate the mass of particles collected daily if the inlet loading is 7.9 grains/ft^3.

Solution

Assuming 100% collection efficiency, the mass collected daily is

$$545,000 \times 7.9 \times 24/7,000 = 14,762 \text{ lb/day}$$

Example 7.6.7

Engineers have designed a filter baghouse for a new plant. The design is based on pilot plant data, the unit in the pilot plant was operated under conditions identical to those intended for the large plant. The engineers assumed that the filtration cycle would allow for cleaning and operating at constant pressure. Their design will give an average filtration rate exactly equal to the required capacity. To add a factor of safety, engineer A wants to use 25% more bags; B wants to make each bag 25% longer; C wants to make each bag with 25% more area; D wants to use 25% more filtration pressure. Rank these proposals in the order in which you consider they would increase the average hourly capacity of the filter. Explain and justify your rank by use of appropriate theory or equations.

Solution

For purposes of analysis, we neglect the resistance of the bag. Engineer A's plan to use 25% more bags will increase the collection area by a factor of 1.25. The time of filtration will be decreased by a factor of $(1.25.)^2$ If the filtration rate capacity is

$$Q = V_G/(t + t_c)$$

the improved rate, QS, to insure a factor of safety is then

$$QS = V_G/[t/(1.25)^2 + t_c]$$

If cleaning time is neglected, we see the rate is increased by a factor of 1.56, i.e.,

$$QS = 1.56 \, Q$$

The same improved rate is obtained using the plans of engineers B and C. For plan D, the time of filtration is decreased by 1.25. The improved rate is

$$QS = V_G/[(t/1.25) + t_c]$$

If cleaning time is again neglected, we have

$$QS = 1.25 \, Q$$

The proposals are, therefore, ranked in the following order:

1. a, b, c
2. d

Example 7.6.8

A baghouse filter is run at a constant gas rate for 30 min during which time 3,000 ft^3 of gas from a cement kiln operation is processed. The initial and final pressure in the unit is 0.5 and 5.0 in. H_2O gauge, respectively. If the filter is further operated for 30 min at the final pressure, calculate the quantity of additional gas treated.

Solution

For constant rate filtration the describing equation is

$$\Delta p = BQ^2 t + CQ$$

At time zero, the data give

$$0.5 \text{ in. } H_2O = O + C \times 100 \text{ ft}^3/\text{min}$$

so that the value of C is

$$C = 0.005 \text{ (in. } H_2O) \text{ (min)/ft}^3$$

Substituting the data at t equal to 30 min gives

$$5.0 = B(200)^2\, 30 + 0.005 \times 100$$

or

$$B = 1.5 \times 10^{-5}\ \text{(in. } H_2O)\,(\text{min})/\text{ft}^6$$

At constant pressure the describing equation for this system is written as

$$t = (B/2\,\Delta p)V_G^2 + (D/\Delta p)V_G$$

where D represents not only the resistance of the bag, but also the resistance of the solids deposited during the constant rate period. The coefficient B remains the same, since it still is proportional to the quantity of solids deposited during this constant pressure period. Coefficient D is calculated from the equation

$$\Delta p = (BV_G + D)Q$$

Since Δp = 5 in. H_2O at V_G = 0, we have

$$D = 0.05\ \text{(in. } H_2O)\,(\text{min})/\text{ft}^3$$

After 30 min of constant pressure filtration, we solve for V_G.

$$30 = (1.5 \times 10^{-5}/10)V_G^2 + (0.05/5)V_G$$

The positive root is

$$V_G = 2{,}200\ \text{ft}^3$$

Therefore, the total quantity of gas filtered is

$$100 \times 30 + 2{,}200 = 5{,}200\ \text{ft}^3$$

Example 7.6.9

The following data were obtained in a carefully run test on a filter operating at constant pressure

V_G (ft³)	172	243	298	365	421
t (min)	10	20	30	45	60

1. What can be said about the resistance of the filter medium as compared to that of the deposited particles? Support your answer by calculations.
2. If the time of cleaning is 10 min, what is the optimum time, in hours, for the filtration cycle? Optimum time here refers to maximum gas per cycle.
3. What is the volume of filtrate obtained in this cycle?
4. What is the percentage increase in the volume of the gas from the filter if the cycle of (2) is adopted in place of the previous (60 plus 10 min) cycle?

Solution

1. The describing equation is

$$t = (B/2\,\Delta p)V_G^2 + (C/\Delta p)V_G$$

Since we only need the ratio of B to C and Δp is constant during the run, we may write the preceding equation as

$$t = (B^*/2)V_G^2 + C^*V_G$$

Substitution of any two data points will provide a relationship between B and C. For example, using the first two data points gives

$$10 = (B^*/2)(172)^2 + C^*(172)$$

and

$$20 = (B^*/2)(243)^2 + C^*(243)$$

Solving the two equations simultaneously gives

$$B/C \approx B^*/C^* \approx 0$$

The same result is obtained by substitution of any combination of two data points. Alternately, the graphical approach suggested earlier gives rise to an (intercept) value of C approaching zero. Therefore, the resistance of the bag *is* negligible.

2. The optimum filtering time for constant pressure operation should equal the cleaning time. Therefore,

$$t = 10\ \text{min}$$

The optimum cycle time is, therefore,

$$t = 20\ \text{min}$$
$$= 0.333\ \text{hr}$$

3. The quantity of gas processed for 10 min operation is 172 ft³ .

4. The original filtering time was 60 min. The volumetric flow rate processed is

$$Q = V_G/(t + t_c) = 421/(60 + 10)$$
$$= 6.0 \text{ ft}^3/\text{min}$$

For the cycle in part 2 the rate is

$$Q = 172/(10 + 10)$$
$$= 8.6 \text{ ft}^3/\text{min}$$

The percentage increase is then

$$100(8.6 - 6.0)/6.0 = 43.3\%$$

Example 7.6.10

A gas from a lime kiln filtered in a bench scale filter gave the following representative results:

	Time, t, min	Vol filtered, V_G, ft³
Constant rate period	0–10	0–35.4
Constant pressure period	10–35	35.4–86.7

A plot of $V_G{}^2$ vs. t gave a straight line over the range of 10 to 35 min. After each filtration operation, the necessary period for shaking and cleaning was 5 min. In the test the fan was running at maximum capacity. In order to obtain maximum daily capacity without changing the maximum capacity of the fan, how many minutes should be devoted to actual filtration in each cycle? How many complete cycles should be run per 24-hr day, and what would be the volume of gas processed? Assume the bag resistance to be negligible.

Solution

There are three describing equations for this system if the bag resistance is neglected.

$$\Delta p_f = B(Q)^2 t; \text{ constant rate period}$$
$$t = (B/2 \Delta p)V_G{}^2 + DV_G; \text{ constant pressure period}$$
$$D = \Delta p_f/Q_o; \text{ initial condition-constant pressure period}$$

The three unknowns are B, D, and Δp_f. Substituting the data and solving the equations simultaneously gives

$$B = 0.411$$
$$D = 14.5$$
$$\Delta p_f = 51.4$$

in consistent units. The describing equations become

$$\Delta p = 0.411 \, Q^2 \, t_Q; 0 \leqslant t \leqslant 10$$
$$t_p = 0.0039 \, V_G{}^2 + 0.282 \, V_G; t > 10$$

The rate over each cycle is

$$Q = (V_{G,p} + V_{G,Q})/(t_p + t_Q + t_c)$$

where the subscripts p and Q refer to the constant pressure and constant rate periods, respectively. The maximum rate is obtained in a manner similar to that described earlier. We set

$$dQ/dt_p \text{ or } dQ/dV_{G,p}$$

equal to zero and solve for t_p or $V_{G,p}$, respectively. We choose the second course of action in order to simplify the presentation.

$$Q = (35.4 + V_G)/(0.0039 \, V_G{}^2 + 0.282 \, V_G + 15)$$
$$dQ/dV_G = 0.0039 \, V_G{}^2 + 0.276 \, V_G - 5.0 = 0$$

The positive root to the above equation is

$$V_{G,p} = 14.66 \text{ ft}^3$$

so that

$$t_p = 5.0 \text{ min}$$

The maximum rate is approximately

$$50/20 = 2.5 \text{ ft}^3/\text{min}$$

The total cycle time is 20 min. There are

$$24 \times 60/20 = 72$$

cycles per day, and

$$50 \times 72 = 3,600$$

ft³ of gas processed per day.

Example 7.6.11

The following data were obtained on a small-sized constant rate laboratory filter:

Area of bag = 0.25 ft²
Number of bags = 4
Volume of gas processed = 412.5 ft³

Time of filtration = 55 min
Final pressure = 10.0 in. H_2O
Initial pressure = 0.01 in. H_2O

Design a unit to filter 8,000,000 ft^3 of the same gas every 4 hr to the same final pressure and using the same type filter. What filtering area is required? How many bags would be required if the net filtering area of each bag is 66 ft^2?

Solution
At constant rate

$$\Delta p = BQ^2 t$$

Substituting the data for the pilot unit gives

$$10 = B(412.5/55)^2 55$$
$$B = 3.23 \times 10^{-3} \text{ (in. } H_2O\text{) (min)/ft}^6$$

For process conditions we have

$$\Delta p = B^*Q^2 t$$

Substituting process data yields

$$10 = B^*(8 \times 10^6/4 \times 60)^2 \, 4 \times 60$$

so that

$$B^* = 3.75 \times 10^{-11}$$

Since

$$B \propto (A)^{-2}$$

the ratio of the two coefficients is

$$B/B^* = (1/A)^2/(1/A^*)^2$$
$$= (A^*)^2/(A)^2$$

For the pilot unit, A = 1. Therefore,

$$(A^*)^2 = 3.23 \times 10^{-3}/(3.75 \times 10^{-11}) = 0.861 \times 10^8$$

and

$$A^* = 0.93 \times 10^4 \text{ ft}^2 = 9,300 \text{ ft}^2$$

If the net filtering area for each bag is 66 ft^2, the number of bags required is

$$9,300/66 = 141 \text{ bags}$$

Example 7.6.12

A sample from a homogeneous furnace exhaust is to be treated in a small single-bag filter at a constant rate of 4.5 ft^3/min. Test data yield the following equation:

$$V_G^2 = 6,500 \, p$$

where

V_G = volume of gas treated, ft^3;
p = pressure, in. H_2O;
t = time, min.

If the run is to be terminated at the end of 5 hr, calculate the theoretical gas horsepower of the blower and the theoretical work for the run in (ft) (lb$_f$).

Solution
The work is given by

$$\int_0^{V_{G,f}} (p)dV_G; \, V_{G,f} = 1,350$$

Since $V_G^2 = 6,500 \, p$ we may write

$$p = (V_G/t)(V_G/6,500) = QV_G/6,500$$
$$= 4.5 \, V_G/6,500$$

Integrating the work equation gives

$$W = (4.5/6,500)(V_{G,f}^2/2)$$
$$= 4.5(1,350)^2/2 \times 6,500$$
$$= 630.9 \text{ (in. } H_2O\text{)(ft}^3\text{)} = 3,281 \text{ (ft)(lb}_f\text{)}$$

The final pressure is

$$p = 4.5 \times 1,350/6,500$$
$$\approx 1 \text{ in. } H_2O$$

The gas horsepower is then

$$\text{hp} = 4.5 \times 1.0 \times 5.2/33,000$$
$$\approx 0$$

Example 7.6.13

A bag filter is operating at constant pressure. The equation describing present operation is

$$t = 0.08 \, p^{-1}V_G^2 + 0.20 \, V_G$$

where

t = time, min;

p = pressure, in. H_2O;

V_G = volume filtered per unit area, ft^3/in^2.

The present cycle consists of a filtering time of 100 min and a cleaning time of 3 min. The operating pressure is 5.0 in. H_2O. It is necessary to increase the overall capacity of the filter. It has been suggested that the operating pressure be doubled to accomplish this. The nature and concentration of the exhaust, the operating temperature, and the cleaning time are to remain unchanged. As a recently hired production engineer, you are asked the following questions. What would be the maximum attainable percentage increase in overall capacity if the operating pressure were doubled? What would be the percentage increase in horsepower requirements?

Solution

The describing equation is

$$t = 0.08 \, (p)^{-1} \, V_G^2 + 0.2 \, V_G$$

At 100 min the volume is

$$100 = (0.08 \, V_G^2 / 5) + 0.2 \, V_G$$

The positive root is

$$V_G = 73.05 \, ft^3$$

If the pressure is doubled, the describing equation becomes

$$t = 0.008 \, V_G^2 + 0.2 \, V_G$$

The volume rate of flow (per cycle) is

$$Q = V_G / (t + t_c)$$

To maximize this rate we set either

$$dQ/dt \text{ or } dQ/dV_G$$

equal to zero and solve for either t or V_G, respectively. If we employ the latter choice

$$Q = V_G / (0.008 \, V_G^2 + 0.2 \, V_G + 3.0)$$

with

$$dQ/dV_G = -0.008 \, V_G^2 + 3.0 = 0$$

Solving yields

$$V_G = 19.31 \, ft^3$$

with

$$t = 6.86 \, min$$

Therefore,

$$Q(100 \, min, 5 \, in. \, H_2O) = 73.05/103 = 0.71 \, ft^3/min$$

$$Q(6.86 \, min, 10 \, in. \, H_2O) = 19.31/9.86 = 1.96 \, ft^3/min$$

We conclude that doubling the pressure and operating at maximum (rate) conditions has nearly tripled the flow rate.

Since the operating pressure (drop) has doubled, the horsepower requirement also has doubled.

Example 7.6.14

A filter now operating on an optimum cycle at constant pressure has an overall capacity of 300 ft^3/sec of gas. The operating equation is

$$t = 0.003 \, p^{-0.8} \, V_G^2 + 1.0 \, p^{-0.4} \, V_G$$

where

t = time, min;

p = pressure, 2.0 in. H_2O;

V_G = volume filtered/area, ft^3/in^2.

Filtering time is 15 min. Because of an accident, 1/5 of the filter area is temporarily out of service. In order to maintain the original capacity during the emergency period, what percentage increase in compressor horsepower will be required?

Solution

The describing equation for the unit is

$$t = 0.003 \, (p)^{-0.8} \, V_G^2 + 1.0 \, (p)^{-0.4} \, V_G$$

For a pressure of 2 in. H_2O and time of 15 min, V_G may be calculated from

$$15 = 0.003 \, (2)^{-0.8} \, V_G^2 + 1.0 \, (2)^{-0.4} \, V_G$$

Solving for V_G gives

$$V_G = 18.98 \text{ ft}^3/\text{in}^2$$

Since the total volumetric flow rate is

$$Q = 300 \text{ ft}^3/\text{sec}$$

The total volume treated is

$$V_G = 300 \times 60 \times 15$$
$$= 270,000 \text{ ft}^3$$

The area is given by

$$A = 270,000/18.98 = 14,226 \text{ in}^2$$

If only 80% is available for filtering

$$A = 0.8 \, (14,226) = 11,380 \text{ in}^2$$

Under these conditions the new V_G will be

$$V_G = 23.7 \text{ ft}^3/\text{in}^2$$

Using the same describing equation, the new pressure can be calculated by

$$15 = 0.003 \, (p)^{-0.8} \, (23.7)^2 + (p)^{-0.4} \, (23.7)$$

Solving for p gives

$$p = 3.5 \text{ in. } H_2O$$

The percent increase is

$$100(3.5 - 2.0)/2.0 = 75\%$$

Example 7.6.15

A furnace product is filtered at a constant rate. Cleaning requires 2.0 min. The cost of filtering is 25 cents/$(ft)^2(hr)^2$; the cleaning cost is 2 cents/$(ft)^2(hr)^2$. Is any additional information required to set up schedules for maximum filtrate per unit time and minimum cost per unit of filtrate? If not, set up the schedules.

Solution

The flow rate, or filtrate per unit time, is set by the operating conditions. This can be increased by either increasing the filtration time for each cycle or (the equivalent of) increasing the final operating pressure.

If we define n as the number of cycles in T min, then

$$n = T/(t + t_c)$$

The cost of filtering per unit of filtrate is related to

$$n \times 0.25 \times t^2/3,600$$

The cost of cleaning per unit of filtrate is correspondingly related to

$$n \times 0.02 \times t_c/60 = n \times 0.02 \times 2.0/60$$

The total cost per unit of filtrate is then given by the sum of the latter two equations. To minimize this cost, we set the derivative of the total cost with respect to t equal to zero and solve for t. The result is

$$0.00425 \, t^2 + 0.017 \, t - 0.04 = 0$$

The positive root is t = 6.0 min. The minimum cost per unit of filtrate is obtained with a cycle time of 8.0 min.

Example 7.6.16

A baghouse is planned for installation on a coal-fired boiler to handle 100,000 ACFM at 500°F. Estimate the collection area required in the collector and the operating brake horsepower of the fan if the pressure drop across the filter is 6 in. of water.

Solution

From Table 7.2.2, choose a fiberglass filter media to withstand the high temperatures. According to Table 7.5.4, the filtering ratio for coal-fired boilers using glass filter media should be approximately 2.0 to 2.3 CFM/ft^2. Use 2 CFM/ft^2.

Collector area required = 100,000 ACFM/2 CFM/ft^2
= 50,000 ft^2

Using a reverse-flow system and choosing bags 25-ft long and 12 in. diameter,

The operating brake horsepower of the fan, assuming a fan efficiency of 68%, is

Area of each bag = 18.055 ft²
Number of bags required = 50,000 ft²/18,055 ft²/bag
$\qquad$ = 2,770 bags

Brake hp = 100,000 × 6 × 0.0001575/0.68
$\qquad$ = 139 hp

NOMENCLATURE

A	Area of filter available to gas stream
A_p	Surface area of particle
c	Particle concentration
C	Cunningham correction factor
C_D	Drag coefficient
C_{DC}	Fiber (collector) drag coefficient
c_i	Dust loading to the filter
D	Particle diffusion coefficient
d_c	Diameter of collector
$d_c{}'$	Equivalent diameter of the collector
D_d	Circular duct diameter
d_p	Particle diameter
E	Electrical energy required
$\overline{E}$	Function of W, collection efficiency
f	Friction factor for flow through a bed of collectors
F_D	Fluid resistance to particle (drag force)
f_f	Fanning friction factor
g	Acceleration duets gravity
g_c	Gravitational acceleration constant
h	Dust layer resistance
k	Boltzmann's constant
K	Permeability coefficient
k'	Kozeny-Carman coefficient
K'	Fabric resistance
K_2	Specific dust-fabric filter resistance coefficient
L	Effective length of particle capture (or depth of dust deposit on filter, where indicated)
L_c	Length of cylindrical collector
L_d	Length of circular duct
L_f	Thickness of filter medium
L_p	Width of deposited particles
m_p	Particle mass
N_D	Diffusion parameter
N_{DI}	Direct interception parameter
N_I	Inertial impaction parameter, dimensionless
Pe	Peclet number
Δp	Pressure drop
Δp_c	Pressure drop across cake
Δp_f	Pressure drop for flow perpendicular to cylinder
Δp_m	Final pressure drop achieved before cleaning
Δp_o	Overall pressure drop across the entire filter system
Δp_p	Pressure drop for flow through a bed of spherical particles (deposited cake)
Q	Gas volumetric flow rate
Q_o	Maximum flow rate through the filter

Q_T	Overall flow rate
r_b	Radius of cell boundary
r_c	Radius of cylindrical collector
R_f	Filter resistance
r_h	Hydraulic radius of the collector
r_p	Radius of particle
Re_c	Reynolds number based on the collector diameter $(\rho_G v d_c / \mu_G)$
S	Specific surface
s_p	Collector surface area
Sc	Schmidt number
Sh_{avg}	Average Sherwood number
t	Time
T	Absolute temperature
t_c	Cleaning time
t_f	Filtering time
t_p	Time period for one cycle
v	Undisturbed stream velocity
V_G	Volume of gas filtered for deposited thickness Δz
v_p	Collector volume
V_p	Particle volume
v_s	Superficial velocity through filter
w	Filter thickness
W	Particle weight on filter per unit of cloth area
W_p	Pumping (fan) work
x_i	Volume fraction of collectors with specific surface S_i
y^*	Ordinate of the starting point of the critical trajectory at the cell boundary
Δz	Cake thickness
α	Filter density
ϵ	Filter bed porosity
ρ_B	Bulk density of filter cake
ρ_G	Gas density
ρ_p	Particle density
η	Single-collector inertial impaction efficiency
η_B	Blower efficiency
η_D	Efficiency of collection by diffusion
η_{DI}	Direct interception collection efficiency
η_G	Collection efficiency from gravity settling
η_I	Inertial impaction collection efficiency
η_{I-DI}	Collection efficiency due to combined impaction and direct interception
η_{I-D-DI}	Collection efficiency due to combined impaction, diffusion and direct interception
η_M	Motor efficiency
η_T	Overall collection efficiency
μ_G	Gas viscosity

PROBLEMS

1. Calculate the inertial impaction number for particles 50 μm in diameter and specific gravity 2.4 in an air stream at ambient conditions. The aerosol is flowing past a cylindrical collector 765 μm in diameter at a velocity of 4.0 ft/sec.

2. Obtain the single-collector collection efficiency for the above system.

3. Estimate the single-collector collection efficiency for the same system if the interception effect is included.

4. The dimensions of a bag in a filter unit are 8 in. in diameter and 15-ft long. Calculate the filtering area of the bag.

5. If the filtering unit in the previous example consists of 40 such bags and is to treat 480,000 ft³/hr of gas from an open-hearth furnace, calculate the "effective" filtration velocity in feet per minute and ACFM per square foot of filter area.

6. The filter unit in the previous example operates at 99.99+% collection efficiency. Calculate the mass of particles collected daily if the inlet loading is 3.1 grains/ft³.

7. In the discussion of the effect of area on the time of constant pressure filtration, it was noted that time was inversely proportional to the square of the area for a constant amount filtered. Thus, doubling the area would cut the time to one fourth the original value. If the effect of the time for the cleaning cycle is neglected, cutting the time to one fourth indicates that the average rate of filtration is four times greater. Now suppose that a company using a filter places a second identical unit in operation alongside the first. Obviously, the capacity (rate of filtration) of the two units will be twice the capacity of one, and the total area will be twice the original. How can one account for the apparent contradiction in which the rate of filtration appears to be proportional to the area squared in the first case and to the first power of the area in the second?

8. A baghouse filter is run at a constant gas rate for 30 min during which period 2,500 ft³ of gas from a cement kiln operation is processed. The initial and final pressure in the unit is 0.4 and 4.0 in. H_2O gauge, respectively. If the filter is further operated for 1 hr at the final pressure, calculate the quantity of additional gas treated.

9. An old bag filter from a discontinued process is to be utilized for constant pressure filtration at 5.0 in. H_2O. The filter has 20 bags of 8 ft² area. Cleaning time is determined as 45 min. For the given pressure the filtration equation is

$$t = 0.013 \, V_G^2$$

where

t = time, min;

V_G = volume filtered/area, ft³/in.².

Determine the maximum overall capacity of this filter in cubic feet per hour under the given conditions.

10. A filter is operating at constant rate on an optimum cycle. The filtration equation is

$$V_G^2 = 6,000 \, t p^{0.65}$$

where

V_G = volume filtered, ft³ × 10^{-3};
t = time, min;
p = pressure, in. H_2O.

The cleaning time is 45 min. The maximum allowable working pressure is 4.0 in. H_2O.

a. What is the maximum overall capacity, in cubic feet per hour?

b. It is necessary to increase the capacity of the filter. It has been suggested that an additional unit identical to the present one be installed. Both units would work from the same compressor which has ample capacity, and filtration would be carried to the same maximum pressure as at present. The time required to shake and clean the two units is estimated at 4.0 min. What is the maximum percentage increase in the overall capacity that could be attained by adopting this suggestion?

11. A sample from a coal-fired burner is to be filtered at a constant rate of 5 ft³/min in a single-bag filter. Filtration time is 4.5 hr. The only test data available come from constant rate runs and indicate that at a final pressure of 5.0 in. H_2O the volume of gas treated, in cubic feet, at any time, in minutes, is given by the equation

$$V_G^2 = 150,000 \, t$$

a. What is the theoretical gas horsepower for the constant rate filtration?

b. What is the theoretical work, in ft-lb$_f$, for the constant rate filtration?

REFERENCES

1. Stanley, S., *Clean Air,* p. 53, August 1973.
2. Billings, C. E. and Wilder, J., *Handbook of Fabric Filter Technology,* Vol. 1, NTIS, PB 200 648, GCA Corporation, Boston, December 1970.
3. Strauss, W., *Industrial Gas Cleaning,* Pergamon Press, New York, 1966.
4. Langmuir, I. and Blodgett, K. B., Report RL-225, General Electric Research Laboratory, Schenectady, New York, 1945.
5. Ranz, W. E. and Wong, J. B., *Ind. Eng. Chem.,* 44, 1371, 1952.
6. Jarman, R. T., *J. Agric. Eng. Res.,* 4, 139, 1959.
7. Langmuir, I., O.S.R.D. Report No. 865, 1942.
8. Bosanquet, C. H., *Trans. Inst. Chem. Eng.* (London), 28, 130, 1950.
9. Johnstone, H. F. and Roberts, M. H., *Ind. Eng. Chem.,* 41, 2417, 1949.
10. Ranz, W. E., Tech. Report No. 8, University of Illinois Engineering Experimental Station, Urbana, 1953.
11. Stern, S. C., Zeller, H. W., and Schekman, A. I., *J. Colloid Sci.,* 15, 546, 1960.
12. Chen, C. Y., *Chem. Rev.,* 55, 595, 1955.
13. Pfeffer, R., *Ind. Eng. Chem. Fundam.,* 3, 380, 1964.
14. Paretsky, L., Theodore, L., Pfeffer, R., and Squires, A. M., *J. Air Pollut. Control Assoc.,* 21(4), 204, 1971.
15. Thomas, J. W. and Yoder, R. E., *AMA Arch. Ind. Health,* 13, 545, 1956; 13, 550, 1956.
16. Ranz, W. E. and Wong, J. B., *Ind. Eng. Chem.,* 44, 1371, 1952.
17. Davies, C. N., *Proc. Inst. Mech. Eng.,* 1B, 185, 1952.
18. Anderson, D. M. and Silverman, L., Havard Air Cleaning Laboratory, U.S. AEC Report No. NYO-4615, 1958.
19. Fair, G. M. and Hatch, L. P., *J. Am. Water Works Assoc.,* 25, 1551, 1933.
20. Williams, C. E., Hatch, T., and Greenburg, L., *Heat. Piping Air Cond.,* 12, 259, 1940.
21. Rao, K. S., Ariman, T., Hosbein, R. L., and Yang, K. T., Collection of dust by fabric filtration in an electrostatic field, Proc. 2nd Annu. Environmental Engineering and Science Conf., Louisville, April 20–21, 1972, 557.
22. Gillespie, T., *J. Colloid. Sci.,* 10, 299, 1955.
23. Kraemer, H. F. and Johnstone, H. F., *Ind. Eng. Chem.,* 47, 2426, 1955.
24. Lundgren, D. A. and Whitby, K. T., *Ind. Eng. Chem. Process Des. Dev.,* 1(4), 345, 1965.
25. Licht, W., *Removal of Particulate Matter from Gaseous Wastes: Filtration,* American Petroleum Institute, New York, 1961.
26. Ergun, S., *Chem. Eng. Prog.,* 48, 89, 1952.
27. Davies, C. N., *Air Filtration,* Academic Press, London, 1973.
28. Brinkman, H. C., *Appl. Sci. Res.,* A1, 27, 1967.
29. Happel, J., *AIChE J.,* 4, 197, 1958; 5, 174, 1959.
30. Kuwabara, S., *J. Phys. Soc. Jpn.,* 14, 527, 1959.
31. Theodore, L., *Transport Phenomena for Engineers,* International Textbook, Scranton, 1971.
32. Harrop, J. A. and Stenhouse, J. I. T., *Chem. Eng. Sci.,* 24, 1475, 1969.
33. Theodore, L., Buonicore, A. J., and Pfeffer, R., ongoing research.
34. Theodore, L., Buonicore, A. J., Giegerich, E., and Pfeffer, R., unpublished work.
35. Theodore, L. and Buonicore, A. J., ongoing research.
36. Carman, P. C., *Trans. Inst. Chem. Eng.* (London), 15, 150, 1937; *J. Soc. Chem. Ind.* (London), 57, 225, 1938.
37. Sullivan, R. R. and Hertel, K. L., *J. Appl. Phys.,* 11, 761, 1940.
38. Theodore, L. and Buonicore, A. J., ongoing research.
39. Blasewitz, A. G. and Judson, B. F., *Chem. Eng. Prog.,* 51, 6, 1955.
40. U.S. Dept. of Health, Education and Welfare, *Control Techniques for Particulate Air Pollutants,* AP-51, January 1969.
41. Dustex Division, American Precision Industries, Inc., Bulletin 311.
42. Vandenhoeck, P., *Chem. Eng.,* 79(9), 67, 1972.
43. Adams, R. L., Fabric Filters for Control of Power Plant Emissions, Paper No. 74-100, presented at the 67th Annu. APCA Meet., Denver, June 9–13, 1974.
44. Culhane, F. R., *Environ. Sci. Technol.,* 8(2), 127, 1974.
45. Thomas, J. W., Rimberg, D., Miller, T. J., "Gravity Effect in Air Filtration", Aerosol Science, 2, 31, 1971.
46. Loeffler, F., "Adhesion Probability in Fibre Filters", Clean Air, 75, 1974.
47. Freshwater, D. C. and Stenhouse, J. I., "The Retention of Large Particles in Fibrous Filters", AIChE Journal, 18, 786, 1972.

INDEX

TITLES OF INTEREST

CRC PRESS HANDBOOKS:

CRC HANDBOOK of Tables for APPLIED ENGINEERING SCIENCE, 2nd Edition
Edited by **Ray E. Bolz, D.Eng.**, Case Western Reserve University, and **George L. Tuve, Sc.D.**, Case Institute of Technology.

CRC HANDBOOK OF CHEMISTRY AND PHYSICS, 57th Edition
Edited by **Robert C. Weast, Ph.D.**, Consolidated Natural Gas Service Co., Inc.

CRC PRESS "UNISCIENCE"^{TM} TITLES:

AIR POLLUTION from PESTICIDES and AGRICULTURAL PROCESSES
Edited by **Robert E. Lee, Jr., M.S., Ph.D.**, Environmental Protection Agency.

BIOLOGICAL MONITORING for INDUSTRIAL CHEMICAL EXPOSURE CONTROL
By **A. L. Linch, M.S.**, Consultant, Environmental Health, Everett, Pennsylvania.

EVALUATION OF AMBIENT AIR QUALITY by PERSONNEL MONITORING
By **A. L. Linch, M.S.**, Consultant, Environmental Health, Everett, Pennsylvania.

FIXED BIOLOGICAL SURFACES--WASTEWATER TREATMENT: The Rotating Biological Contactor
By **Ronald L. Antonie, B.S., M.B.A.**, Autotrol Corporation.

INDUSTRIAL CONTROL EQUIPMENT for GASEOUS POLLUTANTS
By **Louis Theodore, D.Eng.Sc.**, Manhatten College, and **Anthony J. Buonicore, M.Ch.E.**, Wright-Patterson Air Force Base.

NOISE AND NOISE CONTROL: In Buildings, The Community, Industry, and Transportation Vehicles
By **M. J. Crocker, Ph.D.**, Purdue University, and **A. J. Price, Ph.D.**, University of British Columbia.

RECENT DEVELOPMENTS in SEPARATION SCIENCE
Edited by **Norman N. Li, Sc.D.**, Esso Research and Engineering Co.

TRACE ELEMENT MEASUREMENTS at the COAL-FIRED STEAM PLANT
By **W. S. Lyon, Jr., B.S., M.S.**, Oak Ridge National Laboratory.

USE of PURIFIED OXYGEN in SECONDARY WASTEWATER TREATMENT
Edited by **J. R. McWhirter, M.S., Ph.D.**, Union Carbide Corporation.

CRC CRITICAL REVIEWS^{TM} JOURNALS:

CRC CRITICAL REVIEWS^{TM} in ENVIRONMENTAL CONTROL
Edited by **Conrad P. Straub, Ph.D.**, University of Minnesota.

Direct inquiries to CRC Press, Inc.

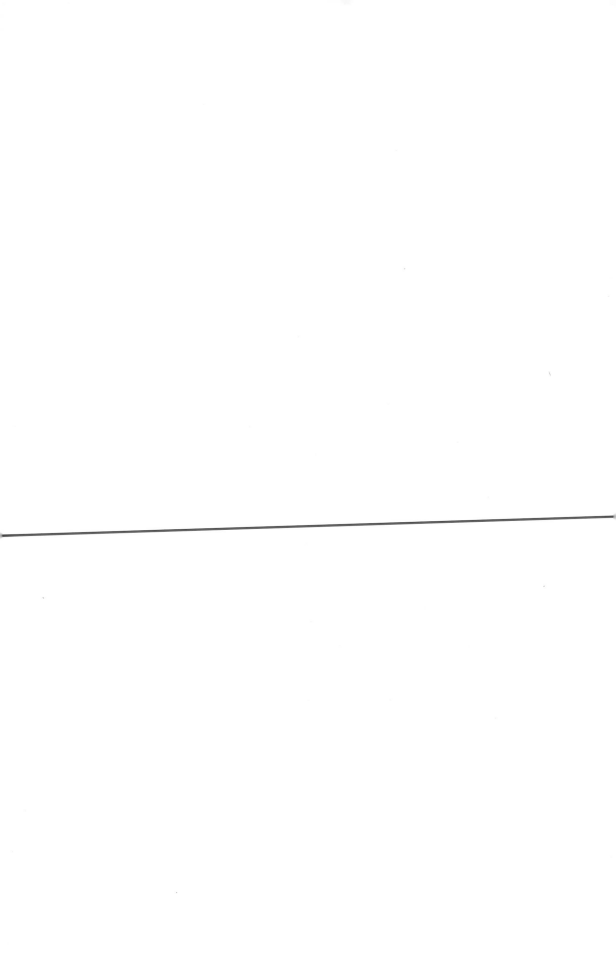